Frank K. Martin

Dear Victor,

On occasion my reputation for being a parsimonious penny pincher leads me to reach certain conclusions that may be considered cockeyed by those few friends on whom this largess is humbly bestowed. On the rare chance that you might get wind of the attached and, far rarer still, seek to satisfy your curiosity about what this semantically challenged fellow could possibly have to write worth reading—this side of a comic book—I display my irrational frugality openly as follows: Since I can purchase the attached paper weight at wholesale, the money saved is simply money saved, to whomever the benefit might accrue! Being the Christmas Scrooge that I am, I expect to recapture the shortfall on volume!

Warmest Christmas greetings, 2005,

Frank

53601 Ridgeview Lane ▪ Bristol, Indiana 46507 ▪ Phone 574-848-4422

(continued from back cover)

"Academia has found a gold mine in transforming the art of investment based on common sense into a science of finance, filling entire libraries of textbooks full of undecipherable equations. In *Speculative Contagion,* however, highly successful value investor Frank Martin shows us with a well-structured, easy-to-read, and focused account of the financial markets' gyrations over the last few years not only how to avoid costly investment mistakes but how to capitalize on the purchase of bargains that investment markets provide from time to time.

"Just in case you lost some money in the stock market in the last few years, Martin's *Speculative Contagion* is the book you must read! Make it compulsory reading for your children and grandchildren as well, as speculative and destructive investment contagions are likely to repeat themselves again and again.

"I boarded a plane in Hong Kong—destination Los Angeles. Twelve hours into the flight, I was still reading Frank Martin's fascinating and insightful account of the investment markets over the last few years. Finally, a true value investor who puts the undecipherable equations of financial academia in their proper place and articulates in a highly readable book the simple but rewarding case for 'common sense' investing."

– MARC FABER,
Editor of *The Gloom, Boom & Doom Report*

"*Speculative Contagion* makes an important contribution to investors' understanding of stock market manias. The most important contribution of this gem of a book is the wise counsel this well-seasoned professional provides to his clients during that tempting and tumultuous period. Frank Martin's message of prudence and patience, in the midst of the late '90s mania, protected his clients' capital and positioned their portfolios to not only survive the 'Bubble' but find real value in its aftermath."

– JOHN MAGINN,
Co-author of *Managing Investment Portfolios: A Dynamic Process*

SPECULATIVE CONTAGION

An Antidote for Speculative Epidemics

Frank K. Martin

authorHOUSE™

1663 Liberty Drive, Suite 200
Bloomington, Indiana 47403
(800) 839-8640
www.AuthorHouse.com

First published by AuthorHouse 11/21/05.

ISBN: 1-4259-0075-5 (dj)

Library of Congress Control Number: 2005910260

Printed in the United States of America
Bloomington, Indiana

This book is printed on acid-free paper.

To my children—Todd, Shannon, and Erin—and their children who are a father's and grandfather's dream come true. And to my wife, Marsha, whose unconditional love and devotion have miraculously liberated a physically challenged man from the bonds of disability. She is the wind beneath my wings.

TABLE OF CONTENTS

PREFACE

The Nasdaq 500, the index most emblematic of the "Great Bubble" and the insidious onset of increasingly heady times throughout the 1990s as investing and speculating gradually merged to the point of being indistinguishable, began its multi-year implosion in March of 2000, during which its value shrunk by almost 80%. The trajectory of the speculative Nasdaq index ever higher into the stratosphere of delusion and its inevitable capitulation to the laws of gravity is graphically depicted on the cover of this book. The carnage, like the speculative contagion that fueled the epidemic of "irrational exuberance," spread to many other quarters of the marketplace as well. To give credibility to the characterization of the speculative delusion with the adjective great, one need only gauge the violent collapse in the aggregate market values of all U.S. stocks that followed.

Throughout the latter half of the '90s, market commentators more or less arbitrarily and, as it turned out, quite irresponsibly, asserted that a decline of 20% would constitute a "bear market," obliquely implying that investors and speculators alike need not anticipate anything worse. The approximate total market value of all domestic equity securities reached its apogee of $17 trillion in the spring of 2000. Two and a half years later, $8 trillion of illusory, inflated value—roughly half of which can be attributed to the savaging of stocks making up the Nasdaq index—had disappeared into thin air as the Bubble collapsed to considerably less than half of its earlier, unsustainable size. The market value of U.S. stocks then stood at a greatly diminished $9 trillion. Therein, I submit, is compelling evidence of the difference between a bear market and the bursting of a Great Bubble. Moreover, the aftereffects of an assault of that magnitude on financial wealth are likely to be felt far and wide, and perhaps for a time span much longer than most people imagine at this juncture.

Relying on the very generalized presumption that the average person learns from his own mistakes and the wise man learns vicariously from observing the behaviors of others, it is the writer's belief that many valuable insights can be gleaned from careful examination of the Great Bubble from within, as each puff of air gradually stretched the ever-more-fragile membrane to the inevitable point of rupturing. What follows are the 1998 through 2004 Martin Capital Management (hereafter MCM, not 1900 in Roman numerals, though some may see my thinking as dated!) annual reports, abridged as necessary to keep the book within tolerable limits. Most additions to the original text are bracketed; a modest number of changes to the original reports were added to improve clarity. In addition, substitutes were inserted without acknowledgment for duplicated pet aphorisms, words, or phrases; and the sometimes annoying repetition of a number of key ideas or concepts (as might logically appear in seven discrete reports) were generally left unattended in order to add emphasis and to maintain the flow of the text. Every effort was made to avoid omitting anything that might cast this book in a more favorable light than it deserves. All MCM annual reports are available in their entirety in the library section of the firm's Website, www.mcmadvisors.com, for those who wish to scrutinize the original documents, including the omitted accounting sections mentioned below. Each report (organized in Chapters One through Seven) will tell, in its own time and in its own way, how it felt to be pulled one way by the temptation to mindlessly join the crowd in its rush for paper gold and the other by the sometimes fragile convictions about what constitutes rational thought and behavior.

Appearing in the Appendix is the lengthy and equally remarkable prequel to the mutating anomalous investment environment, the very fodder that made writing this book obligatory, "The More Times Change, the More They Remain the Same: 1927–33 Through the Eyes of Benjamin Graham." The power of the flashback in revealing the genius and prescience of Graham is even more remarkable when read as a stand-alone section. It originally appeared in the 2000 annual report.

The 1998 annual report (Chapter One) features a long and rather technical discussion of the progressive relaxation of accounting standards as more and more companies sought both to report a trendline of earnings growth that was steeper and smoother than it would have been under a less aggressive interpretation of the rules. "Soapboxing" against these increasingly pernicious abuses continued for three more years (1999 through 2001) under the fitting homemade title of "Ledger d'Maim." Despite the writer's vantage point as an incredulous observer of the daisy chain of chicanery that revealed the full extent of its ugliness in the fall of Enron, those sections were omitted to avoid bogging down the reader in the miasmic muck. The "Ledger d'Maim" sections are not unlike an autopsy: Most readers prefer to be spared the gory and otherwise odious details, generally satisfied with a summary of the cause of death! As noted above, the original annual reports can be read in their entirety on our Website. They have been displaced but not discarded—so that accounting aficionados will not be left bereft and inconsolable.

In Walden, Henry David Thoreau addressed the use of the first person. In most books, the I is omitted, often to avoid appearing egotistical. Thoreau reminds us that "We commonly do not remember that it is, after all, always the first person that is speaking." It is convenience and the obligation to own up for what is said that the first-person pronoun will frequently appear throughout the text. Unlike Thoreau, whose sole resource was the expanse of nature herself, I have had the luxury of drawing on the writings of, and conversations with, countless others far more sagacious than the undersigned, all of which could suggest that we would be the more appropriate pronoun. Feel free, if you wish, to view them as if they were one and the same.

Differentiating this book's perspective from others is that it will not reflect on what happened with the clarity and certainty of hindsight, along with the sanctimonious demeanor often in evidence when events are dispassionately viewed in retrospect. Rather, the book is intended to capture in vivid detail the emotions that had the upper hand as the speculative contagion spread, often rendering rational thought dumbstruck if not impotent. This volume takes a somewhat novel "pre- and *during*-mortem" look at the Bubble as it inflated to its ultimately inimical size from which the process reversed itself, thus offering the reader a unique "you were there" perspective.

And who is in a better position to give an account of the goings-on than someone in the thick of the battle? As an investment advisor, prone to reflect on cause and effect, I came to work in the "Bubble" every business day of the week. I watched and wondered, sometimes nearly overcome with self-doubt, worrying that we as a firm were out of step with a new-era reality. At other times, I was modestly encouraged by some seemingly insignificant piece of evidence that gave us a sign, often little more than a fleeting assurance, that we had not lost our way, that our sense of historical proportion might eventually validate the vision we were pursuing for our clients and ourselves. It was a grueling experience, the likes of which I do not expect to see again, once it has run its course, for many years to come. Too much damage will have been done to the collective investor psyche for a sequel to appear—until the salient memories of the trauma of this momentous episode fade. When the still vivid recollections of the Great Bubble and its aftermath begin in time to wane, it is my hope that the reader will pull this then dust-covered tome from the bookshelf and revisit the investment verities that offer the twin virtues of allowing one to both sleep well *and* eat well. They are by no means the only way by which to "skin the cat" of investment success, but as you read on you will learn of their impressive productivity and durability. These key truisms should be reinforced as one pieces together each annual snapshot of the investment scene, as the "talking picture" rolls on through seven years of investment history.

Aristotle is said to have observed: "We are what we repeatedly do. Excellence, then, is not an act, but a habit." What I hope you will absorb as you read *Speculative Contagion* is that mastery of self must come before mastery of one's investments. Before a foot is placed in the market arena—assuming that one's goal is not to prove once again that a fool and his money are unlikely to remain long-term companions—it is imperative that one have a firm grasp of what it means to be a *rational* decision maker. While a more complete definition of the word will take form as you encounter its many applications throughout the book, please understand that rational thought and behavior require no small reservoir of willpower (to say nothing of knowledge), which the majority do not appear to possess and only a few of those who do seem willing or able to apply it to their advantage. For the fortunate who have both the will and the knowledge, it is within reach. Yet the more important question is "Do they have the desire" to make the sacrifice to acquire and habituate it?

Another essential mental building block is a single-mindedness of purpose or, more succinctly, *focus.* Like rationality, focus, by its very definition, is severely limiting and utterly unglamorous, requiring a generous use of the most unpopular word in the English language: "no." One example of our focus is in winnowing down our universe of investment candidates to a handful of superior businesses—to the exclusion of all others. The investor who zeros in on his clearly defined objectives shows little tolerance, no matter how high the entertainment value or the prospect for easy money, for extraneous and irrelevant information. In fact, he is likely to become a bore as he bores in on his subject.

Beyond the awareness of self, the inner strength of a disciplined will, independence of thought, and the overall knowledge/wisdom that are foundational for rational and focused investing, success is more likely to come to those who have some clue about the counterintuitive way that the thought processes and subsequent behaviors of crowds differ from individuals acting in isolation. There is a sound basis for the famous quote from the poet/dramatist Johann von Schiller who once said, "Anyone taken as an individual is tolerably sensible and reasonable—as a member of a crowd he at once becomes a blockhead." If one is to avoid the allure of the majority, a.k.a. the mythical character "Mr. Market" as defined by Benjamin Graham in the pages that follow, one must have an understanding of the manic-depressive nature of this creature, who may prove to be your best friend or worst enemy depending on how well you get to know him. One should also gain some awareness of an asymmetrical behavioral pattern common to the conduct of crowds as their collective state of mind tends to swing from extreme to extreme. This writer believes that there is a cyclicality to the world of finance that is just enough on the positive side of random to make the study of history relevant. Books like *Extraordinary Popular Delusions and the Madness of Crowds* by Charles Mackay, LLD, put this propensity into a context that leaves the careful reader feeling that delusions and the madness that follows are endemic to the human condition.

Speculative Contagion, from beginning to end, reveals our apprehension when others were greedy, gullible, or gripped by folly, as well as our measured and often agonizing—and sometimes plainly discouraging—detachment from the ever-more-irrational goings-on. This real-time effort will not dwell on a distracting, generalized "I told you so," for history has spoken emphatically, with incriminating, indisputable facts. Footnotes are provided when appropriate to bring the reader up-to-date on still unfolding true stories (or those that can be found in the financial morgue), some of which are more than five years old. Information in the footnotes is up-to-date as of June 30, 2005.

Finally, *Speculative Contagion* serves as a bully pulpit for the author. I found it bordering on the unconscionable to live in close proximity to the latest iteration of the *Den of Thieves* (1992), written by James Stewart and chronicling the Wall Street depredations of the 1980s, without speaking out against the crimes and misdemeanors they were perpetrating. Accordingly, throughout the book the reader will encounter occasional tirades directed at the more flagrant violations of the standards of ethical conduct, rationalizing my outspokenness by turning to no less an authority than 18th-century Scottish economist and philosopher Adam Smith. The book that established economics as an autonomous subject and launched the economic doctrine of free enterprise, *An Inquiry into the Nature and Causes of the Wealth of Nations* (1776), examined in detail the consequences of economic freedom, including the role of self-interest, division of labor, and the function of markets, among others. As a moralist, Smith argued that the system of free enterprise was only as strong as the general ethical character of the society of which it was composed. The more egregious ethical breakdowns that occurred, particularly the abuses of fiduciary trust and power at the highest ranks of corporate governance, threatened to become the weak link in the economic chain. If the chain breaks, chaos is likely to reign. Dare I hold my tongue when the consequences of silence could be so dire?

Acknowledgments

Every tree that withstands hurricane-force winds has unseen roots buried deep in the soil. This book is the tree, but its roots nurture and strengthen it. Countless people are, collectively, the roots. Among those who bent their shoulder to the wheel to get this project rolling included Al Auxier, Warren Batts, Edward Chancellor, Marks Hinton, Janet Lowe, John Maginn, Merle Mullett, Rich Rockwood, and Shirley Terrass, all of whom provided advice, support, and encouragement along the journey. A special thank you goes to Dennis Rocheleau, Mike Stout, and Larry Crouse who reviewed the manuscript with the same critical eye as if it were their own. Thanks also to Bill Monroe for providing the clever illustrations in Chapter One. Aaron Kindig and Tom Dugan, outstanding junior analysts with our firm, accepted the many assignments thrown at them with enthusiasm and produced results commensurate with their outstanding effort. Kristen Smith, who stepped into the project midstream, did a remarkable job getting up to speed in a heartbeat while assisting with the editing and keeping me focused on the task at hand. Stephanie Malcom, the formatting pro, helped package the prose. Wordsmith Dan Shenk, proprietor of CopyProof, was responsible for seeing to it that all *t's* were dotted and *i's* crossed. ☺

During my senior year as undergraduate at Northwestern University in 1964, I had the career-defining good fortune of taking a course in security analysis, taught by a salty and savvy investment veteran, Corliss D. Anderson. An adjunct professor of finance and a retired partner at Duff, Anderson & Clark, Professor Anderson enthusiastically paced in front of the class with a copy of Benjamin Graham's *Security Analysis* (fourth edition, published in 1962) clasped in his hand with the zeal of a Bible-thumping evangelist, breathing life into the dismal science with a seemingly endless stream of commonsensical anecdotes. I was hooked on the simple logic of it all, and how it fit so nicely into my emerging bigger picture of the holistic life. From there the road to Omaha was no more than a hop, skip and a jump. Warren Buffett embodied much of what I learned in the classroom—and so much more. Buffett has established himself, albeit unwittingly, as the consummate capitalist icon. His genius for business and investment, unequivocally confirmed by the marketplace over half a century, is packaged in a persona whose emotional, intellectual, and ethical qualities are generously augmented by great integrity, humility, personality, humor, character, constitution, disposition, spirit, and temperament. Adam Smith would be proud.

We also have drawn much strength and wisdom from clients (*friends* is a more fitting descriptor) with whom our relationship in almost all cases is constructively candid and mutually respectful. Many are older and far more experienced, and their sage advice has often been vitally important, particularly when one's convictions are tested to their core day in and day out. Regular encouragement from virtually every client has kept our spirits high and our desire to persevere undeterred. Those words are not platitudes. There are few men or women alive who reach their potential without the support of caring others.

While I am the oldest of the full-time members of our firm—by some margin—I am humbled by how much I have learned from my partners, associates, and our one-of-a-kind support organization. In more cases than I care to admit, the teacher has become the pupil. While I am deeply indebted to my external mentors, my gratitude is no less to my younger trusted teachers.

In the 2001 annual report [Chapter Four], I addressed the matter of attribution as follows:

> Sources for factual matter include *The Wall Street Journal, Barron's, Fortune* magazine, *Forbes* magazine, various Internet sources, *Bloomberg News,* and others, along with a number of books. Considering the limited audience for which this report is intended, the abbreviated production window, and the fact that most readers already are familiar with my ideas and writings, my words and those of others are freely mixed, sometimes without formal acknowledgment, particularly in the latter sections of the report. It is not my wish to put forth as original the ideas or words of others. To the contrary, I wish to save them the embarrassment of being associated with me! If you find a really great idea in these pages, and you're sure it could not have come from my semantically challenged synapses, give me a call, and I'll find the source and give credit where credit is due.

In reading *The Problem of Pain* by C.S. Lewis, I found he expressed the issue much more succinctly: "As this is not a work of erudition I have taken little pains [pun intended?] to trace ideas or quotations to their sources when they were not easily recoverable. Any theologian will see easily enough what, and how little, I have read." While I must read to compensate for my incapacity to think and reason as Lewis did seemingly without effort, and *erudite* would not be the word to describe this far-from-scholarly exposition, I nonetheless have followed Lewis's lead and not taken pains to trace all "ideas or quotations to their sources." (Permission has been received for the extensive references to copyrighted material from Benjamin Graham and Warren Buffett.) As one observer suggested—with obvious references to the quality of the effort (and therefore the need for *any* attribution, as well as the reason I sought solace from Lewis's book)—"Don't quit your day job!"

Speaking of vocational endeavors, this book's purpose is not promotional. Our firm's nondiversified investment style and human-capital constraints impose severe limitations on the dollar amount of assets that can be effectively managed and the number of clients who can be satisfactorily served. If managed assets exceed $1 billion, we believe that the universe of investment candidates will begin to shrink, which could have an adverse effect on investment performance, an important driver of client satisfaction and the primary impetus behind our revenues. Additionally, we don't think we can serve more than 25 clients per portfolio manager in the manner to which they have become accustomed. Accordingly, the inquest represented by this book is an avocation of yours truly—and a most delightful one at that.

Finally, the opportunities for reflection and contemplation abound for a professional investor for whom success is not measured solely, or even mostly, in dollar terms. It would have been a great loss indeed to the writer if he had sped through the preceding six years in the pell-mell pursuit of the almighty buck and missed the forest for the trees, a lifetime of lessons that were there for the taking. And the lush woods of history blossom resplendent with wisdom and knowledge regarding the periodic, ironic twists in human behavior. Such ineffably sublime gifts are given to those whose senses remain attuned to the juxtaposition of the daily stream of anecdotal tidbits, like so many falling leaves, along with the perpetually repetitious nature of the willful human mind. On an even more personal note, in the reckless rush for riches that characterized the '90s, many were so consumed by the "more is better" mindset that they never paused long enough to ask: "How much is enough?" I hearken to the thoughtful words of Kahlil Gibran in *The Prophet*. "And what is fear of need but need itself? Is not dread of thirst when your well is full, the thirst that is unquenchable?"

Annual historical performance data are included in each chapter, for without it the message would be woefully incomplete. Moreover, there appears to be limited understanding about what Benjamin Franklin identified as one of the great modern discoveries—the theory of compound interest. Returns from equity securities for the author's firm were negative in three of the last 10 years. By the end of the book, the cumulative importance of 30% of the years registering negative returns will become apparent. Performance data, parceled out annually on an as-you-go basis, is provided simply to assist the reader in grasping more firmly this apparently elusive concept. As noted in the preceding paragraph, we are not soliciting new business through this book nor, accordingly, can we respond to inquiries from readers. Rather, the book is offered as a small contribution to the body of investment knowledge. We encourage readers to apply whatever insights they may glean to the management of their own investment assets or what they might look for in selecting a manager.

CHAPTER ONE—1998

Introduction

May Reason Prevail

In June of 1998 Warren Buffett, in a public-television interview with *Money Line*'s Adam Smith, was asked: "Why do smart people do dumb things?" Buffett opined that greed, fear, envy, and mindless imitation of others are among the factors that mitigate the transfer of the mind's horsepower to the wheels that propel us along the road toward business and investment success. Rather than superior intelligence, Buffett confided, it is the capacity for unconditionally *rational* thought—followed by proportional action—that separate the winners from the also-rans. These qualities have distanced him and Charlie Munger from the pack by such a margin that the multitude is no longer even a speck on the horizon.

While reading for the first time the recently reprinted first edition (1934) of *Security Analysis*, authored by Buffett's mentor, Benjamin Graham, to which much-deserved attention is directed in this report, a similar thread was strikingly evident throughout the 700-page masterpiece. Written in the darkest depths of the Depression by a man who personally was not spared its devastation, the volume reveals Graham's genius for almost inhuman objectivity and rationality in the face of a financial and economic storm that wreaked such havoc and mental anguish on a whole generation of investors that most had no stomach for stocks throughout the rest of their lives.

To the extent that the writer is able to view the investment landscape from a similar frame of reference, this report in its entirety will ideally reflect the ascendancy of reason over emotion and fact over folly.

A Reader's Guide

This year's account is organized by topic, prioritized from most important to least important based on the presumed breadth of their appeal. Beyond the discussion of issues of immediate relevance, a lengthy essay [beginning a four-year diatribe against willful, and ultimately shameful, disregard for the necessity of an honest system of "weights and measures"] in accounting for corporate results follows—the value of which transcends the moment. A magnifying glass is used to examine the relaxation of standards in corporate financial management and reporting that came about when executives put pragmatics before principle in their run for the roses in the earnings-per-share-growth-at-any-cost derby. Readers of corporate annual reports know that this is a time to resurrect the Latin expression *caveat emptor*. [Beginning in Chapter One, "The Numbers Game" exposes the progressively widening gap in GAAP (generally accepted accounting principles). Later, Chapter Seven wraps up with "Fully Deluded Earnings," the S&P's initial attempt at putting the creative accounting genie back into the bottle. As noted in the Preface, three accounting sections in between were omitted for the sake of brevity.]

The Year 1998 in Review

The past year brought to the fore an interesting and challenging—but not unprecedented—dichotomy. The most widely referenced equity-market benchmark, the Standard & Poor's 500 stock index, heavily weighted for the big and the beautiful, rose by 26.7% in 1998, achieving in the process a record-setting fourth year in a row of gains in excess of 20%. The Nasdaq index, dominated by big capitalization technology companies, including several that have prominent places in the S&P index, put on an even more impressive show, rising 39.6%. Nasdaq volume, we parenthetically note with undisguised amazement (since we are aware that the companies of which it consists are among the least proven), regularly dwarfs that of the New York Stock Exchange. During that same interval, the Russell 2000, composed primarily of so-called small-cap stocks, told an entirely different story, actually falling by 3.4% for the 12 months.

Surprisingly, despite the handsome showing of most of the major indexes, the majority of stocks suffered a losing year in 1998. Backsliders outpaced winners both on the Big Board and, more dramatically, on Nasdaq, where the 1,690 stocks that registered higher prices for 1998 were handily outnumbered by the 3,351 that fell. The two-tier market that emerged in the spring of 1998 is reminiscent of 1972. We took the "road less traveled."[1]

---

1 Just as the "Nifty Fifty" skyrocketed to eventual oblivion beginning in 1972, so did technology and Internet stocks in late 1999 and the spring of 2000. The mundane "Main Street" companies fared far better in both episodes.

While the prices of the most favored companies rose farther and farther above what we believe to be their intrinsic worth, several fine businesses (but market wallflowers) presented us with attractive purchase opportunities during the late-summer rout. While the S&P 500 and the Dow Jones industrial average backtracked by nearly 20% from July through August, the three that we purchased in larger quantities traded at their lows for prices that were, on average, approximately one-third of their 52-week highs. More importantly, these growing companies were purchased at an average price-earnings ratio of below 10 times trailing earnings. They have since rallied sharply but still trade well below their earlier highs. If we are confident that we (1) understand a business that historically earns high returns on shareholders' capital, (2) feel that its business model is stable enough for us to estimate its intrinsic worth, and (3) conclude that management is both competent and shareholder-oriented, falling prices play to the strength of our business analysis. In each case, our average cost is well below what we think the businesses are worth. If business conditions remain reasonably positive, five-year expected returns for the three companies could average better than 20%, compounded annually. Since the mailing list for this report extends beyond our clients, we are not mentioning the companies by name.

We admit to having an abiding interest in the great consumer-products franchises like Coca-Cola and Gillette, and we would purchase them and others of their ilk if, based on conservative terminal-price assumptions, five-year expected returns approach 15%. Based on our work, at current prices, they are likely to earn little more than the yields available on U.S. Treasury securities for the foreseeable future. That's not enough to get us off the dime.[2]

---

2 We often talk about patience, but Coca-Cola and Gillette have tested our limits. After peaking around $90 per share in mid-1998, Coke began a long stair-stepped descent, hitting $37 in the spring of 2003 and recently traded for $42. In similar fashion, Gillette peaked at $63 at the same time that Coke was reaching for the stars. It hit a low of $27 in the spring of 2001. For whatever strategic reasons, Gillette agreed to surrender its independence (for an 18% premium to the prevailing market price) to Procter & Gamble and is currently selling at $55, pending consummation of the merger.

Investment Performance

Period Ending December 31, 1998	MCM Equities *	S&P 500 *
Five Years	14.3%	24.0%
Three Years	21.0%	28.2%
One Year	-7.4%	28.6%

* Compounded annually, MCM data net of fees

Year	MCM Equities (Net of Fees)	S&P 500
1994	-7.5%	1.3%
1995	19.1%	37.5%
1996	31.8%	22.9%
1997	45.1%	33.3%
1998	-7.4%	28.6%

[The performance data above are compounded annually and also are time-weighted. Common stocks, which during the year grew from 17.5% of assets to approximately 30%, declined 7.4% in value (after fees), conspicuously underperforming the S&P 500 which increased 28.6%, for its fourth consecutive year in a row of producing returns in excess of 20%. Parenthetically, when we speak of aggregate percentage commitment to equities, the reader should be alerted to the fact that pursuant to individual investment policy statements, one investor's portfolio could be totally committed to common stocks, whereas another's might be invested entirely in fixed-income securities. The reluctance to join the crowd and commit more money to equities reflected opportunities forgone as we continued to place far heavier emphasis on the return *of* your capital rather than the return *on* your capital. Fixed-income securities earned their coupon, a portion of which is tax-exempt interest from municipal bonds, and then some. Because of a large commitment to fixed-income securities, the negative return from common stocks was mitigated, and so most portfolios ended up in positive territory, albeit the gains were modest. Not only were we undercommitted to the hottest asset class, our selections in the skyrocketing market were, in our judgment, based more on value than popularity.

In the early years, our focus (and our demonstrated expertise) was primarily in the arena of tax-exempt, fixed-income securities. Beginning in 1994, we felt sure-footed enough to begin prudently tiptoeing up the slippery slopes of equity ownership, increasing our exposure to good businesses, although in 1998 we began to wonder if our disciplined ways would ever be valued in an investment world gripped by a speculative frenzy.

In updating this report, the results above—and in all subsequent chapters—were revised to reflect a significant change in 2003 in our methodology for presenting annual equity performance results in order to broaden the base of portfolios included in the calculation and to make it possible for our calculations to be audited by independent third parties. In the past, the results had been determined by using the performance of several long-standing representative accounts as a shorthand proxy for all accounts. In 2003 we recalculated performance from 1994 through 2003, using data from the master list of all our accounts. The "tracking error" (the difference in results using the two methodologies) was insignificant, as indicated graphically by the chart in Chapter Seven. The returns were calculated on a time-weighted basis. Needless to say, the results are portfolio-size-weighted; that is, the performance of larger portfolios has a greater impact on the consolidated results than smaller ones. We should note that the data on the S&P 500, our self-selected benchmark, are *before* any fees.

No methodology is without its shortcomings. Though we believe our approach's deficiencies to be trivial, in the spirit of full disclosure, we'll summarize them for you briefly. First, we include common stocks that clients select on their own (sometimes after a trip to a barbershop). They are grouped with the companies we have acquired, but these "personal preference" stocks represent less than 1% of the total value of all MCM equities. Parenthetically, while we haven't bothered to keep a detailed record, cursory analysis would suggest that the contribution of those client-picked securities to our overall performance over time has been negative. While it's like a tiny dent in the fender of a new car in terms of its effect on aggregate performance, what caused the dent often serves a useful purpose, which I will let you deduce. Second, we haven't found any practical way to include intra-month money flows in or out of asset classes. There will always be occasions where large money inflows occur during a month. We believe such flows have an immaterial effect on overall results. Finally, there is what is known as a "survivor's" bias, which distorts the S&P 500 as well. When a client terminates a portfolio relationship with us, the entire history of the account is removed from our records. But client turnover has been negligible, and the performance history of those disassociated portfolios is not believed to have been materially different from the majority of portfolios. All in all, we believe that the data provided are a more than acceptable representation of our investment results.]

Short-term market-price volatility is relatively high for mid- and smaller-sized companies found on the road less traveled. While the market prices of the companies we own eclipsed by some margin the performance of the popular averages (and most equity mutual funds) in 1996 and 1997, this past year was a different story. We don't want to appear indifferent to these shorter-term outcomes, be they positive or negative, but our focus remains on the ultimate rationality of markets over time. Today's investor pays a heavy premium for popular big-cap companies. We expect the earnings of the companies we own to grow at a rate no less than the earnings of the S&P 500 index, and yet we acquired them for one-third of the index's price-earnings ratio. To paraphrase Benjamin Graham, in the short run, it's popularity and outward appeal that help a girl win a fellow's attention, but in the long run, it's good cooking that helps her keep it.

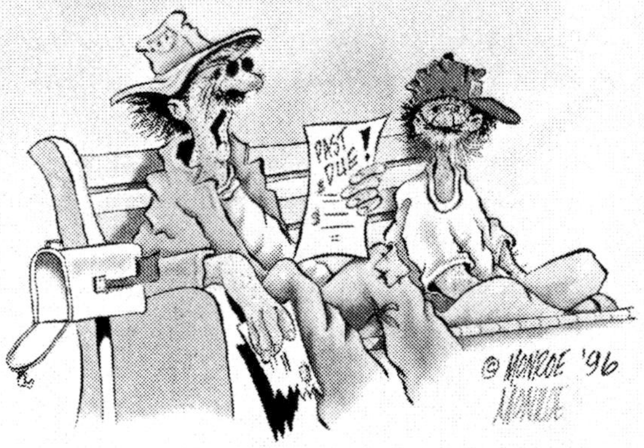

"WHAT WE NEED AROUND HERE IS A POS'TIVE CASH FLOW."

We would be less than candid if we didn't admit to coveting the returns that the S&P 500 and Nasdaq 100 have earned during the past several years. We regret not being able to find ways to fully and prudently share in the explosion of financial wealth that has been created out of thin air. Furthermore, it's a near certainty that if present trends continue, we will lag even farther behind. The high-stakes game of musical chairs that Wall Street has been playing is neither one we understand nor one in which we have any demonstrated competence. In the final analysis, our respect for history's lessons (see "The Dean of Wall Street Revisited" later in this chapter) and our pledge to think and act rationally leave us no choice but to stay our carefully plotted wealth-preservation course.

We have an aversion to investment operations that may lead to permanent loss of capital. In our judgment, permanent loss can result from (1) investment in securities of issuers in which high confidence of their ability to survive particularly adverse economic circumstances is not warranted by the facts and/or (2) an investor becoming so despondent because of the decline in the market value of his or her portfolio that in a moment of all-consuming fear he or she forces the conversion of a paper (and perhaps temporary) loss into a permanent one. We go to great lengths to minimize the likelihood of the first eventuality, a course of action for us that is essentially devoid of emotional forces. The second is more problematic. There is little basis for us to determine in advance how an individual might respond under conditions of such high stress. It has been 25 years since tolerance for wealth-threatening market-price declines was tested in the crucible of high emotion, and there is little precedent, therefore, from which to make such judgments about what form that response might take today should the market fall long and hard. At considerable cost in temporary (if not permanent) loss of opportunity, we have managed portfolios to avoid subjecting our clients to that test.

As we wait (im)patiently for some semblance of order to be restored in equity valuations, the vast majority of the assets over which we have control are invested in the safest-harbor securities available. The money we manage, both yours and ours, that isn't committed to equities is squirreled away in the highest-grade fixed-income securities, including Aaa-rated pre-refunded or escrowed-to-maturity tax-exempt municipal bonds and U.S. Treasury bills and notes. To compromise on credit quality at this juncture in our economic history would be the equivalent of a boat's captain feigning preoccupation with safety as he snugs the vessel alongside the pier. Only he knows that below the waterline the hull is riddled with leaks, and the junk (pun intended) will stay afloat only so long as the bilge pumps keep working. Higher portfolio returns, if they are to be achieved, will be the result of rising interest rates or expanded investment opportunities in equity securities, not compromising on credit quality in fixed-income securities.

Market interest rates fell during 1998. Because we have elected not to expose our clients to the market-price volatility inherent in long-duration bonds (made even longer by lower coupons) as I did in the early 1980s, falling interest rates are anathema to longer-term investors such as ourselves. While short-duration bond prices rise moderately, coupon interest is reinvested at lower rates. The "realized compounded yield," a bond-management term, suffers accordingly. Conveniently, the consumer price index is concurrently wallowing in low single digits, making the yields from fixed-income securities somewhat more palatable. Unfortunately, the bulk of the income and realized gains earned on the wealth we manage is not consumed but reinvested instead. We openly acknowledge the formidable task that lies ahead: We must cope intelligently, on the one hand, with a global deflation that has driven bond-market yields to the lowest levels in a number of years and, on the other, with a virulent price inflation that is sweeping through the U.S. equity markets like a raging inferno. Necessity (with due apologies to Aesop or a lesser-known Latin source) is not the mother of a sound portfolio policy; purchasing quality assets at or below what they are worth is. We can't change the game, but we can determine if and when to play. In all decisions, we pledge to conduct ourselves in a businesslike manner—to be, above all, rational and circumspect. As noted earlier, we will do our best to avoid being held hostage by greed, fear, or the mindless imitation of others.

Analysts, as if there's any doubt, are not always right—even when the logic of our reasoning is theoretically sound. As we ply our trade, modern communications technologies have given us fingertip access to vast amounts of economic, business, and financial information at a somewhat reasonable price. Most of it is reliable. Deliberate falsification, while often sensational, is relatively uncommon. A far more important source for errors is in making judgments about an always uncertain future. Lacking anything more tangible, we feel compelled to proceed on the basis that the past is at least a rough guide to what tomorrow has in store. At times it isn't. Another handicap is the sometimes irrational behavior of market participants, seemingly playing in concert under the direction of a slightly mad imaginary maestro. We must rely on this market to ultimately vindicate our judgments. All too often it is painfully slow in adjusting to our way of thinking! As readers are acutely aware, our contention that there is little or no margin of safety in the current prices of many common stocks is of little relevance in a market where the players are rhapsodizing to an improvised tune, the tempo of which is wildly upbeat. Patience and persistence, we frequently remind ourselves, are virtues, even if they don't feel particularly noble at the time they are called into play. We know all too well why the head of the tortoise rides low until the hare is in sight.

The Fixed-Income Alternative

Forecasting interest rates is surely the most difficult and error-prone assignment that a manager who relies on fixed-income securities to function as portfolio workhorses must accept. Let's begin by examining the bond-yield forecast implicit in the yield curve. The bond market is huge, global, active, and therefore relatively efficient; it represents a good summary of what institutional fixed-income investors around the world think about U.S. interest rates. When we observe that the yield curve is relatively flat, as it is today, in nontechnical terms we mean that market yields for securities due in 30 years are not much higher than those due in just one year. For example, the spread between the 30-year and the one-year yields was 0.58% at year-end. Why, you might wonder, would investors lend money for 30 years for essentially the same annual amount of interest they can earn by lending it for one year? The only reasonable conclusion is that they must think that interest rates will fall and that their total return over time will be higher if they "lock in" the yields available on longer-term instruments. If they felt otherwise, surely they and other investors of similar persuasion would sell longer-term bonds (at the margin, causing their prices to fall and their yields to advance) and purchase short-term bills or notes (resulting in their prices rising and their yields falling), producing an upward-sloping yield curve that tends to be more understandable.[3]

We don't take exception with the yield curve's forecast. It is reflective of the popular deflationary scenario. However, there are two compelling reasons why we haven't ventured into long-dated bonds. First is the unanimity of bullishness that the yield curve implies. Implicit in bond prices (again assuming the market is quite efficient) is the expectation that prevailing inflation and economic winds will continue to be favorable to bond investors. Little provision is made in today's bond prices for the possibility of reflation, or that the Euro will eventually displace the dollar as the world's reserve currency,[4] or any other plausible scenario that might result in rising bond yields.

Second is the matter of duration. *Duration* is a technical bond-management term that quantifies the market-price sensitivity of a fixed-income security to changes in market yields. It makes intuitive sense that the greater the number of years until a bond matures, the more volatile are price changes in response to a given change in market yields. What is less widely understood is that duration is also a function of the size of the bond-interest coupon. The smaller the coupon, holding all other factors constant, the greater the volatility. The roller-coaster amplitude of price fluctuations of zero-coupon bonds, therefore, makes them the most volatile of all types of fixed-income securities. Since the only cash payment made occurs when the bond is redeemed at par at maturity, duration and the number of years to maturity are one and the same. When I purchased long-term zero-coupon bonds in the early 1980s at market yields in excess of 13%, I welcomed the prospect of outsized volatility because I felt it would eventually work in my favor. Conversely, committing capital to 30-year 5.17% Treasury bonds today at par borders on speculation, unless it's the investor's intent to hold the security to maturity. If market yields were to increase by 200 points (2 percentage points), the bond price would fall nearly 25%, in all likelihood

---

3 Five years later, the forecast implicit in the yield curve proved resoundingly correct. In June 2003 the 30-year Treasury bond yielded 4.17% and the five-year, 2.02%, while the Fed funds rate was 1.00%. As of June 30, 2005, short-term rates had rebounded from their lows, and the yield curve was nearly as flat as it was in 1998. Currently the 30-year Treasury bond yields 4.30% and the five-year, 3.83%, while the Fed funds rate is 3.50%. Only time will tell if the bond market has adequately discounted future levels of inflation.

4 After its debut on December 31, 1998, at $1.17 per Euro, the Euro exchange rate sank as low as $.82 in late 2000 and now has recovered and strengthened to $1.20 as of June 30, 2005. The dollar is also weak relative to the yen. The U.S. dollar still reigns supreme as the world's reserve currency, but complacency could eventually topple the mighty buck.

foreclosing on the possibility of selling the bond in order to reinvest the proceeds more opportunistically in, say, common stocks.[5]

Finally, a word about bond quality is warranted. As you may not be aware, the yield differential between high- and low-quality bonds widened dramatically during the year when global economic concerns elbowed their way into the headlines. Russia, in particular, shocked selected domestic money-center banks and hedge funds when it effectively defaulted on its sovereign debt. Our stance regarding bond quality remains unchanged. Unless we can find opportunities in investment-grade bonds that compare favorably with those from investment in well-capitalized and reasonably priced common stocks, we will not compromise on credit quality. We feel confident that the creditworthiness of our clients' bond portfolios exceeds that of those managed by any of our regional competitors—by a wide margin.

Sometimes much can be learned by simply stepping back from the hectic pace of business life and asking the question, "Does all of this make sense?" This report, prepared late each year, affords the writer that opportunity. We make every effort to examine all asset classes through the aforementioned paradigm. The combination of OPEC and rising inflation sent crude oil prices from as low as $5 in late 1973 to almost $40 in 1980. As the U.S. economy moved from double-digit to low, single-digit inflation during the recession in the early '80s, the price of a barrel of crude oil fell from its $40 peak to a recent low of around $10. Conversely, the price one must pay to purchase a dollar's worth of bond interest has risen just as sharply as oil prices have fallen. Bond yields, which exceeded 14% when oil was peaking, have since declined dramatically to 5%. (Bond prices move in the opposite direction of bond yields.) Those who believe that the longest peacetime economic expansion will eventually overheat should be as interested in investments that might benefit from rising oil prices as they are wary of long-term bonds with fixed coupons.[6] To be sure, the highest-quality fixed-income securities, with short durations, will likely remain as portfolio stalwarts so long as

---

5 While such a bet looked risky in light of historical yields (we have warned against rearview-mirror investing, in which we ourselves have been known to indulge), as noted in a footnote above, the shape of the yield curve indicated lower rates ahead. Committing assets to longer-duration bonds of the highest quality would have resulted in performance that handily beat the S&P 500 since then. In Chapter Eight read about the biases that infect all investors to one degree or another.

6 In June 2005 the price of crude oil hit $55.58 per barrel, a handsome advance from the $10 at which it traded when the above comments were made. To be sure, capitalizing on the sixfold increase in the price of crude oil is much harder than participating in a rising stock market. It's difficult to share proportionally in the rising price of crude oil, except in the futures market, and using indirect methods can be problematic since the correlation between the price of crude oil and the stocks of major oil exploration and production companies can be surprisingly tenuous.

they meet our present and well-defined need for preservation of principal. When opportunities for growth in principal appear, without concurrently endangering its safety, the role of fixed-income securities will be greatly diminished. Who knows what will appear in their place?

The Dean of Wall Street Revisited

> "The reign of Antoninus is marked by the rare advantage of furnishing very few materials for history, which is indeed little more than the register of the crimes, follies, and misfortunes of mankind."
>
> – *The Decline and Fall of the Roman Empire*, by Edward Gibbon (1737–94)

Edward Gibbon offers a curious reference in the opening quotation regarding the unremarkable reign of Roman Emperor Antoninus (Marcus Aurelius), who ruled in the middle of the second century A.D. It is noteworthy that the events that account for the decline and eventual fall of the Roman Empire, not an insignificant development in the course of world history, was, as noted by Gibbon, "little more than the register of the crimes, follies, and misfortunes of mankind." As you may recall, the book *Extraordinary Popular Delusions and the Madness of Crowd* was of similar persuasion, insofar as the subordination of the rule of law and the follies of man (i.e., often originating from periodic episodes when common sense is almost laughably deficient). With the insights gleaned from the 1934 edition of *Security Analysis* by Benjamin Graham and David Dodd, we should be able to gain a clearer appreciation for the origins of the *follies* of the late 1920s that led to the *unfortunate unintended consequences* (often presented as unexpected or unprovoked tragedy) in the 1930s. Our interest is, however, more than academic. To the extent that follies are as cyclical as human gullibility—in contrast to science, where knowledge is cumulative and where real progress is possible—perhaps we can put history's lessons to practical use to avoid some of the more costly logical consequences that ignorance of the past periodically teaches.

By way of introduction, Benjamin Graham died in 1976 at the age of 82; it wasn't until 1996 that his memoirs, written in his later years, were published. Graham had a prodigious intellect, graduating from Columbia University in two and a half years and having the distinction of being invited to teach in three departments (Literature, Philosophy, and Mathematics) at Columbia. Instead, Wall Street beckoned in 1915. During the 14 years leading up to 1929, young Graham tasted much success, first as an employee and then as a junior partner at a brokerage firm—and finally as head of his own business.

At the quarter-century mark of 1925, the great bull market was under way, and Graham, then 31, developed what he later described as a "bad case of hubris." During an early-1929 conversation with business associate Bernard Baruch (about whom he disparagingly observed, "He had the vanity that attenuates the greatness of some men"), both agreed that the market had advanced to "inordinate heights, that the speculators had gone crazy, that respected investment bankers were indulging in inexcusable high jinks, and that the whole thing would have to end up one day in a major crash." Several years later he lamented, "What seems really strange now is that I could make a prediction of that kind in all seriousness, yet not have the sense to realize the dangers to which I continued to subject the Account's capital" (Benjamin Graham, *Benjamin Graham: The Memoirs of the Dean of Wall Street*, edited by Seymour Chapman [New York: McGraw-Hill Book Company Inc., 1996] 259). In mid-1929, the equity in the "Account" was a proud $2,500,000; by the end of 1932, it had shrunk to a mere $375,000. The dismay and apprehension Graham experienced during those three long years he summarized by saying:

> The chief burden on my mind was not so much the actual shrinkage of my fortune as the lengthy attrition, the repeated disappointments after the tide had seemed to turn, the ultimate uncertainty about whether the Depression and the losses would ever come to an end. ... Add to this the realization that I was responsible for the fortunes of many relatives and friends, that they were as apprehensive and distraught as I myself, and one may understand better the feeling of defeat and near-despair that almost overmastered me towards the end. (ibid., 259)

What has deeply impressed me about the 1934 edition of *Security Analysis*, which Graham set to work on in 1932 (with publication in May 1934), was his uncanny ability to put mind over matter. He intellectually detached himself from the travails that were wracking his portfolio, his confidence, and his sense of stewardship. While there are a number of hints in the book that tie the author's travails to the text, they are most subtle.

The Rise and Fall of Security Analysis

In the introduction to the scope and limitations of security analysis, Graham described the preceding three decades as a period during which its prestige experienced both a "brilliant rise and an ignominious fall":

> But the "new era" commencing in 1927 involved at bottom the abandonment of the analytical approach; and while emphasis was still seemingly placed on facts and figures, these were manipulated by a sort of pseudo-analysis to support the delusions of the period. The market collapse in October 1929 was no surprise to such analysts as had kept their heads, but the extent of the business collapse which later developed, with its devastating effects on established earning power, again threw their calculations out of gear. Hence the ultimate result was that serious analysis suffered a double discrediting: the first—prior to the crash—due to the persistence of imaginary values, and the second—after the crash—due to the disappearance of real values. (Benjamin Graham, and David T. Dodd, *Security Analysis* [New York and London: Whittlesey House, McGraw-Hill Book Company Inc., 1934], 3)

Even an analyst as well-grounded as Graham failed to account for the severe economic contraction that followed the crash. Its causes have been speculated about ever since. Today, concerns about the "reverse wealth effect," thought to be a force that exacerbated the Depression, are clearly on the minds of Alan Greenspan and other policymakers.

The New-Era Hypothesis

During the post-World War I period, and particularly during the latter stage of the bull market culminating in 1929, the public adopted a completely different paradigm toward the investment merits of common stocks. According to Graham, the new-era theory or principle may be reduced to one sentence: "*The value of a common stock depends entirely upon what it will earn in the future*" [emphasis added]. From this dictum, Graham drew the following corollaries:

1. That the dividend rate should have slight bearing upon the value.
2. That since no relationship apparently existed between assets and earning power, the asset value was entirely devoid of importance.
3. That past earnings were significant only to the extent that they indicated what changes in the earnings were likely to take place in the future.

This complete revolution in the philosophy of common-stock investment took place virtually without realization by the stock-buying public and with only the most superficial recognition by financial observers. (ibid., 306–307)

HE USED TO BE STRICTLY VOODOO, BUT LATELY HE'S MOVED INTO MARKET FORECASTING.

Fast-forward 70 years, and a student of history might logically conclude that the investment landscape is eerily similar to that which Graham described in the late 1920s. The current dividend yield on the S&P 500, at 1.34%, is one-third the yield on U.S. Treasury bonds and is at its lowest ebb in modern history. When capital gains are plentiful, who cares about dividends? After all, if the surveys are correct and the average mutual-fund investor really believes that stocks will provide total returns exceeding 20% annually for the next 10 years, today's minuscule dividends pale in comparison to what the investor must expect from capital appreciation. To be sure, the dividend yield would be higher, although not materially so, were the cash used to fund stock-repurchase programs paid out in dividends instead. In plain English, dividend yields are low because stock prices are high (and bond yields are slightly below their long-term average). The explanation is to be found in the denominator, not the numerator.

Likewise, the price-to-book-value ratio of 6.53 is off the charts. As with dividends, there are plausible explanations. Companies like Microsoft and Dell, S&P 500 heavyweights, are short on physical assets and long on intellectual property. In addition, as discussed elsewhere in the report, corporations have taken massive restructuring charges against shareholders' equity in recent years. The growth in book value has, accordingly, not kept pace with the growth in earnings per share. With regard to earnings, Wall Street has never been more dependent on forward thinking than it is today. And that's in spite of the longevity of the current expansion that has set peacetime records, plus the reality that Japan and various Asian and Latin American economies are groaning and creaking like the timbers of a wooden ship in stormy seas. Given the uncertainties that abound, we wonder whether Graham would characterize the heavy reliance today on future prospects as speculation and not investment.

While the exponential ascension in stock prices during the late '20s was in large measure a self-fulfilling prophecy, it was not without scholarly explanation, however tenuous. *Common Stocks as Long-term Investments* by Edgar Lawrence Smith, published in 1924, was often cited as justification for the ownership of common stocks. Unfortunately, the sound premise was rendered unsound by the dint of prices escalating to speculative levels in the late '20s. In practical terms, Smith's supposition was as sensible at 10 times earnings as it was ill-advised at 30 times. Coincidentally, Professor Jeremy Siegel's book, carrying nearly an identical title, *Stocks for the Long Term*, is the contemporary version of the same phenomenon.

Graham asked the rhetorical question, "Why did the *investing* public turn its attention from dividends, from asset values, and from earnings, to transfer it almost exclusively to the earnings *trend*, i.e., to the changes in earnings expected in the future?" He observed that the tempo of economic change made obsolete old standards. At one time, stability was thought to be a function of a business being long-established. Instead, corporations that had been profitable for a decade lost their edge. In their place, other enterprises, "which had been small or unsuccessful or of doubtful repute, have just as quickly acquired size, impressive earnings, and the highest rating." The parallels with today are unmistakable. Think of IBM, AT&T, General Motors, Eastman Kodak, and Kellogg (to name a few) and the restructuring charges that have revealed cracks in their heretofore impenetrable armor. On the other hand, we all have witnessed the spectacular ascent of technology stocks that has sent the Nasdaq price-earnings ratio soaring to over 100, as well as the flight of Internet stocks that have modest though rapidly growing sales and often no earnings. (ibid., 307–308)

Forgetting to Read Menus from Right to Left

As for the analysis of individual businesses, Graham attached great importance to the purchase price, the only variable over which an investor has control (if he has the discipline to patiently wait, and sometimes forgo purchase altogether, so as to pay no more than a price that affords a satisfactory margin of safety). Graham distinguished between financial reasoning and business reasoning as they relate to purchase price:

> We have here the point that brings home more strikingly perhaps than any other the widened rift between financial thought and ordinary business thought. It is an almost unbelievable fact that Wall Street never asks, "How much is the business selling for?" Yet this should be the first question in considering a stock purchase. If a business

> man were offered a 5% interest in some concern for $10,000, his first mental process would be to multiply the asked price by 20 and thus establish a proposed value of $200,000 for the entire undertaking. The rest of his calculation would turn on the question whether the business was a "good buy" at $200,000. (ibid., 492)

> This elementary and indispensable approach has been practically abandoned by those who purchase stocks. Of the thousands who "invested" in General Electric in 1929–1930 probably only an infinitesimal number had any idea that they were paying on the basis of two and three-quarter billions of dollars for the company, of which over two billions represented a premium above the money actually invested in the business. (ibid., 493)

The market value of GE has grown to $334.9 billion since then, compounding over the years at an average annual rate of 7.5%, plus dividends. The premium above the $37 billion actually invested in the business that an investor pays today is a tidy $298 billion.[7]

Long before modern portfolio theory (MPT) and its mathematical models took root in academia, Graham argued that it was unsound to think that the investment character of an issue was a constant:

> The price is frequently an essential element (of any investment operation), and so that a stock may have investment merit at one price level but not at another. The notion that the desirability of a common stock was entirely independent of its price seems incredibly absurd. Yet the new-era theory led directly to this thesis. If a ... stock was selling at 35 times its maximum recorded earnings, instead of 10 times its average earnings, which was the preboom standard, the conclusion to be drawn was not that the stock was now too high but merely that the standard of value had been raised. Instead of judging the market price by established standards of value, the new era based its standards of value upon the market price. Hence all upper limits disappear, not only upon the price at which a stock could sell, but even upon the price at which it would deserve to sell. An alluring corollary of this

7 At the time of this comment, General Electric was selling in the range of $30 (adjusted for a 3:1 stock split in May 2000). It subsequently rose to $60, revealing, as so often happens, investors' misguided affection with the currency equivalent of exchanging two nickels for a dime. Having backtracked to a low of $21 in early 2003, it has subsequently rallied back to a price of $34. Earnings per share were $.95 for 1998 and $1.61 in 2004.

> principle was that making money in the stock market was now the easiest thing in the world. It was only necessary to buy "good" stocks, regardless of price, and then to let nature take her upward course. The results of such a doctrine could not fail to be tragic. Countless people asked themselves, "Why work for a living when a fortune can be made in Wall Street without working?" The ensuing migration from business into the financial district resembled the famous gold rush to the Klondike, with the not unimportant difference that there really was gold in the Klondike. (ibid., 310)

The Investor's Dilemma

In reflecting on the seven years preceding the publication of *Security Analysis*, Graham pointed out the investor's dilemma brought about by the boom-and-bust market cycles that were emblematic of the most turbulent financial and economic era in the 20th century.

> The wider the fluctuations of the market, and the longer they persist in one direction, the more difficult it is to preserve the investment viewpoint in dealing with common stocks. The attention is bound to be diverted from the investment question, which is whether the price is attractive or unattractive in relation to value, to the speculative question whether the market is near its low or its high point.
>
> This difficulty was so overshadowing in the years between 1927 and 1933 that common stock investment virtually ceased to have any sound practical significance during that period. If an investor had sold out his common-stocks early in 1927, because prices had outstripped values, he was almost certain to regret his actions during the ensuing two years of further spectacular advances. Similarly those who hailed the crash of 1929 as opportunity to buy common stocks at reasonable prices were to be confronted by appalling market losses as a result of the subsequent protracted decline. (ibid., 321–322)

Despite obvious similarities to today, it is virtually impossible to forecast the likelihood that knowledge of history will be of relevance now. Furthermore, in attempting to determine the cause-and-effect correlation between two events, the association can be imaginary. Behavioral scientists call it "illusory correlation." Each reader will have his or her own opinion as to what extent the inferences above are imagined. Nonetheless, wealth management requires that we sacrifice opportunity when its downside, however remote, may be permanent loss of capital (defined in the section titled "The Year 1998 in Review"). The aforementioned conversation Graham had with Baruch, followed later by his words of contrition, are still ringing in our ears.

It's a Numbers Game

In examining the confluence of forces that culminated in the Crash of 1929, Benjamin Graham compared the late stages of the phenomenon with the Alaskan Gold Rush. The blurring of distinctions between Wall Street and Main Street that occurred in the last chimerical years of the 1920s became the fetid bog of exaggerated expectations in which an addictive Gold Rush mentality fermented. The cause-and-effect logic that had throughout history linked effort with reward was thought to be temporarily, if not permanently, suspended. Common-stock paper wealth, gold's modern-day gilt-edged substitute (and lots of it) was to be had by those who simply knew how and where to go to unlock its treasures. Visions of untold riches—made even more seductive because the payoff was far out of proportion to the labor expended to acquire it—transformed plodding and deliberate merchants and manufacturers into wild-eyed prospectors. In their frantic search for the theretofore elusive dream, they gladly swapped their dark suits and conservative ways for a pick and shovel. They abandoned many of the rules of thought and conduct—including reason and common sense—that had governed their lives in what at the time must have seemed like a dull and uninspiring past.

Perhaps Graham's analogy may be applicable 65 years later? What we appear to be witnessing today is a near universal rush for the gold that common stocks symbolize. A sense of urgency tied to the obsessive belief that the bounty is finite and that a drop-dead point looms out there somewhere has sustained the charge at a fanatical pace. Nowhere in this agitated plot is there a speaking part for the rational man—except as a quiet and skeptical spectator.[8]

---

8 As yet another example of the repetitive nature of history, the eternal gullibility of the "madding (and sometimes maddening) crowd," and the parasites who prey on its denizens (see elucidating insights from novelist Ayn Rand in Chapter Seven), let's step back in time to the California Gold Rush, which preceded by about 50 years the longer-lived Klondike Gold Rush. It was on John Sutter's expansive property that James Marshall, Sutter's sawmill contractor, discovered gold nuggets in the American River in 1849. Sutter and Marshall suppressed the gold news so as not to cause interruptions with their real estate development. Not surprisingly, it was a San Francisco merchant and master of hype, Sam Brannan, who got wind of the seemingly well-kept secret and subsequently became the richest person in California—but Brannan never mined for gold. When he started racing through the streets yelling, "Gold, gold in the American River," he wasn't planning to dig for it. He was planning to sell shovels. And the first person who sold shovels got a lot more gold than the person who had to dig for it. The laws of supply and demand were not unfamiliar to Brannan. His wild run through San Francisco came just after he had purchased every pickax, pan and shovel in the region. A metal pan that sold for 20 cents a few days earlier was now available from Brannan for 15 *dollars*. In just nine weeks, he made $36,000. *While there are many stellar exceptions, the sooner one learns that much of Wall Street is actually in the "picks and shovels" business the better.*

The following section examines the lengths to which some corporate executives have gone to massage their corporation's finances and their own compensation programs to seize what they believe to be their share, if not more, of the spoils. All the schemes, however far they stretch credulity, seem to excite little resistance if they are packaged under the pretense of "enhancing shareholder value." The deportment of those who exhibit some or all of the symptoms of Gold Rush fever, when viewed through that fascinating and age-old prism, is made much more understandable. Observed under any other construct, such people must appear capricious.

Some years ago, I asked the CFO of a public company what he thought earnings would be for the year. His facetious reply: "What would you like them to be?" I wouldn't ask that question today because I'm afraid of what the answer might be.

The Supremacy of Earnings

Somewhere along the road to riches the corporate balance sheet was discarded as having little nutritional value, like yesterday's half-eaten McDonald's hamburger and fries. In its place has arisen "earnings power" (more often than not with substantial justification) as the primary determinant of the intrinsic value of a business. Before we lay to rest this barbaric corporate relic—the balance sheet and in particular the shareholders' equity account—let's say a few kind words in its memory. Shareholders' equity (book value when expressed in per-share terms) represents the shareholders' investment in the business, carried on the corporate books at depreciated cost, after all liabilities have been satisfied. While book value represents a reasonable starting point if liquidation of assets is in prospect, it is otherwise a relatively poor measure of the value of a business. For example, the tangible assets of Coca-Cola and Gillette pale in comparison to the value of their brands. The earnings of both companies are derived more from the market dominance and power of their intangible property than from the physical and financial assets that appear on the balance sheet. Nonetheless, when purchasing a business at a premium price relative to its book value—invariably the case today and frequently with good cause—some awareness of the size of the gap is warranted.

The full measure of the premium is better appreciated when expressed in aggregate terms. Returning to our earlier examples, the market value of Coca-Cola is $171 billion and represents a premium of $164 billion over the $7 billion in net tangible assets. Unconsolidated bottlers are carried at cost on Coke's balance sheet. If the market value of the bottlers is used, the $7 billion would increase to something like $15 billion. The equivalent numbers for Gillette are $52.5 billion in market value of the shareholders' equity and $2.5 billion in net tangible assets. (Excluded is the valuable goodwill associated with the purchase of Duracell.) These financial statistics give credence to the earlier observation that most of the market value of these two businesses is derived from corporate assets that are nowhere to be found on the balance sheet. The not-insignificant premiums that the shares of these companies command in the marketplace are more understandable than many less-established companies in vogue today. There is a possibility, however slim (given the lightning pace of change and the general instability in the Internet world), that Yahoo and Amazon.com will dominate their respective markets 10 years hence. But there is relatively little doubt, conversely, that Coca-Cola and Gillette will reign supreme in theirs. He who doesn't understand the difference may ultimately be a victim, not a victor.[9]

Now we turn back to "earnings power." Even here a perfunctory note of caution is justified. Graham offers these thought-provoking observations:

> In recent years increasing importance has been laid upon the trend of earnings. Needless to say, a record of increasing profits is a favorable sign. Financial theory has gone further, however, and has sought to estimate future earnings by projecting the past trend into the future and then used this projection as the basis for valuing the business. Because figures are used in this process, people mistakenly believe that it is "mathematically sound." But while a trend shown in the past is a fact, a "future trend" is only an assumption. The factors that we mentioned previously as militating against the maintenance of abnormal prosperity or depression are equally opposed to the indefinite continuance of an upward or downward trend. By the time the trend has become clearly noticeable, conditions may well be ripe for a change. (Graham, *Security Analysis,* 36)

---

9 (All of the following stock prices have been adjusted for splits.) Amazon.com peaked at $110 in late 1999 and cratered at $5 in the fall of 2001, when the market capitalization was approximately $2 billion, which was down from the high of $38 billion. The stock has subsequently rallied back to $33 (a market capitalization of $14 billion) as of June 2005. Sales have grown to $6.9 billion in 2004, from just $600 million in 1998. In 2004 the company earned net income of $589 million. Likewise, Yahoo skyrocketed to the same lofty price of $110 in early 2000, only to collapse to $4 by the fall of 2001. As of June 2005 it sold for $35. Revenues for 2004 were $3.5 billion, and profits $840 million, or $0.58 a share. The market capitalization as of June 30, 2005, was approximately $48 billion, down from approximately $117 billion at the peak, but still mind-boggling compared with current earnings. Forever chasing the latest great idea, speculators are now ogling Google. Amazon was the creation of a young fellow with an audacious idea, whereas Google is the brainchild of two bright young guys with an algorithm. We are addicted to Google as consumers of information, but not to the stock. As of June 30, 2005, its market capitalization was approximately $82 billion, with earnings for the last 12 months of about $1 billion. Seven years later, my skepticism remains unabated. Remember Darwin ...

The Accountants Are Not to Blame

Accounting is under indictment, in all likelihood unfairly.[10] The task of reducing endless variations of actual business activities to standardized financial reports and protocol is at best not without significant real-life problems. No doubt part of the reason is that accounting is, as it always is destined to be, a step behind an ever-changing business world, the current expression of which is increasingly driven by technology and deal-making. In reality, the Securities & Exchange Commission (SEC) and public accountants are chasing a forever-moving target. It is out of practical necessity that the generally accepted accounting principles (GAAP) allows companies' chief financial officers and their bosses plenty of flexibility—or, in Washington jargon, "wiggle room." The rules rely on honesty and integrity—behaviors that are ostensibly encouraged by the presence and watchful eyes of "independent" auditors—to ensure that financial presentations are both "transparent" and "reliable." Lawrence Revsine, a prominent accounting professor at Northwestern's Kellogg Graduate School of Management, sums up the current state of affairs succinctly: "Accounting stinks." It always will, but through no fault of its own.

Let's face it; GAAP will never be a good match for those who are intent on finding a way around the sometimes flimsy roadblocks against misrepresentations and other abuses that the Financial Accounting Standards Board (FASB) erects. Besides, the seemingly ever-evolving boom in financial assets that dates all the way back to 1982 has put a premium on deception because, to put it bluntly, it pays so well. Which brings to mind the pungent pronouncement attributed to Mark Twain (loosely interpreted) that there are liars, there are abominable liars, and then there are statisticians. The head of auditing at KPMG Peat Marwick, the fourth-largest accounting firm, observes: "There's probably more pressure to achieve results than at any time that I've seen." Earnings growth drives executive bonuses as well as stock options (which of late account for more than 50% of executive compensation), and the ability to make accretive acquisitions, raise money, or even survive as an independent entity. Robert Olstein, a fund manager and former co-author of the respected newsletter *Quality of Earnings Report*, lays part of the blame at the doorstep of security analysts. "Accounting tricks are always going on," he says. "What's changed is that companies are getting away with more now because analysts aren't paying any attention." We agree. Unfortunately, as is human nature, the longer the dry spell, the more likely it is that people will

10 Sadly, some accountants and accounting firms succumbed to the temptations of the times. Independence became compromised when shekels trumped scruples. "He who writes my checks calls the tune I sing" is an old adage for an ageless reason.

stop carrying umbrellas.

The investor's watchdog, the SEC, has begun to rattle its sabers. This past fall, SEC Chairman Arthur Levitt began a rare series of meetings with top corporate CEOs, accounting analysts from investment houses, the FASB, and the Big Five accounting firms, among others. Not only did the midyear stock market retreat prod normally unflappable Federal Reserve Board Chairman Alan Greenspan into action (reaction?), but the SEC's Levitt openly worried that if accounting problems continue, even more damage could be done to investor confidence. It is probably reasonable, although impolitic, to ask: "If the chairmen of both the SEC and the Federal Reserve take their cues from the stock market, why, pray tell, should the captains of industry do otherwise?" Reasoning further, it appears that people in high places sense that the speculative Bubble is inflated to near the bursting point, and no one wants to be remembered by history as the one holding the hatpin.

What's a Company to Do?

If companies aspire to take full advantage of the fruits that this grand and expansive bull run offers, they must demonstrate earnings momentum. Some, whose businesses are simply not up to the test, have relied instead on extraordinary measures, in desperation turning to "cookin' the books" (in most instances on low) in order to remain a player.

Earnings management is the unspoken buzzword among corporate managers as they seek to pull out all stops in responding to the Wall Street edict. For many senior officers of publicly traded companies, the fixation on reporting a steady upward progression in earnings per share is more than academic. The potential for millions of dollars of stock-option profits often hangs in the balance. It is paramount, therefore, that managers win and hold the favor of Wall Street analysts, whose thumbs-down reactions (if managers disappoint by missing their "guided" estimate for quarterly earnings per share by a cent or two) can trigger a flood of sell orders.

The 'Big Bath' Restructuring Charge

Corporate America has finally discovered what the 42nd president has long known. If you put the right spin on (corporate) sin, what was once unspeakable among estimable gentlemen seated in dark leather chairs around a heavy mahogany table is now an acceptable, if not actually fashionable, topic for conversation. Forgiveness for these sins of malinvestment comes freely from an ever-more-blasé investing public whose memories are short and who call for neither confession nor contrition. This state of unquestioned forbearance has not gone unnoticed in the corporate boardroom.

The naked truth is that restructuring charges (often announced in oxymoronic terms as "nonrecurring" charges) are management's public admission that earnings in past years were overstated. They are a confirmation that corporate resources had been committed to an investment or investments that ultimately failed to measure up to minimal expectations—and the time has come to stop the hemorrhaging. A charge or debit is made to shareholders' equity, and a liability reserve of equal size is established. Liquidation of unproductive assets and personnel severance costs are among those future expenses for which reserves are instituted. As costs are incurred in untangling yesterday's bright idea, the liability reserve is reduced accordingly. It is noteworthy that those costs do not appear as a line item on the income statement but rather are shuttled directly to the liability side of the balance sheet.

To be sure, humans, even CEOs, make mistakes. After all, investments are made in the present, but returns are subject to the vicissitudes of the future. A lot can happen between now and then. For example, how a customer, or a competitor, might respond to a new product is often little more than conjecture until the jury of the marketplace hands down its verdict. Good managers can reduce investment risk, but they can't eliminate it.

"HOWEVER, BY USING AN ALTERNATE METHOD OF ACCOUNTING...."

Strangely, it's apparent that investors rarely look back as stock prices often rise when restructuring charges are announced. The rationale? First, the operating-earnings drag of the miscue will cease, and thus future reported earnings, *ceteris paribus*, will increase by the amount of the expenses thereby avoided. Additionally, there is a more subtle gain to be had. As sometimes happens, managers will overestimate the costs to be incurred in the effort to right yesterday's wrong. In fact, since Wall Street is ostensibly impervious to the size of the charge (within reason, of course) and, as noted previously, exacts no immediate market-price penalty, is it not better to be safe than sorry? That's how the so-called "big bath" charge came into being. Here's the benefit. After the damage has been repaired, still undepleted reserves can be used to offset future costs without having those costs leak onto the income statement. In Burger King terms, we think of the twin benefits as a "double whopper" for future earnings. No wonder Wall Street cheers! And it all began with the amputation of a leg or an arm from the body of shareholders' equity. I suppose if anyone ever looked at the restructuring charge for what it is from an accounting point of view—a reduction in assets for which shareholders lay claim—the drum roll announcing the event would be muffled. Main Street investors understand the absurdity of what Wall Street investors apparently thrive on. Think of it as emasculation of the corporate balance sheet; assets only count in liquidation, and who's worried about that?

It gets more troublesome. As hinted above, big charges can become addictive. And don't for a minute think that such chicanery is the exclusive plaything of corporate lowlifes. Such behavior can be found in the best of families. AT&T, the company whose sadistic, omnipresent telemarketers invade my home (seemingly once a week and, like clockwork, always at dinnertime), took multiple write-offs totaling $14.2 billion during the decade ending 1994. All the while, its earnings miraculously grew by 10% a year, from $1.21 to $3.13. Even magician David Copperfield would find that feat amazing. It was, after all, a financial elephant the size of the Empire State Building that AT&T made to disappear in a cloud of accounting mumbo jumbo. The write-offs exceeded by almost $4 billion the $10.3 billion in earnings that the company actually reported. Sometimes it's helpful to compare the growth of a company's earnings over a period of time with the growth in shareholders' equity, before dividends are paid. Don't allow your children to do AT&T calculations unsupervised. We last wrote about AT&T's foibles in the 1995 annual report, and the beat goes on.[11]

Speaking of children, would they clamor for Frosted Flakes if they knew that Battle Creek-based Kellogg Co. has taken charges to "streamline operations" in nine of the last 11 quarters through year-end 1997? Real operating earnings for 1997 were more like $1.29 (down 24% from the year earlier), compared with the $1.70 reported. And the company still commands a price-earnings multiple of 31. At what point, it seems reasonable to ask, should such costs be recognized as recurring and thereafter appear as operating expenses in the income statement?[12]

11 AT&T continues to be a "poster company" in the numbers game. Following earlier spin-offs of Lucent and NCR, it spun off AT&T Wireless (which was later bought by Cingular in 2004) and Liberty Media in 2001. It discarded AT&T Broadband in a transaction with Comcast in 2002 and announced in mid-2004 that it will be shifting focus from residential services to business services. After reaching $94 in early 1999, the stock fell to a low of $14 in late 2004. Because of the number of spin-offs, the decline in the stock price of AT&T overstates the loss in value for shareholders. In the latest chapter, in early 2005 SBC (one of the Baby Bells born from the government breakup of AT&T) announced plans to acquire its former parent for $18 per share. But wait, there's more ... While AT&T no longer exists as a stand-alone operating company, the bloodied but nonetheless venerable AT&T name is likely to survive. In a salute to the power of branding, SBC is considering renaming itself ... AT&T!

12 The year 2002 was the first in the last five that Kellogg did not take a line-item restructuring charge. The stock peaked at $50 in early 1998, later falling to $20 in the winter of 2000. It currently sells for around $42, about 20 times earnings, and appears to have cleaned up its act.

A popular catchall technique, staying with descriptors familiar to children, is the "cookie jar reserve." Companies use unrealistic assumptions to estimate liabilities for such items as sales returns, loan losses, or warranty costs. In effect, they stash accruals in cookie jars during the good times and reach into them when needed in bad times. This practice helps to smooth earnings rather than actually enhance them, as other schemes are able to do.

Some restructuring charges, we hasten to add, actually lead to increased earnings power, thereby enhancing the intrinsic value of the business by pruning dead branches. Our attention here is to the abuses.

Acquisition Reserves

"DUE TO CUTBACKS AND DOWNSIZING, WE HAVE TURNED OFF THE LIGHT AT THE END OF THE TUNNEL."

While different in origin, reserves established as a result of acquisitions can serve much the same purpose. SEC Chairman Levitt calls the practice "merger magic." The number of acquisitions taking place each year has skyrocketed, making the issue increasingly relevant. In-process research-and-development write-offs, unknown a decade ago, have soared since IBM used the technique to write off $1.8 billion of the cost of its 1995 acquisition of the spreadsheet creator, Lotus Development. The capitalized expenditure, in-process R&D, is obviously of indeterminate value to the acquirer. It is frequently written off after the acquisition as a "one time" charge so as to reduce future earnings drag (which, under certain circumstances, we ignore).[13] WorldCom's $37 billion purchase of MCI Communications is another case in point. WorldCom estimated that at the time of the acquisition MCI had $6 billion to $7 billion in R&D under way but

13 IBM traded at about $90 when the above comments were made and traded for $75 as of June 2005. It peaked at $135 in 1999 and sank as low as $54 in 2003. In 2002 the company recorded an after-tax charge of $1.8 billion for "extraordinary" items.

not ready for commercial application, making it the largest in-process R&D charge so far. Since it is possible that WorldCom may never see any benefits from the MCI expenditures, accounting rules allow WorldCom to write them all off at once. Apart from the accounting practice, the Main Street business owner might well wonder why WorldCom paid so much for MCI if there is even a remote possibility that almost $7 billion of acquired assets are worthless. In reality, there is little doubt that WorldCom ascribes great value to MCI's R&D efforts. As WorldCom turns MCI's R&D efforts into salable products, profits therefrom will be juicier without the drag of the amortization of capitalized R&D expenditures. In this instance, expenses and revenues are clearly not properly matched. With regard to the balance sheet, the charges effectively understate the amount of capital invested in the business.[14]

Equally troubling, according to the SEC's Levitt, is the creation of large liabilities for future operating expenses to hype future earnings—all under the guise of an acquisition. Walt Disney, in its 1995 purchase of Capital Cities/ABC, wrote off certain of ABC's programming costs at the time of the acquisition, thereby relieving its income statements of three or four years' worth of additional expenses. From this point forward, the company will have to show legitimate earnings growth, not the kind that comes from accounting machinations—unless it can engineer still more deals, as many banks have done.

Pooling vs. Purchase Acquisition Accounting

Now we're getting a bit technical. At the risk of missing a subtlety or two, I'll attempt to keep the discussion at the lay level. In the case of an acquisition accounted for as a pooling of interests, the acquired company is absorbed into the parent company. The historical financial statements of the parent are recast so as to portray prior years as if the two had been a family for a long time. Stringent tests must be passed for pooling to be used. On the other hand, purchase accounting, as the name implies, means that the revenues, expenses, and profits of the acquiree are aggregated with the parent's income statements from the time of acquisition. If, as is almost always the case, the acquirer pays more than the market value of the net assets of the acquired company, the premium, an asset called "purchased goodwill," must be amortized against earnings for up to 40 years.

14 WorldCom filed for bankruptcy in July 2002. It was charged with overstating earnings by more than $11 billion in the largest accounting fraud scandal ever.

The advantage of pooling is that whatever purchase-price premium might have been paid, it is nowhere labeled as such and therefore is not subject to amortization. By way of an analogy, think of pooling as it might apply to a marriage between NBA clotheshorse Dennis Rodman and actress/model Carmen Electra that, hypothetically of course, lasted several years before irreconcilable differences (he never put the cover on the lipstick) brought an end to the otherwise blissful union. On the date of consummation, Dennis—speaking exclusively in financial terms—may have paid a hefty premium for the 50% of his (and soon-to-be-their) marital estate that he effectively surrendered to the comely lass of *Baywatch* fame, if not fortune. (Assuming Nevada's laws on marriage dissolution are typical, Carmen's equity in the marital estate could approximate a shocking 50% on that sad day, presuming that the brief time between "Let's get married" and "I do" left no time for a prenuptial.) It is doubtful that their balance sheets or income statements were comparable at the time of the merger of unequals. Poor(er) Dennis surely suffered instantaneous dilution unless he was hedging against a possible season-less NBA. Because he pooled, rather than purchased, the "goodwill" arising from his impulsiveness need not be officially amortized even though, in reality, a prudent man would do so. Bankers, Dennis should know, are sometimes prudent.

Unless accounting measures can be employed to reduce or eliminate the purchase price paid above the market value of net assets in a purchase transaction (as addressed elsewhere), the premium must be amortized against future earnings. The advantage of purchase accounting is that, depending on how the transaction is financed, a steady stream of acquisitions may result in earnings growth well above that which is organic. Cendant, one of the more celebrated failures of 1998, stumbled badly in executing its strategy of growth by acquisition. For the curious, it's a cautionary tale of a company that camouflaged slow internal growth with a flurry of acquisitions, the last of which turned a formerly *as-cendant* trajectory into an almost fatally *des-cendant* one.[15]

At MCM, we don't quibble with purchased goodwill if it's readily apparent that the premium paid is equal to or less than the

15 Within a six-month period during 1998, Cendant stock plunged from $42 to about $7. In the five years since, earnings have been irregular, as the company disgorged itself of hastily conceived acquisitions and reorganized as a global provider of complementary consumer and business services. The stock traded around $22 at the end of June 2005.

value received. As far as we're concerned, companies that go to great lengths to avoid amortization charges are squandering time and money. As a matter of practice, we add back amortization charges to earnings in our valuation work if the usefulness of the goodwill acquired is unlikely to decline over time. In this supercharged acquisition environment, however, we suspect that many acquisitors with voracious appetites have grossly overpaid. Paradoxically, one aftermath of the current binge must inevitably be another wave of aforementioned restructurings, including goodwill write-downs, as a result of overpriced mergers.[16]

With regard to the matter of acquisition accounting, in our financial modeling, we attempt to ferret out economic earnings. Accordingly, we make whatever adjustments we feel are justified—regardless of which method is used to account for an acquisition—to reveal economic realities. If the analyst community would do likewise, there would be far less use of smoke and mirrors in the practice of financial reporting.

Revenue Recognition

Although we don't encounter this misdemeanor often, in part because of the practical difficulties in identifying it, the SEC has served notice to companies that try to boost earnings by accelerating the recognition of revenue. Think about a bottle of fine wine. It isn't appropriate to pull the cork until the contents are properly aged. But some companies are removing the cork early, recognizing revenues before a sale is truly complete; before the product is delivered to the customer; or when the customer still has options to terminate, void, or delay the sale.

---

16 Until 2002 FASB (Rule 142) mandated amortizing goodwill generally over a 40-year life. In 2002 FASB flip-flopped and relieved companies of the obligation to systematically amortize goodwill. Instead, it now requires that goodwill be reviewed annually for possible impairment in value. If impairment has occurred, the company takes an immediate charge. For the six years prior to the accounting change in 2002, cumulative goodwill amortized for the S&P 500 totaled $3.91 per share. From 2002 to 2004, goodwill- impairment charges totaled $10.36 per share, with $6.91 charged in 2002 alone. The vast majority of these write-offs were related to acquisitions that failed to live up to merger-frenzy expectations, and their carrying value had to be slashed in a more rational environment. To be sure, the old method of amortizing the carrying value of assets that often appreciated in value—and then charging that expense against earnings—made no economic sense. Under the new rule life is different, but not necessarily better. Large one-time impairment charges permit a company to sweep under the carpet prior dissipations of shareholder capital without typically evoking much of a response from Wall Street. Why? Because of the accounting treatment, the action has a salutary effect on earnings, return on equity, etc. ...

'Stealth Compensation'

The use of stock options as a key component of executive compensation has mushroomed. According to Richard Walker, named SEC director of enforcement last April, stock options outstanding have nearly doubled since 1989, accounting for 13.2% of shares outstanding. *The Wall Street Journal* calls them "the steroids that bulk up executive pay ... the currency of an optimistic and opulent age." From 1992 to 1997, the value of option grants to CEOs and other executives of about 2,000 companies surveyed by Sanford C. Bernstein & Company quintupled to $45.6 billion from $8.9 billion. Also, according to *The Journal*, options-driven CEO compensation has climbed to 200 times the level of the average worker—a fivefold increase from the 1970s. That striking if not unsettling divergence draws little artillery fire during good times, yet the capitalist ideology itself could become the prime target if the cataclysm of serious recession sets in.

With more and more of an executive's pay linked to the upward movement of a company's stock price—in which historically he or she had little cause for direct interest—it's no longer uncommon to see a modern executive preoccupied with financially managing the business for the chief purpose of maximizing the stock price. Such practices may or may not be consistent with the goal of increasing intrinsic value. During a recent analyst conference on another hot topic, fair-value accounting, several participants expressed concern about any changes that would increase earnings volatility. One analyst summed up the sad state of affairs when he said, "Any [managers] not concerned with smoothing earnings [are] not doing their job. You need to manage Wall Street—without being deceptive—while hiding information that could be used ... by competitors."

For financial-reporting purposes, option grants are free money, because in their accounting treatment they are doubly blessed: Options granted do not appear as an expense on corporate income statements, yet they are deductible when exercised as a cost for the purpose of tax reporting. The table [see Figure 1.1 in the Appendix] prepared by Smithers & Company in London reveals the dramatic effect on reported earnings if stock options are considered a current expense rather than capitalized, as they essentially are now. (Smithers' methodology in estimating the annual cost of stock options is admittedly biased in favor of the obvious point he attempts to make. For our purposes, we deduct from operating earnings an estimate of the value of options granted in the current year. We then adjust the denominator in the EPS calculation to account for the dilutive impact of previously issued options.) Smithers arrived at the figures for the hundred largest U.S. companies for 1996 by summing the estimated value of options that were exercised during the year and the estimated cost of immunizing the company against future increases in its stock price, which would have the effect of upping its total option costs. The first 11 companies would have shown losses after the adjustment. The next 13 would have seen their profits cut in half. Curiously, six of the first seven also appear in the table depicting the 24 largest-cap companies in the S&P 500 stock index.

Admittedly working with hard-to-get data (estimated option expense information is tucked away in a company's 10-K reports), Smithers concluded that the 1995 earnings of the 100 companies he surveyed would have been 36% lower in 1996 if full-cost accounting for options had been used. Had the same methodology been used in 1995, earnings would have been 30% lower.

There's another perspective from which to look at the options sleight of hand [see Figure 1.2 in the Appendix]. The major companies listed have issued options that total more than 25% of fully diluted shares outstanding. To the extent that options are issued in lieu of reportable cash compensation, these companies may be seriously overstating their operating earnings, to say nothing of diluting (conveniently rhymes with looting) often unsuspecting shareholders who rarely make it through the annual report footnotes, let alone the proxy statement. Fortunately, several large institutional managers are no longer silent on the issue. Redress, however, is years—or a pervasive bear market—away.[17]

As noted in the table and by way of extreme example, Microsoft has issued options equal to almost 45% of its shares outstanding. Shareholders, including Bill Gates who before dilution owns approximately 20% of the company, will suffer massive dilution unless the stock falls to a fraction of its current price. If the company were to consider repurchasing the shares necessary to fund its options program, they would cost $49 billion at today's market price. Microsoft has $14 billion in cash. Cash flow for 1998 is estimated to be $9 billion. Under that hypothetical scenario, the total of outstanding shares would remain unchanged, but cash on hand and future cash flow would be depleted for years to come. Regardless of its name, options are synonymous with dilution. Now refer back to the previous table to see what might be the effect of Microsoft's largess with its employees with regard to reported earnings.

In 1993, when FASB attempted to rule that the burgeoning use (and

---

17 In spite of heavy resistance from industry lobbyists, FASB 123R took effect at large public companies for annual reporting periods starting after June 15, 2005. Since options are valuable (but unlike cash they can't be precisely valued), an approximation of their expense will appear as a line item on the income statement. This action is clearly a step in the right direction. However, nature may have her way in the end. If stock prices don't heat up again soon, the worth of options as a compensation tool will be greatly reduced. Good ol' cold cash could be restored to its former glory and re-emerge as the "currency of compensation"! What goes around comes around ...

concealed cost) of options should be divulged on corporate income statements, the agency ran headlong into the lobbying steamroller driven by the Big Six auditing firms and much of corporate America. Dennis Beresford, now a professor at the University of Georgia, served as chairman of FASB when the endeavor was flattened. "The argument was: Reduced earnings would translate to reduced stock prices," recalls the then embattled professor. "People said to me, 'If we have to record a reduction in income by 40%, our stock will go down by 40%, our options would be worthless, we won't be able to keep employees. It would destroy all American business and Western civilization.'" *Forbes* magazine cynically concluded: "The bull market is more important than accurate financial reporting." Nobody, as noted previously, wants to be caught holding a hatpin should the bubble burst.

Beyond the absurdity of allowing options compensation to escape being treated like any other corporate expense and the possible backlash from eventual exposure of "stealth compensation" (that skews overall compensation in favor of the executive suite at the expense of the factory floor), we have other misgivings about the use of options. A widely cited argument for their use is that they cause managers to think like owners. As owners of the publicly traded shares of businesses, we find it difficult to understand exactly what it is that option holders have in common with us. When we make an investment, our first act is to write a large check. If the stock price subsequently falls—for any of a host of reasons—and we fess up to our mistake and sell, our loss is painfully tangible, and it represents far more than just the loss of an opportunity that the option holder endures. Ever-resourceful "optioneers" have found a remedy for the one downside of options—the opportunity that's lost when the share price heads south. It's increasingly fashionable to restrike options at lower prices should the stock go begging. Who said there wasn't opportunity in adversity?!

As for granting options to the rank and file, sometimes for the purpose of blunting internal criticism of megagrants on Executive Row, the practice is as widespread as it is unproductive in achieving its desired goals. According to a proxy-statement analysis by William M. Mercer Inc., 35% of the 350 major companies tracked by the firm have stock-options programs for all or a majority of their workers. Another source advises that 50% of mid-level professionals at major companies receive options. Far from promoting an owner's frame of mind or even inspiring loyalty to the company, the vast majority of recipients treat this form of corporate beneficence as nothing more than a windfall. The Lotto mentality moves up and down the corporate ladder with surprising ease. When Citicorp Chairman John Reed was asked how he reacted when Traveler's Chairman Sanford Weill first proposed the colossal merger of their huge financial-services firms, he replied: "My instinct was to say, 'Why not?'" In the wake of the surprise announcement, both companies' stock prices surged, as in lockstep did stock-option paper profits for both Reed and Weill, whose one-day windfall was a cool $67 million and $248 million, respectively. Based on what has transpired subsequently, and presuming that Reed was not distracted by visions of sugar plums dancing in his head, "Why?" might have been a more-reasoned and less-instinctive retort. Boys will be boys, differentiated only by the size of their toys. Our other objections will be saved for another year.

Once again, we acknowledge that option programs have become nearly universal, particularly with technology companies. A company in Silicon Valley, for example, that stands on principle may find it practically impossible to recruit effectively.

In the meantime, rest assured that we comb the footnotes of 10-K's and proxy statements of every company that we research to unearth stock-option or other abuses that may be tucked away there. Recognizing that stock options in this day and age are nigh unto ubiquitous (yes, rhymes with iniquitous), we don't object to companies that use options sparingly—and, in particular, to companies led by a dominant shareholder who doesn't personally participate in the options program. If the presumably knowledgeable insider is willing to suffer with us the cost of dilution at parity, we see no reason to take issue. As shareholders, we find repricing proposals to be an even more outrageous example, fancy explanations notwithstanding, of options simply serving as off-income statement compensation. Apparently, FASB has reached the same conclusion. Early in 1998 it decided that companies repricing options should expense the difference between the lower-share price and subsequent increases. In the end our concerns may be of little consequence. If market participants of the future are like market participants of the past, and if the pendulum is freed again to swing, the next pervasive bear market will close the gap between effort and reward. Options, like stock prices, will fall—out of favor.

Stock Buybacks

Stock buybacks might well be more appropriately reviewed under a different banner. Many, if not most, programs evince a prudent use of shareholder cash. Boards that authorize share-repurchase initiatives at market prices below what the businesses are intrinsically worth per share (without forgoing investment in even more compelling growth opportunities and with due regard for the financial security of remaining shareholders) are clearly putting the shareholders' interests high on their priority list. While trying not to cast unnecessary aspersions on the purity of motives, we nonetheless find a curious circularity to the reasoning behind the calculation of the worth of the business. If the higher-earnings-per-share growth rate that results from the share buyback program in turn causes the board's determination of the worth of the business to be ratcheted up accordingly, where does one get off the merry-go-round?

Furthermore, and of no pressing concern, it also has occurred to us that share-repurchase programs are subject to finite limits. There is conceivably no ceiling on company growth, but a company can retire no more shares than are outstanding. If there are enough shareholders who don't comprehend the value of the business and are willing therefore to part with stock at prices well below intrinsic worth, someday there will be but one shareholder group remaining. That's what we call an MBO (management buyout)—on the installment plan.

Depending on how they're financed, stock buybacks have the effect of increasing earnings per share. If the numerator (after-tax earnings adjusted downward to account for additional interest expense when money is borrowed to finance the purchase) falls less than the denominator (reduced by virtue of the shares acquired and retired), earnings per share will rise. In a catch-22 scenario, once a stock-repurchase program is instituted, discontinuing it becomes problematic. If the stock price surges in part because of the presumed higher rate of earnings growth, terminating the buyback plan will remove the growth catalyst that financial engineering provided, and the share price will likely register Wall Street's displeasure. Letting the air out of stock prices, as noted elsewhere, is anathema in modern-day boardrooms. To the extent that this section addresses techniques by which executives can "manage" earnings, share repurchases must be included. Such programs—many of which we applaud, and a few of which we think are blatant, flagrant, and systematic squanderings of shareholder assets—are nothing more than another arrow in the financial-engineering quiver. Their only income-statement appearances are through an increase in interest expense or a decrease in interest income, relating to the means by which they are financed—and a reduction in the denominator in the earnings-per-share calculation. They have no effect on operating profits.

As is often the case, the tax code ostensibly forces the corporate hand. It is reasoned that because dividends to individuals are taxable as income at rates approaching 40%, whereas gains on long-term capital transactions (including occasions when individual shareholders sell back to the issuing company) are subject to a maximum 20% tax, the latter distribution option is more tax-efficient.[18] The logic is not in all instances bulletproof. For starters,

18 The tax on dividends for most shareholders was reduced to 15% as of May 5, 2003.

shareholders selling to other investors rather than directly to the company also avail themselves of the favorable tax rates on long-term capital transactions. The tax differential is admittedly of particular appeal to a taxable shareholder who sells enough stock each year to equate to a cash dividend, had one been paid. In effect, he or she creates a synthetic dividend that is taxed at no more than the 20% rate. Tax-exempt shareholders, including 401(k), pension, and other deferred-compensation plans, at least from a tax perspective, are obviously indifferent to the form of distribution, whether through dividends or share repurchases.

Finally, little is said about how a company's board of directors views its relationship with passive shareholders. In most instances, it is probably appropriate for the board to think of a shareholder's investment in the company as but one among many similar holdings that make up the shareholder's total portfolio. Such an attitude regarding any obligation that the board might feel toward its constituent shareholders is consistent with the doctrine that holds, "If you don't like what we're doing, you can always sell your stock." This almost universal and impersonal "portfolio of companies" paradigm runs counter to the "partnership" construct that Warren Buffett speaks of in his letters to Berkshire Hathaway shareholders. To be sure, Buffett's ownership structure is as refreshing as it is atypical. His 42% stake in Berkshire represents virtually all of his $30 billion net worth.[19] Likewise, for a considerable percentage of the company's outside shareholders, Berkshire also represents a large part of their wealth. Their Berkshire holding is not unlike a beloved lake cottage that becomes a family heirloom. It isn't surprising then that Buffett takes great pride in the low rate of turnover of Berkshire shares. If turnover were to increase appreciably, it might suggest that the lake is going dry.

Conclusion

The increased reliance of companies on accounting practices that are implemented to give the impression of often unwarranted growth, profitability, and stability is a sign of the times. For us, such hocus-pocus (with a bogus focus) simply mandates more thorough "due diligence." We spend extra time these days with financial-statement footnotes, proxy statements, and other disclosure documents. As noted above, when we attempt to determine the true earnings of a company, we often must recast financial statements to more fully reflect economic reality.

---

19 Buffett's investment in Berkshire had appreciated to almost $42 billion as of June 30, 2005.

CHAPTER TWO—1999

Introduction

The writing of the annual report is a special privilege for the undersigned. In addition to the opportunity it provides to communicate with a wonderful group of people, it also periodically induces me to step back from the fray and reflect on the nature of the causes of which the capital markets constitute merely the effect. Throughout, an atypical attitude toward risk and opportunity is advocated that may make the journey of wealth management less uncertain if not more productive. Much of what follows, as always, pays due homage to Mark Twain's dictum: "History doesn't repeat itself, but it rhymes." More on that later.

Call it philosophical resonance. At some point in our professional lives, we come to the realization that we can't be all things to all people, that we must choose sides. I had the early-career good fortune of being exposed to the writings of Benjamin Graham well before I was introduced to mainstream thinking. That learning experience proved to be an epiphany. The logic and integrity of Graham's thinking enthralled me. Just as naturally as dessert follows the main course, I later came to embrace the teachings of Warren Buffett, Graham's protégé. Buffett is simply Graham raised to the second power. Such singular focus likewise means there is little room in my intellectual library for the volumes of modern portfolio theory dogma, which governs the thinking of many in our profession. It's not so much a matter of right or wrong that separates the two as it is a difference in time perspective. Buffett thinks in terms of buying businesses, while MPT is about buying stocks. The difference is huge.

While many of the views expressed herein reveal the influence of the opinions of learned others, they cannot be entirely separated from my own evaluation of the prevailing facts and circumstances. Intentional or otherwise, they display my imprimatur, as well as mirror my biases and predispositions. As for the order of things, this report will begin with a discussion of the goings-on in both the equity and debt markets. It will then turn to how the MCM ship has navigated them: where we sought deep water and how we avoided possible shoals. Finally, there will be a section that features heretofore unspoken musings by Warren Buffett on the subject of the outlook for the returns from equities over the next decade or two.

A Tale of Two Markets

The defining characteristic of the markets for U.S. common stocks last year was the divergence in stock price performance between those industries favored by investors and those considered passé. The companies leading the information revolution, broadly defined to include communications equipment (computer hardware, software, and services; electronics; and technology services), turned a trend that was well-established in 1998 into a blowout in 1999. The S&P's tech sector jumped 74.7% last year, following 1998's 72% gain. *Technology issues accounted for about 90% of the advance in the overall S&P 500*, which climbed 19.5% in 1999. The venerable Dow Jones industrial average, meanwhile, getting a late-year boost from two of its new members, Microsoft and Home Depot, surged ahead 25.2% to a record 11,497 Reflecting the tidal wave in tech issues, the Nasdaq finished 1999 with a record gain of 85.6%. By comparison, the great mass of companies simply languished.

As we are inclined to do, allow us to cast what is happening in the context of both time and space. The 68 companies that comprise the S&P technology index subset accounted for 13.3% of the value of the entire capitalization-weighted S&P 500 composite index at year-end 1997. In 24 months, it had tripled to 44.4%. The technology-dominated Nasdaq composite index, also capitalization-weighted, has become the market's force *du jour.* (The Internet sideshow is examined elsewhere in this report.) The fact that the companies of which the Nasdaq is constituted are the least seasoned in the American economy does not seem to matter one whit to an investing public whose appetite for technology—or perhaps the rising prices that their shares offer—appears insatiable. The market value of the Nasdaq composite, a mere $220 billion as recently as 1990, has ballooned to an incredible $5.7 trillion. In contrast, the market capitalization of the S&P 500 composite index is about $12 trillion (itself approximately 75% of the estimated $16.4 trillion U.S. equity market). Adjusted for the double counting (Nasdaq companies included in the S&P 500 index), the Nasdaq composite looms large indeed next to the sum of the market values of all the other industries that provide the material side of the American dream—industries that build and furnish the homes in which we live; produce, package, and distribute the food we eat and the pharmaceuticals that fill our medicine cabinets; make and retail the clothes we wear; and manufacture and sell the cars we drive and the planes we fly (and the fuel that makes them go). You know, the incidental stuff!

To be sure, the information revolution is the most important growth driver in our economy. Skyrocketing share prices are a testament to the premium that investors are willing to pay for growth or, in the case of the Internet, the distant expectation of it—or to the extent to which investors have taken leave of their senses. Of the three emotions that periodically sweep through the marketplace like a forest fire fanned by high winds—fear, folly, and greed—which might it be? The price-earnings ratio for the Nasdaq composite exceeds an unimaginable 200. Yes, there are two zeros. The off-the-charts trailing, 12-month, 27 to 33 times (depending on how you keep score) price-earnings ratio at which the S&P 500 sells pales by comparison. Indeed, these are the most unusual of times ...

Growth vs. Value

To elaborate a bit more on the subject, it is widely believed that growth investors tend to focus on technology companies and others with rapidly growing profits, while value managers seek undervalued and beaten-down stocks that often have low price-earnings multiples. If we must be categorized as value investors, it's because we only invest in those securities for which we can reasonably estimate their value and only at prices that are less than that value. We prefer growth but understand that it is but one component of a company's value. Reflect for a moment, if you will, on the airline industry and its profitless prosperity.

As for a rough approximation of the growth in the intrinsic value of the S&P 500 index, we estimate it may have increased by a total of 10% to 15% over the 1998–99 period. It was spurred by the 110-basis-points drop in interest rates in 1998 (using the 10-year Treasury note as proxy) in the face of flat operating earnings. The flip side of the coin appeared in 1999 with operating earnings advancing by 16% while weathering a 170-basis-points uptick in interest rates. In sum, over the two years, the yield on the 10-year note rose by 60 basis points, and operating earnings for the S&P 500 composite companies advanced at an annual rate of 8.1%. The increase in the market value of the index, heavily weighted by technology issues, was more the result of expanding price-earnings ratios than earnings growth. Based on trailing 12-month earnings, from the first day of 1998 to the last day of 1999, the price-earnings ratio of the index advanced from 24 to 33, according to *Barron's*. The S&P value index crept ahead 12% in 1998 and 9% in 1999, more in keeping with the growth in underlying intrinsic value.

The disparity in performance between growth stocks (including both technology and branded consumer-product stalwarts) and value stocks is most pronounced among the smaller and mid-size companies. Looking beyond the S&P 500, the growth stocks in the Russell 2000 index, the small-cap benchmark, were up more than 40%, while value stocks in the index fell 3%. That spread is the widest in 20 years.

The growth/value gap was even more pronounced among mid-cap stocks, with the Russell mid-cap growth stocks gaining about 50% and value stocks unchanged. In the S&P 500, the gap was narrower. The index's growth stocks rose 27.3% last year, and value issues advanced 10.7%.

Hedge-fund manager Julian Robertson Jr., writing to the clients of Tiger Management in December, summed up the value manager's dilemma:

> ... [T]he Internet is a great new technology that will change our lives. But there have been other great developments that created equally important lifestyle changes. In the past, investors overreacted to the promise of these changes ... We're in a wild runaway technology frenzy; meanwhile most other stocks are in a state of collapse. I have never seen such a dichotomy. There will be a correction. As to whether or not this correction will take the form of a total market collapse as in 1929, 1973–74 and 1987, I have doubts. Why? The out-of-phase stocks are just too cheap. ... [T]his would imply a long-term underperformance of technology (believe it or not, it has happened) while the rest of the market continues to advance. Of course, this would be the ideal situation.[20]

As for the last sentence, Julian Robertson hedges more than just his portfolios.

Zeroing in on one of the two most widely recognized investment styles, the following table [see Figure 2.2 in the Appendix] makes clear the what-price-do-I-pay-for-growth dilemma that a man with money in his pockets faces today. He may be damned if he does and damned if he doesn't. If he forks over an ante that discounts the next hundred years of earnings and something unexpected occurs "'twixt the cup and the lip," history may reveal him to be a fool—and a much less prosperous one at that. If "Jack" doesn't,

20 As events unfolded, Julian Robertson proved to be amazingly prescient. A later footnote will tell the rest of this sad but instructive story.

and this bean "stock" grows to the sky, his wealth will grow at the pace of a redwood, while everyone else's imitates a rocket. The unwanted consequence of the first choice is that he may find himself absolutely poor and in the second, relatively so. While neither outcome is desirable, the consequences of the first are more severe. We hope you agree.

Another hallmark of the times is the harsh retribution dealt companies that fail to "make their numbers." An interesting ritual has developed between and among corporate America's and Wall Street's *cognoscenti,* and it ties neatly into the discussion in the section titled "Ledger d'Maim" [omitted, but it can be located in the 1999 annual report on the MCM Website]. Before a company officially announces its quarterly earnings, it is frequently known to "guide" key analysts as they construct their earnings forecasts. So much for independence. Soon a "whisper" estimate mysteriously circulates within the analyst community. Analysts are preconditioned. Understandably, then, when a company's formal release hits the wires, there is precious little tolerance for an earnings shortfall. In the new economy, the element of surprise increasingly has been "managed" out of profits, leaving a smaller portion of the earnings outcome subject to the vagaries of business, at least in the near term. Failure to "make their numbers," therefore, reveals far more about a company's operating results than a penny or two per share would otherwise suggest. If the earnings disappoint, despite the best efforts of the company's managers to massage out imperfections, something must be seriously awry. The palace revolt is as swift as it is sure.

A Study in Contrasts: Debt vs. Equity

The two securities that potentially tie up one's capital the longest are common stocks and distant maturity bonds. Ownership can be perpetual, and the return of principal from a bond can be as many as 30 years away. Either, of course, can be sold in the interim under most circumstances. As noted above, technology stocks have paid off handsomely in the recent past, whether one's investment horizon is near or far. Long-dated bonds (we use the 30-year U.S. Treasury bond as proxy) were the mirror opposite. These "certificates of confiscation," as they are impolitely called, provided a 1999 total return of minus 14.4%, far and away the worst calendar-year performance ever.[21] Yields on Treasury bonds began the year at 5.09% and finished at 6.48%. The Lehman Government/Corporate index suffered a negative return for

21 No sooner had the "certificates of confiscation" been spat upon when the worm, as it so often does, turned. From January 1, 2000, through June 30, 2005, the compounded annual total return of the 30-year Treasury bond with interest payments reinvested at 4% was approximately 10%; the S&P 500, before reinvestment of dividends that would've added a little more than 1% to the total return, was -3.7%; and the Nasdaq, -11.7%. In pretax dollar terms, $10,000 invested in the Treasury bond at the outset would have been worth $17,000 five and a half years later. Sometimes you win by not losing ...

only the second time (1994 was the first) since it was created back in 1973. The miserable showing of bonds in '99 might properly be laid at the doorstep of the booming stock market, with investors accelerating a trend that began five years ago of dumping bonds for stocks. An unprecedented development of the late '90s was that stocks were driving bonds—rather than interest rates influencing equities as they have in the past. The wealth created by the booming stock market is pushing the economy ever higher. Consider that the Conference Board's index of leading economic indicators rose to a 40-year high in November, thanks in part to the sizzling stock market.

Beyond investors' aversion to bonds, other forces had the effect of nudging interest rates higher as well. The economy continued to boil, the Federal Reserve hiked the discount rate three times, and fears of nascent inflation refused to die.

If there were a consensus forecast for interest rates by the end of 2000, it probably would peg the yield on the 30-year bond at 7%. In spite of, or perhaps because of, economists' underestimation of economic resiliency in 1999, they are calling for more of the same in 2000. Upward pressures on interest rates will continue to build under that scenario.

The wild-card argument for higher yields stems from the uncertainty about how foreign investors will react to any changes in perceptions about the dollar and the attractiveness of the U.S. Treasury market. When the U.S. government borrows money these days, the chances are excellent that foreigners will be the ones writing the checks. Foreign investors—insurance companies, pension funds, central banks, individuals—now own almost $1.3 trillion in U.S. government securities, which is 40% of Washington's $3.2 trillion in accumulated marketable debt, according to the latest federal statistics. Five years ago, by contrast, foreigners held $641 billion in Treasuries, just 20% of the total at the time. Foreigners, effectively, have helped finance our imports. Princeton economist Alan Blinder, former vice chairman of the Federal Reserve, says there is "an upside and a downside to borrowing money" from abroad: "The upside is you get your hands on the money. The downside is you have to pay it back."

A good case to be made for lower yields is the "flight to safety" proposition. Pronounced stock market weakness could precipitate a scramble for the safe-harbor alternative that high-grade fixed-income securities offer. Any economic weakness that followed also would reduce the demand for money and, *ceteris paribus*, its cost.[22]

---

22 The enigma of lower long-bond yields remains unresolved and inexplicable. The market-clearing yield on the 30-year Treasury bond as of June 2005 was 4.30%. We wonder aloud what the yield on the 30-year bond will be in 2010.

How We Managed Risk and Where We Found Opportunity

We believe that if you get the risks right, the returns will take care of themselves. As investors who consider patience a virtue and a prudent purchase price an absolute necessity, we looked for a more favorable mix of risk and opportunity elsewhere, given the considerable danger implicit in paying such extraordinary prices for the immensely popular and impressively growing technology companies. And we found such a mix. In our judgment, it resides in a number of well-capitalized companies whose primary appeal is not that they have a hot-wire connection to the information revolution but that their competitive advantages within their industries are defensible. Their historical earnings-growth rates, as well as longer-term prospective rates, are likely to be several times that of the economy as a whole.

Your portfolio reflects our ongoing reluctance to pay unprecedented premiums to play in a game in which we have no demonstrated competence and no croupier's advantage. We feel like an old hand at Las Vegas; our gut sense of the way things work tells us that the longer we stay at the tables, the more likely it is that we'll walk away empty-handed. Our rational side dominating, we watch and we wonder. To be sure, our reticence to sit for a few hands of blackjack has been costly in terms of lost opportunity, made all the more obvious by the run of good luck the fellow over whose shoulder we're looking is having. Make no mistake, we believe investing is the only game of chance where anybody who is savvy and independent enough can *become* "the house" and set the odds. We abide in that conviction. Our judgment, however, has yet to be confirmed. Once again, as indicated in the table below, our equity securities lagged the performance of the S&P 500, although by a considerably smaller margin than in 1998.

Investment Performance

Period Ending December 31, 1999	MCM Equities *	S&P 500 *
Since Inception **	15.1%	23.5%
Five Years	20.2%	28.5%
Three Years	16.9%	27.5%
One Year	18.8%	21.0%

* Compounded annually, MCM data net of fees

** December 31, 1993

Year	MCM Equities (Net of Fees)	S&P 500
1994	-7.5%	1.3%
1995	19.1%	37.5%
1996	31.8%	22.9%
1997	45.1%	33.3%
1998	-7.4%	28.6%
1999	18.8%	21.0%

According to Ben Graham and Warren Buffett, the three most important words in the serious investor's lexicon are *margin of safety.* In other words, the purchase price of a stock should be sufficiently below the investor's estimate of the company's intrinsic worth—in that if the estimate proves to be low, a cushion in the form of the discounted price still remains. The higher the uncertainty about one's estimate, the greater the margin should be. It's really rather straightforward. How interesting it is that teacher and student *nonpareil* are, above all, concerned with managing risk. In the end, that's where the game is won or lost. In the meantime, rest assured. We will not do things with your money that we won't do with ours, the pressure to keep up with the (Dow) Joneses notwithstanding. That portion of your portfolio committed to well-capitalized, growing businesses that we think we understand and that we purchased on average about 10 times earnings typically did not exceed 30% of the portfolio's value at year-end.

Fixed-income securities in our clients' portfolios returned less than their coupons. Rising interest rates saw to that. That translates to about a 3.5% total return from Treasuries and about 2% from municipal bonds. Because of the short durations of our portfolios (average maturities range from one to five years), we were not penalized like long-bond buyers by the rising rates. On the contrary, in 1999 we were able to recycle liquidity at the best yields available in several years. Falling bond prices have actually spelled opportunity for us.

Tax minimization was factored into investment decisions made. For tax-paying investors, the lion's share of the gains realized will be favorably taxed at long-term capital-gains rates, and a varying share of the income earned was from municipal bonds and therefore exempt from state and federal income tax. Interest income from U.S. Treasury securities is also exempt from state income taxes.

As prosaic as this must sound, the 6.5% yield available on five-year Treasury notes and the almost 5% to be earned from Aaa-rated, pre-refunded municipal bonds of similar maturity may provide ample competition for the broader equity market over the next few years.[23] Despite the goings-on in the broad market, we will continue to buy high-return on equity companies (irrespective of the size of market capitalization) that enjoy solid growth opportunities, are well-financed, and are selling at prices that offer an attractive trade-off between risk and opportunity. Our performance-based fee structure means that your portfolio's growth and our revenues are "joined at the hip." Moreover, the "high-water mark" proviso checks any urge we might have to overlook risk in the face of the temptations of greed or folly. We appreciate your continued forbearance and hope that in time both of us will be proved wise.

Finally, when you think of common sense ("street smarts" in the jargon of Wall Street), the words of Mark Twain again come to mind. What may surprise you is that the great 19th-century skeptic was not in real life the sage that his clever aphorisms would suggest. Twain repeatedly squandered his writing income on questionable investments, including a turn-of-the-century version of biotechnology. He appears to have been swayed by investments linked to well-known businessmen or politicians. In addition to the biotech fiasco, Twain's losing bets ranged from a health-food company to a new printing process to an Austrian carpet-weaving machine. At least he was able to make light of his losses, and his experiences spawned some classic one-liners. For example: "There are two times in a man's life when he should not speculate," lamented Twain. "When he can't afford it, and when he can." Fortunately, some lessons can be learned vicariously.

Back to the Future?

It is not uncommon for investors to imagine the future as an extension of the immediate past. That is, their vision of tomorrow is wherever a straight line that connects the dots of yesterday takes them. It even has Sir Isaac Newton's physical principles behind it—an object in motion tends to remain in motion. And yet, financial history, with

23 That is precisely what occurred, with bonds outperforming stocks by an embarrassing margin. Wharton professor Jeremy Siegel, pilloried elsewhere, insists that stocks will outperform bonds in the long run. Roger Ibbotson's voluminous historical account (see reference to Ibbotson elsewhere) lends the weight of historical evidence and precedent to add credence to Siegel's extrapolations. The writer agrees with both. What Siegel, the academic, forgets on occasion is that (to badly paraphrase John Maynard Keynes) while the patient, long-term investor may become "rich" in the long run, if he's foolish he may go broke in the short run!

no regard for our forgetfulness, occasionally reminds us of its cyclical (y)earnings. To be sure, few would disagree with the notion that simple extrapolation of the past is an acceptable beginning point from which to approximate the future—most of the time. But there are moments, inflection points if you will, when and where simply extending the line is a sure prescription for misfortune. It is the line that can be one's undoing. It can lull a person into complacency.

Think of a grandfather clock in slow motion. When gravity gradually and inexorably overcomes momentum, and the pendulum is about to reverse course—when aversion to the mean becomes regression to the mean—linear extrapolation is plainly counterproductive. Periods of linearity are never permanent, any more than are the seasons. In fact, the existence of irregular recurring patterns of events, often well-camouflaged by the abstruse symmetry of their ebb and flow (the timing of which can be annoyingly unpredictable) should at least pique one's curiosity about the possible relevance of the study of bygone days.

This cyclical tendency of business and the free markets is such that by the time a trend is most pronounced and thus most widely embraced, it is also most pigheadedly inclined to reverse itself. It is one of life's poetic ironies that in the depth of darkest winter the buds of spring begin to form. The swinging-pendulum metaphor may also help to make the point.

We surely need not be reminded that history is a tool, relevant apart from the classroom setting, that actually has practical utility—like a head is more than just a hat rack. Of equal importance, knowledge of where we've been frees us from the constraints of having to simply take things as they are for lack of anything else to hang onto. Paradoxically, it is a lack of familiarity with, or a general disregard for, history's tutorial that may well exacerbate its repetitious nature. If you don't know history, says the sage, you're condemned to repeat it.

To be sure, history is a teacher in the abstract for those who want to apply it to the future. While, as Mark Twain said, events of the present sometimes "rhyme" with the past, they nonetheless have their own unique rhythm. It is the timing, then, that often proves most nettlesome for those attempting to apply the events of yesterday to make order of today—and to capacitate a clearer vision of tomorrow. Timing errors may humble the prophet, but they needn't necessarily disparage his prophecy. Read on to learn about two modern-day Cassandras whose warnings should not be dismissed simply because they cried "wolf" when none was at the door.

Where's the Wolf?

The date of a most unusual final prospectus was May 9, 1996. The security being initially offered was the new "Class B Common Stock" to be issued by Warren Buffett's Berkshire Hathaway. The relatively small $500 million offering of shares at $1,110 each (the equivalent of 1/30th of the Class A shares, the highest-priced stock on the New York Stock Exchange) was solely to forestall promoters from issuing low-priced shares of a unit trust designed to track the performance of Berkshire's Class A shares.

Stated Buffett recently: "Our issuance of the B shares not only arrested the sale of the trusts, they provided a low-cost way for people to invest in Berkshire if they still wished to after hearing the warnings we issued." The timing was thus not of Berkshire's choosing. The following is the impassioned "sales pitch" that Berkshire's chairman provided would-be investors, in full view of even cursory readers, on the cover page of the offering document.

> WARREN BUFFETT, AS BERKSHIRE'S CHAIRMAN, AND CHARLES MUNGER, AS BERKSHIRE'S VICE CHAIRMAN, WANT YOU TO KNOW THE FOLLOWING (AND URGE YOU TO IGNORE ANYONE TELLING YOU THAT THESE STATEMENTS ARE "BOILERPLATE" OR UNIMPORTANT):
>
> Mr. Buffett and Mr. Munger believe that Berkshire's Class A Common Stock is not undervalued at the market price stated above. Neither Mr. Buffett nor Mr. Munger would currently buy Berkshire shares at that price, nor would they recommend that their families or friends do so.
>
> Berkshire's historical rate of growth in per-share book value is NOT indicative of possible future growth. Because of the large size of Berkshire's capital base (approximately $17 billion at December 31, 1995), Berkshire's book value per share cannot increase in the future at a rate even close to its past rate.
>
> In recent years the market price of Berkshire shares has increased at a rate exceeding the growth in per-share intrinsic value. Market overperformance of that kind cannot persist indefinitely. Inevitably, there will also occur periods of underperformance, perhaps substantial in degree.

> Berkshire has attempted to assess the current demand for Class B shares and has tailored the size of this offering to fully satisfy that demand. Therefore, buyers hoping to capture quick profits are almost certain to be disappointed. Shares should be purchased only by investors who expect to remain holders for many years.

Buffett, in this instance, was anything but prescient [see Figure 2.3 in the Appendix]. No sooner had he given his "not at this price" warning than the stock began a two-year ascent, during which it more than doubled.[24]

Next we turn to Federal Reserve Chairman Alan Greenspan, the most powerful appointed official in Washington and the most powerful person period when it comes to guiding the U.S. economy. Six months after Buffett pronounced Berkshire stock to be overpriced, the other financial giant of our times, Greenspan, issued his famous "irrational exuberance" statement during a speech to the American Enterprise Institute for Public Policy Research on December 5, 1996. The title of the talk: "The Challenge of Central Banking in a Democratic Society." The chairman of the Federal Reserve Board worried aloud about the economic consequences that might ensue from the collapse of a financial bubble.

> Clearly, sustained low inflation implies less uncertainty about the future, and lower risk premiums imply higher prices of stocks and other earning assets. We can see that in the inverse relationship exhibited by price-earnings ratios and the rate of inflation in the past. But how do we know when *irrational exuberance* [emphasis added] has unduly escalated asset values, which then become subject to unexpected and prolonged contractions as they have in Japan over the past decade? And how do we factor that assessment into monetary policy? We as central bankers need not be concerned if a collapsing financial asset bubble does not threaten to impair the real economy, its production, jobs, and price stability. Indeed, the sharp stock market break of 1987 had few negative consequences for the economy. But we should not underestimate or become complacent about the complexity of the interactions of asset markets and the

24 After reaching a low point of about $1,500—coincident with the peak in the Nasdaq frenzy—the Class B shares rebounded to a high of $3,150 in May 2004. Currently they sell for $2,800. Nobody, not even the most astute and wealthiest diversified investor in the world, is capable of forecasting short-term stock price movements. That's a "tip" worth remembering!

> economy. Thus, evaluating shifts in balance sheets generally, and in asset prices particularly, must be an integral part of the development of monetary policy.

On that date, the Dow Jones industrial average closed at 5,178.25.[25]

Having surveyed the financial-section headlines of major metropolitan newspapers for 1999, it is clear to me that Greenspan's apprehensions about the possibility that the financial markets' collective tail may someday wag the economic dog have not faded in the least. Of particular interest is the speech he gave this past October, in which he alluded to the absence of an equity-risk premium that historically has been embedded in stock prices. The word *risk* appears in the text 53 times, as if in Greenspan's tangential way, he was trying to emphasize the point by innuendo so as to avoid the chance of instigating the very event that he clearly fears.

How could these two men, perhaps the most knowledgeable and respected leaders extant in the fields of finance and economics, be so far off on their timing? How could they turn cautious three or more years in advance of a storm that does not yet even loom on the horizon? Unapologetically, Buffett observes matter-of-factly, "Markets behave in ways, sometimes for a long stretch, that are not linked to value. Value, sooner or later, counts."[26] Peter Bernstein in *Against the Gods* identifies the phenomenon mathematically as regression to the mean. Dependence on reversion to the mean for forecasting the future, he cautions, tends to be perilous when the mean itself is in flux. And yet, without some regard for the eventual central tendency of stock prices, valuation anomalies like the 200-plus times earnings at which the Nasdaq composite sells are possible. Price fluctuations, however random they appear, must be tied to something more stable than themselves. Indeed, they are accepted with equanimity these days—without triggering cries of alarm much beyond the measured exhortations of the likes of Buffett and Greenspan.

Even the smartest and best-informed economists and investors can't pinpoint the extremes to which crowd psychology—sometimes manic, sometimes depressive—will oscillate (or if and when it will lose its oomph and eventually display its opposite side). Don't lose patience or get distracted,

---

25 Three years after Greenspan's warning, the Dow reached a peak of 11,497.12 on December 31, 1999; it sank to 7,591.93 on September 30, 2002, before rallying in the early summer of 2003 to over 9,000. The Dow has since lingered around the 10,500 mark for many months.

26 Once again, the markets have proved the efficacy of Benjamin Graham's adage: "In the short run, the market is a voting machine, but in the long run, it is a weighing machine."

for the race is long. With all of Buffett's "sins" of omission (the most recent being his reluctance to embrace technology or Internet stocks), his net worth is still, shall we say, respectable. Think of him as a $26 billion "loser." But even he admits that his best days may well be behind him, that 15% is more achievable. For years he has warned that size alone militates against the intrinsic value of Berkshire compounding at a rate anywhere near the 23% of the last 35 years. By the way, how impressive is that rate?! A college graduation present of $13,600 to a 22-year-old this spring who can match Buffett's after-tax rates of return will have enough seed money to ensure a $100 million nest egg at normal retirement age. Nonetheless, with Berkshire stock down 23% in 1999, the first annual decline since 1990, the vultures are beginning to circle. *Forbes* columnist and money manager Martin Sosnoff recently took Buffett to task for being out of touch with the new economy in an article titled "Buffett: What Went Wrong?" The feature article in the December 27 issue of *Barron's* posed a similar rhetorical question: "What's Wrong, Warren?" What if it isn't Buffett who's out of touch?!

Warren Buffett on the Stock Market

Buffett is loath to talk about the stock market, despite his belief in the eventual tendency for prices to converge on value. One would think his confidence in the principle of regression to the mean would have been sufficiently shaken after the ill-timed Berkshire Class B advice and earlier pronouncements that high rates of inflation are endemic to our political economy. And yet, on four occasions in 1999, Buffett felt compelled to speak out, giving extemporaneous talks on the subject to private groups. *Fortune* magazine writer and Berkshire Hathaway annual report editor Carol Loomis distilled the contents of the first and the last in a November 22 article titled "Mr. Buffett on the Stock Market." Buffett then edited Loomis. Most of the observations below have their genesis in the article.

Buffett builds a compelling case that today's investors, prone as they are to look at the future through the rearview mirror, have an unsupportably optimistic view of the returns that common stocks in general can deliver in the years ahead. A PaineWebber and Gallup survey released in July '99 reveals that the least experienced investors—those who have invested for less than five years—expect annual returns over the next 10 years of 22.6%. Even those who have invested for more than 20 years are expecting 12.9%. They seem to be able to disconnect themselves from underlying business and economic realities, and that concerns Buffett [not to mention the writer].

Going back 34 years, Buffett overlays a sort of biblical symmetry onto the past to observe the sequential appearance of lean years and fat years. For the first half, from the end of 1964 through 1981, the market's return was indeed lean. The Dow Jones industrial average started at 874.12 and ended at 875.00. Observed Buffett wryly, "I'm known as a long-term investor and a patient guy, but that's not my idea of a big move." This anemic outcome was even more curious because of a GDP (gross domestic product) increase of 370% over the 17-year span. Two other developments completely negated the upward thrust on equity prices that would logically be expected from a growing economy. First, the market yields on U.S. Treasury bonds rose from just over 4% at the end of 1964 to more than 15% by late 1981. Since bonds represent direct competition for all other investment assets, the quadrupling of interest rates had the effect of driving bond prices (and therefore the prices of all near substitutes, including equities) sharply downward. Second, after-tax corporate profits as a percentage of GDP—that portion of the total sales of goods and services in the economy that ends up in the coffers of the shareholders of American businesses—tumbled to 3.5%, well below the average indicated on the chart [see Figure 2.4 in the Appendix]. So, at that point, investors were looking at two commanding negatives: subpar profits and sky-high interest rates. Looking forward by extrapolating the past, investors were despondent, a state of mind amply reflected in stock prices.

The next 17 years (beginning in 1982) were as fat as their predecessors were lean. The Dow skyrocketed from 875 to 9,181, a 10-fold increase. Interestingly, GDP grew less than in the first period, but the precipitous fall in bond-market yields to 5% and the increase in corporate profits' share of GDP to 6% provided much of the impetus for higher stock prices. Long-term bonds rewarded investors with an annual total return of more than 13%, but stocks stole the show. Their annual total return, with dividends reinvested, reached an astounding 19%. But those two fundamental factors only explain part of the rise. The rest is attributable to the change in investor psychology from the despair of the early '80s to the exuberance of the '90s, bordering on the irrational, to which Alan Greenspan alluded. Advancing stock prices soon became a self-fulfilling prophecy. It is from that psychological framework that the current crop of rosy expectations, which the Gallup organization surveyed, has been formed.

What's Ahead?

Staying with the symmetry of the 17-year cycle, what's likely to be in store between now and 2016? Buffett avers emphatically that for an outcome anywhere close to what investors expect—even those with 20 or more years' experience—one or more of the following events must occur. Government-bond yields, now 6.5%, must fall farther still. (If one has strong convictions about that, bond options are the purest and most profitable way to capitalize on that scenario.) In addition, the portion of GDP destined for corporate profits must increase. Regression to the mean is a force to be overcome if that assumption is to have merit. For corporate investors to eat an ever-growing slice of the American economic pie, some other groups must eat less. Political pressures, to say nothing of competition, will likely keep a lid on the expansion of corporate profits. Of course, corporate profits could rise to new highs as a percentage of GDP, but they obviously cannot grow faster forever.

What about growth in GDP? The assumption of a 3% real growth rate is consistent with historical trends and the expected growth rate in the economy's productive capacity. To that we add inflation of, say, 2%, arriving at a 5% nominal growth rate. To the extent the rate of inflation changes, so will the nominal growth rate.

So here we are. Profits growth under the above assumptions would approximate 5%, to which would be added about 1% for dividends in determining the returns investors can reasonably expect. Dividend yields are at record lows, which can largely be attributed to record-high stock prices.[27] Earnings per share would rise faster than profits because of share repurchases, were it not for shares issued in primary offerings and through stock-option plans. They more or less cancel each other out.

If one thinks investors are going to earn 13% a year in stocks, one must assume that GDP is going to grow at 12%, with another 1% coming from dividends. Historical standards, if not the economics of investment, would suggest that little help is going to come from expanding price-earnings ratios. On the contrary, one must acknowledge that future returns are always affected by current valuations. The 500 companies that comprise the S&P composite index represent 75% of the market value of all U.S. corporations. In the last four quarters, earnings for the S&P 500 companies totaled $403 billion; the present market value for the index is $11.7 trillion. Current prices in relationship to earnings are defying history, the laws of economics ... and gravity.

Investor expectations are seriously detached from reality today, according to Buffett, just as they were in the mid to late '60s in the final throes of the great postwar bull market. Even though experienced investors expect annual returns of almost 13% over the next 10 years—and novices believe they will get nearly 23%—in the opinion of the greatest investor living today, common stocks in the aggregate will be lucky to return 6%, or 4% after inflation, in the years ahead.

---

27 The S&P 500 dividend yield has risen to 1.8% from a low of 1.1% in August 2000, due to a combination of falling stock prices and rising dividends.

Investing in Businesses Driving the New Economy?

But, you say, I don't invest in staid old businesses that grow in line with the underlying economy. I avoid the mundane; I am not broadly diversified. Perhaps, you argue, there is an alternative to spreading one's bets all over the board in order to avoid the mediocre returns from sampling a little bit of everything? Maybe if we concentrate our portfolios in technology and Internet issues, where growth is sure to eclipse that of GDP for years to come, we can avoid the curse of the broader malaise? Read on and decide for yourself.

By way of proper introduction, we begin by noting that the 20th century has spawned a momentous series of inventions that have changed forever the way we engage in nearly every aspect of our daily lives. Think of how far Americans have progressed from the snail's pace of the horse, buggy, ship, and steam locomotive to the speed, comfort, and convenience of first the automobile and then the airplane. In communications, we've gone from the Pony Express to the telegraph to worldwide telecommunications. In media, we've progressed from local performances to national book chains and "talking color pictures." Chronicles of the pervasive impact of these marvels of ingenuity on where we live, work, and play would fill a large library. Imagine how different home life would be without the telephone, radio, television, and air conditioning—and white-collar workdays without the high-speed elevators and skyscrapers.

Consider some of the following effects of past technological improvements on business. Marketplace opportunities went from being confined to local communities to national and international markets, which gave rise to the notion of "economies of scale" of mass production. National media introduced the concept of "branding." Imagine the process of manufacturing widgets without the ability to constantly communicate with your customer base. And now comes the information revolution whose backbone is the diminutive computer chip. Computers revolutionized the volumes and means by which we manage and transport data. The latest iteration, the Internet, will forever change the conduct of commerce, both retail and business-to-business, and the mechanisms we employ to communicate at all levels. More on that in a moment.

Surprisingly, as awe-inspiring and life-changing as these inventions have been, almost without exception they were a boon to consumers and a disappointment to investors. At the peak of excitement over the prospects for the automobile, there were 2,000 producers in the United States. Now there are three, if you include Chrysler in spite of its recent sale to German carmaker Daimler-Benz. As of year-end 1998 (chosen so that Chrysler would be included), the market value of the domestic automobile companies totaled $118.5 billion. The industry sold $302.9 billion worth of vehicles in 1997 and earned $25 billion, Chrysler included. We can only speculate about the high point in market valuation that the industry excited at the pinnacle of the public's infatuation with the horseless carriage. If it was in the vicinity of $100 million, the average annual increase in market value approximated an unimpressive 7%, to which dividends should be added or capital infusions deducted.[28]

Widening the scope, there are 230 companies in the FactSet transportation grouping. Included are airlines, air freight/delivery services, railroads, trucking, and marine transportation—the means by which goods sold on the Internet and everywhere else are transported from the manufacturer, through the wholesaler, and ultimately to the consumer. On 1998 sales of $516.6 billion and earnings of $23.3 billion, the mid-December 1998 market capitalization of the industry aggregated $305 billion. Within that segment, the airline and aircraft-manufacturing industries, which numbered 300 companies in their heyday between 1919 and 1939 (undoubtedly the Silicon Valley of that age), have met an investment fate similar to that of the automobile. If the peak market valuation of the airline industry during that span was $5 billion, its current valuation of $46.7 billion would suggest that investors in the aggregate earned approximately 3% before dividends and capital infusions, of which the latter exceeded the former by a huge amount. Further complicating the process, investment in the industry has regularly required special navigational skills as one makes his way through the minefield of business failures. An unnerving 129 airlines

28 General Motors stock reached a peak of $95 in the spring of 2000. In April 2005, nearing the end of 0% financed SUV life support, it dipped below $26, its market capitalization around $19 billion at midyear. Ford topped out a little earlier in the spring of 1999 at $37; it reached a low of $7 in early 2003, sporting a recent market capitalization of less than $18 billion. DaimlerChrysler AG followed a descent similar to Ford's, rising to $110 per share in early 1999, only to collapse to a price in the high $20s in early 2003. DaimlerChrysler AG was valued in the marketplace at about $40 billion at the end of June 2005. While the shares of all three have recovered modestly from their lows, they are far from firing on all cylinders. The combined market capitalization of the three companies totaled $77 billion, compared with the aforementioned $82.1 billion for Google. The three behemoths have 1,072,000 people on their payrolls, whereas Google employs 3,000, less than three-tenths of 1% of its gargantuan manufacturing brethren. Of no surprise, brains are going for a premium over brawn in the information economy! It doesn't appear to matter if all the world's auto companies will continue selling 50 million cars a year (something like 100,000,000 tons of steel, rubber, plastic, etc.) if they can't make money doing it. Still, the three companies nominally earned $8.1 billion against Google's $1.2 billion. However, all of their various and sundry liabilities, marked to market, dwarf their consolidated shareholders' equity. I think Google is probably too expensive. I am at a loss to opine on the value of the auto industry.

have filed for bankruptcy in just the last 20 years [including former industry leaders United, Delta and Northwest].[29]

Moving a little closer to home, if you had invested an equal amount of money in all of the PC manufacturers in the early 1980s, your return would be 4% as of the end of 1999.

Is the Internet the Answer?

All of which brings us to technology's *wunderkind,* the Internet. As a firm and as individuals, we at MCM are active consumers of Internet services. While there is little doubt about the expansiveness of its utility in any number of venues, its capacity to generate corresponding profits is not so clear. Regardless, investors have developed a nigh-unto-obsessive fascination with Internet stocks like no craze in modern history. In 1996 the fledgling industry, then relatively few in number, sported a market capitalization of $12.9 billion, while losing $134 million on sales of $4.4 billion. By year-end 1998 the number of players had multiplied many fold, and the industry's market capitalization shot up more than 10 times to $141.9 billion. Sales tripled to $12.4 billion over the two years, yet losses actually expanded, to $2.4 billion. It was throughout 1999 that the Internet fever rose to the point of threatening to shatter the thermometer. For the last four quarters, sales for the 200 public companies that Bloomberg surveys have increased to $21.9 billion, while losses continue to mushroom—to $4.1 billion. Overlooking the nascent industry's lingering inability to make a buck, all manner of investors and speculators continue to relentlessly clamor for Internet stocks. The market capitalization of the industry reached an astounding $823.1 billion by mid-December 1999. Seizing the opportunity, Internet entrepreneurs and promoters have been quick to satisfy the public's insatiable appetite: Of the record 505 IPOs sold in 1999, more than half derived the lion's share of their revenues from the 'Net. Together they raised one-third of the past year's $66 billion in dollar volume. As surely as nature abhors a vacuum, supply rushes in to meet demand.

---

29 The fallout from the September 11, 2001, tragedy wreaked further havoc on the airline industry. A rough approximation of the market capitalization of the airline industry as of June 30, 2005, was $22 billion (with the industry's anomalous leader, Southwest Airlines, accounting for $10.6 billion of the total!). Anybody want to trade the Big Three automakers—and the entire airline industry thrown in for good measure—for two good geeks and an algorithm? Austrian economist Joseph Shumpeter introduced the concept of "creative destruction" in his 1942 book *Capitalism, Socialism, and Democracy,* a form of industrial mutation that incessantly revolutionizes the economic structure from within, relentlessly destroying the old one, unceasingly creating a new one. Although I read it years ago, its central thesis has not yet fallen victim to "creative destruction"! Great ideas are rather impervious to that sort of obsolescence ...

What do the Internet investors expect for an encore? Taking into account the industry's stratospheric valuations, if the Internet industry earns more profits in 2020 than *all* Fortune 500 companies *combined* earn today, or $334 billion—a most improbable outcome—the survivors must command a terminal price-earnings ratio of 20 if investors in the aggregate hope to eke out even a comparatively pedestrian 10% average compounded return. In all likelihood, you can't get there from here. We, meanwhile, watch from the sidelines with interest.

As for the investment dilemma posed several paragraphs above, I doubt that the Internet will be the answer. Perhaps what we're witnessing is merely the traditional boom/bust cycle for new technologies ... at warp—check that—Internet speed.

With the weight of experience behind his arguments, Warren Buffett contends that "*the secret to successful investing is not locked up in the knowledge of how much an industry is going to alter the way people live their lives, or even in how much it's going to grow, but rather in determining the competitive advantage of any given company and, above all, the durability of the advantage. Products or services that have wide, sustainable moats around them are the ones that deliver rewards to investors*" [emphasis added]. Internet investors, please proceed down the "information superhighway" with caution.

What Buffett Isn't Telling Us

Buffett never spoon-feeds those who dine at his table. He expects his guests to use their intellectual utensils to slice, dice, and then consume and digest the repast he offers. For starters, he does not dwell on the obvious, that the return he expects from common stocks going forward is slightly less than the relatively no-brainer alternative: U.S. Treasury notes and bonds with maturities of two to 30 years offer yields around 6.5% today. Of course, taxation of the interest income from bonds is more onerous than capital gains realized from the sale of common stocks. For those investors whose capital is invested in municipal bonds, however, the returns from tax-free interest are comparable to the after-tax returns that Buffett foresees from common stocks.

Equally important, he only indirectly refers to an alternative approach to achieving above-average returns in the future. In all likelihood, the euphoric state of mind that characterizes today's investor will eventually give way to its polar opposite. Persistently high or low valuation markets have never—ever—lingered indefinitely, despite feelings to the contrary at the time they were seducing the investment public at large. Regression to the mean (and often beyond) is likely to manifest itself again ... and often when least expected. The Dow Jones industrial average will not follow a string from here to 30,000 in 2016. (That's where 6% a year will take you.) The emotional road that leads from "irrational exuberance" to hard reality will most certainly be rocky. Patiently waiting for market prices of the companies he favors to reflect equanimity, if not despair, rather than unchecked optimism, Buffett will surely again snatch opportunity from the jaws of defeat, just as he did in 1973–74. He speaks confidently of 15% returns for Berkshire shareholders in the future. He will achieve them by buying superior businesses when they sell at prudent prices sometime in the future. And they will, as surely as night follows day. He will avoid the great temptations of the day alluded to above. Meanwhile, he sits on hordes of cash. Buffett had this to say as part of the chairman's letter in last year's Berkshire Hathaway annual report:

> At year-end (1998), we held more than $15 billion in cash equivalents [including high-grade fixed-income securities due in less than one year—$36 billion if you include longer-term fixed-income securities]. Cash never makes us happy. But it's better to have the money burning a hole in Berkshire's pocket than resting comfortably in someone else's. Charlie and I will continue our search for large equity investments or, better yet, a really major business acquisition that would absorb our liquid assets. Currently, however, we see nothing on the horizon.

How's that for a well-articulated strategy?!

What's a Long-Term Investor to Do?

Humankind's recurring propensity to unwittingly fall victim to financial fads, follies, and foibles is like a bad dream that we can't get out of our minds. It's a vague but imposing countervailing force that stands in the way of our unequivocally embracing the new economic and capital-markets paradigm. Add to that the utter absence of anything approaching a healthy respect for risk by a large segment of the investor population, and we have more than enough anecdotal evidence to compel us to fly the caution flag—if we truly believe that preservation of capital comes before all other aspirations. In other words, "To win, first you must not lose." The surest way is to press on toward your destination, while at the same time minimizing the risk of a skyjacking when risks of terrorism are running high, by booking yourself on a train until normalcy returns [little did we know what was to happen 21 months later ...]. Of course, the train isn't as fast. A less certain but somewhat speedier alternative is to select another airline and a different route. With short- to mid-term U.S. Treasury notes and pre-refunded municipal bonds coupled with high-quality (but presently unglamorous and unloved) equity securities, we are attempting to keep you on your way via both vehicles. If conditions improve—that is, if prices move closer to value—it will be so much easier and less costly to transfer from train to plane.

Investment Redefined

In the depths of the Depression, chastened by his failure to foresee the stock market crash and the enormity of the economic aftershock, Benjamin Graham reflected on the meaning of the term *investment* in the 1934 investment classic, *Security Analysis.* Years before the surreal madness of the late 1920s rendered rationality temporarily irrelevant, Graham recalled that an "investor" purchased stocks ...

> ... at price levels he considered conservative in the light of experience; he was satisfied, from the knowledge of the institution's resources and earnings power, that he was getting his money's worth in full. If a strong speculative market resulted in advancing the price to a level out of line with the standards of value, he sold the shares and waited for a reasonable price to return before reacquiring them.
>
> Had the same attitude been taken by the purchaser of common stocks in 1928–1929, the term investment would not have been the tragic misnomer that it was. But in proudly applying the designation "blue chips" to the high-priced issues chiefly favored, the public unconsciously revealed the gambling motive at the heart of its supposed investment selections.

Investors' behaviors in the late '20s differed in one vital respect from earlier practices. The buyer made no attempt to determine whether shares were worth the price paid by the application of firmly established standards of value. The market simply made up new standards as it went along by accepting the current price—however high—as the sole measure of value. Continues Graham: "Any idea of safety based on this uncritical approach was clearly illusory and replete with danger" (Graham, *Security Analysis*, 54). Under that line of reasoning, no price was too high to render a security unsafe.

Now that the 1990s have drawn to a close, I wonder what history's verdict will be of these extraordinary times. Will it remember the last decade of the 20th century as the beginning of a new era with fresh rules and modernized standards, or will it expose yet another episode of investment metamorphosing [now "morphing"; even language changes and, yes, morphs] slowly but surely into rank and misguided speculation? Will the children of Generation X learn that their Boomer parents were like the rising sun at the dawning of New Age economics? Or, as Jim Grant has suggested, is knowledge in the field of finance cyclical and not cumulative? Why, we ask, hasn't Holland's Tulip Mania of the 1630s slipped quietly into the obscurity of the archives of financial history? Why did Japan repeat in the '80s the destructive behavior that brought the U.S. financial markets and economy to their knees in the '30s? Are speculation and its inevitable aftermath unavoidable parts of the human condition? As memories of the lessons of the past fade over time, is each new and uninitiated herd of speculators little more than unsuspecting sheep being driven into the shearing barn to be periodically shorn? [Or worse yet, as the cartoon at the front of Chapter Four so eloquently illustrates, are the sheep stampeding pell-mell over a cliff?] Is the casino capitalism of today, at rock(y) bottom, simply a new variation on an old theme?

It is to state the obvious that prices, particularly those of companies probing the frontiers of the new tech-based Information Age, have long been detached from traditional benchmarks of value. But it's not just concerns about the relationship between price and value that put a traditionalist on edge. Rather, it's also about how investors attempt to capitalize on what is taking place. Day trading, like Internet pornography, is a diversion with which most of us are unfamiliar. And yet both thrive right under our collective nose—and both with suspect olfactory emanations. Encouraged by the apparent disregard for the nature of the relationship between the price of an asset and its underlying value, day traders provide additional anecdotal evidence of the prevailing atmosphere of speculative promiscuity. It is increasingly common to think of stocks not as fractional ownership pieces of a real business, but rather as pieces of gilt-edged parchment (or, more appropriately, formless entries on a monthly statement) that are to be bought and sold with impunity, much like baseball cards. Casino capitalism may, in fact, be a fitting moniker.

The cynic describes a long-term investment as short-term speculation gone horribly wrong. But, in our belief, *long term* and *investment* are as compatible and as deserving of one another as love and marriage. Instead, the words *short term* and *investment* create the true oxymoron. Confusion about the difference can be dangerous to one's financial health. It is ironic indeed that the Internet has made possible day trading in, as you might guess, the Internet stocks themselves.

The Internet, of course, is reshaping every segment of the economy, but nowhere does that change occur at a greater pace than in the financial-services sector. Specifically, what's happening in the brokerage industry is a preview of things to come in other businesses. It's happening to brokers first because they aren't selling toasters or cars. Their products are intangible, so the transaction can happen purely electronically. When does affection become infatuation? For some, day trading is simply the new game in town. Conditioned by the lottery, the proliferation of gambling casinos, and now such television shows as Regis Philbin's "Who Wants to Be a Millionaire?," Internet day trading has become the newest "easy money" fad.

The New Tulip Bulbs?

Shortened time horizons have become a fact of investment life. How much has turnover increased? According to *Business Week,* some 76% of the shares of the average U.S. company listed on the New York Stock Exchange turned over last year, up from 46% in 1990 and only 12% in 1960. It was running at 82% through May 1999. On the Nasdaq, home of the greatest proportion of high-tech companies, turnover was three times as high. *Time* magazine's 1999 "Person of the Year,"[30] 35-yearold and delightfully affable Jeff Bezos, Amazon.com's founder and CEO, leads a frenetic and exciting life—and so, apparently, do the shareholders of the company leading the e-commerce revolution. The average share in Amazon.com Inc. is now held for *seven* trading days before being sold to someone else. Yahoo! shareholders stick around for all of eight days. As for the more mature technology companies, the holding periods are longer: Dell Computer (3.7 months), Microsoft (6.3 months), and Cisco (8.5 months). Even the consummate hold-it-for-a-lifetime investment, Coca Cola, sees its ownership turn over every 2.2 years. At the height of Tulip Mania, bulbs were not coveted for the beauty to be derived from their eventual blossoming but to turn a quick profit. Most were never planted. Tulip bulbs were simply the fast-buck medium, incidental to the real objective. They could just as easily have been ... ah ... Internet stocks!

---

30 Telltale signs of exaggerated sentiments were to be found everywhere during the Great Bubble. The "curse of the cover story" befell the enthralled stockholders of Amazon.com and e-commerce wunderkind Jeff Bezos, Amazon.com's founder. (See earlier footnote on Amazon for details.) E-commerce is a small but rapidly growing share of the retail marketplace, but Wal-Mart has yet to be toppled.

Of course, most of the churning today can be traced to mutual funds, which own a higher percentage of stock than ever. Constantly under pressure to achieve short-term performance objectives, fund managers are quick to change horses, often midstream. For investors in the highest brackets, taxes on the gains from shares held less than a year are double those held more than 12 months. The shareholders of most mutual funds include individuals whose gains are taxable, as well as tax-deferred entities, such as 401(k) plans. Taxable investors get the short end of the stick in this high-turnover performance derby.

More Dollars Than Sense

The "Day Tripper" of Beatles lore could well have been the precursor three decades ago of this era's day trader. In August of '99, Alan Abelson, the erudite *Barron's* columnist, looked inside the murky world of day trading. He highlighted the findings of the North American Securities Administrators Association (NASAA), which comprises multifarious regulatory bodies that had spent months probing the seams of the "bucket shop" day-trading world, poking into such delicate subjects as commissions, suitability standards, and the whereabouts of the customers' yachts. (Ameritrade, the online broker, recently lost what could prove to be a landmark arbitration case involving an Indianapolis med-school graduate who was trying to speed the payment of his student loans by trading Internet stocks on margin.) One of NASAA's conclusions, which raised many an eyebrow, was that an estimated "70% of public traders will not only lose but lose everything they invest." Another of the report's striking revelations concerned the "annualized cost/equity ratio." This neat little number "measures the amount of profit required on average equity just to pay transaction costs and break even." That ratio is an astonishing 56%. In other words, on a $100,000 account, you have to make a mere $56,000 just to pay your commissions! Day trading, apparently, is a lot more like gambling than most people think. Fittingly, so are the results.

As long as we're on the subject of illusions, a word or two is in order about the IPO (initial public offering) express train to riches. As anyone who reads *The Wall Street Journal* or watches CNBC is aware, the Boston Chicken-type IPO market is back en masse. You may recall that we expressed our doubts about the Boston Chicken phenomenon in the 1993 annual report. When it debuted in 1993 amid great fanfare, the Chicken's price in the aftermarket rose an unprecedented 150% from the offering price. The Ponzi-like[31] capital structure imploded five years later, and the company, like its stepchild, Einstein's Bagels, sunk into the ignominy of bankruptcy. McDonald's recently purchased the remains of the company for pennies on the dollar. This time it is the Internet that is center stage—and the sellers are more clever than ever. In earlier superheated IPO markets, sellers would be suing their underwriters for underpricing the issue if the price in subsequent trading rose by the kind of percentages that are widespread today. This is not so nowadays because by intentionally keeping the initial offering relatively small, in the face of supercharged demand, a scarcity premium is created, and the post-sale price often skyrockets. It is on the strength of that price that real money is raised in a subsequent "secondary" offering. The illusion is that there is lots of easy money to be made by investing in IPOs. In reality, the people who take serious money off the table are the sellers. As for the buyers, recently disclosed secret "pot lists" indicate that institutions, who carry nearly as many sticks as the commission dollars they spread around like so much grease on the wheel, receive 70% to 80% of the allocation of the first round. In all probability, many of the retail buyers who bite the bullet in the aftermarket or in a secondary offering will be the first to scramble for a chair once the music stops.

As to the seductive appeal of greed and folly mentioned early in the report, need more be said? Finally, when an epidemic of high-turnover speculation has displaced long-term investment as the standard of conduct in the financial markets, the endgame is almost never pleasant.

---

31 Carlo "Charles" Ponzi emigrated from Italy to the United States in 1903. For the next 14 years, he wandered from city to city holding a variety of jobs, including that of dishwasher. Then he hit upon an idea of arbitraging foreign postal coupons. It was easy money until red tape associated with all the transfers ate away all of Ponzi's imagined profits. That didn't stop Ponzi. The scheme that evolved was very simple: He parlayed the original idea into a scam that promised investors would double their money in 90 days. At the height of his scheme, money was flowing in at $1 million per week. Early winners were paid with the money flowing in from new players. The money distributed far exceeded the earnings power of the underlying activity, which in this instance was nil. Eventually, authorities began investigating the too-good-to-be-true scheme, and the operation began to collapse when *The Boston Post* ran a headline story in July 1920, questioning the legitimacy of Ponzi's devious plan.

CHAPTER THREE—2000

Introduction

Risk: No Longer an Afterthought

The first year of the popularly perceived new millennium began with an ironic twist. The much ballyhooed and widely feared Y2K computer meltdown will be remembered (assuming the acronym so symbolic of the amorphous outreach of the tentacles of technology has not already been erased from your cranial hard drive) as the ultimate non-event. Perhaps Y2K's sole redeeming virtue was in once again giving witness to the nearly incomprehensible power of crowd psychology. On the other hand, the largely unexpected and thus not feared disintegration of the technology and Internet stocks was, by chilling contrast, the cataclysmic incident for which the year will not soon be forgotten. The common thread that ties these two incidents together? The willingness of people to submit themselves *en masse* so unquestioningly and with such groundless fear in the first instance and with such "irrational exuberance" in the second. The Internet and computer technology are related ideas from the same school of science: The Internet teems with overcapacity, as the economic efficacy of its many entrants is yet, if ever, to be proved, while most stocks pertaining to computer technology are outrageously overvalued, priced as if endless hyper-growth were assured.

At its most rudimentary level, the featured financial story for 2000 was about speculation in certain favored industries, escalating through the process of contagion to preposterous and ultimately self-defeating extremes. It's a phenomenon that has repeated itself throughout all of human history and which necessarily has been examined in these pages in the past.

If ever-iconoclastic rationalism and uncompromising intellectual independence were called for, the year just past was it. Only you can be the judge as to whether we kept our heads when many about us were losing theirs. Here's the hook: If you expect to make that finding, you'll have to read on!

In the midst of all the wealth-destroying "gore" for which 2000 will be remembered by a horde of sheep shorn naked, we trust that you never lost a night's sleep (or even got "bushed") worrying about the safety and security of your portfolio, about the possibility of a crack that threatens to become a chasm in your nest egg. Wealth management, the markets in their own perverse way occasionally remind us, is not just about eating well, it's also about sleeping well. Perhaps our profession is not unlike amateur tennis: It's usually not the number of winners hit but rather the number of unforced errors that determines the outcome. The rather extraordinary and equally humbling absolute and relative performance of last year, which can be seen in the following section, was in part the result of good defense—we had only one unforced error—and the concurrent but somewhat unexpected good fortune of the market choosing this particular year to recognize how undervalued some of our companies were, resulting in four outright winners as well.

To be sure, it is not our intent to make light of the breadth of financial trauma suffered in many sectors the past year but simply to remind you of its existence because, like a hurricane in the Caribbean, it rendered its devastation elsewhere. Don't be fooled; the storms may not have passed. And the winds of destruction could reach places heretofore untouched. Though your experience may be vicarious thus far, the lessons learned from the stories that follow should be taken with the highest degree of seriousness. And the word "trauma" may well understate the magnitude of the markets' giant sucking sound, like the enormous and indiscriminate vacuum cleaner mounted on the sleigh of "The Grinch" (the wonderful Christmas movie starring Jim Carrey) as the town of Whoville unwittingly surrendered all its accumulated material gifts to a thief in the still of the night before Christmas. Suddenly, it seems, billionaires have shrunk like cheap cotton to millionaires, millionaires slipped into the ignominy of being merely well-to-do, and all manner of speculators—big fish and minnows alike—were rendered, for lack of a better phrase, acutely *un*rich.

Putting numbers to the diminution of paper profits is telling. Overall, it is estimated that the market capitalization of U.S. equity securities fell some $2.5 trillion over the course of the year, against a start-of-year total of approximately $17.4 trillion. The value of all stocks on the New York Stock Exchange, about $12 trillion, was essentially flat for the year, while the Nasdaq lost approximately $2 trillion, compared with a start-of-year total of an incredible $5.3 trillion. From its peak on March 10, 2000,[32] the Nasdaq Composite fell 39.1%. The index itself plummeted from 5,049 to 3,521 in a matter of 34 days, reaching a low of 2,333 on December 20, which translates to a breathtaking peak-to-trough decline of 53.8%. In the euphoria of a year ago, a bear market was thought to be a decline of about 20%. Who, I wonder, after "tout television" picked up on the 20% figure, was originally responsible for suggesting such an arbitrary and foolish metric? The market capitalization of the Dow Jones index of Internet stocks fared even worse. From its peak, also on March 10, the market capitalization declined dramatically from just over $1 trillion to $251 billion on December 21, a shocking 76%. The remediation of speculative excess is often as dramatic as it is devastating.[33]

Lest we overlook it, bifurcation was as evident in 2000 as it was the year before, this time in both the equity and the debt markets, as well as between them. With regard to the equity markets, the players simply reversed their roles. While the technology bashing was under way, there was a resurrection of interest of sorts among the old-economy industries. As for bonds, Treasuries prospered, thanks to falling interest rates, while junk simultaneously sank because of worsening credit quality. Finally, while stock prices went down, quality bond prices went up.

Not only was paper wealth greatly diminished as the Bubble began to burst, what wealth remained (of which there is still plenty) was subjected to a winnowing process known as redistribution. In the relative scheme of things, discerning and prudent investors climbed a rung or two on the ladder of wealth preservation and accumulation, while those who didn't know any better (or if they did, sacrificed rationality at the altar of momentum investing or its variations) dropped a rung or two ... or more. As was noted in the 1999 annual report, there are always

32 Unlike the assassination of the Archduke of Sarajevo on June 28, 1914, which was the "tipping point" for the start of World War I, no single event triggered the massive and soon-to-be cascading reversal of "fortunes" that began March 10, 2000, of which the Nasdaq index was merely the most illustrative. When someone yells "Fire!" in a crowded theater, it is panic and not rationality that inflames the mind.

33 That was only the beginning. At its low point (thus far), it is estimated that the U.S. equity markets lost more than $8 trillion in value. As if to cushion the effect of the reversal in financial market fortunes over the course of the time span of this book, the estimated value of residential housing in America rose from $8.9 trillion to $17.7 trillion, with estimated owners' equity rising from $5 trillion to $10 trillion. Moreover, the net worth of households and nonprofit organizations, as estimated by the Board of Governors of the Federal Reserve, increased from $33.8 trillion to $48.8 trillion over the same time period, inclusive of losses in the stock market and the $5 billion gain in homeowners' equity.

opportunities, but they are rarely found in the obvious places. As for those who fueled the fires of reckless speculation—the men and women of our profession—we'll have more to say about them later.

Investment Performance

Period Ending December 31, 2000	MCM Equities *	S&P 500 *
Since Inception **	17.0%	18.2%
Five Years	22.2%	18.3%
Three Years	12.5%	12.3%
One Year	29.3%	-9.1%

* Compounded annually, MCM data net of fees

** December 31, 1993

Year	MCM Equities (Net of Fees)	S&P 500
1994	-7.5%	1.3%
1995	19.1%	37.5%
1996	31.8%	22.9%
1997	45.1%	33.3%
1998	-7.4%	28.6%
1999	18.8%	21.0%
2000	29.2%	-9.1%

In the words of Aristotle, "One swallow does not a summer make." Although the decisions we made during the course of the last year led to above-average equity-investment returns, we view such decision making as but one brief segment in a long-term continuum. Who knows what tomorrow will bring? We draw some solace from the deeply held conviction that the ideological foundation upon which our security selection and portfolio management practices have been painstakingly built will, at the very least, keep you out of harm's way. At the very best, we may surprise a few people who believe that there is always a correlation between risk assumed and return earned—and that *conservative* is invariably synonymous with lackluster results. In the meantime, if we continue to adhere to our principles, we are likely to avoid many of the temptations that come in the form of folly, greed, and (most critical and sometimes most troublesome) fear, which on occasion precipitates the most irrational and destructive of behaviors. Our approach served us well in the final 12 months of the second millennium AD, but 2001 will be a new odyssey, to be sure. Again, our convictions will undoubtedly be put to the test. As always, we will forsake the lure of so-called opportunity where the flip side of that coin may result in permanent loss of capital.

Equally important is that we provide you with a full explanation of how the investment returns were earned and what risks were incurred with your capital in the process of earning them. First, as has been disclosed on many occasions in the past, and is stated annually as one of our Investment Principles [see Excerpt 3.1 in the Appendix], it is our contention that there is great virtue in limiting the horses in one's stable to a relatively small number of thoroughbreds. Empirical testing has proved beyond a reasonable doubt that the "riskiness" of a portfolio of 12-15 diverse companies is little greater than one loaded with a hundred or more, as is so often the practice among many institutional portfolio managers. In this instance, we define risk as a terribly bad longer-term outcome—and not the extent of annual portfolio price volatility that is the standard by which it is measured according to MPT. We don't subscribe to that popular discipline so much because it is "demented" (in the mince-no-words eloquence of Berkshire Hathaway's Charlie Munger) but rather due to the fact that (1) our investment holding period is ideally very long, and (2) we don't think of ourselves as buying and selling pieces of paper but rather investing in businesses. MPT is simply incompatible with our investment style.

It is also important to disclose that we attempt to further ameliorate risks that may be perceived to be associated with a concentrated approach toward investment by (1) selecting only those businesses that pass through our rigorous filters and (2) purchasing such companies at prices that afford us a significant margin of safety, as explained further in "The Art/Science of Managing Risk." We strongly believe that the supply of great businesses is severely limited and to engage in broad diversification (for the often spurious reasons that others offer as rationale) is dilutive to the implicit purpose of earning above-average longer-term returns. Little that is good comes without cost, however. And the cost of a concentrated approach to portfolio management is (1) much greater relative portfolio price volatility and (2) the possibility that we will look like geniuses on one occasion and dolts on another. Neither is an accurate characterization, but if the eventual outcome is superior to the more commonplace practices, we strongly believe that the end justifies the means, despite the exasperation that may occasionally (and, we hope, temporarily) ensue.

To put real numbers to the abstract concept of margin of safety, the weighted-average price-earnings ratios at the time of purchase of the companies we acquired was 9.7 times, compared to a price-earnings ratio for the S&P 500 that averaged in the high 20s during most of 2000. Our weighted-average, estimated five-year earnings-per-share growth rate for those same companies is just under 15%, compared with an earnings-per-share growth rate for the S&P 500 of less than half of that.

An additional word on "margin of safety" is warranted here, although it will be discussed in greater detail in "The Art/Science of Managing Risk." Purchasing a business at a price that provides reasonable assurance of a generous margin for error is an erudite way of saying to ourselves, "Buy low, stupid." While intuitively appealing, this is by no means easy to implement. It requires that we step boldly into the lion's den, that we take decisive action at the most unpropitious of times. Backed by extensive research and strong convictions, we must purchase the shares of good businesses in the face of the kind of awful news that forces others to throw in the towel as momentum is turning south or when short-term performance mandates do not permit the luxury of endurance. A significant portion of the favorable outcome achieved in 2000 was due to little more than taking advantage of discarded mainstream companies as the Nasdaq, the presumed ticket to success, sucked money away from everything else while soaring to new highs in the spring. We purchased the castaways you own at deeply depressed prices and then looked on with satisfaction as they surged upward toward intrinsic value and, in a few isolated instances, slightly above—at the very time the Nasdaq index had its comeuppance.

What happens from here on with several of our portfolio holdings may well depend more on the quality of our research and less on our ability to take advantage of a schizophrenic market, though we have identified a number of possible new investees whose depressed market prices would suggest that the "rubber band" effect might be salubrious. If the intrinsic value of the companies we own continues to grow according to our projections—even though the fluctuation in market prices may from time to time suggest otherwise—the market value of the equity portion of your portfolio should follow suit in due course. Buying businesses on the cheap takes chutzpah born of strong convictions. Forecasting future cash flows and discounting them appropriately (the basis for the calculation of intrinsic worth) requires appreciable knowledge and skill—and fair winds. We think we are above average in doing the former; as for the latter, only time will tell. While our aversion to assuming high levels of valuation risk (to say nothing of the difficulty of pushing technology companies through our filters) penalized us in 1997–99, it had the opposite effect in 2000.

It should be noted that, for most portfolios during the five-year period, the portion allocated to equities rarely if ever exceeded 50%, except late in 2000—and that was due largely to the bargains finally found in the spring and the appreciation thereafter. See "Goliaths Slain" if, perchance, you're plagued with lingering regrets for not jumping on the bandwagon in 1998–99.

Though there were several minor exceptions, generally those few clients who asked that we purchase according to ideas of their own choosing—or who imposed certain moratoriums on equity purchases beyond what their Investment Policy Statement stipulated—fared less well than those clients who left us to our own devices. While we don't necessarily encourage such behaviors, we gladly accommodate them in the name of making the investment experience a personalized one for each client. While it cost them (and us!) money last year, next year may be a different story. In the long run, however, if we become redundant, I'm sure you will let us know! We're working hard to see that this doesn't happen.

In 2000 we continued our practice of investing in only the highest-grade fixed-income securities, despite the ever-widening spreads between U.S. Treasury notes and junk bonds (now an eye-catching 520 basis points). One can buy Amazon.com 4.75% convertible debentures due in February 2009 at 35% of par for a yield to maturity of 22%—if they continue to pay timely interest and are able to return the principal at maturity, a wager we have no interest in taking. If junk bonds, which we defined as a convoluted form of equity with limited upside potential and unlimited downside risk, appear attractive, common stocks are likely to be even more appealing.[34]

While we aren't aggressively active fixed-income security managers, we do try to eke out a better return (than a passively managed laddered portfolio would suggest) by managing duration within the context of a relatively short-term portfolio construct. Where we do get very aggressive is in the selection of the highest-quality tax-exempt bonds we own. If you don't know that market well—and how it differs from the incredibly efficient market for U.S. Treasury securities—you can be made to look a fool without even knowing it. While it's not apparent to the untrained eye, we believe that we add significant value because of our years of experience and daily activity in the specialized market for municipal bonds.

---

34 From a low of about $35 near the end of 2000, the convertible bonds of Amazon.com rallied to near par in early 2003 where they have generally traded since, as concerns about the company's dire financial straits subsided. Junk-bond investors realized a total return of 240% (based on coupon payments and bond-price appreciation). Amazon.com's stock reached its low of $5 later in the wake of 9/11. By autumn of 2003 the stock had risen 12-fold to $60. Need more be said about relative upside potential ...? The stock settled back to around $35 at midyear 2005.

Another peculiarity of our approach to wealth management is that we see fixed-income securities for the complementary role they play in meeting portfolio objectives and not as a discrete class of security that should be managed by a specialist and measured against a fixed-income benchmark. Our aggregate portfolio benchmark is the S&P 500, irrespective of portfolio-asset class composition, assuming a client has given us discretionary authority to be fully invested in equity securities. In those instances in which a client's Investment Policy Statement specifies a maximum commitment to common stocks of, say, 50%, a blended benchmark is obviously used instead. Because of a limited potential for outsized gains, bonds are used primarily for defensive purposes. And yet the crowning indignity for the badly shaken cult of equity worshipers was that stocks in 2000 were left in the dust not only by bonds—the 10-year note was up 16%—but also by ... cash! Sometimes you win by not losing ...

Investment Strategy

Singles and Doubles

Given unlimited discretion by a client whose return objective is to earn as high a rate of total return as is consistent with preservation of principal, our optimal portfolio would consist of the marketable equity securities of businesses that pass through our rigorous filters. The companies within this ideal group would have a number of investment attributes in common: (1) They have a long and frequently illustrious history of high returns on conservatively leveraged capital employed; (2) they are businesses that we can readily understand and likely will be performing much the same type of activities in five or 10 years as they are today; (3) they are superbly managed by people we like, admire, and respect; and (4) they sell at market prices that give us an acceptable margin of safety, along with its reciprocal—a reasonable expectation of at least a 15% compounded annual total return over a minimum five-year holding period.

We encountered a number of companies that met those stringent parameters this past year. Invariably, they were the companies that were discarded by the hot-money investors who saw what they thought was low-hanging fruit in the technology and Internet orchard. Furthermore, in most cases, their earnings had come under pressure for what we believed were temporary reasons. No momentum investor would touch them. Despite the general loathing for them and others of their lowly class, price-wise they were silk purses that only *looked* like sows' ears. Four of them appreciated in one year to price levels that, at the time of purchase, we had expected to take several years to achieve. Subsequently, over the course of 2000, the expected return from our equity portfolio fell rather dramatically. In other words, don't expect an encore performance next year! While we have a nearly neurotic aversion to saying goodbye to winsome friends, there is little doubt that we'll be making some portfolio adjustments throughout 2001. Taking into account the avoidance of short-term capital gains, our portfolios likely will see some new names, while others are sold.

Our preference has always been for very low rates of portfolio turnover, effectively enjoying an interest-free loan from the U.S. Treasury, thanks to the continuing deferral of the ever-increasing and yet-untaxed unrealized gains. But on occasion, sharply rising market prices (or, on the flip side, estimates of the growth in intrinsic value that prove to be optimistic) require that we take pre-emptive action. There remains a paucity of companies that meet all of the prerequisites outlined above. As for the traditional growth companies, many remain too expensive for our tastes. Using conservative terminal price-earnings-ratio assumptions, expected returns fall well short of our minimum threshold. We are exceedingly patient. Frequently we complete our research and then wait months or even years until the price comes to us. Our enthusiasm to own a company is often inversely proportional to its price. Despite the fact that Coca-Cola, one of the most venerable of franchises extant, is a company we have always wanted to own (and its market price has fallen from a 1998 high of $90 to the current $56), even that price is too high relative to what we think the business is worth.[35]

During the second half of the year, we completed research on four or five companies that are clear candidates for purchase in the year

---

35 Coca-Cola is an example of the patience required of a long-term investor as he awaits the sweet spot pitch (price) for a great business. The stock, worse than dead money six long years later, is changing hands at $43. We long felt that disillusionment would come slowly to Coke's diehard institutional investor cult following. With ample help from the company, that process is clearly under way. The Coke pitch has come across our plate for more than 350 consecutive weeks, and each time we have taken a pass. One of these days we might just get lucky if Mr. Market, in a moment of despair, causes the stock price to fall into that small area of our strike zone where we can swing with confidence. Keep in mind, Coca-Cola, despite its foibles, has produced irregular and overall modest increases in earnings since it sold at $90 per share in 1998. That year the company earned $1.60 per share. For the 12 months ending June 30, 2005, per-share earnings reached $2.

For the seven years beginning in 1998 through year-end 2004, Coke expended $6 billion in shareholders' cash to acquire another 119 million Treasury shares (compared with 2.426 billion shares currently outstanding) at an average cost of approximately $50.40. Apparently impervious to the extraordinarily high valuations that Coke commanded in the marketplace, the board authorized the purchase of Treasury shares totaling $3.3 billion between 1997 and 1999 at prices between $60 and $90, tacitly affirming as prudent price-earnings multiples ranging from 35 to 60 times. While the abysmal judgment hardly seemed rational to the writer in the late '90s (as was noted in annual reports then), it would certainly appear that since 1998 the $6 billion shoveled out to selling shareholders was, admittedly to a lesser extent, to the disadvantage of those who stayed the course as well. The seven-year buyback program reduced shares outstanding by approximately 5%. Not only were long-term shareholders disadvantaged by the company's pathetically ineffective allocation of shareholders' capital to the "earnings management" stock-repurchase program, but (perhaps taking the lead from the company purchases of stock right through the peak) they shared proportionately in the peak-to-trough decline in Coke's market capitalization from the 1998 high of $218.6 billion to the current value of $104.4 billion. As Benjamin Graham admonished 70 years ago, the same company purchased at one price can be deemed an investment, while at another, a speculation. It would certainly appear that the Coke board engaged in some big-time speculating with somebody else's money.

2001. They pass through all of our filters, but they differ somewhat from several of the current portfolio holdings: Their products are a bit more prosaic, their markets somewhat more mature, and their earnings-per-share growth rates average closer to 10% than the 15% average expected from our current holdings. Offsetting that, at their current depressed prices, they are correspondingly cheaper (perhaps more traditional "value" stocks) and thus offer expected returns easily over our threshold. While this represents an opportunistic diversion necessitated by a dearth of "inevitables" at reasonable prices, our research objective continues to relentlessly upgrade the overall quality of the businesses in our investment universe.

Is It Time for Technology?

In the 1999 annual report, we said we had demurred after surveying possible investment possibilities in Internet-related companies. Although it never makes the headlines, sometimes a simple "no" is the best choice. What about technology stocks after the bloodbath? Now that Nasdaq has done its splendid imitation of a swan in full dive, we wonder where opportunity might be found. We are convinced that, like the Phoenix of ancient lore, some (we sorely wish we knew which ones) will eventually rise in spectacular fashion from the ashes of ignominy. Since few, if any, pass through our filters, let me in this instance defer for a bird's-eye view to an observer whose wise and cryptic insights have intrigued me for more than 15 years.

Marc Faber, a man with a truly global perspective and an uncanny knack for not losing sight of the forest for the trees, has made innumerable appearances in *Barron's*, where he first came to my attention. In a recent piece, Faber addresses the question of whether Nasdaq, which is dominated by technology companies, is overvalued and, if so, by how much. The answer to the first part of the question (it won't come as a shock to you) is yes. To get a fix on just how overvalued that wild-and-woolly market is, he recited a little history.

Launched in 1971 with a value of 100, the composite index, he recounts, never topped 200 until 1982. By 1990 it was still below 500. In 1995 it eclipsed 1,000 for the first time and, three years later, reached 2,000. After that, it really went stratospheric, soaring above 5,000 this past March.

"Never before in the history of financial markets," notes Faber with a touch of awe, "has there been such a highly priced large market as the Nasdaq."

OK, after that quick background sketch, he gets down to the nitty-gritty of determining what a proper valuation would be for Nasdaq. Based on current earnings of something in the neighborhood of $25 billion, he reckons the index should be valued between 800 and 1,500. Faber explains that his forecast assumes that earnings either linger around where they are (which would drop the index to 800) or rise to around $40 billion before suffering some major disappointments (which means Nasdaq would be cut "only" in half from present levels).

Another way to assess the future of Nasdaq, he adds, is to assume that it will give back all the gains garnered in the previous five years. That, as it happens, is the average experience of U.S. stocks in [secular] bear markets. If the past is a prologue for Nasdaq, Faber figures, the index eventually will drop to around 1,000.[36] In sum, by any sensible yardstick, Nasdaq remains incredibly inflated and has light-years to go before it bottoms out. To be sure, the Internet and all that it means in the new millennium is a great aphrodisiac for many investors—and Nasdaq, the Viagra of the financial world, may well stay up longer than it has any right to. "Yours till Viagra falls" could well become the updated inscription of choice in yearbooks as high school seniors "anticipate" their senior years.

While Faber's perspective is tops-down—and is helpful to us in framing our investment decisions—at the end of the day, we're still most at home in our bottoms-up price-in-relationship-to-value paradigm. If we don't know what something is worth, how can we possibly determine whether the price is expensive or cheap? Is Microsoft a long-term-investment candidate at its current price of $44, down from a high of $119 in 1999? It sells for 27 times earnings, though as the section on accounting explains [omitted], those numbers contain both fire and smoke. We ask ourselves, particularly in view of the maturation of the PC market, what will be the growth drivers for the company five or 10 years from now? More fundamentally, will its energizing options-based compensation culture implode, with some lag, along with the share price? Will Bill Gates & Co. be able to acquire and hold the talent that has made them a stunning success story in the information revolution as their industry matures and their rewards systems regress toward the

36 The Nasdaq index hit 1,114 on October 9, 2002, a 78% decline from its high in March 2000. It had since rebounded to the 2,056 level as of the end of June 2005. This is still 59% below its high reached more than five years earlier. If that same metric was applied to the S&P 500, it would have to plunge to a devastating, and eerily coincidental, 500 to retrace its steps from where it began five years before the peak. In very approximate dollars, that would imply a drop in the aggregate market value of U.S. equity securities from the current $17 trillion to around $7 trillion. We are not prepared to comment on the consequences of such an occurrence except to say they would almost certainly be calamitous.

mean? Will they be able to monopolize the new venues, into which they are forced to migrate to sustain their growth, as they have the market for operating-systems software?[37]

There is no doubt in our thinking that information technology will remain the fastest-growing segment of the U.S. economy *until* overwhelmed by genetic technology, which is nipping at its heels. Growth, however, is but one component of the value equation. Capitalizing on rapid-growth industries, as the Internet speculators have so painfully discovered, is often fraught with more peril than prize. Easy money is an oxymoron. It is most unlikely that we, as wealth managers, will be placing big bets on little companies attempting to find their niche along the frontiers of science. We think hitting a homer once every hundred times at bat, with dozens of strikeouts in between, will not get us an invitation to the Hall of Fame. We're content to concentrate on singles and doubles. Mixing metaphors (although staying with sports), it's analogous to golfers "driving for show, putting for dough."

Many "Internet" businesses are much closer to traditional media and distribution businesses than their staunchest supporters were willing to admit only months ago. In this context, we may be searching the trash heap for viable business models. In most cases, however, we are increasingly finding "old economy" companies dominating the so-called "Internet space." It seems that having an established customer base, a brand name, a physical infrastructure, and an old-fashioned know-how are still of use in the 21st century.

Is There a Snowball Rolling Our Way, Gathering Mass and Speed?

Of more immediate concern is the possibility that the massive erosion of wealth that has occurred in the last nine months will precipitate an unexpected economic slowdown or worse after this longest of peacetime expansions. The plethora of recent earnings downgrades from companies

---

37 All market prices that follow reflect Microsoft's 2-for-1stock split in February 2003. Microsoft now trades around $26, down from its high of $60 and up from a low of $22, compared with $22 when this footnote was originally written in late 2000. With a mountain of cash building and few opportunities to reinvest it all in businesses that enjoy economics even close to the 40% operating margins of the Windows/Office juggernaut, Microsoft decided to repatriate some of the spoils of its enormous success. In mid-2004 Microsoft announced a payout of $75 billion to shareholders over the next four years through stock repurchases ($30 billion), a special dividend ($32 billion), and an increased annual dividend ($3.5 billion). Parenthetically, the Bill and Melinda Gates Foundation had a net worth of $27 billion at the end of 2004 and paid out $1.5 billion in grants to charities during the year. The foundation focuses on leveling the playing field, in both global health and education, among other endeavors. The aging prodigy, now 50 years old, continues to distinguish himself inside and outside the business world.

representing a broad cross-section of corporate America gives us pause. The acid test will be how the stock market, and later the economy, will respond to what surely will be a kinder, gentler Federal Reserve policy in the months ahead.[38] While we haven't seen it mentioned in print, we don't rule out the possibility that the Fed may find itself pushing on a string. Make no mistake about it, what may be transpiring is as much about the endgame of a once-in-a-generation speculative orgy as it is about the reverse wealth effect. Katie, bar the door if they complement one another. Serious investors would do well to ponder the wisdom of Benjamin Graham as excerpted from a 1934 edition of *Security Analysis* and Graham's memoirs. [While there is some repetition regarding the references to Graham in Chapter One, the timeless purpose of placing a more extensive elaboration of Graham's insights in the Appendix is to offer a sanctuary from temptation—where investors who get the itch to speculate can retire to reflect on the wisdom of this ageless sage. Paraphrasing the nearly forgotten American Express ad, don't leave the safety of your conservative ways without it.] The speculative pendulum is clearly swinging back toward sanity. How far and how long it swings remains the pertinent question. While the catharsis is under way, capital preservation must take precedence over capital enhancement.

Accordingly, despite lower market yields, we will not depart from our practice of owning only the highest-grade fixed-income securities of relatively short duration. We will venture forth from that safe harbor, as we did last year, only when compelling opportunities appear in equity-type investments in which we can reasonably expect to earn considerably higher returns, consistent with our aversion to assuming anything more than moderate risk, as we define it. We will look forward with one eye and backward with the other, keeping close watch on the path and size of the snowball rolling toward us, a metaphor on which we expand as we attempt to debunk the "Baby Boomer" myth in the section titled "Baby Boomers: Whither Goest Thou?" Lest we forget, there *is* a contraposition to the aphorism, "A rising tide lifts all ships."

The Art/Science of Managing Risk

Before we can attempt to argue that we are capable of managing risk, we must first define it. As you will see, there are two conspicuously different definitions in use today. First, *Webster's New World Dictionary* renders precise the meaning of risk (noun) as "the chance of injury, damage, or loss; dangerous chance, hazard," as a verb, "to expose to the chance of injury, damage, or loss." Second, MPT, which

38 Greenspan and company cut the Fed funds rate 13 times since then, to 1%, the lowest since 1958. Fiscal policy has been complementary in the extreme. June 2004 started a round of rate increases that bumped the rate up to 3.25% as of midyear 2005.

emerged out of academia in the 1950s and is highly quantitative in its approach to portfolio management, defines risk as "relative market-price volatility." It presumes that markets are efficient and that investors respond rationally to various stimuli; thus greater company-specific uncertainty (returning to *Webster's* definition) will be reflected in greater market-price volatility than the norm. The term MPT practitioners use to quantify such volatility is *beta*. The S&P 500, the benchmark, has a *beta* of 1. Stocks with *betas* greater than 1 are considered riskier than those with *betas* less than 1. Obviously, the greater the variance, the greater the risk.

At first glance, reconciling the two perspectives does not appear to be overly difficult. However, upon closer inspection, serious questions arise. First, *beta* is deemed to be a constant, regardless of price. Because MPT advocates believe that markets are largely efficient—i.e., the current price is an accurate reflection of the value of the business based on all available information—risk should not be price-related. Speaking of price, in other words, on March 10 when priceline.com peaked at $162 per share, it was no more risky than it is at its current price of $1.50.[39] That's where they lost us! To be sure, such extreme volatility leads one to wonder about the presumed rationality of the investors whose buying and selling in the marketplace set the market-clearing price at both extremes and at all prices in between. Is it possible that a company's fortunes can change so drastically in such a short period of time? Or, heaven forbid, are investors inclined to act irrationally on occasion, thus casting doubts about the efficacy of market efficiency as a primary tenet of the widely embraced MPT?

The "chance of loss" can be broken down further into semi-discrete elements. First, there is business risk, which is largely a function of our free-enterprise system. Our economy is designed to compete away excess profits, usually via lower prices and/or product innovation. Mismanagement also can bring no end of trouble to otherwise fine businesses. Further, there is financial risk, the often catastrophic downside of the excessive use of borrowed money to fund the purchase of assets. And there is valuation risk. Realistically, there is absolutely no way that the future growth prospects of EMC justify a price-earnings ratio of 125. Period.[40] On the other hand, if you pay too much for Coca-Cola, the longer you hold it, the less you will be penalized for being impetuous. Ultimately, earnings-per-share growth will make you look smart.

---

39 priceline.com effected a "smoke and mirrors" 1-for-6 reverse stock split in 2003. As a result, it currently trades for $21, compared with a split-adjusted high of $975 in May 1999 and a low of $7 in December 2000 and October 2002 (a decrease of 99% from high to low!). Priceline delivered its first net profit in 2003 of $12 million on revenues of $850 million.

40 After eclipsing $100 in the fall of 2000, EMC swooned to $3 and change in the fall of 2002. It currently trades around $14, and with the return of positive earnings in late 2003, the stock still trades at a relatively robust P/E multiple of 34.

The following diagram helps to graphically illustrate essential elements of our argument. The left-to-right, upward-sloping, solid linear curve—our approximation of a point value for intrinsic worth over time—is what differentiates our investment approach from those who are inclined toward MPT. It assumes, almost presumptuously, that the marketplace is not the final arbiter of value but that we, and others of a similarly independent and presumably rational bent, are capable of reaching a reasonable conclusion about a company's value without the market's help. To be sure, this is the most critical element of our decision-making model, upon which everything else hinges. It should be no surprise that deriving it places more rigorous demands on us as analysts than any other of our activities or, for that matter, any other analytical approaches should we choose to pursue them. The gaps between the "value line"—a representation that in reality is never linear—and the dashed lines on either side are known as the "confidence interval." The wider the gap, the more uncertain we are about our estimate of intrinsic value; in like manner, the narrower the gap, the more confident we are of such estimates. Most companies with high levels of business or financial risk simply don't make it through our rather exacting filters. The confidence interval would be too wide for us to find any practical utility in the idea.

MCM Model for Risk and Return

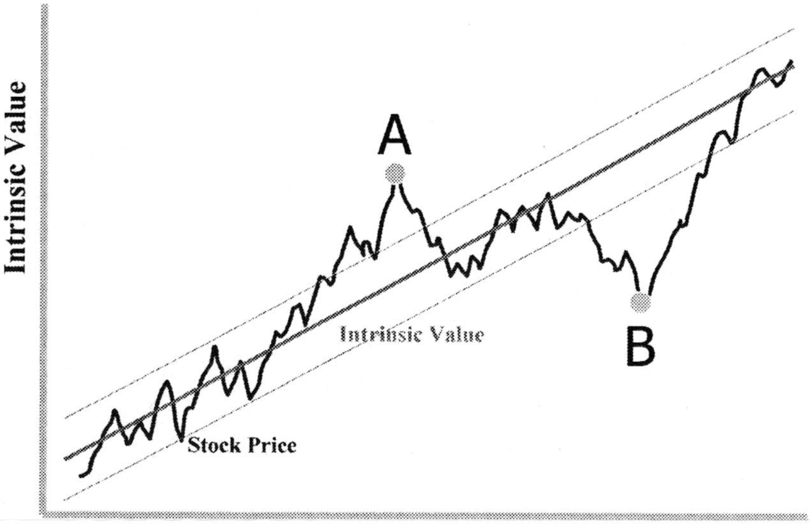

Valuation risk, as implied above, is more problematic. The more linear and upward-sloping the intrinsic-value line, the greater the degree of confidence in extrapolating it well into the future; the tightness of the confidence interval around it mitigates valuation risk for long-term investors. But few businesses offer that optimal package of investment attributes. In reality, most lines are not nearly so straight or steep in slope—nor is the future so certain or the confidence interval so tight. Only government bonds provide similar certainty, and they yield 5.1%, well below our threshold of required rate of return for equities. Working under those conditions of more frequently encountered uncertainty is not without its justification and rewards (as described in the following paragraph). That's where the concept of "margin of safety" comes into play. You'll notice that point B on the diagram is well below the intrinsic-value line immediately above. The spread between what we think a business is worth and the price at which it sells in the marketplace constitutes what might also be called a "margin for error." If our analysis of business, financial, or valuation risk proves to be optimistic, and it becomes necessary to shift the intrinsic-value line downward or flatten its slope (or both), the discounted purchase price gives us a safety cushion to minimize the consequences of our error. Conversely, point A, purchasing a company when it is wildly popular, affords none of the advantages implicit in point B.

There is a corollary to the preceding thesis that appears to us to be entirely logical but puts us at risk of being called heretics. If the corollary is to be believed, it turns on its head the tenet that high risk is the only means to high return. In other words, from our perspective, the world is no longer flat! For the long-term investor who is sensitive to the relationship between price and value, point B affords not only a margin of safety (i.e., lower risk), but the holding-period total return is likely to be greater than the growth rate in intrinsic value as well. As I hope is clear by now, point A promises above-average risk and below-average expected return, unless heroic assumptions are made about an upward shift in the value line. That's what we meant when we said, "If we carefully manage risk, the returns will take care of themselves." Comfortable now in our role as nonconformists, we must confess that MPT's use of price volatility as a measure of risk can be for us, as long-term investors, a measure of opportunity. The greater the volatility, the wider the vertical spread between points A and B is likely to be. If we insist on a significant margin of safety at the time of purchase, above-average volatility may well provide above-average returns. Rather simple, when you ponder it awhile.

Those engaged in investment activities more closely associated with shorter-term speculation are well advised to operate under the high-risk/high-return paradigm. Of course, last year's aberration in technology and Internet issues proves that it is possible from time to time to have the deadly combination of high risk and low return.

A significant portion of whatever advantage we gained over mainstream thinking last year arose because we were able to buy the businesses we longed to own below their intrinsic value. That doesn't happen every year. As with the CEOs of the businesses we own, we cannot escape the reality that capital allocation is a critical and unavoidable responsibility. If long-term returns are determined by the long-term performance of the asset, then we can logically expect to enjoy above-average returns by allocating capital to businesses that earn superior returns on capital, provided we are careful not to be goaded by the seductiveness of popular sentiment into paying too high a price.

Capital Markets

With the proliferation of media sources for financial and market information, rather than regurgitate what has already been digested, in this section we will devote more space to our assessment of the *whys* than the *whats.*

It is a generally accepted orthodoxy within the profession of money management to categorize firms as specialists in this or that, like so many different toy soldiers, some with torch to cannons' wicks and others with bayonets in place, some on horseback, others afoot. The list of possible subsets of investment specialists must number in the hundreds. Those who control the distribution channels to individual and institutional investors alike call the tune, and it's a medley of choices, enough to boggle the mind. It has been a burgeoning market. We hope the investors themselves ultimately prosper to the same extent as the promoters.

Our inclination is to look at all the pieces as parts of a bigger puzzle. As has been argued on these pages in the past, a bond is nothing more in its essential form than a stock with a fixed dividend and a specified maturity date and price. Accordingly, as wealth managers, we view stocks and bonds as interchangeable. Since relatively short-term highest-grade fixed-income securities are, as risk is defined elsewhere, the safest marketable securities available to us, we treat them as the "default class." Nonetheless yielding, with some reluctance, to convention, we will discuss the debt and equity market separately.

Fixed-Income Securities

Despite a similarity in form with common stocks, a bond's designated purpose is to protect capital and produce income. Keeping things simple for the moment, a bond purchased at par promises no chance for profit beyond the coupon earned. Of course, we understand that fluctuations in interest rates or upgrades or downgrades in the credit quality of the instrument will affect the market price, and profitable (or unprofitable) trades can be made to capitalize on those changes. In point of fact, declining interest rates in 2000 resulted in rising prices for fixed-income securities, precisely the opposite outcome experienced in 1999. The interest-rate forecasting record of economists has been so abysmal over the years that we deem it unwise to make big interest-rate bets. In addition, there are esoteric fixed-income security-management techniques designed to juice out a slightly higher total return or meet a defined purpose. We have created synthetic annuities where the fit was ideal, but generally we leave the exotic stuff to others.

The long-term investor might be well-advised to think of a bond as a security that offers no upside (assuming it's not a convertible bond) and unlimited downside. The best a bond can do is provide timely interest and principal payments; at its worst, it can default and leave you with little or nothing (long after the courts and the attorneys are through). To realize the full benefit of the semiannual coupon and the ultimate redemption at par—all that the bond indenture promises—we make no compromise on credit quality. Almost without exception, every fixed-income security we have purchased is either a direct obligation to the U.S. Treasury or, in the case of pre-refunded or escrowed-to-maturity municipal bonds, it is backed by U.S. Treasuries. If we should choose to compromise on credit quality, we (in effect) would be taking equity-type risks with little chance of a big payoff that common stocks have the potential of providing. When we assume equity-type risks, we do so in equity-type securities.

Falling interest rates were especially kind to the owners of the highest-quality fixed-income securities in 2000, as the total returns from your U.S. Treasury and pre-refunded or escrowed-to-maturity municipal bonds exceeded their coupon income. Despite the more favorable interest-rate environment, owners of instruments of lower quality were rendered a cruel judgment by the markets, with prices reacting negatively to deteriorating credit quality. As evidence of another market dichotomy, market yields on junk bonds rose while prices fell when, simultaneously, Treasury securities yields and prices were marching in precisely the opposite direction.

The creditworthiness of U.S. corporations has been in nearly as steep a free fall as the Nasdaq—and for much the same reason: earnings that have failed to meet investors' previous heady expectations. That points to a rising tide of defaults, especially among junk companies. "We've seen a notable decline in credit quality and an excess of downgrades versus upgrades in the last couple of years," says economist John Puchalla, one of the authors of a new report from Moody's Investors Service. The report adds that even better-rated companies have become vulnerable, having borrowed heavily for equity buybacks, mergers and acquisitions, and capital spending.

Barron's editor Alan Abelson makes these observations, with more than a dollop of satire:

> As it happens, corporate buybacks lagged as the year wore on, but that's easily explainable: Companies like to buy back stock only when its price is soaring. Otherwise, the reminder of how the value of their options is shrinking is too painful for the sensitive officers and directors to bear. That billions of dollars of earlier buybacks they authorized are now underwater may have had something to do with the reduced pace of repurchasing, too, although such picayune considerations never stopped them before.

Default rates are in fact rising, and there has been no sign of a letup this year, especially from shakier issuers that sold debt in the more relaxed credit environment of 1997 and 1998. By the end of 2001, Moody's predicts, 8.4% of the junk debt now outstanding will default.

Standard & Poor's also has issued a report forecasting record corporate defaults this year. "Due to the volume of outstanding debt by financially weak companies, we expect defaults to remain high for the next year and the best part of 2002," the company says. So far, $37.7 billion of debt is affected, and S&P expects the total to grow.[41]

The junk-bond market, accordingly, calls for issuers to cough up roughly 13% on their new offerings, as well as throw in equity kickers composed of units with warrants for the issuing company. Even investment-grade companies have found borrowing more expensive. The Morgan Stanley Dean Witter Industrials index, which tracks spreads on five-, 10-, and 30-year investment-grade bonds, stood at 2.17 percentage points over Treasuries in the latest week, up from 2.10 percentage points the previous week. The index is now well above the 1.80 percentage-point spread evident during the 1998 global financial crisis. At year-end the 10-year Treasury note yielded 5.11%.

Risk tolerance by investors is wearing thin. An extreme example of the current travails is NorthPoint Communications Group, whose acquisition by Verizon was canceled last week after the DSL provider had to restate its third-quarter earnings to reflect nonpayment by its

41 According to Moody's Investor Services, global bond defaults peaked in 2002 at $100 billion. From there, defaults declined sharply to a still high $16 billion in 2004.

customers. As part of the deal agreed to on August 7, Verizon was to make an $800 million cash investment in NorthPoint, of which it has already made $150 million. With that no longer happening, NorthPoint's $400 million of 12⅞% senior notes due 2010 plunged 52 points last week to just 10.5 cents on the dollar. As recently as the end of October, NorthPoint's junk bonds were quoted at 94. (There are similar horror stories in the low-grade sector of the municipal-bond market as well.)

Common Stocks

For the year, the Dow Jones industrial average was down 6.2%, its biggest drop since 1981. For all the volatility in other markets, the average actually traded in a fairly narrow band between 10,000 and 11,000 for much of 2000. The Standard & Poor's 500 stock index dropped 10.1%, its greatest swoon since 1977's 11.5% decline. Microsoft's impact on the S&P was huge last year. The stock's 63% plunge accounted for nearly 30% of the index's decline, owing to its market-leading weighting at the start of 2000. Despite the S&P's loss last year, some 249 out of 444 stocks that were in the index at the start of 2000 had actually advanced through December 27, according to analysts at Ned Davis Research in Venice, Florida. The Ned Davis calculations don't include the 56 stocks added to the index this year. Excluding technology stocks, the S&P was down just 0.3% through December 27, and the median stock gained 10.2%. And the Nasdaq composite index fell 39.1% in 2000 to end the year at 2,470, less than half of its March 10 high of 5,049—and its worst showing ever since the index's founding in 1971. At its low of 2,333, the Nasdaq had given back most of its prodigious gains achieved over the last two years (it had closed 1998 at 2,193).

The market action last year amounted to the reverse of what happened in 1999, when the Nasdaq soared 85%, and technology was about the only place to be. During 1999 the S&P 500 rose 19.5% but was up just 4% when tech issues were excluded, says Ned Davis Research. And despite the index's strong performance, the breadth in the S&P was worse in 1999 than 2000: Fewer than half the stocks in the index rose during 1999, while the median stock fell 2.1%.

Foreign stocks, long ballyhooed by financial intermediaries as an essential ingredient for diversified portfolios, did little to further that argument in 2000. As a representative of Latin America, Mexico's Bolsa index declined 21.5% in dollars. As for Europe, Bloomberg's European 500 index fell 10.2% in dollars and 17% in the faltering Euro. The Pacific Rim's largest market, Japan, saw its Nikkei 225 index plunge

27.2% in dollars, 34.7% in yen, to 13,785.[42] Those with long memories will recall that the Nikkei peaked in 1989 at 39,000. We've always been homebodies—and find life easier and our wallets thicker as a result. Besides, mindless imitation of others has never been our style.

The relationship between the total market value of all U.S. common stocks and GDP, until recently, was off the charts, paralleling the Japanese stock market and underlying economy in the late '80s. Such extreme valuations cause us to shiver just a little. What the data tell us is that despite the great damage done to numerous sectors, this American market by any historical or rational yardstick is still no bargain.

The Stock/Bond Dichotomy

We simply can't shake ourselves of the compulsion to view the capital markets as a whole. The corporate-bond market is pricing in a rather high probability that companies will default. The stock market, despite its recent slide, continues to boast historically high valuations. Something doesn't compute here, obviously, since the same earnings that go to equity holders can be used to service debt payments. The quixotic differences in the actions of stocks and bonds tell very different stories.

But it also occurs to us that some of the most robust performers in the equity markets are not overly burdened with earnings either, so their high valuations may be accompanied by equally high probability that they'll default on their obligations. Bridgewater Associates, a highly regarded research firm that invariably asks "why," recently cited Amazon.com as an example of a company on which the stock and bond markets awarded strikingly different valuations. The company had a market cap of some $10 billion ($6.4 billion at year-end), down from $50 billion but still quite noteworthy.

Amazon had around $2 billion in corporate debt outstanding. Of that tidy sum, its nonconvertible obligations due in 2008 were trading at nearly 50 cents on the dollar, offering a yield of over 16.5% (which, as noted above, is somewhat above that on the 10-year Treasury yield).

Observes Bridgewater: "The bond market is saying, in effect, that there's a 54% chance 'the company goes belly-up.' Which isn't exactly consonant with the stock market's insistence that Amazon.com is worth $10 billion." In a sense, Bridgewater commented, in seeking to explicate the paradox of such contradictory valuations, Amazon is a "microcosm of what's happening in the

42 The Nikkei 225 hit a low of 7,607 on April 28, 2003. As of June 30, 2005, it had rebounded to 11,584.

overall equity and debt markets. The debt markets are pricing in significantly high probabilities of default, while the equity markets show little concern." As the year wore on, the equity markets became a little more observant![43]

Baby Boomers: Whither Goest Thou?

Undoubtedly, the most common and adamantly expressed argument I have heard over the last several years in justification of a perpetual cornucopia of stock market riches has as its central thesis the ever-expanding flood of money from the coffers of the Baby Boomers flowing into the stock market. While generally considered even-tempered and understanding, I found that the absurdity of that notion was usually enough to get my juices flowing. First, it focused entirely on demand, with no regard for supply. That most elementary of economic equations, as apparently was overlooked, has two sides. It is price that reconciles the two. Second, and a bit more subtle, is that, metaphorically speaking, in pushing an ever-growing snowball up a hill, it takes more and more muscle for each inch of new territory gained. At some point, the snowball's mass is greater than the muscle behind it. If new muscle doesn't arrive soon, the monstrous snowball may, well, snowball and start rolling back down the hill. That, perhaps, is the question of the moment. Early returns would suggest that you stay out of its path. [This brings to mind the fate of poor Sisyphus of Greek mythology who was eternally condemned to push a rock up a hill, only to have it roll back down before ever reaching the top. Maybe it's the metaphorical Boomer rock/snowball ... and Generation X just may end up being Sisyphus.]

According to *The Wall Street Journal* articles, new cash flowing into stock mutual funds dropped 54% in November—the biggest monthly decline in nearly two years—as investors, stung by falling stock prices, started voting with their wallets. The decline in new stock-fund money was the steepest since February 1999, when the market was still recovering from the global financial crisis.

The preference for safety was underscored by investors' growing attraction to money-market funds, conservative vehicles that gain about 5% or 6% a year, regardless of gyrations in the stock market. That is especially appealing this year with the average stock fund down 5.8%, according to Morningstar Inc., the Chicago fund tracker. In November, for the second month in a row, investors stuffed more money into the cash-like funds than they put into stock portfolios.

---

43 Amazon.com has expanded its merchandising from books to almost everything else. In a sense, it is a proxy for the efficacy of online retailing, which commanded 2.2% of retail sales by midyear 2005 versus 0.9% in 2000. A shockingly low conversion rate of 4.9%—the ratio of visitors to a site who will actually make a purchase—continues to be problematic for the industry. Moreover, traditional store-based and catalog retailers are providing intense competition for the virtual stores.

The final figure came out to $56.19 billion, more than double October's $26 billion total and the highest intake for money-market funds since January 1999.

Indeed, enthusiasm for the stock market appeared to be fading fast in December too. "We're ending the year on a low-key note," said Steve Norwitz, a spokesman for T. Rowe Price Associates Inc., a Baltimore fund firm. In both November and December, he said, the pace of new money coming into the company's stock funds had slowed to a crawl. The firm expected the figures to end December flat, meaning that no net new money will have come into the stock funds.

One area out of favor and staying that way is international funds. Stock funds that invest abroad lost $2.88 billion to investor desertions in November, up from $206 million in October, according to the ICI (Investment Company Institute).

What About the 'Smart' Money?

Steve Leuthold, sage of the Leuthold Group, reports that through July 2000, insider selling of big blocks of stock, which he defines as at least $1 million worth (or 100,000 shares or more), weighed in at $43.1 billion. That's twice as much as sold in the comparable time spans of '98 and '99. As a matter of fact, Leuthold notes, this year's insider dumping in the first half tops the record $39 billion similarly disposed of in all of 1999. And, he warns, judging by filings with the SEC, there's plenty more where that came from: "Mother always told us, 'Don't fight the Fed or bearish insiders.'"

The Internet and IPO Frenzy

Internet analysts were the newest masters of Wall Street's universe. With stunning regularity, they would make an outrageous prediction that, within a year, a stock would double or triple or better—and watch gleefully as the stock sometimes did that in a month. This encouraged the analysts to make even more eye-popping forecasts, which many did (to their great embarrassment today, as most of those stocks now sell for a tiny fraction of the price when the predictions were made).

Then there was the great IPO frenzy. Despite warnings that initial public offerings are risky by their very nature because most IPO companies are so new, investors clamored for them—not just some IPOs but almost all of them. And why not, given that many were doubling on their first day? Many of those highfliers have since imploded, with about two-thirds trading below their offering price—and lots of them way below. See the woeful account of drkoop.com, in "Doctor Doomed." As for the chart [see Figure 3.2 in the Appendix], keep in mind that the performance indicated is recorded from the initial-offering price. Many doubled or tripled or more from the offering price as neophyte investors jumped aboard the train pulling rapidly out of the station. The overall losses, therefore, were far greater than the chart suggests.[44]

Fool's Gold

Last year, taking stock for payment from dot-com start-ups seemed like the path to Internet riches. Maybe it wasn't so brilliant after all. Not long ago, Web designers, lawyers, executive recruiters, landlords, celebrities, professional athletes, and others with goods or services to offer technology start-ups were accepting—in some cases demanding—stock in lieu of, or on top of, cash for their services to up-and-coming companies. It turns out that many ended up with fool's gold. This and the two paragraphs above remind us of two things: (1) Memories are short and (2) an axiom as old and inviolable as death and taxes: "There is no free lunch."

Are There Underwater Mines Everywhere?

In a word, no. We were able to find opportunities, or perhaps it was their falling prices that found us during a year with more crosscurrents than a competitive kayaking course. We believe that generally it will be the headwinds that will prevail, and we will respond accordingly. In the discussion on investment strategy that follows, we will explain how we hope to tack gingerly and cautiously upwind. We would prefer a howling broad reach, but the winds have shifted. We can't control the gales, but we can trim the sails.

Goliaths Slain

> "Many shall be restored that now are fallen, and many shall fall that now are in honor."
> – *Ars Poetica,* by Horace(65–8 BC)

44 The supercharged and frenetic IPO market was a symptom of the speculative Bubble. Its absence from the investment landscape is likewise indicative of the ever-swinging pendulum of investor sentiment. According to available records, bankers priced 543 IPOs in 1999. During the years 2000, 2001, and 2002, a total of 431, 96, and 85 IPOs, respectively, were brought to market. Seven IPOs had been priced from January 1 through June 6, 2003. The pace picked up after the first half of 2003 as a total of 79 companies went public for the full year. There were 233 IPOs in 2004. The lyrics of Willie Nelson's "On the Road Again" are ringing in my ears ... The IPO gang is once again on tour, providing disquieting anecdotal evidence (like mutual-fund cash ratios discussed later) that all is not well with the investor who prefers to buy low so that he might sell high.

Thus appeared the prophetic keynote quotation on the first page of the first edition of the investment classic, *Security Analysis*, published in the darkest depths of the Depression in 1934. The following contemporary eulogy is brimming with insights about how money has been managed—or mismanaged—by the biggest and most prestigious hedge funds in the world. It is also a cautionary tale of the rise and fall of two famed financial-market luminaries.

To begin, these two men—Julian Robertson Jr. and George Soros—are not contemporary scoundrels, nor were they cut from the same cloth as the robber barons of old. To be sure, they were major league speculators, both as bright as they were bold and sometimes brash, yet not so superhuman in the end as to be invulnerable to the risks inherent in those high-stakes and even higher-profile games of chance for which they were so well-known.

Julian Robertson Jr.

Value manager Julian Robertson Jr., the courtly 67-year-old North Carolinian, guided Tiger Management to resounding success since its inception in 1980. Twelve months ago, we had this to say about the value manager's dilemma, quoting from his December 1998 letter to the clients of Tiger Management:

> ... [T]he Internet is a great new technology that will change our lives. But there have been other great developments that created equally important lifestyle changes. In the past, investors overreacted to the promise of these changes. ... We're in a wild runaway technology frenzy; meantime most other stocks are in the state of collapse. I have never seen such a dichotomy. There will be a correction. As to whether or not this correction will take the form of a total market collapse as in 1929, 1973–74, and 1987, I have doubts. Why? The out-of-phase stocks are just too cheap. ... [T]his would imply a long-term underperformance of technology (believe it or not, it has happened) while the rest of the market continues to advance. Of course, this would be the ideal situation.

A few momentous months later, on March 30, 2000, the same week the market sounded the death knell for drkoop.com, Julian Robertson shocked the investment world as he closed down his hedge funds after 18 years of stellar returns and two years of disaster. His lifetime record will always be remembered with awe. Robertson turned his original grubstake of $8 million in 1980 into a personal fortune estimated at a billion dollars, even after the April setbacks. His investors reputedly enjoyed annual returns over that period of 25% (or so he says). Then, in the 18 months preceding his announcement—an agonizing time for value investors—Tiger proceeded to give back half of the gains it had built up over the previous 18 years. While Wall Street neophytes and veterans alike cleaned up in technology issues, Tiger shunned the Internet and stuck largely to old-economy stocks such as General Motors, Unisys, and US Airways.[45]

His decision to close up shop has occasioned a great outpouring of commentary, much of it finding fault with one thing or another. Nobody, though, seems to find fault with his indignant refusal to participate in the bull market for technology stocks. Rather, he has been treated as a tragic hero because his adherence to the "value" rule went unrewarded, while money managers who shamelessly chased tech stocks were treated to vast returns. Instead, he is castigated for letting his $23 billion fund get too big to move in and out of companies without roiling the share price, for neglecting good opportunities because they were too small to make a difference, for forsaking stocks to dabble in the occasional bet on interest rates or currencies ... though his "macro" performance was no less mixed than the other victim of whom I will write shortly.

In announcing that he would liquidate his funds and give back his investors' money, Robertson admitted that he is "out of step with a world in which Palm, the maker of the hand-held Palm Pilot, is valued at more than GM and in which priceline.com (which sells airline tickets but has neither earnings nor planes) was valued at more than US Airways [a company that brought Berkshire Hathaway acute although ultimately temporary pain and in which he held a commanding 22% interest] and most of the other publicly traded airlines combined."

Sadly, for those investors who embraced the priceline.com story as evidence of both the despair and disillusionment that had overcome Robertson at that moment, the prophetic insights that he so often exhibited were disregarded. The price line that priceline.com stock tracked has not been unlike the attitude of a plane before and after it "stalls." The stratosphere-bound shares of the popular and creative auctioneer of airline tickets, hawked on television by celebrity spokesperson William Shatner, perhaps selected because of the public's familiarity with him as an icon from the era of science-fiction fascination, in the end proved that some ideas are, indeed, more fiction than fact when profitability is used as the standard of measure. During the very same week that a disheartened Robertson capitulated and bemoaned the irrationality of the market, priceline.com stock's exponential ascent finally

45 Unfortunately, Robertson's old-economy largest stock picks didn't fare well either. General Motors travails were described in an earlier footnote. US Airways emerged from Chapter 11 bankruptcy in March 2003, only to re-enter bankruptcy in September 2004 with hopes of a re-emergence in the fall of 2005. Unisys fell from $50 in 2000 to a current low of $6.

slowed to stall speed at the altitude of $163. From there, in little over a year's time, it sped toward Earth in a death spiral, currently languishing around $2 per share, $22.5 billion in market value simply disappearing into thin air during the tailspin.[46]

"There is no point in subjecting our investors to risk in a market which I frankly do not understand," Robertson wrote. What's more, he went on, "there is no quick end in sight ... of the bear market in value stocks." That conclusion, sadly for Julian Robertson, was not prophetic.

At the end of 1996, Tiger had roughly $8 billion in capital, 1,000 times its initial outlay but still a manageable pool of money. Then, in 1997, Tiger had its best year ever—up 70%. Overnight, Tiger became Wall Street's sensation—just as Long-Term Capital was ... and just as high-tech funds are today. Tiger's gaudy results attracted billions of dollars from new disciples. "It was fickle money," according to a spokesman for Tiger. "You could say hot money." By August 1998, Tiger's capital had burgeoned to $22.8 billion.

Perhaps intoxicated by his record, Robertson allowed the fund's leverage to balloon to 3 to 1, meaning total assets topped $60 billion. (Of course, leverage also had helped inflate returns on the way up.) With such a bloated portfolio, Robertson knew, as he admitted to a *Wall Street Journal* reporter, that some of his biggest holdings were illiquid. He learned of the terrifying capital erosion at Long-Term Capital, which blew up just as Tiger began to run into trouble. Nonetheless, Robertson apparently was surprised by how fast his fund came undone.

In the fall of 1998, he dropped $2 billion on Japanese yen—a misplaced speculation—and then $600 million more on Russian treasury bonds. Meanwhile, Robertson's cheap stocks kept getting cheaper. In 1999 Tiger had its worst year, losing 19%. In the first two months of 2000, it fell another 14%. The hot money that had so recently pursued Tiger took a flying leap. Some of its old money followed suit. In a relatively brief span, Tiger was forced to redeem $7.7 billion—roughly equal to its total investment and retained profits over its first 16 years. With money running for the exits and losses compounding due to leverage, Tiger had no choice but to sell favored

46 Priceline's market price and market penetration problems are mentioned in an earlier footnote. Palm Inc., early leader in the PDA (personal digital assistant) market, currently sells for around $12, but only after a 1-for-20 reverse stock split necessary to artificially lift the stock price out of the "penny stock" category and avoid the limitations on ownership by certain institutions when the stock falls below a specified price. That equates to $.60 per share when compared with the price noted above. Adjusted for the split, the stock exceeded $3,000 in 2000. PDAs are falling prey to such competition as "smart telephones" or converged devices. Palm has since split itself into two operating companies. PalmOne is the maker of the PDA or hardware, while PalmSource makes the software that goes into the PDA device. Adjusting for this spin-off, the two companies' shares have rebounded to approximately a $38.25 value for the holder of both companies after the spin-off. There is now a rumor that Palm may be interested in acquiring PalmSource.

stocks at depressed prices.

Tiger made three mistakes, dangerous in isolation and fatal in combination: It got too big, it got too exposed to withdrawals from hot-money investors, and it got too leveraged. Despite Robertson's miscalculations, his final letter proved to be prescient: "The current technology, Internet and telecom craze, fueled by the performance desires of investors, money managers and even financial buyers, is unwittingly creating a Ponzi pyramid destined for collapse."

Value investing never becomes irrelevant; it merely goes out of fashion from time to time. Price and value are ultimately reconciled, so the principal attribute required is patience. The flip side of adversity is opportunity. Value investing is more than just purchasing low price-to-earnings stocks as it is conventionally defined; it is also purchasing low price-to-value stocks (a big difference). If properly employed, it also imposes a longer time horizon on the investor's expectations for rewards. Julian Robertson grossly abused the value concept by piling on leverage and by not discouraging hot money from investing in his so-called value-based hedge fund. Robertson's excessive use of leverage as a value strategy was, in a business sense, a contradiction in terms. Robertson gave the impression of a conservative, vaunting his so-called value approach, but in fact was a speculator because of the use of leverage and taking large bets in marginal companies or macro ideas. In the wake of the disaster, there have been some long faces lately in Mister Robertson's neighborhood.

Last year, two of the same factors (leverage and size), coupled with intellectual arrogance, felled another storied hedge fund—the aforementioned Long-Term Capital Management—whose collapse seemed on the verge of toppling all of Wall Street until the Federal Reserve hastily organized a private bailout. To be sure, there are vast differences between the two funds. Long-Term's equity was virtually wiped out, though the fund sputtered on after getting an emergency injection of capital. Tiger is liquidating at its leisure. Even with its losses, a dollar invested at Tiger's inception has grown to a total of $82 (after fees), a sensational compound rate of 25% a year, according to the firm. Robertson's funds are currently so far underwater that it would likely be years before he would exceed the high-water mark and earn performance fees again. His high-overhead operation would surely have exhausted his personal fortune before that day arrived.

Tiger's recent meteoric growth and subsequent implosion harbor a dire warning for today's investors, especially momentum-following mutual-fund investors who are crowding into ever-fewer high-tech growth funds. If you think your favorite dot-com-laden mutual fund is immune, thanks to the new money that continues to pour into its coffers, remember that a short time ago Tiger was all the rage—and that was precisely its problem.

Where does this lethal combination of sizzling profits, followed by astronomical fund flows and huge, concentrated holdings exist today? For many months, tech-heavy mutual funds have been using their outsized gains to attract new money that they promptly reinvest to drive up portfolios and attract still more new money. To cite one example, Janus Capital collected $10 billion (one-fourth of the industry total) in February alone, managing $229 billion by year-end, up from $80 billion at the start of 1999. Unlike Tiger's limited partners, who could take money out only every quarter, thus facilitating an orderly closeout, mutual-fund shareholders are free to sell every day. Will these turnstile investors be any slower to exit than Tiger's were restricted to do, once the performance of growth funds inevitably cools? Put it this way: When it happens, I wouldn't want to be standing in the doorway. For an investor in inflated new-economy issues, bailing out will be the only logical move, because once momentum isn't there to hold these issues up, nothing else—surely not earnings or revenues or even voodoo bewitchment—will be. Janus, despite poor performance this year, is still sticking to its guns. As recently as October, its average price-earnings ratio was 48. We'll revisit this evolving story next year.[47]

George Soros

If Julian Robertson is the Sammy Sosa of hedge-fund managers, George Soros is the Mark McGwire. No pedestal was higher than that of Mr. Soros. A Hungarian refugee from the Holocaust, Soros, now 70 years old, started as a stock-picker in the late 1960s, moving on to "macro" investing—or betting on the broad trends that move stocks, bonds, and currencies around the globe. His style was to wait for big changes in the markets, then take advantage with aggressive moves. Although he turned over the reins of Soros Fund Management to Stanley Druckenmiller in 1989 to concentrate on philanthropy, he continued to keep close tabs on the funds. The firm kept racking up huge gains, creating amazement, even awe, among competitors. Its funds grew so powerful, using borrowed money to magnify their results that their investments moved markets, and their giant bets could be self-fulfilling. For example, in the summer of 1992, it became known that Soros funds were

---

47 As of June 2005, Janus assets had shrunk to $130 billion, owing to stock market depreciation and heavy net redemptions by investors. Janus, whose logo is ironically the Roman god most often depicted with two faces, lived up to its namesake. Implicated in the mutual fund trading scandals, Janus reached an agreement with regulators, setting aside $100 million to be available to compensate investors. In addition, Janus agreed to reduce its management fees by $25 million per year over the next five years.

selling the British pound short, betting on a decline. Hearing this, other investors quickly started doing the same. The short-selling foray in the pound earned Soros the label of "the man who broke the Bank of England." He profited greatly from buying Peru's currency and from selling the Malaysian ringgit, which prompted the most insulting of political outcries from none other than the prime minister himself. Paradoxically, Druckenmiller has since said that the Soros funds actually were buying, not selling, Malaysia's currency during that time. Beginning a couple of years ago, though, this outsized influence began to wane. As global markets swelled, Soros assets—even at the $22 billion they then totaled—no longer could move markets so easily, nor necessarily give the firm access to the best information. Power shifted toward money managers, such as the previously noted Janus Capital, once a third-tier mutual-fund group but now a huge one because of its hot performance in technology stocks.

To be sure, the Soros funds had some fumbles and stumbles. They lost more than $1 billion in 1998–99 betting that Europe's new common currency would rise. Instead, the Euro has fallen 24% since its introduction on January 1, 1999. In addition, despite their big-picture focus, the Soros funds haven't profited from the doubling of world oil prices over the past year or so. Out of necessity, Soros migrated to the newest hot game in town, the venue that catapulted Janus into the big leagues: technology and the Internet.

In spite of larger-than-life images and egos to match, the intrigue surrounding the goings-on within the offices of the great hedge funds was almost palpable—and, at root, most predictably human. Desire for the power and prestige that massive wealth confers can quickly transmogrify into the fear from which no one, no matter how high or low his or her station, is immune. According to *The Wall Street Journal*:

> For months, through late 1999 and early 2000, the Monday afternoon research meetings at George Soros's hedge-fund firm centered on a single theme: how to prepare for the inevitable sell off of technology stocks. Druckenmiller, in charge of the celebrated funds, sat at the head of a long table in a room overlooking Central Park. Almost as if reading from a script, he would begin the weekly meetings with a warning that the sell off could be near and could be brutal. For the next hour, the group would debate what signs to look for, what stocks to sell, how fast to sell them. "I don't like this market. I think we should probably lighten up. I don't want to go out like Steinhardt," Mr. Druckenmiller said in early

> March as the market soared, according to people present at the time. He was referring to Michael Steinhardt, who ended an illustrious hedge-fund career in 1995, a year after suffering big losses.

Soros himself, often traveling abroad on philanthropic endeavors, would regularly phone his top lieutenants, warning that tech stocks were a bubble set to burst. For all the months of hand-wringing, when the sell-off finally did start in mid-March, Soros Fund Management wasn't ready for it. Still loaded with high-tech and biotechnology stocks and still betting against the so-called old economy, Soros traders watched in horror when the tech-heavy Nasdaq composite index plunged 124 points on March 15 to 4,583 (that, of course, was only the beginning; by year-end, it had fallen nearly 2,000 more points to close at 2,634), while the once quiescent Dow Jones industrial average, also on March 15, leaped 320 points. In just five subsequent days, the Soros firm's flagship Quantum Fund saw what had been a 2% year-to-date gain turn into an 11% loss.

Continued *The Journal*: "'Can you believe this? This is what we talked about!' cried a senior trader amid the carnage. Others on the firm's gloomy trading floor busied themselves calculating how much they had lost by aping Soros investments in their own accounts."

Soros pressed Druckenmiller to bail out of some swooning Internet stocks before they sank even farther, while Druckenmiller insisted that the funds hold on.

By the end of April, the Quantum Fund was down 22% since the start of the year, and the smaller Quota Fund was down 32%. Soros had stated in a 1995 autobiography that he was "up there" with the world's greatest money managers, but he added, "How long I will stay there is another question." Now came an answer. Both Druckenmiller and Quota Fund chief Nicholas Roditi resigned. Soros unveiled a new, lower-risk investing style—completely out of character for him—and conceded that even he found it hard to navigate today's murky markets. "Maybe I don't understand the market," a reflective Soros said at an April 28 news conference [using words of bewilderment similar to those uttered by Robertson just four weeks earlier]. "Maybe the music has stopped, but people are still dancing." George Soros may have exhausted his supply of useful insight when he wrote: "I used to get particularly excited when I picked up the scent of an initially self-reinforcing but eventually self-defeating process. My mouth began to water ..."

It is paradoxical that neither of these hedge-fund giants were able to capitalize on the most spectacular speculative Bubble in modern market history. Ironically, Julian Robertson's principle-based and disciplined reluctance to participate in the public's fascination with technology did as much to savage his fund as Druckenmiller's reluctance to withdraw from the same high-tech game before it was too late.[48]

Doctor Doomed

Sometimes a single event can be emblematic of an era. The story I am about to tell may well capture in one singular episode the character of the dizzying spiral of speculative irrationality that ballooned into the excesses of 1999 and early 2000. The flight of fancy was embraced by an enthusiastic public only too willing to believe—and enabled by investment bankers who know only one spelling for the word *principal.* The predictable bust follows a pattern, replicated throughout history, of excess gone unchecked until it plunges back to earth by the weight of its own intrinsic absurdity.

No doubt you will remember the likeness well. His white beard and dignified bearing gave him the air of an Old Testament prophet delivering the word from on high. His name is C. Everett Koop, MD. The good doctor was a 64-year-old pioneering pediatric surgeon in Philadelphia when President Ronald Reagan appointed him to the post of Surgeon General in 1981, back when many of today's 'Net executives were still in knickers. After eight years of public service—during which the bowtie-bedecked, uncompromising, fixed-jaw physician stared down senators as he crusaded against tobacco companies—he became known as "America's doctor." His principled stands on divisive issues (like AIDS) and his proselytizing on behalf of public health made "Koop" a symbol of integrity. Concurrently, in the parlance of the business world, "Koop" had become a

---

48 As a postscript, according to TheStreet.com, Soros's flagship Quantum hedge fund was 90% in cash by May 15, 2000, and has subsequently been reorganized to reflect a lower-risk profile. Several years ago it was reported that Soros still had $4 billion invested in the fund. The 75-year-old George Soros remains ever the outspoken political and social activist. GeorgeSoros.com was established in the months leading up to the 2004 election as part of Soros's campaign to urge his fellow citizens not to re-elect President Bush. In addition to the Website, Soros mailed a personal appeal to 2 million voters; purchased advertisements in more than 50 newspapers (including *The Wall Street Journal*); undertook a 12-city speaking tour; and published his views in a book, *The Bubble of American Supremacy: the Cost of Bush's War in Iraq.*

According to a *U.S. News & World Report* article dated November 8, 2004, Julian Robertson has "retired" to a palatial estate on the coast of New Zealand's north island where he's planning to build a luxury lodge. The development, which features a sunset room tunneled into a nearby cliff and 24 matching chalets, is causing local birdwatchers to squawk. As luck would again have it for the former Wall Street hedge-fund manager, the lodge is apparently too close to the cliff-top sanctuary of the world's largest colony of Australasian gannets (fish-eating seabirds). For a second time he may have to say: "This nonsense is for the birds." Since his Tiger Management fund group returned its money to investors (it still exists to manage Robertson's $850 million fortune and advise other fund managers), Robertson, now 72, has put considerable time and money into the land of the kiwis. His latest passions: golf courses and vineyards.

"brandable" name, his commercial value as an icon thereby greatly exceeding any of the more pedestrian undertakings (such as practicing medicine or even preaching the gospel of good health) in which he might engage.

The impressive skills that Koop so ably demonstrated, first as a doctor then as a public-health advocate, apparently did not transfer automatically, alas, into the business realm. In 1996, in his first business venture after leaving public service in 1989, a health videotape series backed by Time Life collapsed into bankruptcy. He had trusted in business associates, whose motive was profit, as he continued his public-health mission. Shortly thereafter, he teamed up with Donald Hackett, a 20-year veteran of the health-information industry, and the entrepreneur John Zaccaro, neither of whose résumés are particularly distinguished. It was this trio that gave birth to drkoop.com to capitalize on the public's fascination with the Internet, coupled with its reverence for the good doctor.

Fast-forward to March 1999. Koop, then 82, was about to prove that you're never too old to cash in on the Internet craze, that there is no generation gap when it comes to greed (admittedly, perhaps an unkind and unfair characterization in this instance). The company drkoop.com, of which the respected physician was nominal founder, filed a $50 million IPO less than a year after it was formed. To give you some idea of the humbleness of its beginnings, drkoop.com earned a paltry $16,000 in ad revenue in 1998 while ending the year with a $15.2 million retained-earnings deficit. In its offering document, the company attempted to lend credence to its half-baked marching orders: "Our business model is primarily to earn advertising, subscription, and the commerce transaction revenues from advertisers, merchants, manufacturers, and health-care organizations who desire to reach a highly targeted community of health-care consumers on the Internet."

How valuable was his name? Koop signed a five-year contract with the company, granting it authority to use his name and image to market the site and its products. He was to receive 2% of the revenues from current product sales and up to 4% of the revenues from the sale of future products. He received consulting fees of $100,000 in 1998 that escalated upward from there. But Koop's big money was likely to come from a successful IPO. He held more than 1 million shares in drkoop.com, or about 11% of the pre-offering stock.

On June 8, 1999, drkoop.com made its public debut, and the octogenarian former Surgeon General C. Everett Koop became a millionaire 56 times over, reaping the cascade of riches that has become *de rigueur* in the Internet Age. The company's stock was priced at $9 and closed the first day at $16.44. Three weeks later, it peaked at $45.75, soaring to a total market value of $1.3 billion. Not bad for a company that had taken in only $1.5 million in revenues in its entire short history, while at the same time losing buckets of money. Investment banker Bear Stearns underwrote the offering, raising $84 million for the fledgling company while raking off a tidy $6 million in fees for itself and two secondary underwriters, Hambrecht & Quist and Wit Capital. It was a coup for Bear, a perennial underdog trying to break into the first tier of tech underwriters. At what price principle, one might ask? Regardless of where you're inclined to lay the blame for the bloodbath that followed, the investment bankers are the presumed knowledgeable and informed party.

Purchasing a security is not like buying a car: You can't kick the tires. Unfortunately, ethical standards seem to play second fiddle all too often to avarice during manias such as the one through which we are passing. Our industry has been called some ugly names from time to time, and from time to time those names are richly deserved. In another era, the virtual absence of revenues or corporate history, the massive losses, and the less-than-legendary management might have scared off underwriters, but not in the spring of '99. Besides, next to sex, health was the single most popular topic on the Web, and (perhaps most important of all) greed was the creed.

There were some early signs that drkoop.com's managers were not the sharpest scalpels in the bag. Almost from the start, the upstart company cut extravagant promotion and distribution deals with AOL and Disney's Go Network. In April it agreed to pay Go Network nearly $58 million over three years to be the exclusive provider of health content for the Network and related Websites. In early July, less than a month after the IPO, drkoop.com announced it would pay AOL an incredible $89 million over four years in exchange for a nonexclusive yet primary role in providing AOL's health-care content. The AOL deal was for more money than the company raised in its primary offering! The massive expenditures were rationalized as being "critical to growing our brand, building traffic, and establishing market leadership." Investors bought the party line. On the day the AOL deal was announced, the company stock rose 50% to its ultimate and fateful high. Both Bear Stearns and H&Q, as they were "morally" obligated to do (who says there is no honor among thieves?) as a condition of landing the deal in the first place, initiated research coverage in early July, rating the company a "buy" at a price three times that of its initial offering price of $9 a month earlier. The investment bankers were perhaps in some small way drumming up new and presumably less-sophisticated buyers who enthusiastically relieved the favored original-offering customers of the burden of ownership. Indeed, Ponzi schemes come in an intriguing array of guises.

A few weeks after initiating coverage, the Bear Stearns analyst released a 57-page report curiously (and quite erroneously) titled "The Doctor Is In," openly suggesting that there was further upside in the stock driven by the execution of drkoop.com's business plan. The stock was then $25. The analyst was right on one account: There was going to be an execution.

During the third quarter of 1999 (following the public offering), expenses totaled $24 million—much of the money going for promotion and advertising—but revenues came to just $2.9 million. In the fourth quarter, sales rose to $5 million, but expenses added up to another $26 million. Six months after the offering, more than half the IPO proceeds were expended.

The die was cast, despite the toolmakers' (and crapshooters') denials. After the restriction on selling shares lapsed in February of 2000 and the fourth-quarter results had been released, insiders began to unload stock at prices that averaged about $10. Dr. Koop walked away with a mere fraction of his earlier paper profits, a paltry $912,186. The company filed its annual 10-K report with the SEC on March 30 [a date with an increasingly familiar ring to it] (the SEC requires that this important corporate document be filed within 30 days of year-end). Buried in the document was a warning from the company's auditor, PriceWaterhouseCoopers, which shocked investors. "... [S]ustained losses in negative cash flows from operations created substantial doubt about the company's future." On March 31, the stock closed at $3.69; by April 4, it had sunk to $2.

Despite the popularity of the Website, drkoop.com underscores the turmoil afflicting advertising-dependent health sites as the online health industry shifts toward e-commerce and the delivery of medical services. As one unaffiliated analyst noted: "There's not enough advertising to blacken the bottom lines of all the content on six sites out there." Observed another: "drkoop.com has a good brand name and a good amount of traffic, but they haven't figured out how to make money." As noted at the outset, it is also symptomatic of the difficulties in generating profits in this fledgling industry where barriers to entry, until the capital dried up, were nonexistent.

Epilogue

While Dr. Koop remains as titular company chairman, a group of venture investors led by former ExciteAtHome executive Richard Rosenblatt injected $27.5 million into the company in late August and took over management in an ongoing effort to salvage the "brand." On November 3 the company acquired drDrew.com for $1.6 million in cash and stock. My, how prices have come down. Once momentarily wealthy and proud, Dr. Koop is now a defendant in a lawsuit alleging that he and other officers fraudulently sold stock by failing to disclose to shareholders the company's worsening plight. The financial hemorrhaging continues unabated. For the nine months ending September 30, 2000, revenues totaled $9.3 million versus $4.3 million the year before. Losses, however, were a mind-boggling $95.7 million, compared with $36.2 million for the first nine months of 1999. Because of the infusion of additional capital, shares outstanding doubled to 33.8 million from 17.6 million, presumably reflecting part of the dilution from the additional capital. We'll probably have to wait for the next 10-K on March 31, 2001, to learn the full extent of the dilution that the new investors exacted. The stock languishes at $.75 a share, the better part of $1.3 billion gone "up in smoke"—an ironic outcome indeed for the man who put warning labels on cigarette packs.[49]

49 According to the C. Everett Koop Institute on the Dartmouth College Website, Dr. Koop occupies a chair in surgery and heads a small Web-based organization on the campus of his alma mater whose mission is to "promote the health and well-being of all people." In an ironic quote on the Website that had preceded a brief biographical sketch of Dr. Koop, the writer had turned to Mark Twain, who said, "Keep away from people who try to belittle your ambitions. Small people always do that, but the really great make you feel that you, too, can become great." As noted above, this great man briefly fell into the company of "little people." In a recent revisit to the Website, the Mark Twain quote was, alas, missing.

CHAPTER FOUR—2001

Introduction

As the performance table indicates, we have all made it through the minefields of the last two years looking much more gifted than we actually are, waving aside both pans and the plaudits as a matter of course, taking neither seriously.

We must admit that we find it easier to seize an opportunity in the face of generalized fear than to resist temptation while under the seductive and almost irresistible forces of unsubstantiated and illogical greed fomented out of fear of falling behind the pack. The consequences of miscalculations or emotions run amuck in the first instance are far less significant than with the latter, as a surfeit of baneful evidence has made abundantly clear in this increasingly

pervasive down cycle of the markets. We tend to frame such judgments in mathematical terms. Even though there is only one correct answer, some wrong answers are closer to being correct than others. Nonetheless, running counter to the majority is a day-in, day-out test of will, determination, and convictions.

Gazing backward even farther than a year

for a moment, 1999 was particularly hard for us to comprehend or endure because of the unconscious allure of the rampant speculative contagion, the clamor from every direction for action, the epidemic of euphoria over ever-rising prices in already grossly overpriced technology and dot-com shares, the rallying cry that everyone jump aboard the bandwagon or look like a fool. To our good fortune, the latter was shouted by nearly everybody *but* our clients. Suffice it to say, the noise was deafening in the face of all that we knew to be true and conservative. There is an expression that gave some credence to our stand: "Someone who thinks logically provides a nice contrast to the real world." We would agree, though we know the injunction is grossly oversimplified. Since the outcome is never certain, the extent of the logic of one's thinking really isn't known until well after it's too late to reverse one's course. Besides, it's particularly lonely without the comfort and encouragement of the crowd. In truth, investment as we practice it is emotionally taxing: In the course of doing what we think is right, we find ourselves stepping into the fray when the current news is awful and the outlook worse, then doing an about-face and exiting when the sky seems to be the limit. This approach can feel contrary to human nature—that is, until we engage our rational mind and seek solace in the wisdom of its ways ...

Investment Performance

Period Ending December 31, 2001	**MCM Equities ***	**S&P 500 ***
Since Inception **	17.7%	14.0%
Five Years	20.4%	10.7%
Three Years	23.5%	-1.0%
One Year	22.7%	-11.9%

* Compounded annually, MCM data net of fees

** December 31, 1993

Year	MCM Equities (Net of Fees)	S&P 500
1994	-7.5%	1.3%
1995	19.1%	37.5%
1996	31.8%	22.9%
1997	45.1%	33.3%
1998	-7.4%	28.6%
1999	18.8%	21.0%
2000	29.2%	-9.1%
2001	22.7%	-11.9%

For comparison purposes, the above numbers are time-weighted. What that presumes is that we began with a specified amount of investment capital committed to equities and neither withdrew nor added additional funds to that asset class during the measurement period. In real life the dollar results can be markedly different than the above performance percentages would suggest. As a matter of course we take money off the table when prices are unrealistically high and, as noted below, we do the opposite when bargains are plentiful. The data above understate the portfolio wealth effects in 2000 and 2001 because of the huge amount of money we at times committed to common stocks during those two turbulent years. For example, in dollar terms, the $46.1 million in aggregate equity gains that were just achieved in the fourth quarter of 2001—precisely because substantial quantities of funds were shifted from fixed-income securities to discarded equities that offered table-thumping expected returns during the panicky sell-off in September—exceeded the dollar value of all the gains earned in the entire year of 2000. And yet the data above would imply that you did better in 2000 than you did in 2001. I guess it depends on how you keep score …

Far more significant than the numbers themselves is how they were achieved. If the means we employ are irreducible elements of our philosophy, the results will have more weight, possibly more staying power than the will-o'-the-wisp approach practiced by some. While we claimed that 2000 was an aberration, we weren't motivated by some sense of false modesty to make such an assertion. We make the same claim about 2001. We aren't like "Chicken Little" football coach Lou Holtz: Give us enough time, and the full meaning of those words of caution will be known. However, if we stick to the basic elements of rational investing, it is our hope—nay, our expectation—that we won't stray too far from delivering on our goals …

over the long haul. As our record indicates, we take "down" years in stride, so long as our longer-term compounded returns are satisfactory. You should know that no sleight of hand, IPOs, or any other tricks of the trade were used to bulk up our results.

Prelude to Our Investment 'Strategy'

Two and a half years ago, following a July 1999 speech by Warren Buffett on the stock market—a rarity for the Oracle of Omaha who is far more interested in companies than composites—*Fortune* magazine (on November 22, 1999) ran what he had to say under the title "Mr. Buffett on the Stock Market." His logic confirmed mine, and so the self-edited speech was profiled in the 1999 annual report. He must have thought the *Fortune* article worth repeating because he attached it to the 2000 Berkshire Hathaway annual report. In July 2001 he gave a second speech at the same site at which, again with the help of *Fortune's* Carol Loomis (who also edits his annual report), he updated his reasoning from the year before. Don't get too excited; Buffett's "updating" is measured in centimeters, not kilometers.

As you may recall, Buffett identified two 17-year periods—first, the lean years and the second, the fat. The first began at the end of 1964 and concluded at the close of 1981; the second was 1981 to 1998. In the first, the Dow Jones industrial average ended within a fraction of a point of where it began, 875, prompting Buffett to grouse that though he is a patient fellow, *that* tested his limits. In the second span, by contrast, it closed at 9,181, almost a 10-fold increase. Paradoxically, during the lean years, GDP grew by 373%, whereas during the fat years, it rose only 177%. But, as you know, stock prices are influenced by variables other than just economic growth. Corporate profits, a residual, have generally ranged in the neighborhood of 4–6.5% of GDP over the last 50 years. Additionally, prevailing interest rates are part of the discounting mechanism that reduces future income to present value. They tell a story that runs counter to the impetus of the economic-growth data. Interest rates on long-term government bonds at year-end 1964, 1981, and 1998 were, respectively, 4.20%, 13.65%, and 5.09%.

There is a fourth variable—besides economic growth, corporate profits as a proportion of GDP, and interest rates—that holds significant sway over the course of stock prices: the aggregate psychological frame of mind of investors.

So, despite robust GDP growth during the lean market years of 1964–81, interest rates rose dramatically, and corporate profits as a percentage of the GDP pie fell to the low end of their historical range. Investors became increasingly despondent over these double negatives and voted with their feet. The opposite proved to be true from 1981 to 1998. While economic growth was less than half the rate of the first 17-year period, corporate profit margins widened, and interest rates moved sharply lower.

Finally, despondency gave way to euphoria through the process known as contagion (see the section later in this chapter titled "Why History Repeats Itself"), which mutated into an ultimately self-destructive speculative orgy, fueled in its latter stages by little more than rising prices themselves. In my judgment, we are in the midst of hearing the air hissing out of the pricked Bubble. In an analogous reference (mine) to the late '20s, Buffett observed about the era, "What the few bought for the right reason in 1925, the many bought for the wrong reason in 1929."

Buffett went on to examine the relationship of the economy to the market over the entire 20th century as a harbinger of things to come. Mind you, his view is gestalt: Over and over again, he admonishes investors for looking into the rearview mirror to see what's ahead. We call it the "availability bias," which is simple extrapolation of the immediate past to forecast the future. Surprisingly, over most 10-year periods in the past century, the economy grew rather steadily at an inflation-adjusted 2–3% compounded annual rate. The Dow Jones industrial average, however, told an entirely different story. During the 20th century, there were three huge, secular bull markets that covered about 44 years, during which the Dow gained more than 11,000 points. Yet there were three long periods of stagnation, covering some 56 years, during which the Dow actually lost 292 points in the face of the country's solid economic progress. From 1900 to 1920, new innovations in electricity, automobiles, and the telephone formed the backbone of solid economic growth, and yet the market moved at a snail's pace: 0.4% per year, compounded, closing in 1920 at 71.95. The market exploded upward during the '20s, advancing 430% to 381 in September 1929. Nineteen years later, the Dow stood at half of its 1929 highs, despite record-setting per-capita economic growth of 50% during the '40s. For the next 17 years, coincidentally (the Baby Boom years of 1947–64), the Dow advanced fivefold, a nice move but not "fat" by later standards. That brings us to the 17 lean years, followed by the 17 fat years (as detailed above).

How can one explain these anomalies? According to Buffett (whose conclusions largely coincide with my own independent study of the history of investor behavior), investors' perceptions of the future are most heavily influenced by their most immediate past experience—rearview-mirror investing, as he dubs it. Buffett asserts that a book written by Edgar Lawrence Smith, titled *Common Stocks as Long Term Investments*, contains a watershed development in investment theory.

Based on historical data for the 56 years ending in 1922, Smith hypothesized that stocks do better in times of inflation, while bonds do better in times of deflation. It was his reasoning, later confirmed and therefore consecrated and expanded upon in 1925 by none other than John Maynard Keynes, however, that was most intriguing. Begins Keynes: "These studies are the record of a failure—the failure of facts to sustain a preconceived theory." He concludes: "The facts assembled, however, seem worthy of further examination. If they would not prove what we had hoped to have them prove, it seemed desirable to turn them loose and to follow them to wherever they might lead."

While Smith's conclusions about the future of common stocks have been credited with providing academia's blessing, helping to fuel the ever-growing speculative Bubble in the late '20s, his "thinking-outside-the-box" contribution was quite impressive in and of itself—and more so in that it was entirely contrary to the way most investors viewed the future.

When Smith's book hit the streets in 1922, bond-interest coupons yielded less than stock dividends (a relationship that prevailed throughout most of the next 30–35 years). Keynes rationalized that, since a portion of the company's earnings was retained in the business and therefore reinvested, an element of compound interest existed in common-stock investing, whereas it was absent in the ownership of bonds. The double whammy of a higher-dividend yield at the outset, with the likelihood that it would grow as well, lent credence to the idea of common-stock investing and later stoked the fires of speculative desire. Keynes anticipated in 1925 the potential perversity of carrying this reasoning to extremes: "It is dangerous ... to apply to the future inductive arguments based on past experience, unless one can distinguish the broad reasons why past experience was what it was."

Buffett concludes that simple extrapolation of the past is the principal instigator of most investment follies. Smith's study covered a half-century during which stocks generally yielded more than high-grade bonds. The relationship between bond and stock yields on which Smith's theory was predicated has been turned on its ear since the mid-1950s. Even though conditions nearly identical to those on which Smith built his case existed in the late '40s, investors were so hamstrung by their horrible memories of the '30s that they were blind to the opportunity that lay at their feet. Those conditions have never existed since. We note anecdotally that, according to studies, most investors today assume that bonds have always yielded more than stocks.

Buffett then at length makes the case that such "rearview mirror" investing is not merely the asininity of the small investor. He demonstrates convincingly that the great company pension-fund sponsors, actuaries, and portfolio managers repeatedly fall victim to the same malady.

More to our immediate interest, and in the midst of castigating large corporations for being no more astute than the man on the street, Buffett refers to an article he wrote in 1979 in which he made the case that stocks were at that time a better investment than bonds. Bonds were then yielding 9.5%, and the Dow was selling below book value while earning 13% on its equity capital (known as book value, when reduced to a per-share basis). As we have mentioned many times in the past, common stocks are in many respects similar to bonds—and therefore sometimes interchangeable—differing in that their coupons are variable and that there is no set maturity date. Despite these similarities, which are more form than substance, Wall Street, much to Buffett's amusement (and ours), treats them as discrete securities. Admittedly, the amount of the Dow "coupon" is far from fixed, unlike that of a high-grade bond. Still, the opportunity to purchase the Dow below "par" with a variable coupon that had a reasonable chance of averaging 13% over the years had to be conspicuously preferential to owning a bond with a fixed 9.5% coupon. Referring once again to Keynes, Buffett reminds us that the superiority of stocks isn't inevitable: "They own the advantage only when certain conditions prevail."

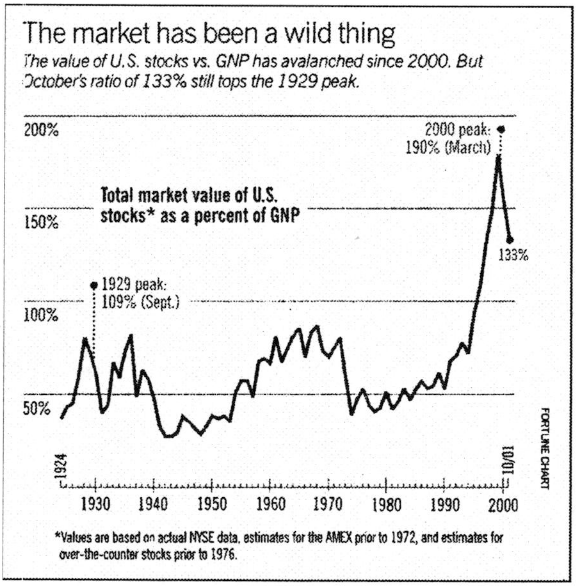

This entire exercise helps to make the case that markets are capable of acting irrationally in the extreme from time to time, and the investor who is forewarned is thus forearmed. Buffett and his alter ego, Charlie Munger, have characterized the widely practiced MPT as laughable. Though MPT isn't mentioned by name in the *Fortune* article, it is damned by implication in the first sentence of this paragraph. Buffett concludes by offering a simple quantitative antidote that investors can administer to neutralize their often emotional "availability bias" assessment of the future. Referring to the 80-year chart depicting the relationship between GDP and the market value of all publicly traded securities, Buffett suggests that when the ratio falls to the 70% or 80% area, "buying stocks is likely to work very well for you. If the ratio approaches 200%—as it did in 1999 and a part of 2000—you are playing with fire."

You will observe that the ratio frequently bottomed out at 50% or below. For those ideal bet-the-ranch conditions to exist there must be a confluence of at least several of the key wet-blanket variables: slow GDP growth, skimpy profit margins, skyrocketing interest rates, and/or pervasive investor despair. Taking a cue from Buffett's behavior in 1973–74, a rational man, who *by virtue of his lack of time, skill, or experience has no prudent alternative but to be broadly diversified*, begins buying when the ratio falls to 70% or 80% and, if he is lucky, still has a little money left to invest when it hits 50%. Since the "bottom" is only declared in retrospect, those who wait for it almost always go away empty-handed. According to our calculus, the aforementioned rational diversified investor would be far better off owning a fully invested portfolio with an average cost of 60% or 70% of GDP than the fellow whose congenital state of agitation and anxiety caused by the presence or imminence of real or imagined danger cannot, in the end, pull the trigger, regardless of price. Invariably, he ends up owning nothing but regrets when the ratio returns to 80% or more. No man is more entitled to buy at the bottom than Buffett, and yet no man is more aware of the foolishness in trying.

The ratio was 133% as recently as October (see preceding chart).[50] Buffett admits that the simple measure has certain minor weaknesses and is hardly precise in terms of timing. But, as a rule of thumb, it's pretty handy. In the long run, if the GDP grows at 5% annually, and you expect the 10% returns from common stocks, then the corporate-profit share of GDP must go off the chart. "That won't happen," says Buffett.

Finally, referring back to his July 1999 *Fortune* article, Buffett ventures that the investing public should expect total annual equity returns (dividends plus price appreciation) over the next decade or two of about 6%, net of frictional costs (such as commissions and fees) of about 1%, along with inflation at 2%. A year later, stock prices are lower and the economy has grown, so he has raised his estimate, accordingly, to approximately 7% for long-term returns. Concludes Buffett: "Not bad at all—that is, unless you're still deriving your expectations from the 1990s."

Making Headway in Headwinds

This exercise in rationality, for which Buffett is renowned and which we also embrace dispassionately, is more than helpful in framing our day-to-day decision making in the context of the prevailing winds. So often investors

50 The ratio was approximately 120% as of June 2005.

suffer great anguish and disillusionment because, unlike the seasoned golfer, they don't bother to toss a few blades of grass into the air before choosing a club. This process of adapting to a new paradigm is evolutionary, not revolutionary. Those most firmly anchored in the immediate past are likely to be among the last to come to terms with the new reality.

Of one thing we are quite certain. Marching headlong, with your bets well-spread, into headwinds is certain to result in outcomes similar to what Buffett expects. Broad diversification, use of index funds that replicate some measurement standard (such as the S&P 500), or other similar so-called risk-management mechanisms simply cannot buck the forces of nature. Those who fathom the shifting secular trend and who correspondingly downsize their expectations will find the broad diversification exercise "not bad at all."

Our inquiry into the nature of markets is based on logical reasoning and has resulted in a style that has been different and will continue to be so. We have set our sights higher, and that requires a different approach to solving the headwind problem. Before an individual company qualifies for purchase by MCM, its five-year expected return[51] must exceed 15%. As the past two years have given ample witness, it can be relatively and absolutely productive. No course of action, however, is without trade-offs. The attendant cost of our nondiversified style is greater inherent portfolio-price volatility. While volatility has been in our favor most recently, we can say with near certitude that it will run against our interests at times in the future—some of them likely to be agonizingly protracted. Ever iconoclastic, we do not subscribe to MPT's reliance upon market-price volatility as a proxy for risk. Rather, we measure risk more like a businessman who owns a private enterprise, whose firm is not "marked to market" on a daily basis. Because there is no group of outsiders valuing his business on a day-to-day basis, and therefore no *beta* (MPT's quantitative measure of risk, i.e., relative price volatility) to numerically approximate business risk, the owner must default to a more Main Street definition: the possibility of an outcome detrimental to his best interests—or at least a result that is less than his expectations at the outset.

But, you say, are you not exposing me to inordinate risks, however they might be defined, by limiting my portfolio holdings to 12 to 15 issues? For that question we have two answers, the first of which is straightforward. Most clients come to us having sold a single business that represented a significant part of their net worth. If we propose an investment policy that expands the

51 [Original 2001 footnote] The expected return is the internal rate of return that reconciles the current price with the estimated future value. The future value, in turn, is the end product of the analyst's estimate of normalized earnings five years hence, multiplied by a terminal price-earnings ratio that itself takes into account an estimate of the earnings growth rate going forward from there.

universe of holdings to the aforementioned number, and if we assume those businesses are at least as inherently profitable and well-managed as the one sold (and are purchased at a price that implies a significant margin of safety), does this scheme not represent a significant reduction in risk?

As introduced in the prior part, the second answer is not so self-evident and may need to be read two or three times to get its full meaning. It is further complicated by the conditional relationship among several variables; for it to bring about the desired result, it relies on the successful execution of certain key activities. Instead of comparing our nondiversified portfolio strategy, at least as conventionally defined, with a single business, we will in this instance contrast it with the S&P 500, which is roughly made up of the 500 most valuable businesses in America, at least in the market's collective judgment.

For purposes of this argument, let's assume that, by number, 75% of the companies that constitute the capitalization-weighted index are average or better businesses, worth owning if purchased at a price discounted from intrinsic value that appropriately accounts for the differences in quality, and that 25% of them are not worth buying at any price above a token amount. That last group would include airlines, steel companies, automobile manufacturers, and the like. Here's where the case could break down. Let's assume that of the 15 businesses that we might select, two-thirds, or 10, prove over time to be well above average and that they were initially purchased at prudent prices. Admittedly, those assumptions are at least moderately heroic! Putting that premise aside for the sake of completing the line of reasoning, were you really more secure in the spring of 2000 buying an S&P 500 index fund at 32 times earnings or the handful of companies we bought at 12 times?

Thus the question becomes: Do you feel safer—are you safer—with two-thirds of the companies in your portfolio being above average, or with 25% (if you purchase an index fund that replicates the S&P 500) regardless of whether the number of companies is 15 or 500? Needless to say, if you accept the proposition, you might logically conclude that not only are you safer in the first instance, but your chances for better-than-mediocre results also are greatly improved. That has been our experience in recent years, but we can give you no binding assurance that it will be replicated in the future. Sometimes small is better—and, yes, safer.

More relevant to a discussion of investment strategy, can this approach be repeated time and again in the future? A simple "yes" or "no" answer will not suffice.

First, change, particularly in the fastest-growing industries (such as technology), seems to be happening at an ever-increasing rate. Many of the companies we examine have wonderful records of profitability, but we have no idea what they will be doing five years from now, let alone next year. Even in the more easily understood and less-glamorous industries, countless slips can occur "'twixt the cup and the lip." Competitive rivalries heat up, managers lose sight of their loyalties ... the list is as long as the imagination is fertile.

Second, even if we find them, can we purchase them at prices low enough to make it possible for the full benefits of ownership of the asset to actually flow through to us as shareholders? You see, while the market is occasionally wacko in the valuation of businesses, more times than not it is quite efficient, pricing them close to their intrinsic worth, leaving us with little or no margin of safety in the event we are wrong in our estimate of their value. In point of fact, we rarely get to seize a true opportunity unless it appears to be just the opposite, forcing us to act precisely at the moment our peers can't seem to unload it fast enough. For instance, just when the technology and dot-com favorites were reaching for the sky in the spring of 2000, many of the companies that we had long wished to own were carelessly discarded as worthless deuces and treys in the frenetic, high-stakes game then under way. Those that were cast aside we picked up at bargain prices. In September 2001, the emotional selling that followed the attacks on the World Trade Center provided similar opportunities, despite the fact that we experienced the same feelings and sensibilities as most other Americans.

Our whole investment life is living the antithesis of the lyrics of Debbie Boone's hit tune of the '80s: "It can't be wrong when it feels so right." Running against the herd makes easy copy, but you need only imagine how frightened you would feel if, instead of "running *with* the bulls" in Pamplona, Spain, you were forced to reverse your direction. Indeed, the Wall Street equivalent of this metaphor has occurred to us more than once [see again the brave, against-the-tide sheep at the outset of this chapter]. All of us are comforted by the affirmation of others. We at MCM, on the other hand, must conjure up our own sense of well-being. Our "buy low, sell high" credo certainly helps. The job we do also is made somewhat easier because we enjoy a significant advantage: Our clients allow us to be patient in the search for ideas, whereas many of our colleagues live in a pressure cooker, enjoying no such luxury of *seeming* lethargy. To quote 17th-century French mathematician and philosopher Blaise Pascal, most human misfortune stems from "man's inability to sit still in a room."

So, you see, it really isn't a grand strategy at all that we follow but rather a simple pattern of behavior analogous to an imaginary game of baseball. We spend most of our time waiting patiently for pitches that cross the plate precisely at our particular sweet spot. In this fictive sport, we can let pitch after pitch whisk by with no penalty for failing to take a cut at a ball in the strike zone, nor will we be forced to take a base on balls if the bat rarely leaves our shoulder. Sometimes the lumber gets a little heavy, and every now and then, we get an itch to take a swing. But most of the time when we get restless, we just step back from the plate, stretch a little, tap the dirt off our cleats, then step back into the box. To be candid, this is a heck of a lot more boring than regular baseball. But the good news is that by changing the rules to our liking, even a minor leaguer can achieve batting averages similar to those that put Ted Williams in the record book.

Our allocation to equities is not dictated by some arbitrary formula, despite the popularity of the practice, but rather by the arrival of the transcendent pitch. While one might apply the maxim [as we have before] "a rising tide lifts all ships"—and its obvious corollary to the buying and selling of stocks—it's rarely that simple. As noted in our discussion on performance, we purchased the castaways precisely as the Nasdaq index was peaking in the spring of 2000. We are far less concerned about a protracted bear market than we are about our ability to identify great businesses and to exercise the patience necessary to purchase them at prices well below what they're worth. Of course, many of the companies we have bought in the last two years have appreciated smartly, effectively closing the "margin of safety" gap between the original purchase price and intrinsic value. Increasingly, the market price, absent market inefficiencies, will depend on growth in intrinsic value. With many of our holdings, the so-called "easy money" has been made.

We are decidedly agnostic when it comes to acting on the majority forecasts for the economy—in part because prognosticators are, at least in the short run, not paid according to the accuracy of their pronouncements. If they were, there would be no economists. To the point, the "recovery beginning in midyear 2002" consensus scenario is, if our memories serve us correctly, simply the reincarnation of the "recovery beginning in midyear 2001." Accordingly, we think it appropriate to partially hedge our portfolios against the possibility, however remote, that the forecasting errors of the last two years will not be the last in this atypical business cycle, if that's what it turns out to be. Rather than cementing our considerable gains by selling companies that no longer go begging for buyers at bargain prices—and in the process incur short-term capital-gains taxes—we will buy long-term put options on the S&P 100 or another more appropriate index. The insurance purchased will not be used to moderate the impact of minor fluctuations in the value of your portfolio. Those "quotational losses" go hand in hand with investing in marketable securities and are of no concern to us. Rather, we will attempt to partially protect your portfolio from, in the vernacular of the reinsurance industry, "super cat" losses. Think of it as earthquake insurance. For your sake and ours, we hope the options expire worthless.[52]

52 [Original 2001 footnote] Try as we might, we could never purchase the put options at premiums that effectively made the insurance a good value. Such an outcome did not come as a big surprise.

Interest Rates: It Had Better Be Uphill from Here

Late in November, two "marker buoys" in the financial history of the United States were passed, collectively signifying where our economy stands in the grand flow of things.

In September 2001 the United States retired a group of Treasury bonds issued in 1981. The bonds carried an interest rate of 15¾%, the highest the government had ever paid on long-term borrowing. It was a nostalgic moment for the undersigned, recalling the 14% *tax-exempt* participation certificates, a hybrid form of municipal bond that we underwrote for the Concord School Corp. of Elkhart. The choice between equity and tax-exempt debt securities was not an easy one.

A month later, on October 31, 2001, with long-term borrowing costs the lowest in a generation, Washington announced that it would "suspend" its issuance of 30-year bonds. Interest rates plummeted, with the yield on 30-year bonds dropping the next day to 4.80% (compared to approximately 5.50% at the end of last year), while the yield on the benchmark 10-year note slid to 4.24% from the 5% range. It seemed that the market was suddenly anticipating the Federal Reserve's decision to lower the federal fund's rate by half a percentage point, to 2%, which actually would come to pass the following week.

After 20 years of declining interest rates (dating back to the aforementioned 15¾% coupon issued in 1981), we have in this country reached the point where we can't reasonably expect rates to fall lower. It's true that the United States is in a recession, and rates tend to decline during periods of retrenchment. But for rates to fall from their current level would suggest the darkest of scenarios. The macro-policy authorities are applying fiscal and monetary stimuli like a drunken sailor buying rounds of drinks for every other inebriate at the bar. This combination has never failed to ignite a rebound in the past—but is the past prologue in 2001–02?

We won't dwell excessively on the possibility that the cyclical recession in which we find ourselves will not be arrested by the application of traditional palliatives, that it will disintegrate (in the face of repeated denials from economists of all stripes and from far and wide) into something more serious. We are loath to draw parallels with Japan because the dissimilarities are as striking as the similarities. Most important, while our readings in classical economic theory would suggest that the possibility for an apocalyptic event is perhaps more likely now than at any time since the Great Depression, there are simply too many variables to assimilate, most of which are unknowable as to the likelihood of their occurrence, to say nothing of how they might interact with other equally unknowable variables. The best minds in the world cannot put this puzzle together; we will not attempt to give you a false impression of our acumen, which could lead to either complacency or fear. Neither is warranted.

Rather, in the face of this shadowy threat, we will respond in the only rational way we know how: with an extra degree of caution. As for fixed-income securities, we will continue our long-standing practice of owning only the best—direct obligations of the U.S. Treasury or tax-exempt municipal securities backed by similar Treasury obligations (pre-refunded or escrowed-to-maturity bonds). We will not even think about junk bonds. If the yield spreads get to be so great that they make the headlines, chances are that equity securities will be even cheaper. Because bond yields are relatively low, particularly when compared to the five-year expected returns from some high-grade common stocks, we will rarely extend maturities beyond five years in this environment for fear of getting "locked in" to a security we would prefer not owning for a long period of time.

We read extensively on the bond market. What we find is that most specialists in this area are merely splitting hairs, an exercise we find unproductive. Whether the benchmark 10-year-bond yields eclipse the lows of 4.16% (hit at the depths of 1998's global financial crisis) by a few basis points strikes us as utterly irrelevant, akin to speculating about how many prima donnas can dance on the head of a pin.

Still, we shall flavor these pages with a bit of history about the bond cycles, largely for the purpose of venturing a guess as to their future course, not so much because we are likely to buy long-term bonds but, rather, because of the effect of interest rates on the valuation of equities.

In a November article in *Barron's*, Richard Sylla, professor of financial history at New York University's Stern School of Business and co-author with the late Sidney Homer of *A History of Interest Rates*, says the market's actions suggest that the two-decade decline in long-term rates may have run its course.

Another self-proclaimed expert and CNBC commentator, Larry Kudlow, head of Kudlow & Co., thinks that if the Fed were to explicitly target the market indicators—commodity prices, the dollar, the slope of the yield curve, and changes in the 10-year Treasury yield—yields could fall back to the 3½–4% range. But absent a change in the mindset of Greenspan & Co., a deeper recession, or a Japanese-style asset deflation (none of which Kudlow sees on the horizon), the benchmark note likely will trade between 4½% and 6½% "over the next bunch of years."

Martin Barnes, editor of *The Bank Credit Analyst* whose service we have read for many years, thinks 4–5% on the 10-year Treasury seems "reasonable." But Barnes believes that corporate-bond yields are likely to remain far higher.

"Don't expect corporates to return to their old [historical] average" of around 4% and change in the 1960s, he says. Top-grade corporate bonds, which now yield around 7%, are back near where they stood three decades ago. Lending credence to our concerns about credit risk, Barnes comments: "Corporate balance sheets are much worse today, requiring the greater risk premium that has been evident since 1998 and limiting the scope for corporate yields to fall."

Neither is it only corporate America's balance sheet that is less than rock-solid. Northern Trust's Kasriel sends a cold chill up my spine when he notes that the federal government faces huge unfunded liabilities. "Whatever happened to the debate over Social Security?" he asks. "It's gone the way of the Chandra Levy story." Paying those future obligations will mean either higher taxes or increased borrowing (most likely the latter). And Ed Yardeni, chief investment strategist of Deutsche Banc Alex Brown, who made his mark in the early '80s by predicting "hat size" bond yields (7–8%) when they were nearly twice as high, thinks the long slide in rates is "pretty close to over."

With the overall economy (current-dollar gross domestic product) on a long-run growth path of around 4–5% a year (3% real growth and 1–2% inflation), 10-year Treasury notes should approximate the same. That leaves scant room for long yields to decline. Indeed, Yardeni uses a 5% 10-year Treasury rate in his long-term stock market valuation model.

Turning more to the anecdotal, if you believe that markets know better than government bureaucrats, there's another clear sign that interest rates have bottomed out: By issuing bonds 20 years ago, Uncle Sam locked in the highest-cost debt in the nation's history; today, Washington eschews borrowing long term, even though rates are the lowest in a generation.

One observer in *The Wall Street Journal* also offered this oversimplified analogy:

> To understand the movement of interest rates over the decades, it's important to note that long-term market trends are defined by a series of cycles with ascending (or descending) peaks and troughs. Think of it as a shoreline. Tides go in and out each day. But if the high-water marks move farther and farther up the beach, there is a definite trend. If the high-water marks start moving down the beach, that trend has reversed. It now appears that the trend of the past 20 years of the tide going out has reversed with a low tide higher than the last.

As for the bottom line, we would be somewhat surprised if interest rates moved dramatically either upward or downward over the immediate future from where they are today. Longer term, we are not so sanguine about subdued rates, more the result of a gut feeling than something concrete we can point to. Accordingly, while we feel reasonably confident that we have a temporary respite from concerns about rising interest rates impacting our earnings-discounting model, that specter may be a reality with which we must deal in the years ahead.[53]

Why History Repeats Itself

History is a perplexing teacher; its lessons often are obtuse, bewilderingly intricate, and complicated. Were they otherwise, the mistakes in the past would not repeat themselves so irritatingly often. And yet, there is much to take away from this school of "hard knocks" for the student who is able to organize the lessons into a variety of models that can be applied in general to events of the future. Unfortunately, what you learn will be of little use tomorrow—or even next year. No sinner is more repentant than one whose transgression is fresh in his or her mind. This is a variation of the "availability bias," the penchant to be disproportionately influenced by more recent events as one gazes too raptly into the rearview mirror.

What we write, therefore, has about the same immediate value as closing the barn door after the horses are already out. Be that as it may, we record the lessons so that you might file them away for future reference in times of recurring grand delusions, recognizing that there is nothing really new in the world of economics and finance. The dismal science is inherently cyclical, bound to repeat itself again and again, with the span between episodes a simple function of the length of memories. By contrast, in scientific endeavors, knowledge is cumulative. Think only of the evolution of the personal computer to gain some appreciation of the difference.

The Power of Popular Delusions

Nothing is more central to the dissection of investment manias than to study those human proclivities common to them all. The capacity for human beings to be readily deluded, to be made to look the fool, is the point of origin from which every seeming behavioral absurdity, at least with the benefit of hindsight, naturally follows.

One of the endlessly fascinating aspects of our participation in the capital markets is the opportunity to witness human behavior in a

53 As of midyear 2005, short-term interest rates had increased on the three-month T-bill from 1.8% to 3%, while the 10-year government yield fell from 5.1% to 4%.

highly charged environment, under conditions that would make a social scientist salivate. On Wall Street one can readily observe individuals whose actions are often the result of especially powerful motivators, such as greed and fear. Further, the abundance of data collected on the transactions that take place permits relatively thorough analysis of those behaviors. While we find the study academically intriguing, our interest relates more to how we can use the information as we ply our trade. We simply think an attempt at understanding the psychology of the marketplace will give us a competitive edge.

Quite pragmatically, much of the practice of psychology is directed toward serving the emotional needs of the individual. Years ago, having read *Moral Man and Immoral Society* by theologian Reinhold Niebuhr, my interest was captured by Niebuhr's different perspective on the study of human behavior. Instead of examining the individual in isolation, he looked at a gathering of individuals and the peculiar impact the group had on the thinking and behavior of its individual members. This was predicated in no small measure by his experience of living through World War II. The general idea certainly is not new. What has great relevance to us as investors, however, is the special nature of that transformation.

Years later, in a search for information on the legendary investor and statesman, Bernard Baruch, I came across the book *Extraordinary Popular Delusions and the Madness of Crowds* by Charles Mackay, LLD; the book was originally published in 1841. Baruch wrote the foreword to a reprinted edition in 1932, as the country reached the depths of the Great Depression. Mackay gives an excellent account of many of history's extraordinary delusions, from the Mississippi Scheme that swept France in 1720 ... to the South Sea Bubble that ruined thousands in England at the same time ... to the Tulip Mania of Holland when fortunes were made and lost on single tulip bulbs. On the other hand, *The Crowd,* penned by a Frenchman, Gustave Le Bon, in 1895, delves into the nature of a crowd that makes human beings vulnerable to its powers. According to the authoritative *Handbook of Social Psychology* (published in 1954), *The Crowd* is "perhaps the most influential book ever written on social psychology."

Of what significance is all of this to us? In 1932 Baruch observed in his foreword:

> Some years ago a friend gave me a copy of *Extraordinary Popular Delusions.* In a vague way I had been familiar with the stark facts of these events, as who is not? But I did not know ... the astonishing circumstances of each of the greater

> delusions of earlier eras. I have always thought that if in 1929 we had all continuously repeated "two and two still make four," much of the evil would have been averted.

But still one is likely to question the relevance, arguing that 1929 was truly an exceptional period, one not likely to be repeated during our lifetime. And in fact, much to our good fortune and to the preservation of our capital, most popular delusions of the financial variety never reach the pervasiveness of the spectacle in common stocks that ran rampant in the late 1920s. It is interesting to note, however, that Mackay offered in the preface to the 1841 edition the observation that "popular delusions began so early (in recorded history), spread so widely, and have lasted so long, that instead of two or three volumes, *50* would scarcely suffice to detail their history." We have taken the position that if we become the victim of a lesser-known delusion, we'll feel not one whit better than if we were swept up in the folly of one of extraordinary notoriety. (One bolt of lightning is of no great national consequence, but it may more than command your personal attention if you are directly between it and the ground!)

In 2000 a week's worth of evenings was consumed reading Robert J. Shiller's just-released and well-written book *Irrational Exuberance*, its title lifted from a phrase for which Alan Greenspan was roundly castigated until eventually a crashing market silenced his critics. Were the Fed chairman to author a book, it might be titled *From Castigation to Vindication*. Shiller, an economics professor at Yale and author of *Market Volatility* and *Macro Markets*, which won the 1996 Paul A. Samuelson Award, was generally right—and for the right reasons. I commend him for his scholarly and timely work. The final sentence on the inside cover of the book contains both an admonition and a note of uneasiness; it reveals a shadow of doubt about a future that is never certain: "It will be studied by policymakers and anyone from Wall Street to Main Street who doesn't want to be caught sitting on the speculative bubble if (*or when* [italics added]) it bursts." In truth, we never know, but we do become more confident as the weight of evidence gets heavier and heavier.

An Ounce of Prevention ...

[Acquiring knowledge of the psychology of crowds not only teaches one about the beguiling and insidious dangers of embracing crowd-think—sometimes termed groupthink—but, forewarned and thus forearmed, the *erudite* investor is less likely to succumb to its often ruinous reasoning.] Because of the incredible gains in communications technology in the 20th century, individuals no longer need to enjoy physical proximity to function as a crowd. Despite their disparate locations, investors around the world can become, thanks to modern technology, an instantaneous and homogenous lot, to which October 19, 1987 (and, more recently, 1998, 2000, and 2001!), painfully attests. Our past and our future have been and will be filled with popular delusions to which many will fall victim, ranging from the inconsequential to the extraordinary; the challenge to us is to learn more about how people become such unwitting victims. Indeed, "An ounce of prevention is worth a pound of cure."

Before turning to the "how" and "why" of our apparent capacity to be collectively deluded, let's recall several episodes from the recent past in the security and commodity markets. Such an exercise should lead us to the obvious conclusion: We are as susceptible as our forefathers were (and our children will be) to the suggestions, however reasonable or unreasonable, of the crowds with which we allow ourselves to become joined at the "lip." Each new generation throughout history, armed as it is with more accumulated knowledge than any generation before it, proves with the same certainty as the march of time itself that knowledge is not necessarily wisdom.

During the summer of 1987, the stock market was on a roll, having built a strong base in the second half of the '70s and having been further stimulated by an injection of easy money in the fall of '82. The popular averages were assaulting new highs with reckless abandon, with stock prices advancing almost exponentially. The market prices of companies seemed gloriously uncoupled from the plodding performances of the underlying businesses themselves. The Dow Jones industrial average reached its zenith of nearly 2,750, and Bob Prechter, author of a popular investment letter that had captured the imagination of Wall Street during the '80s much the same as Joe Granville did some years before, confidently declared that the Dow would finally peak at 3,600 before the party ended.

The stark reality of the fundamentals permitted only one rational conclusion, but the steamroller of sentiment, unmindful of the quiet warnings that history had to offer, crushed under its weight and momentum the logic and reason that stood in its path. While we're aware that averages, particularly in this instance, can be deceiving, examine the following statistics and see if the message that the fundamentals told should not have at least raised some serious questions.

Standard & Poor's 400 Stock Industrial Index

Measurement	Average (annual) (1950-87)	High (1987)
P/E	11.90 - 14.90 *	19.4
Price/Book	1.66	2.93
Yield	3.54 - 4.43% *	2.20% (low)
T-Bond Yield	6.28%	10.50%

* Average of annual lows and highs

One must wonder why most participants did not seek a safe harbor when the storm flags flew. Or why so many allowed themselves to get caught up in the riptide of popular sentiment that carried them to a turbulent sea when surely they must have known better ...

More Fool's Gold

In the late 1970s and early 1980s, there were two popular delusions that grew, at least in part, out of the virulent inflation of that period: gold and oil. Gold, which traded as low as $100 per ounce in 1976, skyrocketed to $850 by January 1980. Except for an aborted rally in late 1980, it fell relentlessly to $300 by the summer of 1982 and currently trades around $360. Rereading popular periodicals of the era helps one gain a sense of time-and-place perspective. *U.S. News & World Report* carried an article on October 8, 1979, titled "Gold Craze—It Sweeps the Country." The author wrote, "Modern day gold fever is gripping the nation as jittery Americans grope for ways to beat inflation. Every day, thousands of people are flocking to coin shops, jewelry stores, and gold dealers to put their cash in precious metals. Consumers who waited in gas lines only months ago are now in line to buy gold coins, bullion, and bracelets in hopes of protecting their savings." And: "This is the biggest gold rush since 1931," said the president of one of the largest gold dealerships in New York, whose "customers have lately been overflowing into the hallways of the Empire State Building."

The speculation in gold in the late '70s is an interesting case study. The yellow metal is difficult to intrinsically value (and in that respect is similar to collectibles) since it does not grow internally as a business might nor does it provide any current cash return to its owners. Conveniently, the very absence of a benchmark freed the speculators from having to deal with an ever-present fundamental reality. Many elements of crowd psychology can be found in the study of that modern gold rush.

Oil Slicks and Beyond ...?

Oil, which itself rose in price 1,500% from late 1973 to 1981, was an even more interesting and economically widespread delusion. In February 1980 *Forbes* magazine carried an interview with Kenneth Arrow, Stanford economist and Nobel Prize winner, who confidently predicted, "We are heading into a world of higher [oil] prices. It will have a major impact on housing by 1983, and I'd be surprised if gasoline is less than $2 per gallon plus whatever inflation adds ... Whether Saudi Arabia will be around in four years I can't predict. It is a very uncertain world."

The oil-rig count, according to Hughes Tool, was up to a record 2,600 at Christmastime in 1979. "Just about everywhere you go you stumble over someone pushing a drilling rig," said the senior vice president for land and production at Chevron USA, who went on to observe that Chevron had not been this busy since the great Texas oil boom in the '50s. The fever was not confined to Texas. Penn State's petroleum engineering classes saw their enrollment surge from 65 to 220 in three years. Most of the major companies in the industry were optimistic, some forecasting the price would hit $90 per barrel by 1990. Why, even conservative Standard Oil of Indiana raised its exploration budget three times in 1979. Money-center banks, active in financing the exploration, were no less upbeat. Chase Manhattan estimated domestic exploration at $15 billion for 1977, $28 billion for 1980, and a whopping $60 billion for 1985. Unfortunately, the widespread bullishness quickly gave way to despair. By 1986, the price of crude had fallen below $10—to less than 25% of its high. Idle rigs and befuddled oil industry executives [including a Texan named George W. Bush], investors, and bankers were more plentiful than politicians at a pig roast.[54]

Fast-forward to the late 1990s. The mania in technology and Internet stocks is simply the latest iteration of this timeless phenomenon. The exponential price curve of the Nasdaq index leading up to its peak in March 2000 was a near carbon copy of those for gold and oil two decades earlier.

We may be witnessing today a number of delusions that have not run their

---

54 In Chapter One (1998 report) we alluded to the possibility that the lack of interest in oil at $10 per barrel might present investment opportunities. Out of the ashes of despair and indifference, opportunity, like the crocus beneath a blanket of snow, irrepressibly grows ...

course. The takeover mania will surely go down as one of the great delusions of the 20th century. It could even prove to be the ultimate financial excess—making for a dramatic, if not tragic, end to the great post-World War II credit boom. When we finally conclude that the old rules no longer apply, they invariably do! In the same vein, one wonders whether a $50 million price tag for a splash of paint on a piece of canvas will not be remembered as a flight of fancy …

The Blockhead

Let's turn now to the somewhat surprising metamorphosis we experience as we become one with a crowd. The poet/dramatist Johann von Schiller once said, "Anyone taken as an individual is tolerably sensible and reasonable—as a member of a crowd he at once becomes a blockhead." That is a provocative statement, one that Le Bon examined with great clarity in *The Crowd.* He suggested that the most striking peculiarity presented psychologically by a crowd is the following: "Whoever be the individuals that compose it, however like or unlike be their mode of life, their occupations, their character, or their intelligence, the fact that they have been transformed into a crowd puts them in possession of a sort of collective mind which makes them feel, think, and act in a manner quite different from that in which each individual of them would feel, think, and act were he in a state of isolation."

Le Bon further observes, as does Schiller (though Le Bon stated it more delicately), that we are likely to function at a lower level—intellectually, morally, and emotionally as a result of submission to the will of the crowd. "Men the most unlike in the matter of their intelligence possess instincts, passions, and feelings that are very similar. From the intellectual point of view an abyss may exist between a great mathematician and his bootmaker, but from the point of view of character the difference is most often slight or nonexistent."

Membership in the crowd brings an egalitarian leveling to the ignorant and educated alike, largely because of the substitution of the unconscious behavior of crowds for the conscious activity of individuals in isolation. Le Bon also describes crowds as emotional and says that, when in them, the individual begins to feel and express the emotions of a "primitive being." [Think lynch mobs at various points in this country's history, and you realize that Le Bon's insights are not confined to any particular time or place.]

The Monster with the Pea Brain

Individuals often become "lost" in crowds and perform acts they wouldn't perform were they alone. In addition to having a collective mind, a crowd is irrational. Moreover, it is worth repeating that the process of capitulation downgrades an individual's capability for intellectual processing to the diminished level of the crowd, effectively the lowest common denominator. The crowd is a mighty monster—usually with a pea brain!

According to Le Bon, three mechanisms are responsible for creating this monster. First, because the individual is anonymous, he or she loses the sense of individual responsibility and thus participates in acts in which he or she would not normally engage. Second, the process known as contagion leads to the reduction of an individual's inhibitions, making it acceptable to behave as a role model behaves. And third, people become more susceptible to suggestion in crowds; the crowd effectively hypnotizes the individual, who then follows the suggestions of other members or the crowd's leader. Behaviors become impulsive, emotional, and difficult to terminate. Simplicity of suggestion is mandatory and paves the way for exaggeration of the sentiments; the throngs are burdened neither by doubt nor uncertainty (at least till later, at which point some members of the crowd begin to wonder "what happened").

Deindividualization

The process known by contemporary social scientists as "deindividualization" takes place, partly because of the aforementioned group anonymity and a heightened state of arousal. (Remember China's Tiananmen Square in 1989?) These conditions lead individuals to become submerged in the group, losing their own sense of identity. When this loss occurs, people no longer feel responsible for their behavior; their attention is drawn to the group and behavior becomes regulated by fleeting cues in the immediate situation.

The Mind of Crowds

A crowd thinks in images. It accepts as real the images evoked in its collective mind, though these images generally have only a very distant connection to the observed fact. Bob Prechter unintentionally encouraged the easily grasped and seemingly boundless image of vast riches with his prognostication of 3,600 for the Dow during the summer of 1987. The collective observations of the crowd frequently are erroneous and most often merely represent the illusions of an individual who, by the process of contagion, has influenced his fellows.

Another example of the difference between image and reality can be found in the proposed acquisition of United Airlines Inc. Do we for a minute think the United Airlines pilots see anything beyond images of great wealth as they assume the awesome responsibility of repaying $7 billion in debt? Marvin Davis, Carl Icahn, and others have created the appearance of a fantasy from a very serious business. The pilots show every sign of being caught up in the crowd. They have risked much—their pension assets, salary cuts, and no-strike clauses. The risks that these people have assumed, we fear, are more foolish than calculated. The pilots have no doubt allowed themselves to believe that the transaction has been legitimized by the presence of Citibank and Chase, who have committed to lend $3 billion and have promised to raise another $4.2 million from others. But some of us remain skeptical. For the pilots' sake, we hope the bankers know more about the airline business than they did about oil, real estate, and Latin America. Some of us can still recall when the airline business was considered cyclical.

As a postscript, after three failed efforts (beginning in 1987), the employee unions of United Airlines finally gained ownership control on July 12, 1994. Despite smatterings of dissenters among sectors of each of the unions, the employee stock-ownership plan was pushed through and approved by shareholders. Employees received 55% of United Airlines' stock in exchange for $4.9 billion in wage and benefit concessions. The buyout was aimed at enabling United, which lost $50 million in 1993, to better compete with lower-cost airlines.

After two and a half years, the transaction seemed to be a success. Adjusting for stock splits, shares had risen from $22 to nearly $60, but it appeared as though the honeymoon was over. In early 1997 pilots voted down a contract offer and demanded a 10% wage increase over four years. Similar deals also were rejected by other United Airlines unions. As is the case with most deals made under financial duress, all parties seemed to regret concessions they made under pressure. It seems as though the pay cuts employees agreed to while they were deindividualized in the group became quite personalized when the new compensation program came home to roost, so to speak.

United Airlines stock began to steadily fall in the fourth quarter of 1997. While the stock has languished around $10 following the tragic events of September 11, 2001, terrorist activity is not the only factor that has contributed to United Airlines' downfall. The U.S. Department of Transportation ranked United last in service in 1999 and second to last in 2000. Due to ongoing labor disputes with its pilots, mechanics, and flight attendants, United had the worst on-time arrival percentage in 2000: a dismal 61%. United Airlines' three biggest rivals—American Airlines, Delta, and Northwest—all ranged from 73% to 77%. United was next to worst in mishandled baggage and in customer complaints filed with the DOT. Perhaps the shared imagery of impending riches that spurred on the union members in the early going grudgingly caved in under the weight of reality: Collective dreams turned to individual despair, and group enthusiasm fizzled into apathy.[55]

Might May Not Be Right

If we subscribe to Le Bon's findings and conclusions, we can see the crowd for what it is, rather than for what it appears to be. Despite the persuasiveness inherent in numbers and the implied power of size, the crowd may be a toothless tiger when it comes to certain tasks that require something other than brute force. Le Bon leads us to believe that as individuals we may in fact be functionally superior in many important respects to the collective mind of the crowd. We are apt to think on a higher plane (no pun intended in light of the previous section)—and to do so more logically. We are likely to weigh with greater care the consequences of our actions. Our problem-solving capabilities will no doubt be at their best, leading to decisions that reflect our optimal level of reasoning. We will operate more on the conscious level, being better able to control our emotions. Facts, not images, will tend to take precedence as we problem-solve.

To be sure, we're quick to acknowledge that separation from the crowd does not protect us from thinking and acting quite stupidly. However, as part of a crowd, we have little or no opportunity to be the best we can be. We need not be intimidated by crowds if we only understand the transformation that takes place in the functioning of the individuals that compose them. Indeed, crowds have their rightful place in history—and they are capable of incredibly heroic deeds, as the young Chinese students at Tiananmen Square demonstrated. However, investing is a cerebral endeavor, dependent on intellect and not force, reason and not impulse, self-control and not high emotion.

Sometimes when we observe uncharacteristic behavior from someone with whom we're acquainted, we say, "He's just not himself." When we see people we respect taking on the telltale behavior patterns of a crowd, we are probably justified in reaching a similar conclusion. They may be particularly competent when functioning as individuals, but as members of the crowd, they may become … well, blockheads, a state of mind to be avoided, not admired.

---

55 United Airlines, another victim of the "stadium-naming jinx," filed for Chapter 11 bankruptcy protection in December 2002. Almost three years later (after successfully *jet*tisoning its pension obligations, ultimately dumping them into the collective lap of U.S. taxpayers, who will see their obligation deferred when, in all probability, the U.S. Treasury will sell more bonds to foreign entities to fund the shortfall …!), United is hoping to emerge from Chapter 11 in the autumn of 2005. The loss for all shareholders will be total.

During the second half of the 1980s, the junk-bond scam reached a fever pitch. The takeover crowd was populated with grand and powerful names, busily, if not blindly, leveraging everything in sight. The end to that unfortunate debacle was as predictable as rain in April. Because of the crudeness and undisguised greed for which it will be remembered—from big cigars to puffed-up egos—and because the episode is relatively fresh in our memory, as are its trademark characters Michael Milken, Ivan Boesky, and a host of other "*Barbarians at the Gate*" [see Chapter Six], we won't rehash that disgraceful moment in economic history here. Those who would not have done it were it not "the thing to do" were likely its hapless victims. We may be no smarter than they—except that we possess a little knowledge about "The Power of Popular Delusions"!

No Chain Is Stronger Than Its Weakest Link

Turning now from the abstract to the concrete, we see how crowd theory applies to everyday activities.

Not beholden to anyone but our clients, we can utter heretical declarations with equanimity and without fear of reprisal. One of the great myths born of the long bull market is that middlemen—in their many iterations, from financial planners to the institutional consultancies—actually add value in the aggregate. What they add, without a scintilla of equivocation, is another layer of costs. Even investment managers, among whom we must be counted, in total are more of a cost than a benefit. Referring once again to the section on investment strategy, if Warren Buffett's prognosis of 7% returns from equities over the next decade or two proves correct the overhead burden of 2–3% in frictional costs will soon gleam brightly on investors' radar screens. During the '90s, that cost, while still considerable in an absolute sense, was more easily buried in the aberrant and therefore unsustainable performance results of that decade.

There are, of course, exceptions to the rule that costs exceed benefits up and down the entire food chain; otherwise, the mean, median, and mode would be one and the same. For our sake, I hope you conclude that a bell curve exists and that we are an "outlier"! If we expect to continue to hold our position, we must be vigilant in avoiding mechanistic imitation of others. We must always think counterintuitively, as we again do in the paragraph immediately following.

The middlemen helped create another myth that "more is better." The proliferation of mutual funds of every imaginable stripe and the bewildering boardroom rationale to "downstream" decision making regarding retirement-plan investments to those least qualified is part of the grand masquerade. Again, you will find our challenge to the popular custom of diversification among asset classes, styles, and stocks of so many varieties that they defy description in an essay of this length. We have never understood the truism that most first-generation wealth is created on the strength of one idea or company, and then concludes with the dubious (in our judgment) assumption that in order to preserve it, it must be spread among a thousand other companies. There's more money than truth in that widespread practice. Compelling financial motives for free(fee?)-loaders up and down the food chain, coupled with often gullible investors, make for a most profitable exchange, at least for one of the parties. If you've been in the game for more than five minutes and haven't yet identified the patsy . . . guess what? You're it.

Perhaps most grating to us is the issue of accountability. Because we're investment managers, that subset of our services falling under the quantitative descriptor, investment performance, is incontrovertible in its factuality. It is what it is, and that's that. Not so with the fuzzy notion of value added by the middlemen. Playing adroitly to the well-cultivated illusion that safety is found in the sampling of a smorgasbord of choices, the middlemen cleverly avoid being accountable for anything beyond taking the naïve and hungry client to the table spread with enough variety to choke a horse. To be sure, justice may not be swift, but it is sure. If the tide continues to ebb, they will in due course be exposed as an unnecessary cost for which the value is *de minimus*.

Surprisingly, those who appear to be most astute are equally eager to embrace this negative-value-added proposition. Almost every endowment fund for a college, university, or community foundation within range of our offices (to say nothing of other pools of organizational money, big and small) uses the consultancy model. The common denominator is the committee structure. As indicated above in the section titled "The Power of Popular Delusions," a committee is an odd potpourri of people whose collaborative idiosyncratic behavior is often in no way reflective of the brilliance or sagacity of any of the individuals of which it is made. A person's capacity changes, and usually not for the better, when he or she submits to the will of a group. Thus what is said below applies only to committees and not to those of whom it is composed. The problem is structural, not personal.

Continuing in this vein, after years of firsthand observation, I am convinced beyond a shadow of doubt of the counterintuitive notion that one astute individual has five times the investment decision-making capacity of a committee of five persons who, individually, are equally endowed intellectually. This metamorphosis—from incisive, decisive individual to mealy-mouthed group member—is not without explanation. No single member shoulders the ultimate responsibility, so a CYP (cover your posterior!) decision-making cloud hovers over the group and often disrupts collective clear-headed thinking.

The lowest-common-denominator syndrome, given enough time, will assert itself. The meeting rarely begins before the last and most harried member arrives, and the tenor of the deliberations is usually established by the member who is both least knowledgeable and most vocal! The group, rarely self-selected and ever-changing, is often so diverse as to talent, level of interest, and amount of experience that effective decision making is rendered nearly impossible. The idea of laying off responsibility to a third party as an antidote to the inherent structural ineptitude of a group of individuals (attempting to carry on business as a unit) often gains respectability by default. Add to that the obligatory consultant's flippant use of the vernacular of modern portfolio theory, dropping such terms as negative covariance, the efficient frontier, *beta,* and the esoteric math that ties it all together (none of which most consultants could explain with much lucidity), and you have the perfect prescription for a group that looks and functions more like the Three Stooges than what the grand theoretical design would have you believe. What more susceptible prey could a consultant hope for!

Pay close attention to the next consultant's presentation. The charts and occasional histrionics aside, consultants are in the business of collating and cataloguing massive quantities of historical data and trying hard, sometimes almost desperately, to impart some sort of unique spin to other consultants' warmed-over and rehashed verbiage. The sheer amount of material is intended to convey an image of the consultant's facility for thought and reason—and the committee frequently finds the comfort it needs buried in those numbers. Conspicuous by its absence, though, is any subjective reference to the future. Most consultants have a propensity for looking backward, citing the performance of yesterday's darlings who, by the very nature of the ebb and flow of investment fashion, are likely to be tomorrow's dogs. In so doing, they do little more than perpetuate the herd mentality.

While some of the above may seem unkind, you need only hear Charlie Munger rant on the subject to realize that we are in fact falling all over ourselves trying not to offend!

CHAPTER FIVE—2002

Introduction

This year's truncated offering is respectful of Einstein's admonition: "Make everything as simple as possible, but no simpler." Accordingly, you will find this report a little light on numbers and a little long on opinion. Reasoned judgment has been in short supply in recent years, and this monograph may be a (subconscious?) attempt to help fill the void. All of us are inundated with information about recent events or happenings, especially as reported by newspapers, periodicals, radio, or television. Regurgitating the facts of yesterday may bring a form of catharsis, but it adds little value. On the other hand, reactions to essays that challenge conformist thought might well run the gamut from raising the reader's ire to piquing his or her curiosity.

Investment Performance

Period Ending December 31, 2002	MCM Equities *	S&P 500 *
Since Inception **	13.7%	9.3%
Five Years	8.6%	-0.6%
Three Years	11.1%	-14.5%
One Year	-13.6%	-22.1%

* Compounded annually, MCM data net of fees

** December 31, 1993

Year	MCM Equities (Net of Fees)	S&P 500
1994	-7.5%	1.3%
1995	19.1%	37.5%
1996	31.8%	22.9%
1997	45.1%	33.3%
1998	-7.4%	28.6%
1999	18.8%	21.0%
2000	29.2%	-9.1%
2001	22.7%	-11.9%
2002	-13.6%	-22.1%

The Roller Coaster Took Us for Quite a Ride

Relatively benign annual performance data provided in the tables above often betray the sometimes brutal and other times benevolent roller-coaster-like movements of the markets and individual securities between the dates that mark the beginning and the end of any calendar year. While the speculative technology and Internet Bubble was being pricked in the spring of 2000, bargains galore were found among the unglamorous, if not mundane, businesses that were discarded willy-nilly as the gamblers drew for a hotter hand. The bifurcated market provided opportunity for some, imminent disaster for others—largely depending on whether they were going against the grain or with it. By contrast, the emotionally charged sell-off following the tragic events of September 11, 2001, visited its temporary carnage largely indiscriminately. It had the same effect as a mile-wide tornado approaching a small town.

While different in character from the market-rocking events of both 2000 and 2001, the year just completed dished out its own concoction of challenges and opportunities. The first quarter, a follow-through of the emotional whiplash that often accompanies events that are shocking in both magnitude and unpredictability, saw stock prices rise. Emotional equilibrium was restored during the second quarter, when the ground gained in the first three months of the year was given back. Come the third quarter, fear reigned supreme. The economy appeared to be in dire straits as a seemingly desperate Federal Reserve Board initiated the 11th consecutive cut in the Fed funds rate, driving it down to an unprecedented 1¾% level. Unilateral war against Iraq loomed on the horizon. Corporate governance scandals reached epidemic proportions.

The free fall in stock prices had a take-no-prisoners ferocity about it. From the close of the markets on June 30 until the quarter ended on September 30, the Dow Jones Industrials, the S&P 500, and the Nasdaq fell 17.9%, 17.6%, and 19.9%, respectively. Record or near-record quarterly percentage declines were established for several popular indices. The metamorphosis in the mood of the players in the market was palpable.

One week into the fourth quarter, investors' cyclical capacity to seemingly overnight swing like some mad primate from one emotional limb to another manifested itself once again for two months. By December, however, the ardor had cooled with the weather, and at the turn of the year, the three indices mentioned above had regained some of their losses, rising 14.5%, 13.3%, and 19.9% from their October lows. When comparing the percentages just cited with those in the paragraph above, don't forget that the mathematics of compounding require a 100% gain to offset a 50% loss.

All the above intra-year pyrotechnics notwithstanding, the three indices registered losses of 16.8%, 23.4%, and 31.5%, respectively, before dividends. As has been our practice in the past, we chose not to follow the lead of "Mr. Market," a notably unstable fellow afflicted with an apparently incurable form of bipolar disorder. During his manic phases, we either sit back passively or, if his hunger for equities borders on the insatiable and the prices he's willing to pay approach the absurd, we may attempt to satisfy his appetite. When his despair reaches the point of wild-eyed and irrational action—as it did during the third quarter—we feel obliged to ameliorate his suffering by taking off his hands some of the stock he is so insistent on dropping like a hot potato. Accordingly, during the third and fourth quarters in the aggregate, we committed another $25.5 million to a number of the companies that Mr. Market was only too willing to sell.

As absolute-return-oriented advisors, we are not at all pleased because our negative return for 2002 was less than that of the S&P 500. In that respect, we performed miserably. Short-term market price volatility is a consequence—deemed as favorable or unfavorable depending on the temperament of the person—of being an investor in marketable equity securities. Some investors attach great importance to the daily or even hourly ups and downs, while others, like the undersigned, pay them no heed except when they present us with a mouth-watering opportunity *to do something.* As we mentioned last year, we expect to have negative years on occasion (and our record makes that point clear!). Those who take a longer-term perspective—and the shorter-term fluctuations in stride—tend to be amply rewarded in the long run (our record makes that clear as well).

Time- vs. Dollar-Weighted Returns: Subtle but Significant

The fourth quarter's gain in the dollar amount of aggregate portfolio wealth was thus the combination of two contributing factors: First, the market price's appreciation in the companies we had owned for some time, and second, the surge in price of the companies just purchased during the third- and fourth-quarter slump. While no precise estimate is practical, we reckon that approximately 87% of the gain in aggregate equity portfolio wealth resulted from the first factor, with the remainder from the second. The time-weighted performance reporting convention that we're obliged to follow in the tables at the beginning of this section makes no allowance for the wealth-effect benefits of taking money off the table when the odds are against us or committing additional capital when they seem to be in our favor. In each of the last three years, your wealth has fared better than the time-weighted percentages would suggest. And if performance were measured on a dollar-weighted basis, the difference would disappear.

One more subtlety needs to be brought to your attention. As we have become more fully committed to equities—a rational response, we would argue, to a generally widening margin of safety—sharp slumps in stock prices do not provide the conspicuous opportunities that they once did when we were loaded with cash. To return to a favorite sailing metaphor, if you are flush with cash, you may remain safe in the shelter of the harbor until the storm passes. If, on the other hand, you have a significant commitment to equities, you must ride out the storm at sea and, if necessary, "heave to" in the teeth of a gale. If your vessel is sturdy and seaworthy, and you have your sea legs, you can face Mother Nature in all her fury with equanimity and not trepidation. Moreover, when the weather clears, and the fair winds return, you will find yourself miles ahead of the ever-cautious bloke who's still securely tethered to the pier. The spoils of victory rarely go to the fainthearted. To conclude the analogy, it seems more sensible for long-term investors (such as ourselves) to devote our energies to finding sturdy ships than attempting to predict the erratic weather.

Nearly repeating ourselves verbatim from last year: Little has been said—and little needs to be said—about the performance of our fixed-income assets. Since we never compromise on quality, and we keep our durations quite short, suffice it to say we generally expect our returns to match the note's or bond's yield to maturity at the time of purchase. We enjoyed a modest bump in total return in the last several years because of falling interest rates, but it was a "borrow from Peter to pay Paul" kind of give-and-take, and it's therefore nothing to crow about.

Investment Strategy

Although this report is annual, the formidable task of formulating a rational investment strategy in a chaotic world is like warily tiptoeing back and forth along a gymnast's five-meter balance beam. Forces from all sides persistently threaten to knock you off your perch. They include:

- The ongoing nightmare, aggravated by fear of the unknown, of another surprise attack by fanatical terrorists.
- Possible war with Iraq that could explode into a regional or global conflict of unknowable proportions.
- A schizophrenic economy that seems to defy diagnosis (and therefore effective treatment).
- A global economic malaise that threatens to spread like a pandemic disease.
- A destructive bear market, savaging stock market wealth and leaving policymakers without precedent to anticipate its effect on consumer behavior.
- A dollar that has rested on its laurels far too long.
- A political environment that, at least in terms of a coherent macroeconomic policy, has yet to define itself.

The ledger of "macro maladies" continues to grow. Moreover, the prices of businesses, on average, still seem rich relative to the plethora of ambiguities, real and imagined—and respected investors, not the least of whom is Warren Buffett, have made broad-brush prognostications about the relatively anemic performances to be expected from the popular averages for some years to come.

Every business day we face the daunting task of enhancing the value of your capital without putting it in harm's way. In so doing, however, we are fortified by the simple wisdom of John Maynard Keynes: "It is better to be generally right than precisely wrong."

Dow 36,000: New Strategy for Profiting from Coming Rise in Stock Market

By way of backdrop, a sea change in a deeply ingrained perception about what constitutes investment is upon us. The profound catharsis, deleteriously reversing the treacherous and insidious transition from investment to speculation (and all the accoutrements that distinguished the capital markets and its various links to the economy during the '90s) is firmly under way.

To begin, let me set the scene in 1998–99. Following are a few symptomatic indications of the pervasive susceptibility and concomitant euphoria that led to the emergence of "irrational exuberance" in many popular industries, stealthily and progressively biasing the reasoning of the horde of investors who, "at the margin" (those actually doing the buying and selling and therefore setting prices), pushed prices higher and higher as the bull market of the '90s reached full flower, surging relentlessly toward its own demise. A crowd, as we have often written in the past, is amenable to suggestion, the simpler (and often the more preposterous) the better. What stage-whispered prompting could be more explicit, understandable, and forceful to a layperson than the one made by James K. Glassman and Kevin A. Hassett, co-authors of *Dow 36,000: The New Strategy for Profiting from the Coming Rise in the Stock Market* that hit the bookstands in September 1999, just months before the wild-eyed ride ended in stunning collapse. *Dow 40,000: Strategies for Profiting from the Greatest Bull Market in History*, hurriedly penned by money manager David Elias, trumped the Glassman and Hassett effort, only to be overtrumped by Charles Kadlec, chief investment strategist for Seligman Advisors Inc., who wrote *Dow 100,000: Fact or Fiction.*

The latter two expect their Dow targets to be met in 2016 and 2020, respectively, implying historically palatable compounded annual returns of 9% and 11.1%. The latter authors' analytical methodology is fairly standard. On the other hand, Glassman, a *Washington Post* columnist, and Hassett, an economist and resident scholar at the American Enterprise Institute (AEI) where Glassman is also a fellow, must have roundly embarrassed AEI—and possibly herded gullible investors by the thousands to their financial slaughter—because of impossible forecasts supported by cockeyed reasoning. Straining investors' credulity to the limit, they foresaw the Dow reaching 36,000 in three to five years, implying ludicrous annual rates of return of 52% and 28%, respectively. Among other transgressions, they coined a new acronym (that perfectly symbolized the absurdity of the times): "PRP"—a "perfectly reasonable price."

As for the investment eggheads, a conference was conducted in Palm Beach, Florida, in December 2000 for the senior executives of investment advisory firms (where, because of some breakdown in the screening process, I found myself in attendance). One would be quite right in concluding that such an august gathering would insist on more substance than the so-called investor who gets his tips from CNBC's boundlessly blathering broadcasters. Among the featured presenters at the conference was the obligatorily upbeat Jeremy Siegel, professor of finance at the Wharton School of the University of Pennsylvania and author of the much ballyhooed book *Stocks for the Long Term.* As you may recall, we took Siegel to task in the 1998 annual report

[Chapter One] for repackaging the generally sound concept that Edgar Lawrence Smith introduced in 1924, under the nearly identical title, *Common Stocks as Long-term Investments*, and (disregarding Keynes' admonition) for trumpeting the virtues of common stock investing *at precisely the wrong time.* This atrocity of timing was not unlike the Ford Foundation-funded, well-reasoned, and scholarly study persuasively endorsing the concept of "total return" investing, maladroitly rolled out on the eve of the 1973–74 bear market. While Siegel's demeanor was a little less ebullient because of the Nasdaq's eight-month plunge leading up to the conference, he remained the prancing Pollyanna that December in Florida.

As a postscript and with the benefit of hindsight, Siegel just didn't get it, as the table below reveals. Ironically, though, in the long run Siegel will be right, just as Edgar Lawrence Smith was. For many of his fans, however, the reality of greatly diminished wealth in the meantime is proving nettlesome if not downright troublesome.

	12/29/00	**10/9/02**
S&P 500	1,320.28	776.76
Dow Jones Industrials	10,786.85	7,286.27
Nasdaq Composite Index	2,470.52	1114.11

Such was the mindset of both the small and the mighty as we approached the precipice in the late winter of 2000. The signature mental attitude or disposition that predetermines a person's responses to and interpretations of any monumental speculative bubble is a compulsive preoccupation with a fixed idea. For the soon-to-be-humbled investment professional, the polite word was *return*, whereas for the untutored, the bourgeois word *greed* was operative. Both manifested symptoms of restlessness and irritability. Conspicuous by its absence was any awareness of the storm cloud of mushrooming risk looming ever larger on the horizon. In reality, a form of unabashed envy, the thought of being left behind as the freight train of unimaginable riches pulled out of the station, was more than many investors could stomach. Where it was going, or how it might get there, was of little importance. The fact that it was leaving the station was all that mattered.

Remember how CNBC, the continually televised "tout sheet," whose commercial commission (ethical standards were generally suspended wherever a buck could be made) was to opine on whatever investors were craving to hear, came out of nowhere to remorselessly cater to such copycat speculating? Nature abhors a vacuum. The CNBC of today, its programming milieu exuding a reactive case of economic self-righteousness—always solicitous of the viewers' mood—seems more contrite than it did two years ago and will likely, in this writer's opinion, be a shadow of its former self five years hence. That said, CNBC, like a chainsaw, can be a useful tool in the right hands.

The Reckoning

As night follows day, a speculative binge, like a drunken spree, must come to an end—and for many of the same reasons. Overnight exhilaration gives way to disillusionment and despair. The investor who had asked, "How much *will* I make" now, with an anxious look in his eyes, nervously poses the question, "How much *can* I lose?" *Risk* replaces *return* as the operative word. Preservation of capital displaces enhancement of wealth as the prevailing objective. Focusing on our ever-aging population, according to surveys by the American Association of Retired Persons, a Washington advocacy group for people age 50 and older, the universe of affected investors is surprisingly large. The portion of people 55–64 who invest in stocks climbed to 58% in 1998 from 28% in 1989. "Where you once had home value as the largest asset for many people, now it's often stock value." Among investors surveyed between the ages of 50 and 70, fully 77% said their holdings have dropped in the last two years, with 37% losing between 10% and 25%, and 25% losing between one-quarter and one-half. About one in five older Americans who lost money in the stock market during the past two years has postponed his or her retirement date, and 10% of those already retired are at work again because of stock market losses. Overall, two-thirds of older investors with losses, including those who haven't retired at all, say they are making lifestyle adjustments—from budgeting more carefully (59%) to taking fewer vacations (34%) to postponing a major purchase (30%). And 43% worry that, in the future, they will be less comfortable in retirement than they previously had expected. One in five fears that he or she may have trouble paying for healthcare and prescription drugs. Whether it's the AARP—or, perhaps more fittingly, the urp—generation or the Internet day trader, the relentless erosion in wealth is not a trifling matter, and, as noted below, the full extent of its economic repercussions is yet to be known. Will Rogers' famous dictum will once again be resurrected: "I'm more concerned about the return *of* my principal than the return *on* my principal." This change in general psychology will occur, as always, long after its relevance has peaked.

Sober in the Morning

That last sentence, a natural segue, lays the groundwork for our strategy. Among Warren Buffett's pithy sayings, the following is particularly apropos:

"We are fearful when others are greedy, and greedy when others are fearful." Having generally avoided the epidemic of excessive or uncontrolled speculative indulgence, we, unlike the hung-over party animal who is likely to upchuck at the mere offer of another drink, have a relatively clearheaded thirst for opportunity. Moreover, and equally important, in contrast to party surroundings where liquor flows freely, no one is shoving a drink into our hand every time we turn around. We are liberated not only from libations but from the crowd's bothersome banter, freed from the urge to mindlessly imitate others, as we go about our business. If one is to have any hope of making headway in the emotional-roller-coaster world of investment, one must avoid distractions that will get in the way of keeping an even temperament, thereby truncating both the highs and the lows. Investment teetotalers that we are, there will be no "bellying up to the bar" on our watch.

Bottoms Up

The title of this section refers to our preoccupation with microeconomics (a focus on the firm) rather than macroeconomics (concentration on the system) as we attempt to rationally find our way through the maze that will lead us to durable investment success. Our first turn in the labyrinth—and one that separates us from much of the crowd—is that we spend the great portion of our time and energy studying businesses as opposed to the myriad forces that constitute the external environment in which those businesses operate. Admittedly, businesses do not function in a vacuum. It's just that we're inclined to stick with the knowable and avoid spending too much of our time speculating about what is unknowable. For example, we have absolutely no idea whether, when, where, or how another terrorist attack might be launched in America. No amount of rumination will add one percentage point to the probability that we can pinpoint such an event. Not to downplay the tragedy of 9/11, which affected us as it surely affected you ... but (for the most part) it was "business as usual" within days of the attack.

Every single business we own kept running as usual, right through the maelstrom. None, to our knowledge, ever considered closing up shop. Berkshire Hathaway, the only one affected in a meaningful way, took a $2.5 billion hit (against a start-of-year equity capital base of $61.7 billion) as the insurer of several of the assets that were destroyed and due to the workers' compensation claims that arose. The record shows that well-managed and well-capitalized businesses with durable competitive advantages, like the seaworthy ship mentioned earlier, survive—and often thrive vis-à-vis their weaker competition—in environments of manifold uncertainty. This kind of information is most valuable because it is in the realm of the knowable.

The "macro trap," because it is so generalized and nonspecific, helps to agitate our anxieties, which is precisely why we don't let it dominate our thinking. Various sectors of the economy were directly affected by 9/11, of course. Commercial airline travel was sharply curtailed in a knee-jerk reaction. Again, truly hoping not to appear callous in my attempt to be coolly analytical, the "rearview mirror" mentality helped fly United Airlines right into bankruptcy court. Fears notwithstanding, in all likelihood the safest time in years to fly commercially was immediately after the attacks when vigilance at all levels was at its peak—and yet the airports were empty. More importantly, having expended the critical element of surprise in one venue, the terrorists would surely have chosen another if subsequent attacks were in the offing. But the public reaction was indicative of human nature in times of crisis. We "fight the last war" because our vision of the past is always clearer than our foggy notions of the future. That propensity is, as discussed above, at work in the capital markets today.

The Margin-of-Safety Paradox

Not wanting to appear nonchalant, we must face up to some hard decisions in this possibly atypical but not unprecedented economic environment. Remaining rational and circumspect in the months if not years ahead will largely determine how well we fulfill our mission to our clients. Are we in a cyclical economic contraction from which we will soon emerge or something more insidious and protracted? A quote from Benjamin Graham is indelibly imprinted on my mind:

> But the "new era" commencing in 1927 involved at bottom the abandonment of the analytical approach; and while emphasis was still seemingly placed on facts and figures, these were manipulated by a sort of pseudoanalysis to support the delusions of the period. The market collapse in October 1929 was no surprise to such analysts as had kept their heads, but the extent of the business collapse which later developed, with its devastating effects on established earning power, again threw their calculations out of gear. Hence the ultimate result was that serious analysis suffered a double discrediting: the first—prior to the crash—due to the persistence of imaginary values, and the second—after the crash—due to the disappearance of real values. (Graham, *Security Analysis*, 31–32)

Parallels with the malaise that has garroted Japan since 1989, not so much the means but the end, cannot be dismissed out of hand, even though we realize that the "availability bias" (the tendency to give disproportionate weight to more recent or readily available experiences or events) is at work here. Listening to Alan Greenspan's words, as well as being very attentive to his inflections, we find it clear that he wonders and worries about whether he has inadvertently taken us to the economic precipice.

If "real values" disappear, how does an analyst get a handle on the intrinsic worth of a business if his "confidence interval" for that swing variable is a mile wide after allowing for the possibility, however unlikely, that "the extent of the business collapse which later developed, with its devastating effects on established earning power, again threw their calculations out of gear"? If the estimation of intrinsic value is deemed substantially unreliable, there is simply no way to determine the extent to which the current market price affords a margin of safety.

Countless technology and dot-com companies serve as vivid contemporary examples of the valuation conundrum that Ben Graham described 70 years ago. Even today, after stocks of many companies of that ilk have withered to less than 10% of their highs, we still cannot determine whether they are cheap or dear. But do not despair, for that example is of limited utility. Companies in those industries were just as difficult to value in the best of times. The dilemma was captured in a Christmas cartoon picturing a frustrated reindeer complaining to one of the elves: "We give away all our products. We don't make a dime. I'm telling you, Santa runs this place like a dot-com."

Waiting Patiently for Those Hanging Curves

We at MCM are ever mindful that the size of our paycheck is in direct proportion to the amount of increase in your wealth above and beyond that pesky but ethically critical high-water-mark hurdle, which is also a convenient daily reminder that "in order to win, the first thing you must do is not lose."

Returning to our well-worn (think of your favorite glove) baseball metaphor, there is little to be gained—if the economic contraction proves to be persistent—by going after every pitch. It's in your best interest, as well as ours, to wait patiently for the sweet pitch, refusing to swing at anything else. Thanks to the forbearance of our clients, in this game we'll never lose our place at the plate by being forced to take a base on balls. How simple, you say. But we would beg to differ. Even if the game of baseball were scored this way, batters' egos would soon take over, and they'd flail away. After all, the athlete who is paid to swing, "wood." Steely self-control is the operative phrase in times like these. Patience is the order of the day. To be sure, if this contraction transcends the cyclical, it will be much more difficult to tell the slider from a fastball headed for our sweet spot. And yet it isn't impossible. There are many hard-to-read pitches—and a few juicy ones, the hanging curves, that leave the pitcher's hand destined for solid contact with the bat. Those are the ones we wait for. The many pitches we can't clearly decipher we let pass without regret.

Returning to the task at hand, the economic environment forces us to narrow our focus to those companies that are easy to understand and *relatively* simple to value and whose competitive advantages, including a rock-solid capital structure and level-headed yet opportunistic corporate leadership, enhance their chances of coming out on top whenever the contraction ends and the next expansion begins, even if it's some years away.

Let's Get Mathematical

"The value of any stock, bond, or business today is determined by the cash inflows and outflows—discounted at an appropriate interest rate—that can be expected to occur *during the remaining life of the asset*" [emphasis added]. That foundational one-size-fits-all investment maxim is older than Methuselah. Please note that this valuation model applies to all investments. The pricing of common stocks, of course, is less exact than bonds: Their "coupons" are variable, and there is no predetermined maturity date or price. Let's frame the challenge investors face in terms of the mathematics of finance, using the above present-value model. Several assumptions, however, must be made (prior to concluding with an obvious question). The assumptions are:

- An investment is made in a first-class company that has earned 15% on its unleveraged equity capital, approximating the long-term American industry average.
- Economic hard times exacted their toll, resulting in the company losing money for three years and causing its net worth to shrink by a third.
- The stock was purchased at 15 times earnings and subsequently falls by 50%.
- After the storm has passed, the company returns to its historical profitability ratios, and 10 years later the stock sells for 15 times earnings.

Now, the question: "What was the holding-period return during those turbulent times?" The answer, for which we will happily provide details for those who are interested: 7.9%. For the mathematically challenged, a simpler example would be if we assume that the economic hard times were such that the company earned a lower-than-historical average return on its unleveraged equity capital of 12% over the 13 years. If we argue that, at the end of the period, the stock again sells for 15 times earnings, the annual return rises to 12% (the same return as the underlying business earned on its equity capital). Regardless of the example, the investment return hinges on the earnings power of the business and the price the market is willing to pay for those earnings at the beginning and the end. If our ship is seaworthy, we can take each storm as it comes with equanimity, never losing sight of our destination.

Warren Buffett, after a long hiatus following the liquidation of his partnerships in 1969–70, came back in 1973–74 with a vengeance. He summarized his enthusiasm, rather impolitely we must admit, for the bargain-priced equities he was gobbling up. Said he: "I feel like a sex-starved man in a harem." What few people know is that at the time the market reached its low point, Buffett's holdings were a full 50% underwater.

Sometimes percentages can distort an investor's perception of reality. The following is a theoretical example: Let's say a stock falls 50% in year one, from $10 to $5. (Let's assume intrinsic worth was able to be approximated and was constant over the three years at $5.) The next year it declines another 50% to $2.50. Finally, after another 50% decline in the third year, it reaches $1.25, a decline of 87.5% from its first-year high, similar (though not so orderly) to the Dow Jones industrial average during the crash and subsequent bear market of 1929–32 or the Nasdaq's total reversal of fortunes from 5,050 in March 2000 to just over 1,100 this past October as indicated in the table several pages ago. Using the example to hypothetically and approximately index Buffett's experience, after avoiding the lion's share of the 1973–74 bloodbath, he missed what turned out to be the bottom by a mere $1.25, and, undaunted by his paper losses, he kept making purchases.

How would you judge Buffett's overall perspicacity? First, and most important in this writer's judgment, his initial stroke of genius was in doing nothing when there was nothing to do—i.e., committing capital to the folly at $10 … *or $12 or $15 or whatever price at which the stock eventually peaked.* He just stood there flat-footed, with the bat on his shoulder, watching pitches whiz by. Admittedly, those times are rare when the pitcher is throwing you nothing but junk. Mind you, Mr. Buffett wasn't asleep; he was simply thinking instead of swinging. As important as that decision was, because no transaction took place, *it was never even recorded.* And yet it counted—avoiding impossible pitches or knucklehead pitchers plays a huge role in the pursuit of investment success. Likewise, his brilliance was not diminished whatsoever because he didn't pick the exact bottom. Those who unrealistically aspire to the impossible, a la Don Quixote, inevitably go away empty-handed, as we noted previously. In fact, Buffett's genius was confirmed again when he persistently took advantage of the ever-widening gap between the market price and intrinsic value.

There is little doubt in my mind that, had the market continued to fall beyond its eventual 1974 lows of 62.28, for the S&P 500, Buffett would have stayed at the plate, the same gleeful look on his face as a kid in a candy store. Each new low would undoubtedly represent opportunities to add some of his existing holdings at even more attractive prices, as well as to make initial purchases of new ones that appeared on his radar screen for the first time as their prices fell. *Although the percentage decline was identical three years running, its investment consequences in absolute dollar terms diminished with each successive year.* If the preceding statement troubles you, test it with your trusty calculator. While we hope not to find ourselves in this position, if we do, count on us not to forget what we are here to do: namely, to honor our responsibility to you.

The Bottom Line for Equities

There are purposes served by these two examples. First, remember the Keynesian quote in the third paragraph of this section. Like Buffett from 1965 to 1972 (and later in 1973–74), we believe we have been "generally right" about what brought us to this time and place, and we will conscientiously apply our best efforts to stay ahead of the curve as we look through the windshield and not at the rearview mirror. In the abstract sense, if we are any more precise than Buffett in our timing, it will be more coincidental than intentional. The cost of obsessing on precision is to often miss the forest for the trees. Second, we will always try to look across the valley to the foothills beyond, to visualize our destination. At last we can say to long-chastised Jeremy Siegel, this may be your moment, the time to "stock" the bookshelves at Barnes & Noble with *Stocks for the Long Term.* Predictably, if none is to be found, it wouldn't be audacious to surmise that one would be "generally right" buying "stocks for the long term"! Sometimes one's trust in the basic precepts of investing seems foolhardy, only to be proved prudent some years hence. As Blaise Pascal said in another context about the ever-present dilemma with which the opportunistic investor must live: "Too much to deny and too little to be sure." Nobody shoots a gun to start this race.[56]

---

56 This statement was written at the lowest point in the market over the last seven or eight years. As for Jeremy Siegel, we searched for words of encouragement from him, but none were found. In a November 30, 2004, interview with *Money* magazine he remained the unrepentant optimist. Siegel has always navigated the investment highways and byways while looking backward—to wit, his latest revelation: "My research finds that investors consistently overpay for growth. I want people to think about investing this way: The great growing companies are not often the ones that give you the best returns. The tried and true triumph over the bold and new."

As for the tangible, the mathematics of finance bridges the gap between conjecture and reality, putting meat on the bones of the theoretical skeletal framework. We know there is much uncertainty we must accept with a wary eye—and yet also with educated equanimity if we expect to earn acceptable returns from the asset class with the most productive history and, in all likelihood, the most productive "long term" future. Ultimately, the "bottom line" for equities must be the "bottoms up" orientation.

Last But Not Least: Fixed-Income Securities

As for fixed-income securities, we will continue to treat them as the default class for the investor who authorizes us to commit as much of his or her capital to equities as are available at prices that imply tantalizing expected returns. For the investor who is less tolerant of price volatility, there will likely be a cap on the percentage of the portfolio that can be invested in equities. In the second instance (as in the first), we would be fully invested, within the defined limits, only if such action is justified on the grounds of prudence. For the investor who might specify that no more than 50% of his or her portfolio be committed to equities, under certain circumstances as much as 100% could be invested in fixed-income securities. Under the most unusual of circumstances—not encountered since this firm's inception—the same could be said for an account that is authorized to be fully invested in equities. Accordingly, we take our investments in fixed-income securities very seriously. We always have been sticklers for the highest-quality fixed-income securities. In that regard, we're confident that no other investment manager in our market could measure up to our standards. While compromising on quality will almost certainly produce an incrementally higher current yield, bonds offer no growth in intrinsic-worth opportunities comparable to equity securities. A bond indenture makes two primary promises: to make generally fixed semiannual interest payments and to redeem the bond at par value on the maturity date. If there is no upside, it makes no sense to us whatsoever to expose our clients to risk on the downside.

Within our high-grade fixed-income portfolios we attempt to add value through "duration" management—i.e., we will own shorter-duration (industry jargon that quantifies the sensitivity of the bond's price to changes in interest rates) notes or bonds if we think Treasury note and bond interest rates are more likely to be heading up than down, which is what our admittedly cloudy crystal ball is telling us now. We also manage fixed-income securities in an effort to maximize tax efficiency. We constantly monitor taxable and tax-free yield differentials in order to steer our high-tax-bracket clients' portfolios toward maximum tax efficiency. In short, the choice between municipal bonds and U.S. Treasury bills, notes, or bonds is not as cut and dried as it appears.

CHAPTER SIX—2003

Introduction

The Rogues' Gallery, 2003 Vintage

Early 2003 provided a somewhat unexpected respite from the plethora of deplorable corporate disclosures in 2002, which included the WorldCom debacle, where megalomaniac Bernie Ebbers and his apparently dumbstruck board recklessly leveraged WorldCom into the largest bankruptcy in American history. In the professional service sector, the once proud but ultimately disgraceful bust of Arthur Andersen was beheaded by its own sword. These are but two of the more conspicuously reprehensible examples. Momentarily taking center stage, the public relations and military buildup preceding the blitzkrieg in Iraq on March 19, 2003, commandeered the headlines during the first quarter.

Wall Street was back in the limelight on April 28, when a historic $1.4 billion settlement was reached between the Securities & Exchange Commission and 10 Wall Street firms for their fiduciary misconduct during the Bubble days when business ethics were conveniently suspended and the lust for fool's gold made a mockery of morals. Of course, no firm or individual has admitted guilt, continuing a ritualistic dance of "repentance" that takes place between the SEC and the accused, wherein the "not guilty" parties are more than willing to cough up the cash to burnish their tarnished reputations—or at least sweep their misdeeds under the carpet in exchange for the judge turning a deaf ear. For aspiring felons, we note offhandedly, "white collar" crimes stand head and shoulders above most others, without much bothersome dandruff. On June 4 aspiring near-billionaire Martha Stewart, the "diva of domesticity," was caught with her hand in the cookie jar reaching for a chump-change "chocolate *tip*." Reports have estimated she saved between $40,000 and $57,000 by selling prior to the Food & Drug Administration announcement. Five days later Freddie Mac reported that it had underreported earnings and would thus have to restate the previous three years' earnings. While underreporting clearly is better than the alternative, earnings squirreled away today will propitiously reappear when Freddie "Kruger-rand" Mac is money-hungry to shore up results in the future. The rub: The slippery slope of earnings management can easily morph into flat-out misrepresentation where the numbers and reality take divergent paths.

On September 3 New York Attorney General Eliot Spitzer announced evidence of widespread illegal trading in the hedge-fund and mutual-fund industry that proved to be the first volley in a legal/political battle that continued to rage at year-end. On September 10 former Enron treasurer Ben Glisan pleaded guilty to a single count of criminal conspiracy and was sentenced to five years in a federal minimum security prison. Oh, how slowly turn the wheels of justice. Former Enron chairman and CEO Ken is still *Lay*ing low more than two years after the news broke, thus far untouched by the rubble that continues to cascade down around him.[57]

Only weeks later, on September 17, Dick Grasso, chairman of that bastion of free enterprise, the New York Stock Exchange (the roots of which date back to a first meeting beneath a Wall Street buttonwood tree), resigned amid protests that his $140 million pay package was generous to a fault. Not coincidentally, on September 16 the not-for-profit NYSE had reported "earnings" for the first half of 2003 of $27 million on revenues of $540 million. Graciously, Grasso abstained from pressing for the $48 million still owed him. Truth be known, Grasso was merely the fall guy, though with his golden parachute the landing will be pillow soft. What, we might legitimately ask, was the NYSE's 27-member board—which includes executives from listed companies, Wall Street brokerages, and specialist firms—thinking when the proposed looting came to a vote? If this doesn't reek of all manner of conflicts of interest, your olfactory sensors may have become desensitized by the repugnant, pungent odor endlessly emanating from bored (yes, the spelling is correct!) rooms across the country. As you will read later, the widespread abdication of fiduciary duty by those who hold the highest seats of power in corporate America is, in this writer's judgment, ground zero for much that is out of whack with this otherwise wonderful economic system of ours. As to who put these board members in office in the first place, we'll attend to that later. With the exception of the Martha Stewart fiasco, it seems unlikely that any of the ships mentioned above

57 As of June 2005, Ken Lay and former Enron CEO Jeffrey Skilling had been ordered to stand trial on conspiracy and fraud charges. The trial is set for January 2006, more than four years after Enron collapsed in the fall of 2001.

would have run aground had a qualified and diligent board been on watch.

On September 29 jury selection finally began for former Tyco CEO Dennis Kozlowski and sidekick, CFO Mark Swartz. They have been charged with grand larceny, enterprise corruption, conspiracy, and falsifying business records. Altogether they stand accused of pilfering a measly $600 million from Tyco shareholders. Kozlowski, with his outlandish purchases of $6,000 shower curtains and a $2.1 million birthday bash for his wife (half of which was paid for by Tyco and its shareholders), may retain the distinction of being appointed the poster child for this generation of rogues. At Kozlowski's party in Sardinia, a "streaming" knockoff of Michelangelo's David—a statue of limitations if ever there was one—is a metaphor for much of corporate America: Too many CEOs go through investors' money like water (or, in this case, vodka). That may not be urinalysis, but it's my analysis. The long and the short of it? I hope there's no statute of limitations for prosecuting people like Koz-*louse*-ski. As with Martha Stewart, he was exposed for a "relatively" minor misdemeanor: evading roughly $1 million in sales taxes on art he purchased for his New York City digs. Psychologists doubtless have an explanation as to why, despite the consequences, those who are apparently pathologically predisposed to larcenous urgings seem indifferent as to whether their crimes are grand or petty.

Like Robber Barons of Old

As is readily apparent, the 2003 chapter in the "book" on capitalism reads like a litany of woes. The chronology above is perhaps most appropriately described as a *Who's Who of Robber Barons*, reminiscent of the stories of the venal vipers of old who are remembered by the same name: the American industrial or financial magnates of the latter half of the 19th century who became wealthy by unethical means, in those days engaging in questionable stock market operations and exploiting labor. Even though the base of their fortunes was the railroad industry, they were (for the most part) more manipulators of finance than builders of new track. They also were, with few exceptions, ruthless and corrupt, as was the system in which they were embedded. Although the term *robber barons* is barely a century old, their *modus operandi* is as endemic to the human condition as the lust for money and power. Long before capitalism, a feudal lord who exacted stiff levies on travelers passing through his domain was known by the name "baron" [not entirely unlike the local constable who sets a ridiculously low speed limit in his somnolent hamlet, lies in wait behind some shrubbery for unsuspecting out-of-town motorists, and then rakes in the revenues]. ☺ In reality, the barons of yesteryear were not much different from the contemporary class of charlatans mentioned above, who themselves resemble a slightly different iteration of the characters depicted in the best seller *Barbarians at the Gate: The Fall of RJR Nabisco*, originally published in 1992.

The nature of this preamble implicitly presages the common thread that runs through the 2003 MCM annual report: The history of financial markets is predictably cyclical, somewhat like the tides, though *un*predictably asymmetrical in their ebbing and flowing, with the superimposed wind-whipped waves blown in to confuse those viewing the happenings through their bifocals. In the figurative canyons of Wall Street, learning is not cumulative—in large measure because ignorance, greed, fear, and folly indigenous to the human species regularly impede the process of acquiring wisdom. Today's follies are little more than yesterday's foolishness adorned in different finery.

Not only do the gyrations lack symmetry, there is often a related disconnect, occasionally for extended periods, between the prices of stocks—individually or in the aggregate—and the underlying profitability upon which they ultimately must find their justification. Frequently, in the short and intermediate term, external factors rather than earnings are the primary driver of stock prices. (In the long run, however, we believe profitability prevails as the pre-eminent determinant.) Those who are unaware of this propensity toward temporary uncoupling, or who choose to overlook it by allowing themselves to get caught up in "pop" investing, may do so at considerable peril. Headlines lead to headaches for the unfamiliar. The relentless onslaught of front-page news of the widespread betrayal of trust by the captains of industry and the attack on Iraq, extraneous noise in terms of their relevance to the earnings power of American industry, proved to be a disconcerting head fake to those investors whose knee-jerk reaction to the media's shrillness trumped rational analysis in dictating investment strategy in early 2003. Even if you are more fundamentally grounded, and your touchstone is price-to-value relationships, you will find little on the S&P 500 earnings-per-share chart to give full credence to the 28.7% march uphill to 1,112 on December 31 in that bellwether index during calendar year 2003. Even short-term earnings fluctuations may qualify as extrinsic noise. Impressive as the rally may appear (and no doubt the cause of great celebration, as well as relief for maligned money managers), it's well down the mountainside from the peak of 1,527 reached on March 24, 2000. We will attempt to restore some order to this seemingly random walk down Wall Street.

Investment Performance

Period Ending December 31, 2003	MCM Equities *	S&P 500 *
Since Inception **	15.6%	11.1%
Five Years	16.9%	-0.6%
Three Years	12.4%	-4.1%
One Year	33.9%	28.7%

* Compounded annually, MCM data net of fees

** December 31, 1993

Year	MCM Equities (Net of Fees)	S&P 500
1994	-7.5%	1.3%
1995	19.1%	37.5%
1996	31.8%	22.9%
1997	45.1%	33.3%
1998	-7.4%	28.6%
1999	18.8%	21.0%
2000	29.2%	-9.1%
2001	22.7%	-11.9%
2002	-13.6%	-22.1%
2003	33.9%	28.7%

To be sure, as the data above reveal, we have been able to first protect and then enhance wealth reasonably well in the trying and turbulent early years of the new millennium. When contrasted with mutual-fund equity managers, according to data gathered or prepared by Lipper, an affiliate of Reuters, we stack up favorably. While Lipper offers more than 50 categories of equity-fund groups, we chose the three Multi-Cap categories that we believe come closest to investing in the same type and size of companies we do. The Multi-Cap categories are Core, Growth, and Value. Over the five years ending December 31, 2003, their compounded returns were 2.5%, -1.3%, and 5.0%, respectively, compared with 16.8% at MCM. We must point out, however, that the comparison is not apples to apples, since we are far less diversified than the funds. Furthermore, our flexibility enables us to step outside the bounds of traditional "value investing," which often limits the investment advisor to substandard companies, to say nothing of never feeling obligated to pay exorbitant prices for the popular growth companies. Our results also compare favorably to the passive S&P 500 index, which can be reviewed in the tables above.

The appearance of success often begets unwarranted and potentially destructive hubris. Having been an active participant in the security markets since 1966, as well as a certified graduate of the "school of hard knocks," I have confessed on several occasions in the past that we are not nearly as smart as the occasionally manic-depressive markets make us appear during up cycles nor, by inference, as dumb as we must look when they are punk. Fortunately for us, if we should begin to feel a little smug or self-satisfied as we reflect on the progress made in 2003, we need look no farther back than to last year when most of our portfolios were less-well-off at the end of the year than at the beginning! Markets move of their own unpredictable and inexorable volition, never asking our permission first.

It would be heresy for a steward of wealth to talk about investment performance without alluding to the risks assumed in generating the results. We have long lived by the adage that if you manage the risks carefully, the returns will take care of themselves. As noted in prior annual reports, the prices we paid for most of the companies we own (relative to their underlying earnings) were comparatively inexpensive—in relation to a market and, more importantly, to levels at which the individual companies traded in the past. A significant portion of the margin of safety resided in what we believed to be the market's undervaluation of the company's shares. The 2003 top four performing industry groups in the S&P 500, with their contribution to the 28.7% total return listed in parentheses after each, were information technology (6.7%), financials (5.7%), consumer discretionary (4.9%), and industrial (3.4%). Together they represented more than 72% of the gain in the index for the year. While it's difficult to support the following conclusion with the detail necessary in summary form, suffice it to say we believe that the companies we owned throughout 2003 generally sold at lower price-earnings multiples (much lower in the case of information technology) than the companies that led the S&P 500. Our companies also were generally better capitalized. Warren Buffett, citing an observation by Benjamin Graham, identified something that's relevant to current tech valuations: "Companies with mystery are worth more [i.e., sell at a higher price-earnings ratio in the marketplace] than those without mystery." Those companies that elude understanding simply do not make it through our filters.

With several recent additions to our portfolios, a subtle shift in risk management is evident as it relates to those specific companies. With them we have been willing to pay a higher price relative to earnings in exchange for what we believe is a higher degree of certainty about future earnings. Thus the margin of safety is more dependent upon our judgment about the sustainability of the company's competitive advantages and its ability to effectively apply those advantages in the marketplace to sustain earnings growth. To be sure, while we're still quite sensitive to the price-earnings ratio at the time of purchase, it isn't the primary consideration in these instances. To paraphrase Warren Buffett, we would rather pay a fair price for a great business than a bargain price for an average or poor business. This does not represent a sea change in our thinking, but it is still meaningful enough to bring to your attention. Future results will prove or disprove the efficacy of the practice.

Every strategy has its trade-offs: On the positive side, time is the ally of the great company and the enemy of the bad. Even if you pay a price that proves to be temporarily rich, the great companies often handsomely reward patience and persistence. On the flip side, a full price paid for admission carries a double penalty when the projected future growth rate in the company's earnings errs on the side of being excessively optimistic. The injury of lower-than-expected earnings is usually compounded by the insult of a lower price-earnings ratio.

There's another trade-off associated with our relatively concentrated approach to portfolio management (versus spreading our bets all over the board, as is the more common practice). Keep in mind that our implicit goal is long-term safety of principal and above-average returns. The trade-off, of course, is often above-average portfolio price volatility. Modern portfolio theorists associate higher volatility with greater risk, and apply *beta* as their quantitative measuring shtick—to individual securities and portfolios alike. In regard to a single security, we obviously have observed heightened relative volatility in the shares of unproven companies. Likewise, in the portfolio context, the day-in and day-out price volatility of an aggregation of 12 holdings is certain to be more pronounced than an array of 250, *even* if the average established quality of the 12 companies is greater than the 250. The inverse relationship between the number of issues in a portfolio and its volatility, assuming comparable quality, is simply a derivative of the law of large numbers. If you believe, as we do (and on the strength of compelling back-tested evidence), that the random "bad apple" risk against which broad diversification is designed to provide protection can be 90-95% alleviated with the smaller number of dissimilar issues, then we notice another countervailing trade-off that is rarely factored into the investor's calculus. With the risk of an unpredictable outcome—say the unexpected bankruptcy of a company in your portfolio that you presumed solvent—minimized within prudent limits by a relatively nondiversified portfolio, then you stand a chance, at least in theory, of reducing your exposure to another peril: market risk. A broadly diversified portfolio will tend to mirror the "market," replicating its performance up or down with minimal tracking error. Specifically, the risk that a broadly diversified portfolio would lose half its value from peak to trough in the 2000–02 bear market's 50% retrenchment was as close to a near certainty as you can get. Here's where the two approaches to diversification part company. Beyond differences in short-term volatility, divergence in the dollar value of the two portfolios, accentuated by the passage of time, is highly likely. Obviously, this divergence can be either negative or positive. For a real-world example, look at the preceding performance tables and notice the difference between MCM's nondiversified portfolio performance and that of the broadly diversified S&P 500, particularly in 2000 and 2001. That outcome could not have occurred had we been broadly diversified, we state emphatically. What about the probability that the difference would have been negative? If we thought the probability to be 50%, a "random walk," we wouldn't go there. We believe that by confining ourselves to way-above-average businesses and purchasing them at prices that imply a significant margin of safety, we expect more positive differences than negative ones. It also implies that we count on doing better than "the market" over the long haul. Those statements are consistent with our past record and, we trust, will not be invalidated by our future results.

Improvements in Our Performance Reporting Methodology

In preparing this report, we made a significant change in our methodology for presenting annual equity performance results in order to broaden the base of portfolios included in the calculation and to make it possible for our calculations to be audited by independent third parties [as introduced in Chapter One in the section on performance]. In the past the results have been determined by using the performance of several long-standing representative accounts as a shorthand proxy for all accounts. We recalculated performance from 1994 through 2003, using data from the master list of all our accounts. The "tracking error" (the difference in results using the two methodologies) was insignificant, as indicated graphically on the chart below. The returns were calculated on a time-weighted basis. Needless to say, the results are portfolio-size-weighted; that is, the performance of larger portfolios has a greater effect on the consolidated results than smaller ones.

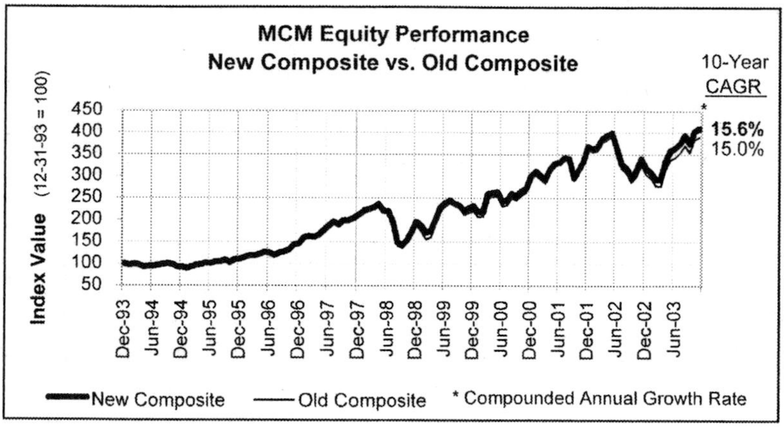

To enable us to make the next point, please refer again to the chart above. It represents the same 10-year time-weighted data from the table above plotted on a monthly basis in chart format. Graphically presented, the numbers tell a slightly more complete story: You'll notice that the trend is generally upward but far from linear, as evidenced by the 21-month trough between the peak reached in March 2002 and the new high achieved at 2003 year-end! Time-weighted results (the reporting standard) assume no cash flow into or out of the account during the measurement period. In practice we make every effort to add to our positions when prices are low and sometimes sell entire holdings when their prices rise to the point where the expected return for the next five years is in the mid- to low-single digits. Accordingly, your dollar-weighted returns—the actual dollar amount of increase in your wealth—is greater than the time-weighted data we are required to report would imply. The time-weighted chart would suggest that you are back to where you were in the spring of 2002, whereas your much heavier pocketbook speaks convincingly otherwise.

Making Headway in the Post-Bubble Environment

This essay seeks to objectively reduce the surfeit of frequently conflicting market information bombarding us from all sides to something that is useful and practical. Specifically, we hope to very roughly approximate where we are along the continuum from investment bliss (where value grows solidly and prices are low relative to value, both implying high expected returns and lower risks) to the other extreme: investment misery and agony, the woeful state of affairs in 2000–02.

You may recall in the 1999 annual report that considerable attention was directed to Warren Buffett's well-reasoned macroeconomic market analysis as published in *Fortune*, in part because he has historically redirected questions of that sort, declaring himself an agnostic on the market in general. His tone was uncompromising as he warned investors to downsize their expectations, arguing that earnings growth is not likely to exceed 3% (to which we add 2% for inflation) unless one uses heroic and historically unsupportable assumptions about interest rates, GDP growth, and expanding profit margins. To that we add a 1% dividend yield and arrive at a nominal 6% total return from a broadly diversified portfolio of common stocks well into the future. Buffett revisited the subject in July 2001, which we again summarized in our 2001 annual report, incrementally raising his hypothetical expected return to 7% because stock prices were lower and the economy had grown. With the S&P 500 finishing 2003 some 28.7% ahead of the preceding year's close, it's no wonder that in a *Barron's* October 27 article a patient Buffett admitted he is sitting on an enormous cash hoard—more than $24 billion—awaiting investment opportunities in the stock and bond markets. In the wide-ranging interview, Buffett said he's "not finding anything" in the stock market and isn't enamored with Treasury bonds or junk debt. His market-related comments are consistent with those made in Berkshire's 2002 annual report, which was released in March 2003, and at Berkshire's annual meeting in early May. In the annual report Buffett wrote that "despite three years of falling prices, which have significantly improved the attractiveness of common stocks, we still find very few that even mildly interest us."

While this writer's unabashed respect for Warren Buffett is manifestly evident, it is not sycophantic. Since Berkshire's annual report is published several months after MCM's, I critically review his chairman's letter to make sure his thinking is straight! *This* report takes a look at the "where we are on the continuum" issue from a perspective somewhat different from Buffett's.

There is no more comfortable place to start than with the long-term relationship between price and value. Parenthetically, we would have preferred to begin with a forecast of the future prospects for growth in the underlying value of American industry but found that daunting task well beyond our, or for that matter anyone else's, capabilities.

The first S&P 500 chart presents earnings per share going back almost 50 years. It's very important that you notice the legend is logarithmic, where the value assigned to each equally spaced point on the vertical axis is 10 times the numerical value of the one below it. Compared with the arithmetical grid scale (1, 2, 3 ... and so on), which is most commonly used, the logarithmic scale is better for showing percentage changes over time, with a straight line representing a constant rate of change. We calculated the trendline—or average compounded rate of earnings-per-share growth over the 47 years—to be approximately 6%. Using this method of presentation, and viewing a half-century of progress from our bird's-eye vantage point, one should get a sense of the relative linearity of the overall trend, at least until 2001. In retrospect, the carnage of 1973–74, for those who take the long view, doesn't seem to be an event worth losing sleep over. As an aside, from 1957 until 1985 dividends yielded 4% on average, which, when added to the growth rate in earnings, equaled the oft-referred-to 10% total return from common stocks from 1926 through 1985.

While one can make a science of trying to precisely explain the drop in earnings in 2001 and 2002, we'll attempt a simple explanation. Here we aren't trying to make points; we're trying to make *a* point. Beyond the obvious effects of the recession, it is our general view that in many instances earnings were overstated for any number of years, depending on the company, leading up through 2000. The last seven years' worth of MCM annual reports discussed in great detail the preoccupation of a number of companies with managing earnings. Many of the sins of the past were recognized with goodwill impairment and a host of other charges in 2001 and 2002. We have no idea how much of the dirty laundry has been aired, but we would hazard a guess that what is hanging on the line represents the majority of it. The reader should be reminded that many companies toed the mark during the period of great temptation, thus ameliorating the repercussions of the most egregious offenders.

So, using S&P data, and relying on an earnings forecast for 2004 of $46.50, which is estimated by fitting a linear trendline to the earnings-per-share chart, is probably a reasonable place to start analyzing to what extent the market is generally cheap or dear in terms of the relationship between price and " trendline" earnings. The S&P index closed 2003 at 1,112, resulting in a price-earnings ratio of 24 on 2004 estimated earnings. You'll notice from the price-earnings ratio chart that numbers in the mid- to upper-teens prevailed between 1957 and 1973 when interest rates and inflation were relatively low and earnings growth slightly above average. The period from 1975 through 1990 was marked by higher-than-average interest rates and lower-than-average growth rates in earnings.

Next examine the relationship between the S&P 500 index, the index's annual earnings, and the index's annual high/low price-earnings ratio on the charts provided. As you can see, the spike in the price-earnings ratio around the turn of the century is partially explained by the doubling of the index (numerator) and the sharp drop in earnings, the denominator.

Since today's stock prices are an approximation of the discounted present value of future cash flows, there are three unknowns that must be estimated:

(1) cash flows many years hence, (2) the estimated cost of money (the underlying Treasury bond interest) over that same time frame as one component of the discount rate, and (3) the equity-risk premium added to the underlying cost of money to arrive at the total discount rate to be applied to reducing the future cash flows to present value. By comparison, a Treasury bond (currently considered to be the highest-quality fixed-income instrument available) is priced using the same methodology, though all variables are known. Assuming a bond currently trades at par, only future fluctuations in market interest rates will cause its price to deviate from par.

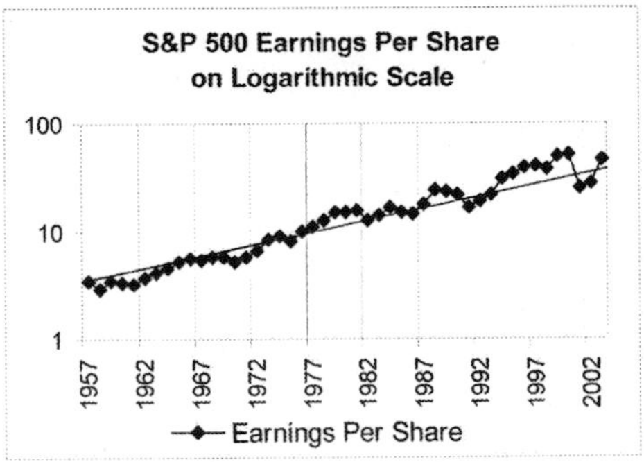

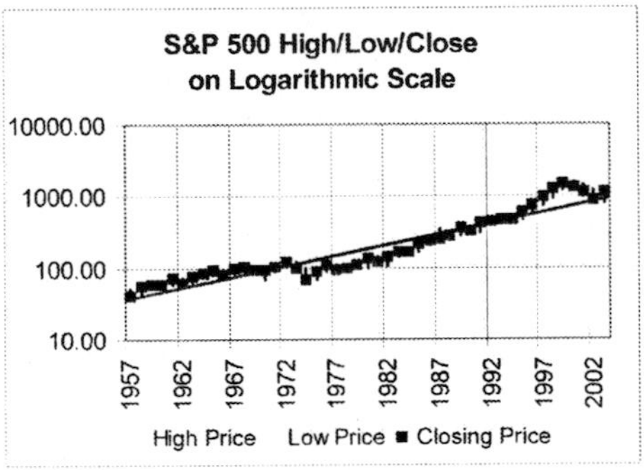

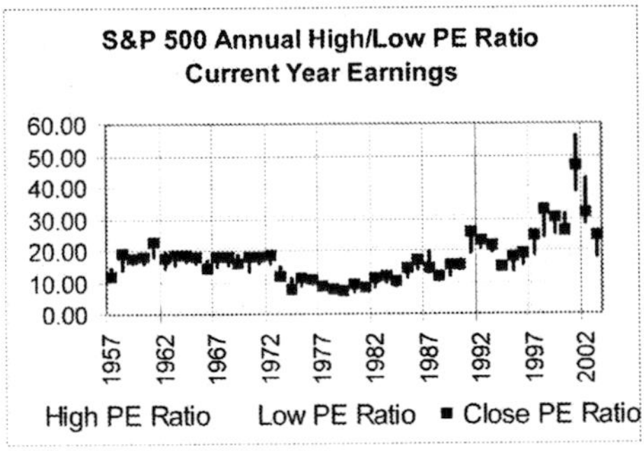

Returning to the pricing of common stocks, as for the first and very important variable, we are at a loss to forecast the growth rate in earnings (a rough but convenient proxy for cash flow) years into the future with any degree of confidence. Precision is difficult to achieve even in the near term. In a recent *Barron's* poll of 12 Wall Street analysts, S&P 500 earnings growth forecasts for 2004 were as high as 16% and as low as 9%, in part because of differing earnings measurement metrics. Beyond telling us that the sheep rarely wander far from the flock, we can say the above numbers don't allow much to hang your hat on. And yet the long-term forecast, where the potential for the most uncertainty exists, is usually based on the simple extrapolation of historical growth rates—and generally for good reason. Sometimes, though, as was the case during the Great Bubble, the extrapolation of wildly optimistic (and ultimately fanciful)

distant growth rates for many historically high-growth-rate companies led to extreme overvaluation. When visions seen through rose-colored glasses collided with reality, the stocks plummeted.

Looking back at the 47-year history of S&P 500 earnings, simple extrapolation was undoubtedly the most accurate forecasting methodology. While we can think of a number of major evolving forces that could knock the extrapolation train off the tracks, we're inclined to stay with the average 6% growth rates for the time being. Nonetheless, we offer a serious note of caution here. In testimony before Congress during the second half of 2003, Alan Greenspan added a new wrinkle to his macroeconomic management formula that appears a lot like "Pascal's Wager."[58] In justifying maintaining the discount rate at the 1% level, he admitted that he would rather err on the side of being too easy than too tight, because the consequences of the latter are much more dire than the former. Thus, even though he assigns a relatively low probability to the deflationary scenario, its consequences are so grave as to cause him to "overweight" that possibility in his policy calculus. And so it is with us. However remote the likelihood of an economic meltdown might be, we, as stewards of your wealth, must overweight it in our portfolio decision making because of the extreme and unacceptable severity of the fallout should it by chance occur. Over the years, we have always positioned ourselves so that if we err, it will generally be on the side of excessive conservatism, otherwise known as forgoing opportunities. Generally, we have compensated by limiting ourselves to good businesses purchased at reasonable prices.

Finally, we turn to the cost of money and the premium in return that one should expect from investment in common stocks vis-à-vis the more predictable U.S. Treasury security. If you view the chart of U.S. government bond yields, it's hard to draw a conclusion about what is normal. If you were to overlay a consumer price index (CPI) chart, you would see the logical connection between the rate at which the purchasing power of the currency is being debased through inflation and the rate of interest lenders demand for the rental of their money. Once again, we are at a loss. Intuitively, if we expect trendline economic growth and take into account anecdotal indicators like the price of gold and the exchange rate of the dollar, inflation should rise, perhaps significantly, over time, from current levels. While there is no direct

58 [Original 2003 footnote] Blaise Pascal, the great 17th-century French mathematician, became a devout Christian in his later years. As one of the original probability theorists, he rationally explained the pious life using mathematics rather than simple faith. He argued that if heaven and hell exist as discrete outcomes in the afterlife and that the probability of each was arbitrarily assigned to be 50%, one must still choose the virtuous life. His rationale rested on the difference in the severity of the outcomes: He reasoned that an eternity of heavenly bliss was infinitely preferable to one of never-ending damnation. That, in a nutshell, is Pascal's Wager.

connection, interest rates should follow—or even lead—the rate of change in prices. As for the equity-risk premium, we feel qualified to prognosticate with more conviction. As we have so often written, investors are inclined to view the world through the rearview mirror. The rocky recent past and the widespread distrust of those who used to report but now manage earnings tarnished the image of equities as the sure-bet road to riches. The equity-risk premium, thought to be largely irrelevant a few years ago, should regain its lost credibility, if not actually overcompensate.

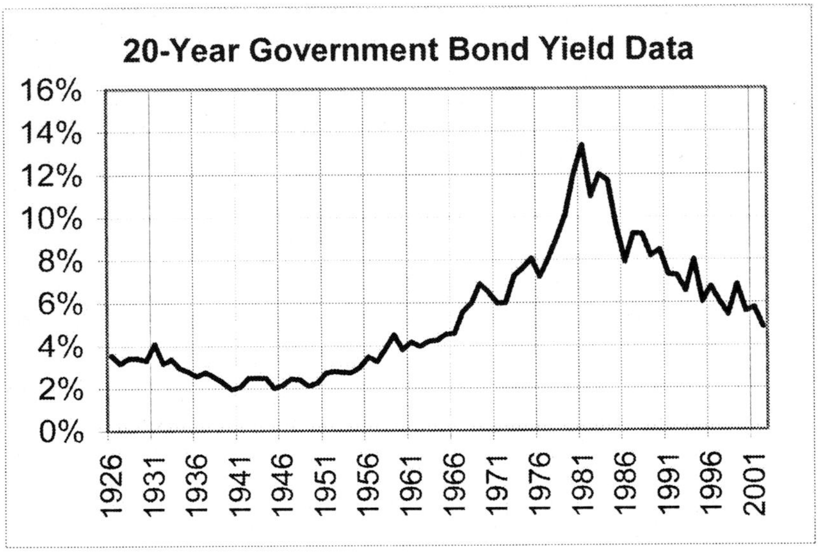

Taking all of the above into account, we must conclude that common stocks, *in general*, as measured by the S&P 500, which tends to somewhat overstate the results because of the survivor's bias mentioned earlier, are at the high end of the valuation continuum. How or when they regress to an approximate mean of, say, 15 times earnings is unknowable. So long as earnings stick reasonably close to their historical trendline growth rates, we believe that the best-case scenario is lumpy total returns from equities that average little more than the underlying earnings growth rate. The likely price-earnings ratio compression may be offset by an ever-rising dividend yield.

From the risk perspective, the most optimistic observation we can offer about the margin of safety is that it is razor-thin. Likewise, the key impetus behind stock prices going forward must be earnings growth since the probability of a significant expansion in earnings multiples is slight at best. In summary, even the best-case scenario is not particularly appealing. No wonder we're finding it difficult to identify companies that meet our threshold return requirement.

How Did We Get Here in the First Place?

Robert Shiller, Yale professor, seasoned market observer, and author of the prescient and timely book , published in March 2000, the very month the Nasdaq Bubble burst, offered a number of "structural" causes in explaining how exuberance eventually became irrational. By dissecting those causal forces, perhaps we can speculate as to whether their power remains potent or whether it is on the wane.

He begins with the invasion of the Internet, delivering leading-edge technology (and presumably serving as confirming evidence of the "new era" in prosperity led by America's worldwide technological dominance) right into our homes in the second half of the 1990s. Visions of sugarplums, however unfounded, danced in just about everyone's heads. Merrill Lynch's slogan, "We're bullish on America," symbolized the triumph of capitalism over other less-effective economic ideologies, the fall of the former Soviet Union being the quintessential case study. Shiller points out that materialism re-emerged and business success, measured most conveniently in dollars, gave rise to the proliferation and eventual abuse of stock options as the quickest road to pre-eminence. Instead of being embarrassed by the polarities brought into *bas-relief* by their wealth, the newly ascended super-rich scrambled to the newsstands, like students to the bulletin board after final-exam results are posted, to see if their name had shown up on the *Forbes* list of the 400 wealthiest families in America. How much our values have changed from the wisdom of Ralph Waldo Emerson: "Great men are they who see that spiritual is stronger than any material force, that thoughts rule the world."

Tax cuts and the latter expectation of further cuts on earned income, capital gains, dividends, and estates provided encouraging and tangible evidence of a pro-business attitude within the Republican-dominated Congress. The powerful Baby Boomer myth, which was more about public perceptions than demographic logic, gained increasing credence during the decade of the 1990s. Proliferating media coverage of the financial markets only fanned the flames of exuberance, transforming once bland business periodicals into televised tout sheets. Who would have imagined broadcasted stock tips, 24 hours a day? After reading the above, again turn to the S&P 500 earnings-per-share chart to see how much, if any, of all this fanfare percolated through to affect higher rates of earnings growth over the last five years.

Wall Street's *modus operandi* adapted easily—and in fact far too effortlessly—to the times. The independence of analysts was compromised with the crumbling of the "Chinese wall," the imaginary barrier that in theory but rarely in practice separated researchers from investment bankers. Power gradually shifted from the analysts to the chief financial officers of corporations, whose profitable investment banking business was doled out with obvious partiality.

The growth in popularity of the defined-contribution pension plan since 1981—when the 401(k) plan came into existence—greatly increased the public's awareness about stocks, even if indirectly through mutual funds. The short- and long-term consequences of the transfer of decision-making authority to the employee, the emergence of the mutual-fund family that offered a cornucopia of investment alternatives, and the relative decline in the traditional defined-benefit plan are examined later in the report.

Returning to Shiller, the decline in inflation in the 1990s to levels not thought possible in the early 1980s bolstered investor confidence since steady prices are perceived by the public as a sign of economic stability and social health. Declining nominal interest rates added to investors' sense of economic well-being, irrespective of whether the more relevant but harder to understand "real" (inflation-adjusted) rates were relatively high or low.

Gambling has prospered in its many other forms over the last 20 years. For example, in 1975, only 13 states permitted lotteries; the number had increased to 37 by 1999. Until 1990 casinos were legalized in Nevada and Atlantic City only. By 1999 riverboat and dockside casinos numbered over 360, according to Shiller's research. Cable and the Internet have piped gambling right into our homes, and the waiting lines at local convenience stores to buy lottery tickets speak volumes about the mesmerizing hold "easy money" has on the popular imagination. Shiller makes a strong case that gambling fosters an inflated estimate of one's own potential for good luck that may well spill over to its more upscale form, speculation in securities.

Trading volume nearly doubled between 1982 and 1999, with annual turnover exploding from 42% to 78%, as casino capitalism stormed the barricades of rationality. The groundwork was laid on a memorable day in May 1975 when fixed commission rates were at long last forbidden by the SEC, as deregulation fought its way through heavy resistance to Wall Street. Trading costs stair-stepped down only to collapse like toy soldiers as online trading took *people* out of the process. Discount brokers and day trading proliferated as the speculative mania, like machine-gun fire, indiscriminately hit more and more targets, ranging from the vulnerable and vigilant to the vile and villainous. Dramatic changes in the volume of trading are almost always positively correlated with major bull and bear markets.

The Complementary Role of Behavioral Economics

From the structural changes that were foundational to the Great Bubble, we must look further to behavioral economics to understand how those forces were amplified and exaggerated in the minds of investors. In prior annual reports we have devoted discussion to individual and social psychology as a means of attempting to explain the seemingly irrational behavior of investors from time to time. More than that, we have relied on it heavily in our decision making. The subject of *behavioral economics* has, in the academic world where change is a lagging indicator, gained ground grudgingly as its struggle to obtain acceptability is symbolized by the oil-and-water character of the words themselves, conveying as they do two different strains of ideology. The science of psychology is as soft as economics is concrete. By way of illustration, it's the rare engineer whose library is filled with books on philosophy. Nonetheless, this cross-thinking is gaining credence in leading academic institutions like Harvard and Yale, the latter where Robert Shiller preaches this gospel, in large measure because ... it works!

Shiller does a masterful job of blending the two sciences in explaining the energy that gave rise to irrational exuberance, not coincidentally the title of his 2000 book. The subject is far too comprehensive to be covered other than superficially here, and we therefore strongly encourage you to purchase the book if you find your appetite sufficiently whetted to induce you to venture out onto the frontiers of economic thought. While the boundaries of the discipline are not well-defined, and perhaps never will be, for the sake of expediency I'll boil them in the same pot, though I won't necessarily toss the ingredients into the stew in the same order he did.

Shiller refers to the herd instinct and naturally occurring Ponzi processes as "amplification mechanisms," often causing the pendulum of investment sentiment to swing to extremes not remotely justified by rational analysis. My affinity for these mechanisms can be traced to many pleasant and engaging conversations with my friend and former associate, Albert Meyer.[59] Ponzi schemes, in one form or another, have been around and will be around forever because of (1) their simplicity and (2) the natural instinct (gullibility?) of groups of people all too willing to embrace the improbable. Generally, they are launched with a promoter putting forth a plausible, although usually improbable, proposition that large gains can be had from investing in the

---

59 [Original 2003 footnote] Albert Meyer was a gifted accounting professor at Spring Arbor University in south-central Michigan when he earned national renown (at great personal risk) for exposing the New Era Philanthropy Ponzi scheme in 1995. Albert, who was recruited as an analyst by our firm shortly thereaftear, now runs his own independent research firm (Second Opinion Research), after spending four years with Dallas-based David Tice & Associates as a research analyst.

venture being hyped. In fact, there is rarely little if any investment merit behind a promoter's assertions. In reality, once the idea gains a toehold of credence, "feedback" mechanisms pour fuel on the fire of desire and the money flows in, motivated almost entirely by the prospect for riches, the "investors" having long forgotten whether or not the original investment thesis was efficacious. Since there is no underlying asset truly capable of generating the earnings at the rate promised, new-money inflows are the primary means of making good on promises to earlier investors. The scheme must come to an end and does so when exposed, often unexpectedly, but certainly no later than when the inflows slow to a point that they don't cover the promised outflows. The whole charade then inevitably collapses like a house of cards.[60]

In its advanced stages, the market (especially Nasdaq) in Internet, technology, and Telcom stocks took on the characteristics of a classic Ponzi process. The underlying earnings power of the companies that made up the industries was minuscule compared with the astronomical valuations placed on them in the mad scramble for paper gold. As with all Ponzi schemes, the first sellers are almost always the most fortunate. As discussed in the 2002 annual report, the conspiracy (I don't think that's too harsh a word) to optimize the "rake" for insiders became perniciously more refined with each new IPO (initial public offering). In any other venue, such behavior would be considered criminal.

The *Zeitgeist*, the spirit of the times, can and often does become irrational because of herd behavior, epidemics, and "information cascades," as Shiller explains. "Groupthink" frequently causes an individual to capitulate to crowd thinking simply because he or she finds it difficult to believe that such a large group of people could be wrong, particularly when an authoritative figure lends his or her stature to the proposition. Shiller argues that the behavior of such individuals may in fact be predominantly rational and intelligent, even when the views to which they subscribe conflict with their own matter-of-fact judgment. The reason: the lasting lessons learned from past errors when going against the majority view. The spread of epidemics and information

---

60 [Original 2003 footnote] Within days of the end of the year, news broke about one of the most outrageous Ponzi schemes ever originated—out of Sacramento, no less, perhaps a modern-day rendition of the 19th-century Gold Rush—according to an Associated Press story. Sunday church regular and picture-waving grandfather, 57-year-old Paul Lewis Jr. illicitly amassed $813 million in his Southern California investment funds on the word of a few friends. Many heard about Financial Advisory Consultants through fellow churchgoers. Prospects marveled at Lewis' reported 20% to 40% returns over 20 years in several of his funds, seemingly confirmed as periodically a few investors cashed in as much as $250,000. Not surprisingly, the firm never provided clients with any details on how it invested their money, nor was the firm ever licensed or regulated as required! Former ZZZZ Best carpet cleaning company scam artist Berry Minkow, who spent seven years behind bars, spoke with authority about Lewis's deceit: "It will go down as the longest-running Ponzi scheme in history—and the mutual fund that didn't exist."

cascades—where a faulty thesis proliferates by word-of-mouth like a forest fire leaping from tree to tree, without the validity of the original thesis again being contested—further explains the suppression of the constraints of rational and independent thought.

Shiller also discusses the psychological factor of "anchoring," a behavioral response that would not be possible if the markets were truly rational (and, by inference, efficient). Anchoring is not so much the result of ignorance but is more attributable to how the human mind works. For example, most of us are quantitatively anchored in the present; in making judgments about the level of a stock's price, the anchor is likely to be yesterday's price. In the qualitative dimension, anchoring takes the form of "storytelling and justification," both of which defy quantification. Liken it if you will to the growing fascination with gambling mentioned above: The vocabulary makes the subtle shift to vague expressions like *lucky day* compared with far more precise terms like *probability.* The emphasis gradually migrates from logical analysis to intuition.

Hand in glove with the above is what we have described in the past as the *overconfidence bias,* the near universal human tendency toward excessive and unjustified confidence in one's beliefs. While the association is a bit tenuous, overconfidence has been deemed a force in promoting the high volume of trading that is indigenous to speculative markets. A companion affinity is the *hindsight bias* that causes one to see the world as far more predictable than it actually is.

By now you must feel a little overwhelmed by all this soft-science stuff and are no doubt wondering the point of it all. Well, it comes full circle to the centrality of the efficient-market thesis to mainstream investment thinking. For if what is commonly believed in academia is in fact true, much of this report is poppycock, worthless nonsense. "Might does not make right," and we're thusly inclined to resist the temptation to blindly take any thesis at face value, no matter how many Nobel laureates plaques are hanging on the office wall. Does it not stand to reason that if indeed the markets are efficient, and all information publicly known is imputed in current market prices, then markets must be immune from excessive exhilaration, of which bubbles are the end product? As a sidebar, it is presumed that one also can infer that people who have differing abilities cannot produce dissimilar investment results, since the superior understanding of some is already incorporated in share prices. What about Warren Buffett? The authorities have pronounced him an aberration. Without belaboring the point, to my knowledge, no modern portfolio theorists have yet to venture forth to argue that the overblown market boom/bust cycle that began in the late 1990s in any way confirms the validity of the efficient-market thesis. All we hear is silence. To this writer, the thesis is damned by faint praise ...

To such practitioners as your servants at MCM, we admonish ourselves to never say "never." Despite the intimidating mathematics of modern portfolio theory, of which the efficient market thesis is an essential building block, real-life experience teaches us that free markets have always shown a disposition toward irrational behavior when the stars of exaggerated sentiment are in alignment. Being aware that the market price pendulum can swing—in both directions—to extremes well beyond what our "anchored" thinking would deem possible, we must remain steadfastly independent and rational in our thinking. No mean feat ... certainly in 1999 ... and perhaps no less so today.

Back to the Future Redux

Thus armed with additional data, we return to the original question: Where are we on the continuum between exuberance and despair? Turning first to Robert Shiller's structural factors, let's highlight a few in the order they appeared in the earlier section titled "How Did We Get Here in the First Place?"

The public has always been justifiably enamored with new technologies, as was the case with radio, television, and the personal computer in their respective heydays. It's hard to believe that on the 20th anniversary of the revolutionary technology that became the personal computer, the *wunderkind* is past its prime, relegated to the characterization of technologically passé. Once yesterday's remarkable innovations became commonplace, they understandably lost their luster as the "new and unusual," a fate that will surely befall the Internet. We need only recall that the productivity enhancements that followed the introduction of the PC in the early to mid-1980s economically benefited the user far more than the producer. Despite the impressive 2003 rallies in the stocks of a number of the leading Internet companies, the earnings power of the industry—compared with early projections and because of the industry's competitive construct—remains suspect.

Of course, we must make full allowance for the likelihood of some new technology piggybacking on existing scientific developments, which may go from obscurity to near universal acceptance in less than 10 years, just as the Internet rode into town on the PC infrastructure horse. Highly regarded futurist John Naisbitt opines in the well-documented, insightful, and cautionary book *High Tech/High Touch* that genetic technologies will overwhelm all other technologies in the 21st century. He reminds us that all of our technological innovations appeared on the scene long before a full attempt was made to understand their ethical and social consequences. Like the Internet, the economics of genetic engineering are not as compelling as they first might seem. Moreover, ethical dilemmas may, and perhaps should, impede the progress of otherwise unbridled scientific zeal. In sum, in this writer's judgment the Internet was a great catalyst only because it worked well in conjunction with other complementary factors, including earnings growth, managed or otherwise. As we look forward five years into the nascent economic recovery's clouded crystal ball, the list of key macro earnings drivers is indeed short enough that the forces that may cause another contraction not too far down the road should be of greater concern.

Another structural factor that gave rise to the Bubble has not abated to any noticeable extent. Worship at the altar of materialism seems rather deeply embedded in our culture. Spiritually uncomfortable allusions notwithstanding, the production and accumulation of *stuff* is, after all, the practical end objective of our capitalist system. And it is unlikely that materialism will be dislodged except under the most economically discouraging of circumstances. Should the tide turn, there is a higher order always beckoning us (the calling of most religious groups from time immemorial), as Emerson affirmed above.

As for macro policy, it's hard to imagine a fiscal/monetary policy mix more supportive of investment than is currently in place. Barring the unexpected, fiscal policy should be a plus for at least another five years.

Although Shiller's earlier discussion of the vaunted demographic shift was comprehensive, as it should have been, we'll summarize its current relevance in one sentence. The Baby Boom stimulus (a fallacious one-sided equation, we would argue) is a little long in the tooth anyway, and in less than a decade, it may be the Baby Bust (that began soon after the development of the birth-control pill in the mid-1960s) that will impregnate the collective consciousness of editorial writers.

Turning to investment analysis—on the assumption that the cathartic process (a thorough cleansing of the pervasive speculative inclination) is not complete—we envision a long period of involuntary contrition that should linger until the speculative sap begins to flow freely again. It might even be possible that respectability may once again become, shall we say, respectable, at least for a time. As for the Chinese wall, count us among the diehard cynics. It is built of beach sand and will always crumble when the waves of greed roll in.

Regarding the continuation of economic utopia (a flat consumer price index and a Fed funds rate of 1%), we state emphatically that it will not persist and can present a host of reasons why, but we can't offer a scintilla of evidence in support of precisely when or how the state of affairs might change. We all know the antonyms for the word utopia. To that we can add nothing more.[61]

---

61 Inflation has remained relatively tame. For the year ending June 30, 2005, consumer prices increased 2.5%. The Fed, however, backed away from its open-the-floodgates "accommodative" policy, boosting the Fed funds rate by 200 basis points.

With respect to Shiller's comprehensive examination of the contribution from the media to the exuberance, as a bold prophecy in the 2002 annual report, the undersigned suggested that in due time CNBC will be a shadow of its current self. It has been a child of the 20-year bull market that culminated in the bulimic disgorgement beginning in March 2000, and its ratings will move in lockstep with stock prices, which, we need not remind our readers, fluctuate! The good news is that the fair-weather financial media, the existence of which is dependent on rising prices and whose emergence was celebrated with such fanfare during the bull market, will die a quiet death. Nielsen ratings will see to that. Don't, however, sell the Dow Jones company short!

Another structural factor is likely to turn from a positive to a negative. The huge spike in overall trading volume is both cause and effect of rising stock prices. Parenthetically, it's a common occurrence in the shares of individual companies, with above-average trading volume most often associated with high and rising prices, when broad attention is drawn to the stock (at least partly due to the self-reinforcing mechanism of the rising price itself). After stocks have cratered—at the very time when some offer the most inviting profile of risk and return—trading volume invariably becomes lethargic. This common phenomenon has not escaped our attention.

That aside notwithstanding, low commission rates and Internet-enabled day trading promote the erroneous perception of easy money. Evidence abounds to the contrary. Frenetic trading, made more risky by the fulcrum of financial leverage, is, for the vast majority of players, a devastating loser's game. As volume slows and price volatility follows suit, the speculators at the margin will gradually drift away. "The lottery" and other forms of gambling may moderate, at least in terms of how we know them today. To be sure, human nature's mostly futile propensity to defy the odds will never, and should never, go away. Some of the greatest innovations in history have come from the minds of such nonconformists. Gambling at its current pace, though, is a social sickness that may have reached epidemic proportions. Eventually all epidemics subside, each for reasons unique to itself.

Because of the relative importance of what follows as a potent swing variable, lengthy ensuing discourse is devoted to the interconnected maze of mutual funds, defined-contribution plans, and corporate governance, after which we'll attempt to answer the question posed at the beginning of this section. (Are you intrigued by the suspense?!)

Sensing the Winds of Change

The subsequent commentary is longer, more taxing, and more controversial than the relatively superficial survey of the structural factors immediately preceding, with the writer begging your indulgence in hopes that the end will justify the means. To begin, certain elements of the capital markets and all their assorted subsets are woven together like the tapestry of a finely crafted Persian rug. The attempt will be to unravel some of the mystery of this complex entity so that several potentially radical hypotheses can be presented that may be relevant to the central issue of this essay. The tentative and untested explanation that accounts for the facts selectively presented below—my theory, if you will—does not necessarily reflect the opinions of my partners and associates. ☺

The Apogee of the Mutual-Fund Boom

Where the process of unraveling begins is itself subject to debate. Exercising the writer's prerogative, I'll start with investment companies if for no other reason than their relative mass and resilience, like the cat with nine lives. Mutual funds in one form or another have been fixtures on the investment landscape since the early 1800s, far longer than most of us would have imagined, anchored as we are in the present. Despite mutual funds' dramatic growth in popularity since the early 1980s, the public's interest in them has historically waxed and waned concurrent with major bull and bear markets. Investment trusts proliferated in the 1920s, only to fall into disrepute during the 1930s because of disastrous investment results and disingenuous promoters whose blatant acts of self-enrichment took precedence over their fiduciary obligation to shareholders (deeds more reprehensible, to be sure, than the malfeasance for which the industry is currently being castigated, as noted below).

The Investment Company Act of 1940 helped to legitimize what became known as mutual funds and, along with the passage of time, to restore investor confidence. Laws are rarely a leading indicator! The Employment Retirement Income Security Act of 1974, ERISA, which gave birth to the individual retirement account (IRA), paved the way for investing tax-deferred dollars in mutual funds, only to be delayed by another episode of mutual-fund misconduct and the bear market of 1973–74. The net exodus from mutual funds lingered well into the 1980s until awareness of the rising market spread to the backwaters of investor consciousness. The impetus that mutual funds received from the declining relative importance of the defined-benefit pension plan as money flowed into the defined-contribution 401(k) pension plan in the early 1980s belatedly, but undeniably, took root in the great bull market that followed. Although the vast majority of equity mutual funds failed to match the performance of passive indices (according to Lipper data, over the 30 years through December 2002, diversified U.S. stock funds returned an average of 9.5% per year compared with 10.7% for the S&P 500), aggressive advertising and more than a 10-fold increase in the Dow during the next 18 years helped polish the image, even if largely undeserved, of "experts" at the helm.

To put the last 22 years in perspective, in 1980 a comparatively minuscule 4.6 million U.S. households owned mutual funds, a 5.7% penetration rate. By 2002 these funds had become well-nigh-ubiquitous, owned in one form or another by nearly 50% of all households, or 54.2 million families. Nature, or in this case mutual-fund sponsors, abhors a vacuum. No surprise then, like the proliferation of pesky dandelions in the spring, 4,682 equity mutual funds (8,231 funds of all types) sprouted in the ensuing years, as tallied in the current Investment Company Institute (ICI) Fact Sheet, a 12-fold increase since 1982. (ICI is the chief advocacy organization of the mutual-fund industry.) In 1982 equity mutual-fund assets totaled $53.7 billion, a mere 2% of the $2.7 trillion at year-end 2002. The peak was reached in 1999 when equity funds exceeded $4 trillion. In the aggregate, funds of all stripes—equity, hybrid, bond, and taxable and tax-exempt money market—grew from $297 billion in 1982 to $6.4 trillion by December 31, 2002. No less telling with regard to the pervasiveness of the mutual-fund phenomenon in actual interrelations or comparative importance is the following fact: The number of mutual funds eclipses the total number of individual companies listed on the New York Stock Exchange. Does not the phrase "absurd redundancy" come to mind? When the middlemen outnumber the largest grouping of stocks they ostensibly manage, something, to understate the point, is askew.

On the heels of a bear market that lasted from 2000 to 2002, mutual-fund ownership declined only slightly. In all, a July 2003 ICI survey found 53.3 million households, or 47.9%, owned mutual funds. That's down slightly from 54.2 million households, or 49.6%, in July 2002. The survey reported that the total number of individual investors owning mutual funds declined to 91.2 million in the 2003 survey from 94.9 million in the 2002 survey. At the same time, the survey found that a record number of households, 36.4 million, owned mutual funds inside employer-sponsored retirement plans. That figure represents 32.7% of all U.S. households.

"The harsh financial environment and weak performance in equity markets starting in 2000 contributed to the decline in overall household fund ownership," says Matthew P. Fink, ICI president. "Despite difficult equity markets, ownership of mutual funds within employer-sponsored retirement plans increased to record numbers" (more on this development below). On the surface, the turnover rate in stock funds indicates feverish activity, but the data are likely to mislead. Annual redemptions and redemption exchanges, as a percentage of average net assets, reached 43.9% for the 12 months ending October 2002 and 34.8% for the year ending September 2003. Most of this is believed to be attributable to a small but frenetic subset of the mutual-fund shareholder population who turned their funds seven times a year on average, as well as a steady departure from foreign funds since 1993. The heavily promoted illusion of limitless riches begging to be mined within the lesser-developed countries was demythologized by the earlier Asian and other foreign bear markets. In point of fact, the vast majority of shareholders rarely alter their portfolio allocations. Institute research confirms that shareholder response to long-term declines in stock prices has been "measured and gradual." Gradual, yes, but measured ... hardly the word to describe often simple reactive behavior that, by virtue of its momentum, changes course with the quickness of a battleship under full power.

Fund-Owner Demographics

Who are these people who have embraced the mutual fund as the means of realizing the American dream? Most mutual-fund-owning households have moderate incomes and, as you might expect, fund ownership increases with income. As of July 2003, according to ICI statistics, 28% of households with income less than $50,000 owned mutual funds, compared with 70% with incomes of $50,000 or more.

The vast majority (83%) of mutual-fund households are headed by individuals age 25 to 64 years; with 52% of all mutual-fund households from the Baby Boomer generation (those born between 1947 and 1964), 23% from the "silent" generation (pre-1946, which includes the undersigned, who has been referred to by many names, none of which even resembled "silent"!), and 25% from the post-1965 Generation X'ers. Thirteen percent of households owning funds are headed by individuals age 65 or older; 4% are headed by individuals younger than age 25. A broadly based, middle-class, younger- to middle-aged demographic if I ever saw one ...

Fink recites the mutual-fund sponsor's mantra on the ICI Website: "Mutual funds offer investors an unparalleled combination of benefits, including professional management, diversification, strict regulations and affordability." Adds Fink: "Funds play a prominent role in helping Americans achieve their significant long-term financial goals, including financing education and retirement."

Disquieting Changes in the Distribution Channel

Beneath the surface of the burgeoning, decade-long surge in mutual-fund sales, subtle changes have been taking place that may well have wide-ranging, long-term ramifications. Direct sales of new funds to individual investors declined from 23% in 1990 to 13% in 2002. The traditional brokers' share of the shrinking direct-sales channel has dropped from 50% to 25% over that same time span. Indirect sales through company-sponsored plans have filled the gap. All the while the power has been shifting to the bigger organizations that enjoy economies of scale and the competitive edge of a panoply of product offerings. The top 25 mutual-fund complexes have consistently controlled about 75% of the assets over the last five years. The top 10 declined from 56% to 46%, owing to the fact that the larger fund complexes have a preponderance of equity offerings that fared poorly from 2000 to 2002 compared with the smaller fund families, which are more heavily weighted toward fixed-income products. In this writer's judgment the distribution mechanism, for the reasons mentioned above, has become more automatic and impersonal, rendering it ill-equipped to stem the tide of disillusionment should mutual funds continue to fail to meet investor expectations, which likely remain higher than what might be thought justified, buoyed by the lingering belief that whatever goes down must come back up—reinforced once again in 2003. When an investor's confidence flags, and when there is no human being whose name you know on the other end of the phone line to reassure, emotions sometimes overcome the rational decision-making process. Additionally, as for direct sales, it has long been understood that mutual funds are not bought, they are sold. Direct-sale distribution is the costliest alternative, and pricing pressures mentioned below play havoc with this important, albeit shrinking, channel.

More 'Barbarians at the Gate'

Not altogether unlike the 1920s or the 1960s, the mutual-fund barbarians are once again storming the gate—in the historical context an ominous sign indeed. (The apparent 40-year cycles are no doubt coincidental, unless four decades represents the time span required for a new generation of sheep, heedless of history's tutorial, to huddle together in a stupor, ready to be shorn.) Scandalous behavior, likely to be emblematic of the naughty '90s, metastasized to the mutual-fund industry, which has been largely without blemish since the late 1920s, as the malfeasance witch-hunt continues. Let us not overlook, simply because of the order of magnitude (or insult the memories of old-timers such as the writer), the "go go" 1960s when Bernie Cornfeld and the other mendacious mutual-fund managers ran recklessly wild, and sullied, with understandable consequences, the industry's good name.

Parenthetically, *Barron's* learned and lettered editor, Alan Abelson, opined recently on the oxymoronic self-righteous political response as big and small funds alike were "splattered by scandal, featuring fine, upright fiduciaries who scalped an eighth here and an eighth there from their own shareholders. And politics was transformed from a cruddy business into a poisonous one. Congress, whose resemblance to a deliberative body has always been accidental, more and more has come to resemble a sack of spitting cats." An investigation carried out ostensibly to uncover unethical or even illegal activities, but actually used to further political agendas, can become uncontrollably ugly—like some episodes of aggravated crowd behavior. Joining the chorus with moral indignation and a proposal for swift justice, the Investment Company Institute president in November "Fink-ed" on his minions, whom he legitimized with lavish praise only a few paragraphs above, as he doubtless feigned disgust, admonishing his wards with these whimsical words: "... I am outraged by the shocking betrayal of trust exhibited by some in the mutual fund industry" and those who have violated criminal laws "... should be sent to prison." He went on to caw in testimony before the U. S. Senate Committee on Banking, Housing & Urban Affairs, "I am appalled by the circumstances that caused you to convene this hearing. Like you—and the constituents you serve [This fellow can patronize with the best of them, demonstrating also that he is at least loyal to a pet phrase, to wit:]—I am outraged by the shocking betrayal of trust exhibited by some in the mutual fund industry." Yes, Mr. Fink repeated himself, word for word.

While on the surface the magnitude of the malfeasance seems to pale by comparison to Enronitis, the public reaction seems to run parallel. Pushing the limits of fiduciary etiquette, so-called investment professionals in positions of power and trust have come to treat the individual investor as the hapless stooge. Any fermenting backlash—lest we forget, there is plenty of yeast in the pot—against the very institution of capitalism, as happened during the 1930s, could have grave and irreversible consequences. As Franklin D. Roosevelt put it rather bluntly in the 1930s, "The money changers were cast down from their high place in the temple of our civilization." A more immediate concern is that fund shareholders, apparently the last to get the word, could, in keeping with their typical delayed-reaction response, vote with their feet.

The Witch-Hunt Disposition and Crowd Psychology

Alan Abelson's observations above speak to the legislative overreaction that sometimes escalates into a sordid cycle. A lawyer friend took careful notes in early December during consecutive programs sponsored by the

Subcommittee on Investment Companies and Investment Advisors at the fall meeting of the ABA (American Bar Association) Committee on Federal Regulation of Securities. The first topic was the rule-making decisions rendered by the SEC the prior week. The new rules (most of them like Sarbanes-Oxley) offer, by the SEC's own admission, a very mixed bag of trade-offs for investors—much like chemotherapy: If it doesn't kill you, it may be worth the suffering. The extra-strength dose of regulatory medicine, with history as our guide, is generally the wrong remedy to restore the patient to good health. The SEC contends that the rules must be inviolate in order to restore investor confidence that mutual funds are operating in a "fail safe" environment, justifying the heavy-handedness with the following inflammatory language: "The pervasiveness of prohibited practices within the mutual-fund industry emphasizes the need to adopt extraordinary measures."

The second topic—the proposed rules and even more onerous regulations still on the docket—look like the snarl of a rabid dog. The third topic of discussion was the ongoing litany of enforcement cases. The recent Morgan Stanley settlement was characterized by Mike Eisenberg, the SEC's deputy general counsel, as the most important case, comparing the Canary Capital settlement with the New York attorney general's office as a "wake up" call similar to the fraudulent behavior at, perish the thought, WorldCom. Mr. Eisenberg, according to my friend's notes, remarked that the SEC commissioners were "shocked, angered, and surprised" at the depth and breadth of venality in the mutual-fund industry. Posturing? Perhaps ...

What's Next?

Certainly by now you are wondering about the purpose behind the preceding history lesson. For most of the last 20 years the mutual-fund industry has been the ever-burgeoning channel through which billions (and later several trillions) of dollars have found their way from the savings accounts and the money-market funds of individual investors into the equity markets, many of them from the much ballyhooed Baby Boomers. As entrenched as this phenomenon is, nothing in the business and financial annals would suggest that it cannot be slowed or even reversed. In fact, in this writer's opinion the burden of proof rests with the naysayers. Affection with the stock market that rising prices propagate, as expressed by the weed-like growth of mutual funds, is often followed by disaffection when prices retrench.

Not only are investors likely to exit, but close on their heels will be the funds themselves. Recently the spotlight of regulatory revulsion has focused on the heretofore well-camouflaged and lucrative economics of the mutual-fund industry. Unbeknownst to most lay investors, fees average about 1.48% of assets on stock funds, according to Lipper. While New York Attorney General Eliot Spitzer and the SEC are squabbling about whether fees should be reduced by edict or market forces, respectively, the near certainty of increased fee transparency in a possible low-return environment is likely to give rise to aggressive price competition as fund-management companies grapple with one another to hang onto the assets of disenchanted investors.[62] Fund misconduct and performance results that have left disillusioned investors wondering what happened to the "experts" who are going to lead them to the Promised Land may be the big first step toward commoditizing the industry. Under that scenario, deteriorating economics will drive the weaker players out of an industry teeming with overcapacity. As for the pace, "batten down the hatches" if the ride we're experiencing is not a new bull market. Later you'll read that one man's bust is another's bonanza. Disaffection with mutual funds may well provide MCM with the best risk-adjusted investment environment we've seen in years.

The Great Abdication of Fiduciary Responsibility: the Defined-Contribution Plan

Mutual funds, possibly unwittingly but nonetheless concurrently, have played an important role in another subtler, and therefore less-publicized (but no less ignoble), activity. The proliferation of funds coincided neatly with what this writer considers an abdication of corporate fiduciary responsibility by shifting investment retirement plan decision making from the knaves in the boardroom to the naïve on the factory floor; a.k.a. the "dumbing down" of the investment process. To be sure, most boards simply went along with the crowd, as unacceptable an excuse as that given by the funds that chased the *dot.con* (a book worth reading, by the way) craze right into ethereal cyberspace. If corporate boards of directors cannot be expected to lead rather than follow, who, pray tell, will be the keeper of the gate? Is there a higher corporate authority of which we're unaware? Perhaps with malice aforethought, mutual-fund promoters trumpeted the illusory virtues of the opportunity to control one's own destiny when surely those who were of sound mind must have known it was doomed from the start. Having been

---

62 The first shot in a potential management-fee price war was fired by industry behemoth Fidelity in August 2004. Acknowledging that equity index funds are a commodity, Fidelity lowered fees on the $40 billion invested in its equity index-funds to 0.10%, down from a range of 0.19% to 0.47%. This salvo was aimed squarely at Vanguard, the reigning index-fund king with around $300 billion invested in index funds alone. Surprisingly, Vanguard has not returned fire. The flagship Vanguard 500 Index Fund has held its management fee at 0.18%, almost double Fidelity's fee.

listening and watching for 35-plus years, the undersigned is convinced that the vast majority of participants in company-sponsored 401(k) plans are not, and likely will not be, prepared to make informed judgments about how their retirement assets should be allocated. Furthermore, there doesn't appear to be a practical and realistic solution to the problem.

Before the 401(k) plan came along, the corporate pension plan, aided by Social Security since the 1930s, was the primary means by which corporations did their patriarchal, post-retirement duty toward those employees who had served their companies long and well. Defined-benefit plans, like Social Security or an extra blanket on a cold night, helped reduce the anxiety about how employees were going to maintain some semblance of their former standard of living after the Friday paychecks stopped. The companies met their contractual obligation to dedicated workers by segregating and investing funds from operations. In a not entirely ironic twist, poorer-than-expected investment performance obligated many companies to cough up more money to meet their contractual commitments. The pension system was slow in reacting to the inflationary debasing of the purchasing power of the dollar in the 1960s and 1970s. In all likelihood, the seed of the defined-contribution plan was planted and grew out of the stark realization that corporations would have to bear much more of the cost of maintaining viable defined-benefit plans than they had originally anticipated. The twofold culprit: overestimating investment returns and underestimating the escalation in wage and benefit costs. Defined-contribution plans, whereby the corporation's responsibility is front-end-loaded, assuaged the nervous Nellies and corporate executives of the fear of a large and unknown future pension fund liability, as well as the continual embarrassment of looking like wet-behind-the-ears participants themselves. In all fairness, they also underestimated the mushrooming future costs of healthcare benefits that were promised to retirees. Clearly it's a catch-22 situation. The industries with the greatest liability are, more often than not, the manufacturers of durable goods; their ability to pass on these costs to their customers through price increases is severely limited in the competitive marketplace. Regardless, in a very literal sense, and with empty pretense, boards passed the buck and the liability appurtenant thereto. Harry Truman, known for placing a plaque on his desk in the Oval Office that said, "The buck stops here," must be revolving rapidly in his grave.

From 1990 through 2002 corporate defined-contribution plan assets have grown fourfold from $637 billion to $2.333 trillion, net of the boost of a steady stream of contributions and diluted by the stock market losses from 2000 through 2002, while corporate defined-benefit plans grew by little more than half during the same 12 years: from $924 billion to $1.642

trillion. Moreover, that number is down more than $500 billion from a high of $2.150 trillion in 1999, leaving many pension funds underfunded. Recently General Motors borrowed $14 billion to shore up its underfunded plan and, with adroit accounting gimmickry, made the transaction appear accretive to both earnings and shareholders' equity.[63] An apparent babe in the woods myself, I stopped ranting about accounting gambits when I concluded that, once doused by the spotlight of public opinion, they would soon shrink like unsanforized fabric. Again a voice is heard, "Yeah, right ..."

Pension funds—and GM is far from alone—do not have stellar investment records. That is a board problem and, given GM's "expanded investment strategy" as thumbnailed in the footnote, is likely to remain one. If that's the case, then at the end of the road it's actually the board that's the problem. We address this dilemma below. Investment-savvy boards or otherwise, the defined-benefit-plan obligation ostensibly has corporate muscle and goodwill behind it. The defined-contribution plan has neither. One of the arguments in favor of the defined-contribution plan is its portability. It doesn't strike me as a herculean undertaking to find a way to make the funded portion of defined-benefit plans transferable as well. If the idea ever gets a toehold, competition will ensure that it spreads rapidly. Of course, retirement benefits will differ from company to company, but that's the kind of choice a prospective employee is reasonably well-equipped to make. How this affects the future growth of the 401(k) plan and the mutual funds through which much of the money is invested is anybody's guess.

Minus Two Plus Minus Two Equals ...?

The use of double negatives is considered bad form in the King's English. In the world of money, the math of double minuses is straightforward, and it sums to bad business. What do we make of the likely slow but relentless reversal of fortunes that may lie in waiting for the mutual-fund industry?

---

63 General Motors' pension fund, the nation's largest corporate fund, became also the largest underfunded plan in 2002 largely because of stock market losses totaling almost $10 billion in 2001 and 2002. Robbing Peter to pay Paul, the company issued $14 billion in debt in June 2003 to prop up its plan that provides retirement benefits for 452,000 retired U.S. workers. While the additional funding and strong equity returns in 2003 helped restore the U.S. pension plan, the non-U.S. plan still carries a shortfall of $9 billion as of year-end 2004. In a case of bad news first, GM's large and growing unfunded retiree medical plan totaled $61.5 billion as of year-end 2004. As a benchmark that might give you pause, GM's highly leveraged shareholders' equity totals a paltry $27.7 billion. An assembler of millions of rearview mirrors, the company's decision makers looked squarely into one in fashioning their future investment policy. But let's lend an ear to GM itself: "GM also plans to expand its investment strategy to include increased allocation to asset classes, such as emerging market debt, high-yield bonds and real estate, which should diversify its pension portfolio while reducing global equity allocation to less than 50%. The Company believes these actions will reduce the volatility of annual asset returns and still achieve its targeted return of 9%." This, believe it or not, is a true story. Some things never change ...

Already individual investors are beginning to exit, though the institutionalized momentum of company-sponsored plans continues, albeit at a slowing pace. What if the popularity of mutual funds subsides even more, tracing a pattern from the past? What if the number of households that own mutual funds keeps shrinking, retracing its steps from the current record 50% penetration rate (almost 55 million households) in the direction of the under 5% of 20 years ago? Stranger things have happened ...

Where the Buck Really Stops

The defined-contribution/defined-benefit conundrum is no less perplexing as noted above—and goes begging for a workable solution. In my opinion, Social(istic) Security as it exists today can and should be nothing more than an income supplement and a diminishing one that, despite its utility as a powerful political tool to extract votes from senior citizens. Privatizing Social Security, a contradiction in terms as proposed, does not, nor did it ever, strike this writer as anything more than a harebrained scheme. The Social Security transfer tax exacted from today's workers, given the drag of an aging population, will make it increasingly difficult for them to afford to single-handedly bear the burden of funding the retirement of the multiple taxpayers who go to pasture before them. Speaking of stretching, there also are practical limits as to how far the age for Social Security eligibility can be extended, the older folks busing tables at McDonald's or serving samplers at Sam's Club notwithstanding. Governmental decrees postponing retirement, coupled with a shrinking standard of living, does not make for a happy electorate.

The owners of American industry (you and I), for whom millions of Americans labor for a working lifetime, must insist that the boards we elect discharge their duties to this worthy and dependent population forthrightly, honestly, and with the intelligence and collective wisdom that is to be expected from such an august body. We shareholders are ultimately where this buck stops. Collectively, we have been grossly negligent. Paraphrasing a quote about democratic governments, the corporate electorate gets the leadership it deserves. Let there be no mistake about it, we have come to know many boards whose conduct is exemplary, whose stewardship is beyond reproach in virtually every regard. Often these corporations are governed by small boards whose ownership stakes are large. Their passion for the business, their integrity, and their sense of personal accountability are not at all unlike the hallmark of many small privately owned businesses. These are not the people at whom we are pointing the accusatory finger.

As a close-to-home example, we (as most readers know) owned a substantial stake in Clayton Homes before it was recently acquired by Berkshire Hathaway for $12.50 per share. There was loud and flamboyant debate, with lawsuits flying like paper in a hurricane, about whether the price was fair to the selling shareholders. I was astounded by the absurdity of the demonstration. Founder Jim Clayton, his now CEO son Kevin, and the board of directors—the first two of whom I know personally—were, in my judgment, not only eminently qualified to make an informed decision, they also had more financial incentive than any other shareholder to negotiate the highest selling price possible: The board owned 39.7 million of the 138.6 million shares outstanding; 95% of shares owned by the board were in the hands of Jim Clayton alone. While Ken Lay was looting Enron and Dennis Kozlowski was stealing the Tyco shareholders blind, a band of misguided malcontents were trying to take Clayton to task. Folks, when the savvy founder's masterpiece, reputation, and considerable net worth are on the line, second-guessing his judgment is not only an insult to him but an utterly unproductive use of everyone's time as well. Critics, with the full benefit of hindsight, have claimed parliamentary procedure improprieties as the Claytons scrambled to consummate the transaction with Berkshire. There is little doubt in my mind that in the heat of the battle to defend their beliefs and with the outcome uncertain, natural instinctive reactions, resulting from a sudden urge or feelings not governed by reason, may well have occurred. I have found myself in that situation more than once. Regardless, none of the faultfinders' critiques I have read has put forth plausible ulterior motives that would explain why the Clayton board's decision was for any other purposes than to meet its fiduciary obligation to shareholders. We hold companies like Clayton in high esteem.

The process to which we are referring is evolutionary. Everything, it seems, has trade-offs—including business growth. When the founder's stake is whittled down because the company needs additional equity capital to support its enlarging asset base, or the founder or heirs sell stock for a host of personal reasons, a subtle metamorphosis often takes place. In time, those who govern the corporation move away from the wealth creator toward the so-called professional manager. Sometimes that's a good idea, particularly when the progenitor is better at originating ideas than managing people. But often the successor, frequently well-educated but rarely from the school of hard knocks and betting with someone else's chips, has aspirations and a propensity to assume risks that are different than if the money on the line were the product of his or her own business acumen. This will certainly come as no revelation to the reader.

Concurrently, the size and composition of the board of directors is often gradually transformed, generally a function of the company's size, age, and absence of a dominant personality or owner—an unwieldy organizational construct for which a logical explanation is not immediately transparent to most observers. The conspicuous political correctness and politely perfunctory deliberations are often little more than empty pretense at some Fortune 500 companies—fertile ground, it would appear, for corruption to take root. A domineering CEO sometimes emerges when the system of checks and balances is structurally weak. In the *Essays on Freedom and Power*, Lord Acton wrote late in the 19th century that "Those in possession of absolute power can not only prophesy and make their prophecies come true, but they can also lie and make their lies come true." He is better known for his maxims on the abuse of power largely within the realm of politics, though it seems reasonable to apply them to concentrations of power in business as well: "Power tends to corrupt and absolute power corrupts absolutely." Although the thought does not end there, that's where the quotation is usually concluded, and perhaps for good reason ... What remains is provocative and leaves us feeling a bit uneasy: "Great men are almost always bad men, even when they exercise influence and not authority: still more when you superadd the tendency or the certainty of corruption by authority." The quote was included not because I submit it as an incontrovertible truth, but because it just might simulate some interesting dinner-table conversation!

Needless to say, the kind of company described immediately above where accountability is questionable is where the risks of mismanagement, and perhaps corporate misconduct, are the greatest. Where necessary, we shareholders must redefine how and for whom our boards work, which will initially entail purging the deadbeats and deadwood from the boardrooms. I would be so bold as to conjecture that more than half the people who fill board seats at America's public corporations add only one thing: extra expense with no offsetting contribution. Worse even than that, a few bad apples can have a deleterious effect on the whole bunch.

If you find this subject interesting, I strongly suggest you download the 2002 Berkshire Hathaway (berkshirehathaway.com) annual report's 20-page chairman's letter and read pages 15–18. Granted, Berkshire may be the gold standard, but by grasping the meaning of the company's 2002 chairman's letter you will have some idea of how far off course much of U.S. corporate culture has strayed. Warren Buffett has served on many boards over the years and offers a disconcertingly frank assessment of how they function in real life. Stealing some of Buffett's thunder, other corporations could follow Berkshire's lead and make the strongest statement possible about their attitude toward corporate integrity by simply doing away with directors' and officers' liability insurance. Under that scenario, those left standing—surely small in number—would be standing tall. It'll never happen because there are at least 20 parasites with nefarious conflicts to every Hank Reardon (the capitalist's capitalist from Ayn Rand's *Atlas Shrugged*). If it did, we could say *sayonara* to Sarbanes-Oxley and a truckload of other burdensome and ill-conceived laws, rules, and regulations ...

Concluding Thoughts at This Point on the Continuum

Despite the wandering nature of this dissertation, the hoped-for result is that the conclusion would have become self-evident by now. The confluence of structural forces that gave rise to the great bull market did not appear overnight and their unwinding, unless we're in a most unlikely "new era" where prices remain permanently elevated above value, will likely be prolonged as well. The behavioral forces that amplified the advance are apt to cause the pendulum to swing farther than it might have under that scenario. We have no rational choice but to conclude, therefore, that we are dangerously far from investment bliss on the aforementioned continuum.

Lest you throw up your hands in dismay, please be comforted in the knowledge that through the interaction of supply and demand, the free markets are a self-correcting mechanism, constantly adjusting to new realities. Just as mushrooming demand begat an ever-increasing supply that in its own time helped sound the death knell for the Bubble, shrinking demand will just as surely quell supply. The next chapter in the ever-changing book on the history of capital markets may be the emergence of a recycled class of assets that will temporarily dethrone equities as the king of the hill (if you doubt this is possible, see preceding footnote outlining General Motors' prospective investment strategy), and another middleman, perhaps the next iteration of the investment company, will make a buck wedging itself in between the investment idea and the individual investor. Under that admittedly out-of-the-box sequence of events—and so far as capitalism survives the slings and arrows almost certainly to be hurled its way—the ownership of American business and industry will remain safely in the hands of individuals and institutions, and the stock market may be healthier, albeit far less popular, than it is today.

Common stocks, alive and well but no longer the talk of the town, may then sell at compellingly attractive prices relative to intrinsic worth rather than at the premium they have gradually but undeservedly come to enjoy. Assuming we can get there without too much travail for our portfolios, such an environment is nirvana for investors like us. The margin of safety is almost sure to be increasingly generous. If corporate earnings make a respectable long-term showing, it could be the best of investment worlds. We are in agreement with Sir John Templeton who used to say he liked pessimism because of the prices it produced.

Finally, a nondiversified approach to portfolio management, with its unavoidable (and, we might add, largely irrelevant) volatility, has the potential of working particularly well if the popular averages are either marking time or giving ground. Make no mistake about it, the strategy is sound, but the implementation is the equivalent of driving between the potholes that pepper a poorly maintained northern Indiana road come late winter. We shall do our best to make our way prudently down that treacherous road, knowing that, when least expected, springtime arrives.

CHAPTER SEVEN—2004

Introduction

What is it that characterises the thinker? First of all, and obviously, vision ... The thinker is pre-eminently a man who sees where others do not. The novelty of what he says, its character as a sort of revelation, the charm that attaches to it, all come from the fact that he sees. He seems to be head and shoulders above the crowd, or to be walking on the ridge-way while others trudge at the bottom. Independence is the word which describes the moral aspect of this capacity for vision. Nothing is more striking than the absence of intellectual independence in most human beings: they conform in opinion, as they do in manners, and are perfectly content with repeating formulas. While they do so, the thinker calmly looks around, giving full play to his mental freedom. He may agree with the *consensus* known as public opinion, but it will not be because it is a universal opinion. Even the sacrosanct thing called plain common-sense is not enough to intimidate him into conformity. What could seem nearer to insanity, in the sixteenth century, than the denial of the fact—for it was a fact—that the sun revolves around the earth? Galileo did not mind: his intellectual bravery should be even more surprising to us than his physical courage. ... Einstein's denial of the principle that two parallels can never meet is another stupendous proof of intellectual independence.

By the time you reach this sentence you may well have surmised that the above quotation is neither original nor autobiographical! Rather, it is the keynote statement of this annual message, prescribing the rigorous perceptual framework from which to view the past and present for what it may portend for the future. At every branch on the decision tree, doctrinaire logic will be challenged with facts and practical wisdom. The quotation above was extracted from *The Art of Thinking* by Ernest Dimnet, the last of many printings distributed, paradoxically or perhaps prophetically, in 1929. A used copy—it has long been out of print—was procured through Amazon.com, its tattered cover and musty smell conjuring up an image of an amended title more appropriate to commemorating that year, with the noun "Art" preceded by the adjective "Lost." Who would've guessed that the book should've been a best seller 70 years later? It's obvious the publishers weren't thinking either. British philosopher Bertrand Russell summed up the nature of humankind rather well: "Most men would rather die than think. Many do."

And while on the subject of thinking, another feature of this annual labor of love is the intention to make every effort to present facts as the primary raw material for thought. Accordingly, now that nearly four years have come and gone since the speculative fabric began to unravel and the famous millennium Bubble started to split at the seams, a number of scholarly books have been written on the subject, several of which I have voraciously consumed. Repeated reference will be made to several of them for the factual backdrop they'll provide in assisting the writer's attempt to "see where others do not see." It is hoped the reader will conclude that the outcome reflects a sincere preference for truth over opinion.

Gilbert Chesterton, biographer for Dickens, argued that the French Revolution was predicated on a false notion of "new ideas": "It was not the introduction of a new idea; there are no new ideas. Or if there are new ideas, they would not cause the least irritation if they were introduced into political society; because the world having never got used to them there would be no mass of men ready to fight for them at a moment's notice." While Chesterton died before the great information revolution, I think he was right in one sense. We seem to be slower to embrace new ideas in science—who was not skeptical of the round-earth proposition that Columbus set out to prove?—than reworked variations on old ideas in finance, which we often embrace with reckless abandon. In fact, it is this story of the repetitious reincarnation of financial fancy that is both the essence of this report and the nub of opportunity for those who comprehend it ... and the bane of those who do not.

The text of the report begins with the facts of our investment performance dating back 11 years. The data will be followed by a suggestion on how performance records should be examined in view of our investment philosophy: differentiated from the majority by the fact that we are an independent, self-owned partnership, enabling us to be free and uncompromised thinkers. Most others follow the standard protocol: They measure their performance against an index, are broadly diversified, and see risk as a constant and markets as efficient. We, by contrast, seek to earn a solid, average absolute return by rational means, avoiding the mythological Sirens' call to follow the relative-return crowd. Diversification is only practiced to the point of containing within reasonable bounds the effects of an outsized random risk. Believing that risk and return are inversely correlated and that the markets can be both efficient and irrational (that will take a bit more explaining later), we insist on a purchase price that offers a compelling margin of safety to minimize the effects of bad judgments and maximize the results of good ones. In the high-volume, wildly popular financial markets of today (tomorrow is always another story), finding equities that are priced far below intrinsic worth—and thus offer the comfort of a generous margin of safety—is extremely difficult.

As for the essays, we have researched financial and economic history in an effort to affirm or negate the central thesis of Maggie Mahar's recent best seller, *Bull! A History of the Boom, 1982–1999: What Drove the Breakneck Market—and What Every Investor Needs to Know About Financial Cycles.* Is there, we will inquire, any discernible symmetry to the longer-term ebbs and flows of the capital markets? Are there, as Mahar unequivocally states, "financial cycles"? Next, if we conclude they exist, is it possible to draw real-time and practical approximations about when the metaphorical tide is nearer its high or low point?

Adding to the arsenal of knowledge, understanding, and wisdom hierarchy, we attempt to demystify S&P 500 earnings, in part to counter the often malicious effort that was and is being made to obscure the truth, which, by the nature of the beast, only comes in shades of gray. More to the point, there is pronounced, and equally adamant, polarity about whether the S&P index is cheap or dear. By seeking to truly understand the strengths, weaknesses, and assumptions that morph into the denominator of the price-to-earnings ratio (P/E), we are likely to synthesize the data and knowledge—with more informed judgments the hoped-for result.

We will develop further an essay from last year, using data on the behavior of the so-called "retail investor" to corroborate other findings above.

Finally, we turn to the question that is highly relevant to us: Is this report's top-down perspective at all relevant to a bottoms-up firm that is known more for picking stocks than for opining on the state or condition of markets? Are we, in reality, on a mission impossible, trying to get our arms around a macro environment so gestalt-like in its complexity that its properties cannot even be known through a summation of its parts? Must we forever be financial agnostics, seekers hopelessly encumbered by the "unknowability" of what we seek?

As an editorial aside, readers sometimes inquire about how much effort goes into these annual missives. Typically, I have responded that the writing is done in the early-morning hours and the weekends of December. This year, however, I must confess to laboring much harder and longer. Not only that, but I was aided and abetted as well by associates Aaron Kindig and Tom Dugan, whose research assistance and constructive debates were invaluable. The depth and breadth of this year's subject matter was such that no amount of research could do it justice. Having read at least 2,000 pages of text in preparation, I made the researcher's common discovery that the deeper I dug, the deeper yet was the hole. Moreover, the farther I plumbed the depths, the smaller the hole appeared through which I had descended. In those depths I discovered (to my dismay) the heart of synergism—namely, that the *hole* is greater than the sum of its parts. I might also note that the essence of Martin Luther's admonition was taken seriously—although, regrettably for the long-suffering, in the end not *too* seriously(!): "The fewer the words, the better the prayer."

Frequent references are made to annual reports of prior years. On the outside chance that original hard copies may not be at your fingertips, ☺ please avail yourself of the library on our Website, www.mcmadvisors.com, and download them as Adobe files.

Investment Performance

Period Ending December 31, 2004	MCM Equities *	S&P 500 *	Nasdaq Composite
Since Inception **	17.0%	12.1%	11.60%
Five Years	14.0%	-2.3%	-11.50%
Three Years	6.6%	3.6%	4.10%
One Year	4.7%	10.9%	9.20%

* Compounded annually, MCM data net of fees

** Decenber 31, 1993

Year	MCM Equities (Net of Fees)	S&P 500
1994	-7.5%	1.3%
1995	19.1%	37.5%
1996	31.8%	22.9%
1997	45.1%	33.3%
1998	-7.4%	28.6%
1999	18.8%	21.0%
2000	29.2%	-9.1%
2001	22.7%	-11.9%
2002	-13.6%	-22.1%
2003	33.9%	28.7%
2004	4.7%	10.9%

In 2003 the prices of our equity securities outperformed the underlying businesses by some margin. For the year ending December 31, 2004, the opposite was true. Aggregate, weighted-average, reported earnings per share of our portfolio holdings increased by an estimated 22%. Be careful, as that reported number overstates the true economic value added. Using "normalized" earnings (the more consistent measure), the weighted-average growth rate approximated 12–14%, with the difference between the two numbers indicating that some of the growth in reported earnings for several companies was from depressed levels the prior year.[64]

64 For some readers, percentages are confusing. Accordingly, let us restate the above outcomes in dollar terms. In addition, this will allow us to make several points about compound interest. First, let's look at the total returns since the bloodbath began. We'll use December 31, 1999, as a starting point. For the five years ending on December 31, 2004, a $10,000 investment in the Nasdaq composite, S&P 500, and "MCM Portfolio" would have compounded to $5,439, $8,903 and $19,209, respectively. The lesson to be learned over the last five years is that large negative returns play havoc with long-term compounding of wealth. Over a longer period of time, the differences are likely to be mathematically muted. The same dollar amounts for the *10*-year period ending in 2004 for the two indexes and MCM would have been $29,839, $31,229, and $48,161, respectively. Instructively, the outcome would have been exactly the same if you reversed the two time periods. Finally, to revisit an important theme, the above dollar outcomes misrepresent, in the real world, actual results because of the difference between time-weighted and dollar-weighted performance measurement standards. Time-weighted performance assumes all of the money is invested at the outset. Our investment discipline, which typically has us investing more money the lower prices go and selling more stock the higher prices levitate, means that our dollar-weighted returns typically exceed our time-weighted returns. In summary, time-weighted portfolio performance percentages can be identical for two different portfolios, but the dollar outcomes can be dramatically different.

Barring an economic contraction,[65] the weighted-average, anticipated earnings-per-share growth rate for our current portfolio companies for the next five years is expected to be in the range of 12–13%. Once again, we offer a caveat—although this one will have a favorable bias. As of this writing, we are in the process of selling all or part of three of our holdings that have appreciated to prices that no longer provide an adequate margin of safety. We estimate that the weighted-average earnings growth rate of those companies will be less than the ones that remain in the portfolio. Accordingly, the continuing portfolio's estimated earnings growth rate should modestly increase.

The year 2004 was the first since 1999 that our equity returns, while positive, did not match the benchmark S&P 500. We bring this shortfall to your attention—assuming you didn't make note of it in the table above—to re-emphasize the importance of focusing on our primary investment strategy: purchasing superior businesses at prices that assure us of a generous margin of safety. Such a strategy is likely to lead to above-average results over time, but certainly not each and every year.

Another issue, and a key element of this report, is the valuation of businesses in the main. As I'll note in the section "Fully Deluded Earnings," the S&P 500 closed the year at about 20 times trailing (2004 estimated earnings), well above the historical *average* 15-16 times and about 23 times S&P's newly devised "core" earnings. Just as price-earnings ratios are currently above the historical average, at other times they have been far below. Factors that influence the level of price-earnings ratios include returns on competing investments—specifically bond yields—as well as the extent to which earnings are above or below the aforementioned "normalized" levels (somewhat analogous to the long-term earnings trendline) and the prevailing investors' mood of enthusiasm or disenchantment with equity securities in general.

Although the following notion is both vague and utterly imprecise as to its timing, we feel that the opportunity set of "tomorrow"—ideally, although with no certainty, sometime within the next two or three or so years—may be more propitious for long-term investment in general than it is today. This might even be termed the central thesis of this report. However, we have

65 [Original 2004 footnote] We continue to benefit from the longest relatively uninterrupted peacetime expansion of the past 100 years and, according to most economists, no ominous storm clouds loom on the horizon. As a result, a potentially dangerous hubris is in evidence as most commentators and prognosticators seem to suggest that the long-standing trend will continue indefinitely. While we are in no position to forecast the future of the U.S. economy, we think it foolish to deny the existence of business cycles as though they are antediluvian, a relic from the past. Unfortunately, we can be no more precise than to suggest that they are not antiquated—and that such cycles still have relevance in the 21st century.

no idea whether it will be "marginally propitious," casting doubts on why we would forgo today's relatively marginal opportunities for tomorrow's, which may not be much better—or whether it will appear as "magnificently auspicious." It has not escaped our attention that you hired us to attend to such matters! Unlike flowers, opportunities to invest in great businesses at prices that imply a generous margin of safety (i.e., high expected returns and low risks), don't always come in bunches. When we see "magnificently auspicious" investment flowers, we will pluck them one by one, in hopes of eventually presenting you with a beautiful bouquet! If investment flowers should bloom *en masse,* we will be busily plucking with both hands. Either way, we expect to reach the desired goal.

Financial Cycles or Random Events?

A Rhythmic Pattern to Mind and Matter?

In the financial markets are there such identifiable phenomena as boom-bust, boom-bust cycles, or is history little more than a series of random events that we try to put into neat and tidy boxes, stereotyping and compartmentalizing them for our own deluded convenience? Turning to a metaphor from physics, is a child on a swing at the park, once in motion, similar to the seemingly cyclical nature of markets? Is the invisible "magnetism" of gravity comparable in effect to the tendency of financial markets to regress to the mean, though in the latter case the relationship between cause and effect is imprecise in the extreme? If we assert that the interaction of exaggerated supply-*or*-demand forces occasionally and, sometimes for protracted periods, causes the price of virtually anything to depart from its mean (or, more subjectively, intrinsic worth), is the opposing inclination for price to ultimately regress toward its underlying value equally valid? In the process, can it be presumed that the emotional impetus behind the pricing imbalance often fades (feelings being much more fickle than facts) in favor of rationality? Is it time and dispassionate thinking that overcome and ultimately reverse the prevailing mass sentiment that has been set in motion, pulling it back toward its position at rest, that theoretical state of psychological balance? In the process of returning to normalcy, does the reversal of sentiment accelerate such that its velocity and mass, analogous to the properties of a physical object—called momentum, which refers to both the physical and emotional realms—carry it to the other extreme of its arc? Is there a reason why the pusher of the swing always lingers well back from the center of the arc (the worn area in the grass that we who are mathematically inclined call the mean), never rushing forward but rather patiently allowing the swing to come to him? Does experience not tell him painfully that in one's enthusiasm to impetuously advance to where the swing normally resides at rest is to risk getting knocked down? And thus does it go, cycle after cycle? If you agree that the action of the swing on which the gleeful child sits is comparable to the waxing and waning flow of investor sentiment at a margin, is it also reasonable to assume that the harder you push the child—analogously, the more extreme the prevailing sentiment—the greater is the arc of the swing of sentimentality?

How many long paragraphs do you recall reading where each sentence ends with a question mark?!

If, as you read on, you find yourself open to using this simple and observable metaphor from physics as a perceptual framework, the discussion of the subject for which this section is titled will be all the easier.

The Reluctant One Steps into the Batter's Box

Switching from the park place to the marketplace (I'm thinking Monopoly, you may be thinking ... monotony?), Warren Buffett, the epitome of "to win, you first must not lose" rationality, overcame his celebrated reluctance to opine on the stock market and stepped uncharacteristically out of his bottoms-up enclave into the often ruthless public spotlight in 1999, giving his own brand of carefully crafted commentary to the concept of financial cycles. As the capitalist's icon of probity, Buffett may have worried that by not putting forth his feet-firmly-planted-on-the-ground cry for reason he might be giving tacit approval to the madness that had become the new reality. Not unexpectedly, his appeal to rational thought, a veritable straw in the wind, blew by virtually unnoticed. Applying the reasoning of Bertrand Russell, one of the most important logicians of the 20th century, Buffett's appeal was destined not to move the sentiment needle a tick, for the audience was and is infinitesimally small: "It has been said that man is a rational animal. All my life I have been searching for evidence which could support this." A careful rereading of pages 15 through 20 in the Martin Capital Management 1999 annual report is recommended [see Chapter Two]. Those pages include "Warren Buffett on the Stock Market" and "What Buffett Isn't Telling Us." Ample evidence will be found of Buffett's capacity to not only retrospectively, but also concurrently, identify "secular" (in this context meaning "occurring once in an age") trends amid all the distractions of shorter-term, so-called cyclical fluctuations. (It may be helpful to imagine the comparable and equally confusing motion of the sea: The inexorable, and admittedly incremental, ebbing/flowing of the tide is often unnoticed by the bleary-eyed fisherman, transfixed instead by the relentlessness of the crashing waves and foaming surf. Behaviorists have a fancy phrase for this phenomenon: the "availability bias.")

In 1999 Buffett flashed back 34 years to overlay a sort of biblical symmetry onto the past to highlight the sequential appearance of lean years and fat years. For the first half, from the end of 1964 through 1981, the market's return was indeed lean. The Dow Jones industrial average ended the 17 years within 5 points of where it began. The next 17 years, ending in 1999, were the antithesis of the first, as fat as their predecessors were lean, the Dow skyrocketing from 875 to 9,181, a 10-fold increase. Buffett's analysis in our 1999 report of the "why" is an essential segue into what follows.

As you will read ... Relying on a coldly rational look at history through the eyes of an investor whose unequaled record is visible to all, Buffett concluded that stocks, for the first 10 or 15 years of the new millennium, on average, would likely provide anemic returns compared with the stellar but terminally unsustainable record of 18.4% compounded annually for the prior 17 years (or even the long-run average return for the S&P 500 of 10.4% dating back to 1926). Quantifying his conclusions, he found it difficult to justify stocks returning more than 6% before inflation, 4% after, including dividends. All he knew was that speculation was rampant, and stocks were therefore dangerously overpriced relative to the underlying economy from which they sometimes become detached. Armed with that knowledge and his belief in the irrefutable tendency of price and value to converge over time, Buffett needed nothing more to conclude that if one expected a bountiful harvest some years hence, 1999 was not a propitious year for sowing—unless one was in the market for wild oats. His remarkable record of compounding wealth at more than 20% for nearly 50 years (the second-wealthiest man in the world was not an overnight success, nor did he get there by riding a one-trick pony!) would suggest that he must work his money pretty hard. Right? Wrong. Nothing could be farther from the truth. Buffett is a man who is in touch with what's important by staying *out* of touch with the insignificant, and often distracting, noise that's so endemic to the information revolution. He owns a computer—but largely so he can play Internet bridge with his friends. As for a Palm Pilot, that would be like asking him to trade in his heavy, plastic-framed eyeglasses for a pair of lightweight contemporary specs or, heaven forbid, contact lenses or laser surgery! Might eyewear from antiquity be in some sense symbolic for this nonconformist? "If principles can become dated," he says, "they're not principles." Using his now legendary baseball metaphor, he insists that no matter how long it takes he will wait for perfect pitches to cross the plate at his "sweet spot." Buffett's investment style is as boringly predictable as it is productive. For baseball fans, there's more to come.

Maybe the Markets Are Not Random?

Is it coincidental that Buffett has identified two sequential bust-boom secular cycles of similar length? More important to the present case, he uses oblique language that provokes thought but lets the reader's level of understanding determine how deep to dig. It doesn't, in my judgment, require much of a leap to conclude that in 1999 Buffett foresaw, at least in a comparative sense, another secular bust. Please reread "What Buffett Isn't Telling Us" in the 1999 annual report. While he carefully avoided any forecast, I doubt that the collapse in the Nasdaq index from 5,050 to almost 1,000 came as any great surprise to him. Although "one swallow does not a spring make," three might give a person pause. Neither Buffett, I am quite sure, nor I would be implying that 2016—or any other date—will mark the start of the next secular upswing. History is not so neat and tidy. Parenthetically, as wealth is misallocated and thus often squandered—while simultaneously being redistributed from weak hands to strong (and sometimes dishonorable) ones during these apparent sweeping cycles—it's not a stretch to argue that such cycles are as natural as the seasons. To be sure, the economy would be much more efficient over time if it could be cycle-free, but such an outcome is inconsistent with the nature of humanity ... or perhaps the nature of nature. Excess capacity and low prices are the very conditions indigenous to the bust that makes the season ripe for sowing. The wise crocus sticks its neck out before the last snow. It instinctively knows the seasons. On the other hand, booms result in reckless spending and high prices, begging those who have sown wisely to harvest while fools plant. Neither booms nor busts are inherently bad if viewed in the larger cyclical context; the same could be said for rainy or sunny days. The trick is understanding the order of the seasons.

Buffett: One 'HelluvAnomaly'

Before "slanging" (yes, it rhymes with the appropriate word "hanging")—with a title like the one above, surely I can turn a noun into a verb—on Buffett's philosophical coattails much farther, it's time for my annual disclaimer. Trusting that those who know me well don't consider me a shameless sycophant (is there a reason why I would, or even could, curry Buffett's favor?), might it be argued that my apparently slavish devotion to Warren's World is nothing more than blind imitation, showing no originality? I'll not attempt to answer my own question—or the question others may have on their minds that they have yet to articulate to me. I'll present the evidence and let you be the jury. I'm comfortable and trust you are too.

To be sure, opinions on Buffett run the gamut, largely depending on how long and how well someone has known him. Bill Ruane, among Buffett's many longtime friends and one of the original 1950s "Superinvestors from Graham-and-Doddsville" whom you'll meet in the paragraph following, climbed out onto the thin branches of the heretic's tree when he uttered: "[Graham] wrote what we call the Bible, and Warren Buffett's thinking updated it. Warren wrote the New Testament."

Nassim Taleb, in his provocative yet vituperative book, *Fooled by Randomness—The Hidden Role of Chance in Life and in the Markets*, is not so willing to buy into Buffett, whom he dubs a "random statistical anomaly." My reaction is to match fire with fire, igniting my response with statistics of my own. Nowhere does Taleb mention, let alone attempt to reconcile, the six-sigma records of the other "Superinvestors from Graham-and-Doddsville," all nine of whom studied under Benjamin Graham at Columbia in the early 1950s. In a speech at the University in 1984, Buffett turned to statistics himself to refute the generally held claim that his performance record was a random occurrence, comparing coin flipping with the benchmark-beating records of his fellow superinvestors as proof. As an aside, I was instantaneously attracted to the logic of Buffett's price-versus-value philosophy years ago after studying Graham's famous textbook as an undergraduate at Northwestern in the mid-'60s. Buffett has said, "I've never seen anyone who became a gradual convert over a 10-year period to this approach. It doesn't seem to be a matter of IQ or academic training. It's instant recognition, or it is nothing." Equally important, the "Superinvestors from Graham-and-Doddsville" gave me adequate empirical assurance that I have picked a mentor who's *not* a statistical anomaly. Three of the superinvestors ended up at two geographically far-flung firms, Tweedy, Browne Partners and Ruane, Cunniff & Goldfarb Inc. We keep track of both of these fine organizations, exchanging ideas on occasion with Bob Goldfarb, managing partner of Ruane, Cunniff & Goldfarb Inc. The companies' stellar records remain intact. If you don't take the path of least resistance in this exciting and challenging profession, if you can shake yourself free of the almost irresistible pull of conformity, the logic of the best teachers will find you. As this report and others before it make abundantly clear, I never stop learning from those who never stop teaching. It's no more than the application of common sense: If I wanted to learn how to hit baseballs, I'd buy a copy of Ted Williams' *The Science of Hitting* long before I picked up a bat.

Despite Taleb's off-putting and condescending style, as well as wrong-headedness regarding Buffett on several fronts, his observation that past events will always look less random than they were (the "hindsight bias") should not be dismissed out of hand. While I think it not true (at least insofar as it might apply to me!), he prefers to look at people in the investment world as if they were "deranged subjects." He argues that much of what appears as someone's discussion of the past is nothing more than just "backfit explanations concocted *ex post* by his deluded mind." Taleb's book will sit on my desk throughout the writing of this report as a constant reminder to be vigilant in seeking to discern the difference between skill and chance.

Back to Buffett. A few years later, in the 2002 Berkshire Hathaway annual report released in late February 2003, he lamented:

> Despite three years of falling prices, which have significantly improved the attractiveness of common stocks, we still find very few that even mildly interest us. This dismal fact is testimony to the insanity of valuations reached during the Great Bubble. *Unfortunately, the hangover may prove to be proportional to the binge* [italics added]. The aversion to equities that Charlie and I exhibit today is far from congenital. We love owning common stocks—if they can be purchased at attractive prices. ... But occasionally successful investing requires inactivity.

Twenty months later—November 5, 2004, to be exact—in a *Bloomberg News* article that hit the wires just prior to the release of Berkshire's hurricane-depressed third-quarter earnings, reporter David Plumb reasoned that low returns on the company's growing cash hoard that was $40.2 billion as of June 30 would contribute to the disappointing results. The company's later SEC filing indicated the cash balance was $38.1 billion, but the comparison may not have been apples to apples. Regardless of a paltry return of approximately 2% on liquid funds languishing longingly for a permanent and productive resting place, Buffett said he was "willing to wait years for an opportunity," according to an August interview to which Plumb referred in the article. In that same interview Buffett allowed that the $19 billion in foreign currency forward contracts that Berkshire owns serves as a hedge against a dollar weakened by the ballooning U.S. budget and trade deficits. This reflects a long-standing apprehension about the continuing exportation of claims on America's wealth. "That's a long-term position," Buffett said. "I have no idea what currencies are going to do next week or next month or even next year. *I think I know over time.*" [Italics added to place additional emphasis on this unusually prophetic sentence.] The SEC filing showed the contracts worth $20 billion at the end of the third quarter. Buffett is seldom seen running with the herd—and for good reason. "Madness is the exception in individuals but the rule in groups," observed Friedrich Nietzsche, the 19th-century German existentialist philosopher.

A 'Robbing Peter to Pay Paul' Macro Policy

Is it any wonder that Warren Buffett continues to sit on his hands? My guess is that he sees both the Fed's action and the Bush tax cuts, as discussed a page or so hence, as no more than futile attempts to forestall the inevitable by robbing Peter to pay Paul.

The investment community may not have taken Buffett's words of reality seriously in 1999, but it is doubtful that Fed Chairman Alan Greenspan turned a deaf ear. And, going full circle, when the world's most influential central banker unsheathes his mighty sword, Buffett, intent on keeping his head, does not turn a deaf ear either. This long aside into the secretive world where trade-offs are constantly being weighed and macro policy is formulated is essential for understanding why Buffett, despite the passage of time, is yet loath to place an unmistakably bullish bet, indicating that we have come upon the once-in-a-generation barrel stocked with fish. By way of background, and thanks to various articles in *The Wall Street Journal,* in 1998 Greenspan was feeling intense pressure within and without the Fed to prick the stock market Bubble. He demurred, reluctant to second-guess millions of investors on the right value for stock prices. Moreover, it is believed he was concerned that permanently ending a bubble required rates so high they'd also wreck the economy. Those who think Greenspan's job includes direct intervention to rescue investors from their periodic episodes of lunacy have studied neither the man nor his job description.

The Bubble began to deflate—perhaps too many people had taken the English fairy tale "Jack and the Beanstalk" literally—in the spring of 2000. According to *The Journal*:

> When the economy weakened, the Fed cut rates sharply, following Greenspan's analysis of what the Fed did wrong in 1929. It cut rates twice in January 2001 and five times more through August. After the September 11 attacks, it cut four more times, and did so again in 2002 after corporate scandals undermined investor confidence. In 2003, when the Iraq war and threat of deflation hung over the economy, the Fed cut rates again. By June 2003, the Fed's key rate was at 1%, the lowest in 45 years.

This time, however, debate still rages over Greenspan's strategy. For now, it appears to have worked. The U.S. escaped with a mild recession instead of a 1930s-style Depression or Japanese-style stagnation.

According to the *Journal*, tax revenue, which for 50 years had usually fluctuated between 17% and 19% of GDP, surged to 21% in 2000. Greenspan apparently didn't appreciate how much of that would reverse once the stock

Bubble burst. Shortly after the first Bush tax cut passed in May 2001, which Greenspan supported based on the above miscalculation, tax collections fell short of projections. Still quoting *The Journal*:

> By 2004, after a recession and three rounds of tax cuts, tax revenue fell to a 45-year low of 16% of GDP. In the past three years, the budget swung to a projected 10-year $2.3 trillion deficit from a projected surplus of $5.6 trillion with no prospect of a turnaround.
>
> Greenspan's grasp of economic data and his political instincts came up short this time. Instead of accelerating productivity growth acting as the main driver of higher tax revenues, the most significant contributor was the 1990s stock bubble, which produced a tidal wave of [capital gains] taxes from stock-trading profits, Wall Street bonuses and [taxable] withdrawals [liquidations] from retirement savings plans.

Greenspan also may have miscalculated the gap between himself and Republicans in the White House and Congress over the deficit's significance. Republican politicians embraced Greenspan's endorsement of tax cuts but ignored and sometimes undermined his nagging about the deficit. Greenspan has repeatedly urged Congress to renew a rule first implemented under Bush's father that required tax cuts be offset with spending cuts. It expired in 2002. Greenspan's fellow Republicans defeated his renewed efforts on a party-line vote. In a statement that may haunt Republicans for years, Committee Chairman Jim Nussle, an *Iowa Republican*, rationalized: "We don't believe that you should have to 'pay for' tax cuts." (Until I read that statement, I always thought there could be no one more conservative than a corn-fed Iowa Republican. George W. Bush, irrespective of the true extent of his commitment to federal budget deficit reduction and the presumed power of a congressional majority, will have an uphill fight in making Greenspan's job, as well as that of his successor, easier.)

The U.S. Current-Account Deficit

Finally, in a speech on November 19 in Frankfurt, Germany, Greenspan joined his central-bank colleagues in appraising an increasingly important issue—the globalization of trade *and finance*. He noted that "the volume of trade relative to world gross domestic product has been rising for decades, largely because of decreasing transportation costs and lowered trade barriers. The increasing shift of world GDP toward items with greater conceptual content has further facilitated increased trade because ideas and services tend to move across borders with greater ease and speed than goods."

Greenspan framed the U.S. current-account deficit in the following context: "Foreign-exchange trading volumes have grown rapidly, and the magnitude of cross-border claims continues to increase at an impressive rate. Although international trade in goods, services, and assets rose markedly after World War II, a persistent dispersion of current-account balances across countries did not emerge until recent years. But, as the U.S. deficit crossed 4% of GDP in 2000, financed with the current-account surpluses of other countries, the widening dispersion of current-account balances became more evident. Previous postwar increases in trade relative to world GDP had represented a more balanced grossing up of exports and imports without engendering chronic large trade deficits in the United States, and surpluses among many other countries.

"So far, foreigners are willing to lend the U.S. money to finance the current-account imbalances," Greenspan continued. "The worry, however, is that at some point foreigners might suddenly lose interest in holding dollar-denominated investments. *That could cause foreigners to unload investments in U.S. stocks and bonds, sending their prices plunging and interest rates soaring* [emphasis added]. Moreover, the persistence of bloated U.S. trade deficits over time can pose a risk to the thus-far-resilient U.S. economy."

In short, Warren Buffett's vision of the world is not as narrow as some think. His actions speak volumes about his awareness of both the micro and the macro environments.

Never Lose Sight of the Forest for the Trees

Standing amid the giant sequoias, one can easily lose one's bearings, unlike the eagle soaring and surveying overhead. As an earthbound creature, I must depend on my trusty compass. Moving from the forest to the sea (and mangling a metaphor en route), if the tide truly is ebbing, the overarching tidal wave of macro stimulus seems to have lifted the spirits of the majority, at least until (or if) it crashes on the beach. Excluding the drag of the still-way-down-in-the-dumps Nasdaq composite index companies, the inclusive Dow Jones Wilshire 5000, defined below, is at or near all-time highs. But Buffett's not buying, so to speak. Steering clear of "mindless imitation of others" has kept him out of harm's way many times in the past. How will we judge his actions five years from now? (Though it may be dated, we at MCM, along with our clients, owe him more than a debt of gratitude for the insights he shared five years ago. When you wonder if you're way out in left field, a smile from the consummate coach in the stands can make all the difference. While many of the conclusions reached in the 1999 MCM annual report were not directly attributable to Buffett, his imprimatur was clearly in evidence.)

Returning to an earlier utterance in 2003: "*Unfortunately, the hangover may prove to be proportional to the binge.*" Buffett suspects, as I believe the last sentence confirms (and made all the more certain by his interpretation of the last-trump-card-played desperation implied by the monetary and fiscal policy initiatives outlined above), that the tide has turned, that the game—like the earlier swing metaphor—may once again come to the patient, those who know the market's herd-like psychological proclivities and its tendency to regress to the mean and beyond. What we do know is that he will take advantage of the waves of investor sentiment from which occasional short-term (but presumably long-term for capital-gains-tax purposes) opportunities arise, but he never takes his eyes off the stage of the tide. His foray into $8 billion in junk bonds in 2002 and his flirtation with silver a number of years ago are but a few examples. What Buffett really longs for, though, are times like 1974 when he can throw caution to the winds and fill his plate to overflowing with bargains. To switch metaphors, those who know the difference between wheat and chaff will likely reap harvests an order of magnitude greater than will those to whom stalks (or "stocks") of wheat all look alike. The seeds that Buffett planted in the dark days of the take-no-prisoners bear market of 1973–74 later grew to heights unimaginable as the sun, as it always does, overcame the darkness—about the time the clouds of despair became so pervasive that nobody cared anymore. For those already beaten and bloody, the dog days of the fall of 1974 conjured up many images, none of which looked like opportunity. Is Buffett perhaps finding cause to prepare for what might lie ahead?

> Once to every generation
> comes the moment to decide;
> in the clash of truth with falsehood,
> all must choose and all must side.[66]

Who knows whether one of those defining moments awaits just beyond a bend in the road ... It appears that Buffett, ever-rational and ostensibly devoid of greed and avarice, has, at least for the moment, concluded that the risk of loss is greater than the opportunities forgone. That isn't a forecast—rather a nonspecific, tacit reference to the stage of the tide as he sees it. Unlike a forecast, there is no time dimension. Earlier in this section he used the same logic in explaining his bet against the dollar: "I have no idea what currencies are going to do next week or

66 [Original 2004 footnote] Lyrics from Richard Bewes' hymn "Once to Every Generation."

next month or even next year. [But] *I think I know over time.*" Money, as Buffett proves time and again, seems to find its way to the pockets of those who are its worthy masters. Either you rule your money or it rules you; there is precious little middle ground. If you're not sure, you already know the answer. A wag wiser than I once proclaimed: "Money is a good servant but a poor master."

Buffett's for*bear*ance is not new. He had not been seduced by the rally that followed his exit in May of 1969. From 1969 through 1973–74, while the bear played with investors' hopes as a grizzly toys with a landed salmon, Buffett hibernated, passing on the one-decision-growth-stock "Nifty Fifty" craze. In a radical turnabout in his long-standing policy of "holding forever," in an October 27, 2003, *Barron's* interview he publicly lamented not selling Coke and Gillette at 50 plus times earnings in the late 1990s, when (I presume) they had become so expensive that they could no longer be considered "one decision" growth stocks, even though they were charter members of his sacrosanct "Sainted Seven." Whether Buffett also thought that both companies had lost some of their long-term luster is a question for another time. As a "value" investor,[67] committed to buying low and selling high, "Buffett understood that everything depends on the price you pay when you get in" [and apparently now at extremes, when you get out]. Loosely paraphrasing Maggie Mahar, author of *Bull! A History of the Boom, 1982–1999*, a value investor stops buying at the end of the cycle, when prices are the highest. Flashing back, in Buffett's view prices were still exorbitant in the early '70s, six years after the broad market began its long and jerky 180-degree barrel roll. Again quoting *Barron's*: "While most investors are motivated by a desire to make money, Buffett focuses first on not losing money."

An Investor's Unheralded Virtue

Let us now respectfully pause to consider an uncommon trait that is common among many great achievers: patience. In *Patience: How We Wait Upon the World*, author David Baily Harned attempts to resurrect this lost virtue, one that has served Buffett so well. Harned laments the popular disregard for waiting. Most of us do not consider cooling our heels as occupying a place "at the core and center of human life." In the world as many of us would want it to be, there should really be no "time wasted" at all

67 [Original 2004 footnote] Buffett refuses to be pigeonholed by the dogma of the day that insists that growth and value are separate and distinct investment styles. He believes that growth is a component in determining the value of an asset. Watch for Peter Bernstein's comments on the subject toward the end of this section.

(my words, but think of the irony of the phrase in this context). Gratification should be instant. Images of cell phones, Palm Pilots with Internet access, and the aggravation of long lines in airports following 9/11 raced through my consciousness. Moreover, we are unable to equate waiting with "doing anything." Harned observes that what now counts in life is "activity, agency, getting things done." As an antidote, Harned defines four dimensions of patience, upon which one might reflect in a report such as this, taking a few seconds to customize the message as it might be applied by an investor, so as to grasp for one's own benefit its everlasting and practical relevance: "endurance (suffering without discontent), forbearance (bearing with the faults of others), expectancy (a willingness to wait), and perseverance (constancy)." We can understand the virtue better by reflecting on its four polar opposites: "Impatience and apathy (the extremes of which patience is the mean), boredom, and displacement (loss of touch with one's purpose in life)." A meaty mouthful, best consumed in small bites ...

While the following was aired three years ago, I can't resist repeating the astute insight of Pascal, one of my favorite characters from history: "I have discovered that all human evil comes from this—man's inability to sit still in a room." One of my mentors offers sage advice when he admonishes to "measure twice, cut once." The ratio of thought to action seems way out of balance. An investment veteran is one who remembers the long-forgotten tagline, "Investigate before you invest."

The Interdependence of Patience and Pitches

In a quick transition to allow your overheated cerebral cortex to cool down, we will take another quick trip to the ballpark. No serious conversation about baseball would be complete without reference to the two most prodigious sluggers of all times, Babe Ruth, whose record of 714 home runs stood for 39 years until broken by Hank Aaron in 1974, and Ted Williams, whose career began shortly after the "Babe" retired, earned a lifetime batting average of .344 and hit a total of 521 home runs, despite time away from baseball defending his country in two wars. Nicknamed the "Splendid Splinter," Williams was one of the greatest natural hitters of all time. Buffett, who frequently uses Williams' "sweet spot" analogy in explaining how he decides when to swing his golden bat, has drawn upon the techniques of the great ballplayers, as well as the great executives. Michael Lewis in *Moneyball* describes the atypical way Billy Beane, general manager of the Oakland A's, acquires players, along with the results his approach has produced in recent years. The A's have sported the second-best record in the Major Leagues the past four years (just one win behind the Seattle Mariners), with salaries a mere one-third of what George Steinbrenner, an obvious proponent of "financial determinism," has been paying the New York Yankees. Beane learned the secret of why so many rich men cannot buy success in baseball: "In professional baseball it still matters less how much money you have than how you spend it." In Buffett's league, having too much money actually reduces the likelihood of outsized success. (Beane is Buffett in baseball cap and spikes.) That Buffett takes the mound to throw out the first pitch at Omaha's Rosenblatt Stadium, home of the AAA Omaha Royals, before each year's Berkshire annual meeting is perhaps more symbolic than it appears at first blush.

In any event, Buffett was selected as the leadoff "hitter" because he is the investor's equivalent of Babe Ruth and Ted Williams, rolled into one. (It also doesn't hurt that he, Walter Scott, and the Union Pacific Railroad own the team!) Taking what appears to be a reasonable swing at an old adage, if you really want to learn how to hit a baseball, don't start by asking a rookie. In fact, avoid a rookie even if you have no alternative. Bad advice is worse than no advice at all. On the practical side, unlike any others to follow, Buffett doesn't sell advice but rather takes his own, for which he is in every sense accountable. His batting average is measured with the same precision as Williams'. He is the spirit and soul of Berkshire Hathaway—the storied history of the name even implying that in the right hands a silk purse can come from a sow's ear ("He that hath a will *hath a way*")—a holding company with some $190 billion in assets, second only to General Electric in that metric. Since the mid-'60s Buffett has allocated an ever-growing capital base with unparalleled skill and unequaled results. His 31% stake in Berkshire, approximately 99% of his net worth, is invested at absolute parity with outsiders, such as you and me.

Buffett's salary, so paltry as to make him unworthy of an invitation for membership to any CEOs club, is $100,000. Perhaps even more off-putting to members of the club is that he would be, to inject a Buffett aphorism, as out of place as a "belch in the boardroom." Having never received a bonus or a stock option, what possibly could he contribute to the boardroom blather? Buffett exudes integrity in a business world where duplicity, incrementally but insidiously, has become the *de facto* standard. From my perspective, what makes him so unique is his willingness to share his wisdom with all who will listen, his sagacity so valuable that were he not incredibly charitable with his most valuable asset, people would pay a king's ransom to sit at his feet. Figuratively, we do. Each year a growing throng of us, a standing-room-only 19,500 or so last May, make the pilgrimage to Omaha to soak up the folksy, commonsense wisdom that is so deeply ingrained in the mental framework of Buffett and his sidekick, Charlie Munger, that it flows effortlessly and consistently as they subtly use six hours of questions from shareholders as a springboard to expound on their philosophy. It's like a Little Leaguer having Ted Williams as a coach. Buffett is, no fizz intended, the "Real Thing."

What About Other Major-League Iconoclasts?

While admittedly stepping down a rung on the credibility ladder, I have chosen not to neglect the facts, and opinions, of several admittedly self-selected independent thinkers whom I respect, but whose batting averages are not as well-known as I continue to zero in on the controversial issue raised by the title of this section: "Financial Cycles or Random Events?" An erudite maverick, Marc Faber, whose contrarian philosophy I largely embrace, warns investors when worldwide investment themes have become widely accepted and are, therefore, highly priced and risky.[68] He, meanwhile, continuously and assiduously searches for opportunities in unloved and depressed markets. While most of us are just waking up to the sleeping giant, Hong Kong-based Faber is way ahead of us on the curve: He has been managing money for wealthy Chinese investors for years.

Faber, like Buffett, finds secular-cycle significance in the following 80-year chart depicting the relationship between GDP and the market value of all publicly traded securities. Applied to an individual company, it would equate to the market-price-to-sales-per-share ratio, a rough and ragged secondary valuation technique. If you return to our Website, you'll find the same chart on page 23 in the 2001 annual report, which first appeared in a November 22, 1999, *Fortune* article penned by Buffett [it also appears in Chapter Four of this book]. Faber offers the graphic as a "simple quantitative antidote that investors can administer to neutralize their often emotional 'availability bias' assessment of the future."

---

68 Generally, I am most comfortable with investors where our shared fundamental beliefs include the positive correlation between price and risk, as well as the negative correlation between risk and return. "One of the many unique and advantageous aspects of value investing is that the larger the discount from intrinsic value, the greater the margin of safety and the greater potential return when the stock price moves back to intrinsic value. Contrary to the view of modern portfolio theorists that increased returns can only be achieved by taking greater levels of risk, value investing is predicated on the notion that increased returns are associated with a greater margin of safety, i.e., lower risk." Thus saith the partners of Tweedy Browne, who grew up in Graham-and-Doddsville.

Market Cap vs. GNP 12/31/24 – 12/31/03
Consensus Forecast for 12/31/2003

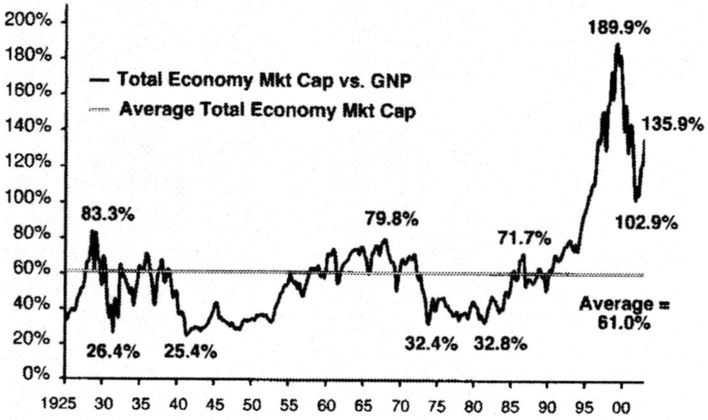

Source: Blue Chip Econometric Detail Consensus Forecast, NYSE, NASDAQ, AMEX, BEA

Total Credit Market Debt
(All Sectors) as % of U.S. GDP

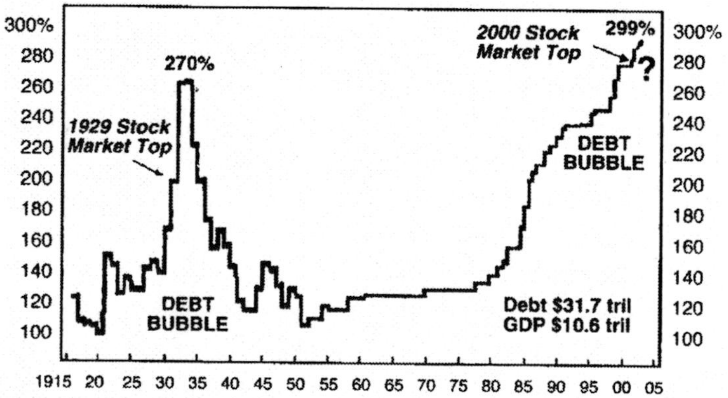

"When we are living on this much borrowed money, we are also living on borrowed time." — Paul Volcker, Federal Reserve Chairman, 1979-1986

Source: St. Louis Federal Reserve, FRED II, BEA

Source: *Outstanding Investors Digest*, April 30, 2004

By adding a second and complementary chart, along with using the same denominator, GDP, Faber compares total debt outstanding to the economy's capacity to service it. Using both tools, he points out the fundamental difference between what he describes as a "real economy" in 1982 and what he sees as the "financial economy" of today. In a real economy, the debt and equity markets as a percentage of GDP are small and their principal function is to serve as the conduit through which savings flow into investments. In a financial or easy-money economy (often encouraged by both low-cost equity and debt capital), the total market value of the equity market is far larger than GDP—and not only channels financial resources into economic investments, but the massive overflow gives rise to colossal speculative bubbles. Faber observes that malinvestments do occasionally occur in a real economy, but they are infrequent and their impact relatively insignificant. Certainly in 1982 the cost of both debt and equity capital was so high as to make most projects funded thereby appear conspicuously imprudent. Incidentally, given Federal Reserve Board Chairman Paul Volcker's willful intent to crush inflation, the high-probability bet was that interest rates would eventually come crashing down. As those for whom I worked at the time will recall, it was the bet I then made with virtually all of my investment capital, and rates did fall. The pitch was clearly in my "happy zone." And the results were proportional.

Please examine these charts carefully. A picture may be worth, who knows, billions of dollars for Buffett? In 1981 domestic stock market capitalization as a percentage of GDP was less than 40%, and total domestic credit market debt as a percentage of GDP was 130%. By contrast, at present the stock market capitalization and total credit market debt have risen to more than 135% and 275% of GDP, respectively.[69]

We believe that the link between the two charts makes their message even more ominous. Nonetheless, as persuasive as these charts appear to be, in our profession every snippet of evidence must be viewed skeptically. The practical genius of Benjamin Franklin is apparent in the following cryptic remark: "'Tis easy to see, hard to foresee." With that caveat firmly implanted in your mind, I will proceed. Net

---

69 Careful examination of year-end 2004 Government Accountability Office (GAO) and first-quarter Federal Reserve data indicates total U.S. debt outstanding of approximately $29.5 trillion. In order to avoid double counting, domestic financial companies (approximately $12 trillion) are not included. Also excluded is the GAO's calculation of the present value of Social Security and Medicare obligations, which are, respectively, $12.5 trillion and $24.6 trillion. While the Social Security and Medicare obligations are real at this point, they can be legislatively reduced at the will of Congress. We find those obligations noteworthy but, because they are not hard numbers, inappropriate to include in the total debt figures. The Dow Jones Wilshire 5000, perhaps the most representative index of all publicly traded, domestically based U.S. corporations, totaled an approximate market capitalization of $15 trillion at year-end 2004—or 128% of GDP.

debt outstanding has risen dramatically in recent years. While an extreme example, Fannie Mae, the $950 billion mortgage lending giant that finances more than a quarter of U.S. residential mortgage debt, reported enthusiastically on its 2003 results, the "greatest year for housing in America's history. Housing sales were at all-time highs. Mortgage interest rates dropped to their lowest level since the late 1960s. Mortgage originations were up more than 40 percent from just the year before, coming in at a remarkable $3.7 trillion, as consumers bought homes or refinanced their existing mortgage." Hold your horses! This is in an $11.5 trillion U.S. economy and, compared with an increase in total mortgage borrowing of just over $1 trillion between 1990 and 1996, the binge in borrowing in 2003 certainly seems unpropitious if not preposterous! Frank Raines, CEO, was unreservedly optimistic. (Prone to hyperbole, Raines neglected to point out that *net* mortgages outstanding increased by a much smaller $735 billion during the year. The net figure is the result of adjustments for refinancings, mortgage principal payments, and defaults.) Following the strongest year in the history of the U.S. housing market, Raines pours it on: "The American people are unsurprisingly bullish on housing and homeownership. Two-thirds of Americans believe now is a good time to buy a home, compared with only 47 percent of Americans who are optimistic about the economy as a whole." (See the "Run for the Roses" section later in this report for insights on how investors chase the "last best thing.") As a sorry postscript, a year later, on the heels of Freddie Mac's "managed" accounting scandal (see 2003 annual report), Mae got her Fannie "spanked."[70]

We have no idea how much debt the economy can service. Flashing back to 1982 ... If, for whatever reasons, interest rates rise sharply henceforth, certain borrowers (like some households overloaded with consumer credit-card, other installment, and/or mortgage debt) are likely to be stretched pretty thin. What we do know is that the purveyors of financial-service

70 [Original 2004 footnote] On December 22, 2004, *The Wall Street Journal* reported the forced departure of Frank Raines, CEO, 56, who took the blame for a shortfall in capital because of accounting changes imposed by the SEC and OFHEO (Office of Federal Housing Enterprise Oversight) that will require Fannie to recognize $9.18 billion in losses on derivative contracts, which were used for hedging interest-rate risks. A key issue for any new auditor will be whether the company's hundreds of billions of derivative financial instruments are valued properly on the company's balance sheet, given the wide latitude that companies receive in estimating the fair-market values of such instruments. Companies have been known to use the valuation of derivatives to manage earnings. Alan Greenspan is a fan of derivatives and refuses to regulate them, arguing that they reduce risk, whereas Warren Buffett warned at the 2003 annual meeting that "derivatives are advertised as shedding risk for the system, but they have long crossed the point of decreasing risk and now increase risk. As with every company transferring risk to very few players, they are all hugely interdependent. Central banks are exposed to weaknesses." Let's hope Greenspan is right, for his successor may have a tiger by the tail.

products, including those financial institutions that deal in the black-box world of derivative products whose notional totals[71] don't appear in the above figures, have seen their earnings skyrocket, along with the debt outstanding. To be sure, money greases the skids of commerce, and easy money lubricates the engine of excess. In simple terms, financial bubbles, driven as they are by human folly, are often the result of too much money chasing too few worthy ideas, leading to overinvestment and excess supply. According to Martin Feldstein, CEO of the private National Bureau of Economic Research (and among several leading candidates to step into the shoes of Alan Greenspan in 2006), "Business spent $4.7 trillion on equipment and software from 1995 to 2000, 37% more than the prior six-year period. Now [2003] utilization rates of this beefed-up capacity are the lowest in 20 years." Add telecommunications and certain regional housing markets (try to reconcile the aforementioned explosion in Fannie Mae originations above with underlying household formation growth), and you begin to get the picture.

Lest we become too enamored with money—and the grand profits that can be earned by its changers—it's helpful to remember that it is also the ultimate commodity. There is very little room for differentiation in the long run. As for commercial banks in general, their history is resplendent with the uncanny capacity to play "follow the loser," mindlessly jumping from one folly to the next. After years of miscues, have they finally seen the light? I wouldn't take that bet if the odds were 10 to 1!

If debt as a percentage of GDP should eventually shrink—which we think is probable, though we wouldn't begin to speculate about when—financial-

71 [Original 2004 footnote] According to FDIC data, of the $71 trillion in derivatives outstanding early last year, 86% were interest-rate contracts. The remaining 14% of the derivatives in the mentioned FDIC study are foreign-exchange contracts and equity, commodity, and other contracts. Approximately 96% of derivative contracts are transacted through commercial banks. The dealer J.P. Morgan Chase Bank is by far the biggest player, representing more than half the market. [Parenthetically, even more striking is the growth and use of derivatives globally. According to the Bank for International Settlements' 75th annual report, published in Basel, Switzerland, June 2005, the notional value of derivatives outstanding at year-end was $320 trillion compared with $199 trillion the prior year.] There are three main areas of derivative activity: hedging, dealing, and speculating. For example, hedging is done by businesses to limit their risk exposure to interest-rate changes. Dealing is the market making by banks to earn fees on derivative contracts and provide the market for businesses to hedge or speculate. Speculation is the entry into a derivative contract without some or all of the offsetting components that are in hedging contracts. Derivatives are basically big bets made with heretofore unattainable leverage—and in amounts that are simply astounding, even to financially savvy mindsets. They expose not only the holders of the derivatives contracts to the risk, but the dealer banks as well if the holders default (counter-party risk). The LTCM (Long-Term Capital Management) crisis resulted from the unexpected defaults of Russia, and the holders of the derivatives related to those defaults experienced cascading losses, resulting in defaults and counter-party defaults. Life, however, is too serious to be taken seriously, so let's end with a smile. Bob Rubin, former Wall Street banker who served as Secretary of the Treasury under Bill Clinton, assumed the Clintonesque vernacular with ease as he explained the difficulty in protecting oneself against the unexpected. "Condoms aren't completely safe," he said. "A friend of mine was wearing one and got hit by a bus."

sector earnings are almost certain to decline as a percentage of S&P 500 earnings as well. And here's the connection. With stock prices currently at a ratio of 136% of GDP, they might become obscenely expensive without the support of unsustainable earnings from the financial sector, *ceteris paribus*. It would appear that a sharp decline in either of these GDP ratios (debt or equity) could have a communicable and sympathetic effect on the other.

Notes another seasoned observer: "There have only been three times in the last 80 years where all elements of the stock market, the economy and debt structure have come together like they have today." Others are not so circumspect. Frederick J. Sheehan, in his bold and brash "An Investor's Manifesto," pointedly presents the nightmare scenario. "We are living at the long end—if 'end' it is—of gross financial imbalances. Most people don't understand this, or won't acknowledge it. This fog of extremity and perplexity is a financial maelstrom that has been building for a generation." We don't attempt to forecast the unknowable, nor should we discount it offhandedly as though it were not a possibility, however remote. Will we look back 10 years from now and call this the "perfect storm"?

The force behind secular cycles that can last for years seems always to be the same: human nature. Secular bull and bear cycles begin slowly because there is always a disposition in people's minds to think the existing conditions will be permanent. With this paragraph we segue into John Kenneth Galbraith's theory on cycles that is based more on the emerging science of "behavioral economics."

A Short History of Financial Euphoria

Galbraith's satirical wit makes this Canadian-born economist enjoyable to read. *The Great Crash, 1929*, considered the definitive work in some circles on the economic devastation of 75 years ago (and never out of print, thanks to new speculative episodes that would bring it back to the public's attention), has been helpful, along with other books, including *Security Analysis* (photographic reprint of the 1934 edition) and *Benjamin Graham: The Memoirs of the Dean of Wall Street*, both quoted extensively in earlier annual reports. Graham penned his remarkable tome while in the thick of battle, when the lingering pain from the slings and arrows were the measure of his defeat—and when absolution was nowhere to be found. His intellectual detachment, his ability to rationally assess the damage and identify its proximate causes (all the while almost mortally wounded financially and deeply distraught emotionally) demonstrated extraordinary will and self-control.

Galbraith, less a warrior and more a historian, waited 20-plus years until the dust had settled. By then the public, roundly chastised, finally wanted answers. He wrote *The Great Crash* in the 1950s, whereas his *A Short History of Financial Euphoria*, published in 1990 (with a second edition in 1994), used the extravagant '80s as a chance to revisit the inevitability of recurring episodes of financial euphoria. Prime malefactors to whom Galbraith referred—complete with accounts of their shameful falls from grace—were junk-bond king Michael Milken; Donald Trump, gambling's Tower of Babel (whose greatest virtue is chutzpah and greatest vice, bad hair); and Canadian real estate moguls Robert Campeau and the Reichman brothers, not to be confused with Rock 'n' Roll Hall of Famers the Righteous Brothers, whose "You've Lost That Lovin' Feeling" holds the distinction of being the most-played song in the history of radio. Wisdom is often found in the strangest places. Investors would be well-advised to listen to the simple, six-note opening line "You never close your eyes ..." Though written for the '80s, Galbraith's observations were inadvertently prophetic and poignant for the decade to follow.

More inclined toward pragmatism than prophecy, Galbraith was leery of the image that a seer rubbing a crystal ball conveyed. "There are, however, few matters on which such a warning is less welcomed," he wrote. "In the short run, it will be said to be an attack, motivated by either deficient understanding or uncontrolled envy, on the wonderful process of enrichment. More durably, it will be thought to demonstrate a lack of faith in the inherent wisdom of the market itself." Galbraith recounted how Paul Warburg, a founder of the Federal Reserve System, and investment author Roger Babson were vehemently criticized in the 1920s; the reactions from the investment public were bitter, even vicious, regarding Warburg and Babson's warnings of ultimate collapse and depression if the speculation continued unabated in the late '20s.

Galbraith warned that investors must resist two compelling forces if they are to avoid speculative manias, of which the late 1990s surely qualifies: "One, the powerful personal interest that develops in the euphoric belief, and the other, the pressure of public and seemingly superior financial opinion that is brought to bear on behalf of such belief." Both stand as proof of the great 18th-century German literary figure Johann Christoph Friedrich von Schiller's famous dictum that the "crowd converts the individual from reasonably good sense to the stupidity against which," as he also said, "the very Gods Themselves contend in vain." As has been repeated time and again throughout these reports—and to which Galbraith lends his two cents' worth:

> History may not repeat itself, but some of its lessons are inescapable. One is that in the world of high and confident finance little is ever really new. The controlling fact is not the tendency to brilliant invention; the controlling fact is the shortness of the public memory, especially when it contends with a euphoric desire to forget.
>
> The rule is that financial operations do not lend themselves to innovation. What is currently so described and celebrated is, without exception, a small variation on an established design, one that owes its distinctive character to the aforementioned brevity of the financial memory [assumed to be around 20 years]. The world of finance hails the invention of the wheel over and over again, often a slightly more unstable version. All financial innovation involves, in one form or another, the creation of debt secured in greater or lesser adequacy by real assets.

This sameness, seldom recognized at the time as such, lends itself well to cyclical yearnings, with the rhythm rooted deeply in the human psyche. Buffett points to the facts and Galbraith to the mind; both reach the same conclusion.

Riding the Train: When to Get On, When to Get Off

As the equity market gradually got its legs after being pummeled for the years leading up to 1982, the road from despair to eventual irrational exuberance had so many detours, switchbacks, and sideshows that only a steely eye on the compass could keep one on course. Having entered the industry as a neophyte in 1966 at the age of 24, I furthered my education in the school of reality, participating fully in both cycles to which Buffett has referred. By 1982, at the age of 40, the undersigned had logged 15 years of experience in the industry. No longer a novice, I lived history in the making, every day. The market gradually picked up speed at the pace of a tired locomotive pulling a full load, huffing and puffing as it snaked its way up the mountain. Later, as the grade leveled out a bit, it traveled at an ever-increasing pace as "financial news TV" and eventually the Internet invaded our homes and offices to the point where it was nearly impossible to resist jumping aboard the train to sure riches. Unfortunately, when the rolling stock reached the crest of the mountain few realized it was time to detrain. When you don't know where you're going, it's hard to know where to get off. They don't blow the whistle for that. Once the train picks up momentum on the other side of the mountain, most everyone looks back up at the mountaintop from whence they came—and not to where they're going. By the time the passengers realize their mistake, it's too late; they've already punched their ticket at a high price. The locomotive is careening around curves, out of control, ironically down toward the valley of *opportunity* below.

As the economy evolved from real to financial from 1982 to 2000, many what now appear to have been minor bubbles occurred: IPOs in the early '80s, Michael Milken's junk bonds, the leveraged-buyout craze in the second half of the '80s, and the so-called (and largely forgotten) "Crash of '87" were but a few of the more obvious examples. Undeterred, the longest peacetime expansion on record chugged along, seemingly impervious to interference from the various and sundry financial episodes, with the salubrious, long-run, threefold effect of generally falling interest rates, stable commodity prices, and generally rising stock prices serving as a tailwind. According to Marc Faber, when bubbles burst in the real economy, the collateral damage tends to be limited. In a late-stage financial economy, on the other hand, investment manias and stock market bubbles often grow to be so large that, when they come apart at the seams, considerable economic fallout follows. It should be noted that in the almost four years following the Bubble of the late 1990s, the main front of economic distress that was expected to follow has yet to pass through. It appears that Greenspan may have engineered another perfectly soft landing ... or, as mentioned earlier, has he simply "robbed Peter to pay Paul"?! If memory serves me correctly, Buffett took to the high ground in 1969, five years before the recession of 1974–75, the sharpest economic setback since the Great Depression.

2005: Mirror Image of 1982?

Another prognosticator for whom I have high regard weighs in below. Octogenarian and brilliant thinker Peter Bernstein, author of *Against the Gods*, observed in the spring of 2003 that the old rules no longer apply. Bernstein is a realist. "For now, equities aren't the best place to be for the long run," he wrote. "The long run here is not necessarily going to bail you out, or even if it does, the margin by which equities will outperform could be too small to compensate for the volatility. ... The hard truth is that the market cannot grow that much faster than GDP." Using the same data that brought Buffett and Faber to their feet, Bernstein echoed: "In March 2000, stocks were valued at 181% of GDP, up from 60% just over 10 years earlier [and 40% in 1982]. Of course, an investor could gamble that dividends would climb higher or that investors would push price-earnings ratios back to stratospheric heights, boosting capital gains. But that's not a risk I would want to take under any circumstances," making it clear that he was opining exclusively on the long run. "Yet," Bernstein acknowledged, "it would be extremely difficult for most investors to realize that 'the world has changed'—that we had entered a new era of investing: boom and bust." Finally, Bernstein cautioned against assuming that tomorrow will be pretty much like today.

What Have We Learned?

I hope you have learned from the evidence and arguments presented in this section that long-term "secular" cycles, like the tides, do exist. Although I don't think the timing of these cycles can be predicted, it does seem to be much easier to recognize the top of a boom or the bottom of a bust than it is the great expanse in between. When those heady or harrowing occasions arise, there's little else you need for making rational investment decisions than to "get physical" by swinging back to the first paragraph of this section a dozen or so pages ago. Fixate on the motion and the message of the simple playground swing. The waves are relatively random and benign, unless taken for more than they are. The behavioral impetus in which cycles are deeply rooted is discussed in a later section, "Run for the Roses."

As for where we are in the long-term cycle, I turn to Benjamin Graham to frame the perspective: "If you see that a man is very fat, it makes little difference that you are able to precisely calculate his exact weight to enhance your conclusion." Synthesizing all that I have read, no other conclusion could logically follow than that the markets are likewise "very fat." How fat? We attempt next to put the S&P 500 earnings on a justly and fairly calibrated scale.

Fully Deluded Earnings

Penance(?) in the Cuff-Links Cooler

The phrase "Fully Deluded Earnings" was coined by Jim Grant, editor of *Grant's Interest Rate Observer.* We venture into this misty landscape at the risk being deemed delusional ourselves. Grant, with whom I have corresponded on occasion, is a "permabear" who, in the '90s, willingly shouldered the brunt of the abuse from those who took delight in ridiculing bearishness, like the haughty patrician Louis Rukeyser, before he was bear-clawed and summarily fired as 31-year host of the most popular financial news program ("Wall $treet *Weak*," in the opinion of this wonk, was always the more fitting moniker). "Bear" with me, but guess who got the last laugh? Michael Lewis, who wrote the Wall Street best sellers *Liar's Poker* and *Moneyball* (the latter got a nod several pages ago), calls Grant "one of the most interesting market analysts alive."

Lewis says there's a tendency to exaggerate the importance of bullish sentiment, even if proffered by a dimwit (not Dim*net*; see opening quotation in this chapter!), and denigrate those (some of whom are first-rate thinkers) who speak to the contrary; see the similar opinions of John Kenneth Galbraith toward the close of the preceding section, "Financial Cycles or Random Events?" Why this phenomenon of human nature, you ask? To update Willie Sutton's alleged dictum ("Why did you rob banks?" "Because that's where the money was"), most of the money is on the bullish side of the street. Likewise, fabricated earnings became the wellspring of greenbacks galore for those for whom crossing over the ethical line was a baby step. Sutton, who actually stole the title for his book *Where the Money Was* from a reporter, was thereby handcuffed to a lie for eternity. Sutton was romanticized for his Robin Hood-like flippancy, whereas today's turnabout "robbin' hood," who deftly picks the pockets of his (relatively poor and, thanks to his actions, getting even poorer) family of shareholders to line his *own* pockets, does short, and certainly not fatal, penance in the cuff-links cooler.

It doesn't take a Harry Houdini to escape the chains of FASB (Financial Accounting Standards Board). By the same token, FASB can't hold a candle to the great magician when it comes to escaping the capricious clutches of Congress, after the politicians reach that fork in the road when they must choose between the deafening, palm-greasing, clamor of lobbyists and the squeaky but clear voice of reason. Accordingly, the game of deluding—first earnings and then those who relied upon them—became well-nigh-ubiquitous. In this short section, and with the help of those with whom we spoke at Standard & Poor's, along with the vast amount of data available on the S&P Website and the periodical *The Accounting Observer,* we'll try to make some sense of how we think earnings should be determined and presented to shareholders.

The Benchmark S&P 500 Index

The S&P 500 index is the generic benchmark against which most U.S. equity performance is measured. It represents 70% of all U.S. publicly traded companies. Lest you think the S&P 500 is flawless, please refer to the 1998 annual report section titled "The Friendly Brute with No Brains." [This section has been omitted from the book but can be found on our Website, mcmadvisors.com.]

Is the Market Cheap or Dear?

In the normal course of our reading it's not uncommon to come across substantial, sometimes shocking, variations among market commentators on the richness or cheapness of the market in general. We thought it might be useful to delve more deeply into the numbers in search of what may approximate the truth of the matter. According to Standard & Poor's, the average P/E ratio from 1935 on a *trailing four quarters, as reported, basis* is 15.63. Some market commentators have argued that with the S&P 500 at approximately the 1,200 level, and since *operating earnings estimates for 2005* are close to $73, the market is valued at just over 16 times earnings, only marginally above the long-term average and thus not overly expensive.

There are two problems with this line of reasoning that makes it a comparison of apples and oranges. First, while operating earnings is an important metric that can speak to the profitability of the core business, this approach essentially treats income and expenses not directly tied to the day-to-day functioning of the business as forever irrelevant to the calculation of earnings. The most important expenses excluded from this calculation would be interest, adjusted for tax effect, and "extraordinary" charges or credits. The definition of "extraordinary" has been vitiated. That's the first example of the apples-and-oranges confusion. Second, the P/E ratio of 15-16 is frequently compared with one using "forward" and not "trailing" earnings. We've always believed "a bird in the hand is worth two in the Bush." The (desired?) effect in using forward earnings is generally to understate the P/E ratio.

S&P's estimate for 2004 *reported earnings* is currently $58.63. The S&P 500 index closed 2004 at 1,212, which puts the estimated trailing *as reported* P/E at 20.7. Using these metrics the S&P 500 PE ratio is 32% higher than the aforementioned mean. Stated another way, if the S&P 500 would have closed the year at the long-term mean P/E (based on the estimate of trailing as reported earnings) it would have been 916, or 24% below the actual year-end close. Granted, we have no compelling argument that the S&P 500 should, forthwith or even anytime soon, regress to its long-term average P/E of 15.63, particularly with the discount rate (of which prevailing bond yields are a component) as low as it is historically. Yielding to our obligation as wealth managers to muse about future opportunity sets that may be dramatically different from today's, the possibility of both rising interest rates and equity-risk premiums, to say nothing of deteriorating assumptions regarding future earnings prospects, could put us in the most uncomfortable position of looking *up* wistfully at the "mean" P/E.

The reader may not need to be reminded that while the numerator of the P/E is calculated with exactitude every few seconds by S&P, the denominator—the earnings variable—is as malleable as the imaginations of those who concoct it. Going beyond the apples-and-oranges issues cited above, let's spend a few moments trying to further demystify earnings.

S&P 500 'Core' Earnings

In an attempt to cut through the clutter of the various (and often confusing) numbers presented as "earnings," Standard & Poor's has developed a "core" earnings figure for the S&P 500. The basic goal is to adjust *reported earnings* to get to a number that better reflects the core profitability of the 500 businesses, which in the aggregate represent the index. Here's the overview. S&P:

- Starts with the as-reported number.
- Reduces that number for the approximately 75% of stock-option issuance that does not appear as an expense on the income statements.
- Subtracts various pension-related expenses that have in good times often been treated like "cookie jar reserves."
- Adds any goodwill-impairment charges.[72]
- Adjusts for gains and losses.
- Adds settlement and litigation expenses to get to a core earnings number.

As can be seen from the chart below, over the relatively short time period supplied by S&P where these adjustments were made, the core earnings number has always been less than the *as reported* number. (Reconstructing earnings prior to the 2002 FASB 142 ruling on the treatment of goodwill is a task too daunting even for S&P.)

---

72 As noted in an earlier footnote, in 2002 FASB ceased requiring corporations to amortize goodwill over (typically) a 40-year period, a change with which we were in general agreement. Instead, it is the responsibility of the company and its accountants to determine when goodwill is permanently impaired. It is then immediately written down to its post-impairment value. Since the goodwill-impairment charge is a non-cash and presumably nonrecurring expense, S&P adds it back to arrive at core earnings. More commentary on the subject in the text later in this section ...

S&P 500 Core-Earnings Adjustments

	1996	1997	1998	1999	2000	2001	2002	2003	2004 Est.	2005 Est.
Operating EPS	40.63	44.01	44.27	51.68	56.13	38.85	46.04	54.69	67.21	73.66
As Reported EPS	38.73	39.72	37.71	48.17	50.00	24.69	27.59	48.74	58.63	65.00
Option Exp PS	(0.49)	(1.12)	(1.56)	(2.50)	(3.62)	(5.31)	(5.31)	(3.92)	(3.40)	
Pension Int Adj.	(0.12)	(0.05)	(0.33)	(0.14)	(2.66)	(5.07)	(5.01)	(0.29)	(3.98)	
Other Net Pension Adj.	(0.90)	(1.11)	(1.42)	(2.28)	(2.69)	(2.26)	(1.99)	(1.71)	(1.42)	
Goodwill	0.03	0.18	0.24	0.16	0.83	2.47	6.91	1.77	1.34	
Gains & Losses PS	(1.36)	(2.50)	(4.45)	(4.24)	(3.26)	1.58	1.19	0.45	(0.06)	
OPEB PS	0.03	0.05	0.07	0.13	(0.34)	(0.39)	(0.35)	(0.32)	(0.70)	
Sett & Litigation PS	(0.01)	0.16	0.47	0.76	0.90	0.40	0.63	0.91	1.73	
Reversals PS	(0.01)	(0.03)	(0.11)	(0.14)	(0.06)	(0.10)	(0.19)	(0.08)	(0.06)	
Core EPS	35.90	35.30	30.62	39.92	38.86	16.01	23.67	45.55	52.04	

As for more details, the first adjustment (and probably the one with which most people are familiar) is option expense. Reported earnings are reduced by the estimated amount of options expense that companies choose not to include in their reported earnings.[73] The next modifications to consider would be the pension-expense adjustments, which are not so black or white. The several pension adjustments, while important, are too complex to discuss here. We believe we understand the issues and recognize there are legitimate arguments on both sides. What is not supposition, however, is the extent to which pension funds, in the aggregate, are underfunded. That number, as of the end of 2003, was $165 billion. As of August 2004, S&P estimated that "funding should improve but at the end of the year S&P companies will still be underfunded by $112 billion." Returning to the subjective, in our judgment pension actuarial asset return assumptions are generally on the high side and, accordingly, pension expense is likely to be a drag on earnings for some time. As for the potential snake-pit promise of post-retirement healthcare benefits, we'll save that discussion for another time.

Goodwill impairment is the next adjustment to consider. While it's true that the actual goodwill impairment is a non-cash charge, it is at least debatable whether this means it should therefore be added to the reported earnings and, all other things being equal, increase the core earnings number. Thought of in its entirety, an impairment charge means that there have been real economic losses. Value (cash and/or company stock) has been exchanged for an asset that is deemed now to be worth less than the original price paid. To be sure, to allocate the entire charge to any one quarter seems arbitrary

73 Recently about 25% of S&P 500 companies expensed the issuance of options, typically using the Black-Scholes pricing model. As a result of mandatory expensing beginning in 2006 and the possibility of stock market returns not matching those that gave rise to the proliferation of options in the first place, I believe that options will eventually amount to no more than a shadow of their former self in terms of their importance as a component of executive compensation.

when the decisions that culminated in the recognition of the loss were often years in the making. More on goodwill later …

Apart from the core-earnings adjustments, there are other considerations in determining the sustainability of after-tax earnings, of which the following is but one. According to the Bureau of Economic Analysis, the third quarter's seasonally adjusted corporate profits as a percentage of GDP were 6.8%. Were it not for the combined effects of the 2002 and 2003 Tax Acts—amounting to corporate tax savings of $123 billion for the annualized, seasonally adjusted data as of the third fiscal quarter of 2004—the after-tax profit margin would've been a much smaller 5.7%. With the budgetary constraints that Congress will ultimately have to address, it may be irresponsible for an analyst to presume that the tax breaks are permanent. You do not have to take our word for this. The General Accounting Office said as much in a December 14, 2004, letter to the President, the President of the Senate, and the Speaker of the House of Representatives.[74]

Let's return briefly to the subject of "goodwill" so as not to slight the importance of historical perspective. The widely accepted definition of the value of a business is the discounted present value of all the cash you can take out of it over time. Cash expended to purchase businesses in excess of tangible assets (the bulk of the purchase price for most companies these days) is recorded on the balance sheet as purchased goodwill. If, for whatever reasons, the goodwill is later deemed to be impaired, the cash expended earlier becomes money poured down a rathole. The present value of that malinvestment of cash should logically reduce the current value of business. Likewise, cash expended to repurchase shares in the market—to offset options issued or to manage earnings—at prices that are to the advantage of the departing shareholder (and therefore to the detriment of the one who stays the course) also should effectively reduce the current value of the business. Not so, according to contemporary Wall Street reasoning, where earnings, however measured, are the final arbiter of value. (Forget

74 [Original 2004 footnote] "… [T]he federal government's gross debt as of September 2004 was about $7.4 trillion, or about $25,000 for every man, woman, and child in the country. But that number excludes such items as the gap between promised and funded Social Security and Medicare benefits, veterans' healthcare, and a range of other unfunded commitments and contingencies that the federal government has pledged to support. If these items are factored in, the current dollar burden for every American rises to about $145,000 per person, or about $350,000 per full-time worker. GAO's fiscal policy simulations illustrate that the fiscal policies in place today—absent substantive entitlement reform or unprecedented changes in tax and/or spending policies—will result in large, escalating, and persistent deficits that are economically unsustainable over the long term. Without reform, known demographic trends, rising healthcare costs, and projected growth in federal spending for Social Security, Medicare, and Medicaid will result in massive fiscal pressures that, if not effectively addressed, could cripple the economy, threaten our national security, and adversely affect the quality of life of Americans in the future." This is a direct quote, folks, from the Government Accountability Office. I'm not making it up.

the cash? Not so fast. Doesn't everything ultimately get reduced to cash? Isn't it the lowest common denominator?) Sacrificing a chunk of often hard-earned shareholders' equity for past sins is deemed to give a bracing boost to profitability. Getting rid of the drag on earnings from the impaired assets with the stroke of an auditor's pen gives a lift to earnings. Similarly, the downsized shareholders' equity causes return on equity to rise. No wonder stocks rise on such public admissions of past errors. This nonsense is nothing new. See Benjamin Graham's comments on "'Stock Watering' Reversed" extracted from the 1934 edition of *Security Analysis* [Excerpt 3.3 in the Appendix]. As for the earlier iteration, here follows his summary of the same practice more than 70 years ago: "The idea that such sleight-of-hand could actually add to the value of a security is nothing short of preposterous. Yet Wall Street solemnly accepts this topsy-turvy reasoning; and corporate managements are naturally not disinclined to improve their showing by so simple a maneuver" (Graham, *Security Analysis*, 418–419).

Where does that leave us? The preceding discussion was simply a subjective look at some of the adjustments the S&P folks make to arrive at their core earnings figure, which is their attempt to demystify earnings. There are arguments for increasing or decreasing the adjustments for several line items. For 2004 specifically, some of these arguments seem to counteract each other, and we would (netting them out) arrive at a figure very close to S&P's core earnings of $52. Putting this back into the context of valuations, the core earnings above would result in a market multiple of just over 23 times. You may scold us here for committing the same sin we accused others of committing earlier—of comparing apples to oranges—in that we are contrasting core earnings with reported earnings. Despite the difficulty in reconstructing core earnings well into the past, we don't believe the variance would be extreme. In our judgment, by any reasonable measure, the market is not cheap. You might recall Warren Buffett's statement: "We would rather be generally right than precisely wrong." As for us, if we are to err, let it be an error of excessive conservatism. You don't lose real money by forgoing opportunity. Remember also, as the dairy farmer put it, "To err is human, to forgive bovine."

Venturing a look into the future, we'll conclude this section by offering a comment or two about profit margins and earnings growth. First, after careful study, we see nothing structural that will impede the gradual regression of net margins toward their long-term mean of around 5%. The mean itself seems to reflect some long-held tacit acceptance of the sharing of the GDP pie among capital, labor, and government. Second, we are equally unimpressed with arguments that GDP growth will accelerate to rates heretofore unseen. Accordingly, despite all the earnings management nonsense of the 1990s, we think the historical trendline growth in earnings is the most optimistic metric to use for extrapolating earnings into the future.

As for how we cope, in our opinion, with an overvalued market and the difficulty many financially leveraged companies will have in "goosing" dividend payout ratios—particularly in light of the most favorable taxes on dividends, at least for another four years—up to the levels that support arguments of a 10% return from common stocks, please refer to other sections of the report.

Run for the Roses

Of Pawns, Guinea Pigs ... and 'Retail Investors'

> Each age has its particular folly, some scheme, project or phantasy into which it is plunged, spurred on either by the love of gain, the necessity of excitement, or the mere force of imitation. ... Money has often been a cause of the delusion of multitudes. Sober nations have all at once become desperate gamblers and risked almost their existence upon the turn of a piece of paper. ... Men, it has been well said, think in herds; it will be seen that they go mad in herds, while they only recover their senses slowly and one by one.

This passage is from Charles Mackay's *Extraordinary Popular Delusions and the Madness of Crowds.*

Returning once again to our baseball metaphor, a "changeup" may keep you, the batter, from dozing off at the plate. Getting right into the swing of things, let's begin with the end in mind. Picking up where the 2003 annual report left off, let's take a look at the denouement of (for lack of a better description) the *average* retail investor as described in the next paragraph. Throughout this section we infer that the adjective "average" modifies the stereotypical characterization "retail investor," respectfully realizing that an individual outcome may fall anywhere on the bell curve, on either side of the mean, which distribution no doubt has a large standard deviation. The final resolution of the sequence of events, almost as though following a well-worn script that calls for generous improvisation, could be stated more politely, but not with more succinctness.

It might be noted that the subject appears two years running as testimony first to the writer's belief that everyone in the know should come to the aid of the least informed, like the crowd that on occasion pursues the purse snatcher. Second, though the pieces of a chessboard include the stately Kings, Queens,

Bishops, Knights, and Rooks, of which there are 16 in all, there are an equal number of pawns who, metaphorically, represent the "retail investor." The pawn is the chess piece of lowest value and, as chess masters know, every pawn move creates a weakness beside it or behind it. The parallels abound. Rooks (also called Castles—what fun we could have with that if only we had the time!), another word for swindler outside the game of chess, are (so much for chivalry) more valued than Knights. Not all is hopeless, however. While the pawn is the first line of defense to be sacrificed to protect the King, if he survives to reach the eighth rank, he can be promoted to any piece other than a King, including the all-powerful Queen. Can you feel Darwin's presence in this ancient game that predates him by centuries?

One is at a loss to stereotype the so-called "retail investor" in terms of cause, but perhaps less so in effect. Those who ended up empty-handed or nearly so, who had little to show but regrets for whatever effort and savings they expended during the great "Run for the Roses," may fit the characterization of the effect. (Dan Fogelberg's 1981 song, a favorite with some Derby fans, is rich with irony, beginning with the album title, "The Age of Innocence." The lyrics in the first stanza in the chorus tell it all:

And it's run for the roses as fast as you can.
Your fate is delivered. Your moment's at hand.
It's the chance of a lifetime in a lifetime of chance.
And it's high time you joined in the dance.
It's high time you joined in the dance.)

As for cause, some retail investors of the '90s were artless, venturing without either plan or purpose; others exhibited a credulity that impedes effective functioning in a practical world; still others were congenitally uncritical; while many were found lacking in worldly wisdom. The crafty were "too smart for their own good by half." A share was surely greedy or slothful, failing to realize that a person cannot consume more than he has produced. Wealth, many learned the hard way, is the product of an individual's capacity to think. Most regrettably, a not insignificant number of these investors were pawns in a social/economic construct where, increasingly, corruption is rewarded and honesty becomes self-sacrifice. As for "retail investors" taken as a whole, Thomas Carlyle sardonically observed: "I do not believe in the collective wisdom of individual ignorance."

The retail investor in this drama about financial cycles is not a bit player, though in the posthumous analysis of a mania that reached bubble proportions (before its ultimate demise), he went largely unnoticed, especially in the early acts. By a series of unintended consequences—following the introduction of the self-directed 401(k) plan in 1981 and the coincidental rebirth of the mutual-fund industry—he found himself standing center stage, with a look of astonishment on his face, holding the proverbial bag when the curtain began to fall.

For purposes of this study, mutual-fund investors, as a group, are the best guinea pigs to be found. (It is not our intent to demean any participant or group of participants in the capital markets. One definition of "guinea pig" is "a person who is used as a subject for research," and that's how it's used here. In the rough-and-tumble world of investment where disciplined rationality may be the most important trait that keeps an investor and his money from being separated, the more we can surmise about the behaviors of the person on the other side of the trade, the better our chances of surviving or even prospering. For the truly patient, it is not a zero-sum game. In the short run, though, it can be brutal.) Not only are "retail investors" deemed to be among the least experienced participants in the financial markets, there is a plethora of data available on their behavior, thanks to the Investment Company Institute's (ICI) statistical and research work in quantitatively supporting the mutual-fund industry's "asset gathering" (remember the pawns?) marketing efforts. By carefully examining the data and thus gaining an awareness of this process that seems to forever migrate toward the demise of the retail investor, we will acquire another shred of evidence about the nature of financial cycles and, more importantly, gain a better understanding of whether we're closer to the beginning or the end of the run. For the retail investors who read this rather disheartening saga, may they gain wisdom as a result so that when history repeats itself they will promote themselves to the eighth rank and become imbued with a new sense of power.

While the drama begins in 1982, a prologue is necessary to set the scene. From the vantage point of today, anyone with a yen for the practical lessons history can teach will look back to that year and see it as one of the most opportune times to commit one's savings to marketable securities during the last 100 years; it was the equivalent of fishing in a stocked pond. More importantly, the rational (not to be confused with retail) investor would have reached the same conclusion—contemporaneously in 1982 when he could and sometimes did seize the moment. Stocks and bonds were so stunningly cheap that an abiding conviction about a rather understandable universal principle is all that would have been necessary to induce the wise man to throw in his lot: the natural tendency of price and value to converge (think again of the child-on-the-swing analogy). Price-value convergence? Mathematicians call it regression to the mean, and physicists, when describing the pendular movement of stock prices (thanks to Newton), note their inclination to gravitate toward the albeit vague notion of "intrinsic value," the point of the arc where they would come to rest without external agitation. Unfortunately, the retail investor was anything but rational when the opportunity arrived. He had lived through the torturous 17 years before, a long span of history, memorable for its violent shorter-term waves. While the tide, the Dow Jones industrial average, ended literally within a pathetic 5 points from where it began, the typical retail investor had been regularly whipsawed, often completely consumed in trying to stay afloat in turbulent seas.

Exhausted and disoriented, he eventually succumbed to despair, in his desperation thinking he had been rescued by the life raft of high, short-term nominal interest rates. Unfortunately, the raft had a slow leak. Three years into the bull market, individuals remained guarded, accounting for only 11-15% of the daily volume on the NYSE, compared with more than 40% in 1975, just 10 years earlier. As for household assets, according to the Federal Reserve, in 1968, when under the mattress would've been a better place, 35% were invested in common stocks, directly or indirectly. In 1989 by contrast, well into the next secular bull market, skittish investors had committed just 13% of their assets to equities. Always chasing yesterday's winner in stocks or the highest current yield in fixed-income securities, most Americans throughout the 1980s found safety initially in money-market funds and CDs, then later in bond funds. Fortunes would have been made had they simply reversed the order. Later to become ubiquitous in the 1990s, mutual funds (profiled extensively in the MCM 2003 annual report)—after years in a torpid state following the abuses of Bernie Cornfeld and his gang of scalawags in the "go go" 1960s—cycled back into favor. To be sure, mutual-fund ownership grew fivefold during the '80s, albeit from a small base but, as noted above, for the majority of investors, mutual funds were not yet synonymous with equities.

Pension Funds, Managed for Mediocrity

Pension funds, lest you be led astray by concluding that in *all* cases money and brains are positively correlated, after throwing an average 55% of new money at equities during the 20 years leading up to 1982, finally chastened, collectively they timidly parceled a relatively paltry 24% of fresh money into common stocks when they were as cheap as they had ever been. Pension-fund managers are the institutional equivalent of the retail investor. As discussed in earlier reports, investment committees invariably oversee pension funds. Committees are small crowds and, according to my favorite book on crowd psychology [despite it being published in 1895 and out of print for years], *The Crowd* by Gustave LeBon, when smart men and women combine their intellects to presumably optimize a solution, the result tends to be surprisingly counterproductive. Rather than being boosted by brilliance, groupthink has a perversely dilatory effect on collective reasoning. When a group is unable to foster an atmosphere of independence and diversity of opinion, which includes free-flowing exchanges of ideas, it often falls victim to the plague of the lowest common denominator. Henry David Thoreau turns the common into the eloquent: "The mass never comes up to the standard of its best member, but on the contrary degrades itself to a level with the lowest." We may be coining a new word, *un*synergism, wherein the whole is *less* than the sum of its parts, but this is not a new idea [see Chapter Three]. Mark Mobius, author of *Passport to Profits*, punches the clock: "A committee is a group of people who keep minutes and waste hours." Read on, and you'll discover how corporations have responded to this dilemma.

'Willful Ignorance'

As examined in last year's annual report, under the title "The Great Abdication of Fiduciary Responsibility," the 401(k) plan was conceived and marketed ostensibly to give the individual investor more flexibility and control over his or her financial destiny, which admittedly it did in spades. Prominent on the hidden agenda, though, was the mad scramble to pass the "hot potato" of the risk and responsibility for managing the assets from the employer to the employee. American sociologist Robert K. Merton's first and most complete analysis (1936) of the concept of unintended consequences helps to explain what happened. As will be apparent below, Merton would likely describe the corporate desire to cede responsibility for managing retirement assets (as noted above, the abysmal performance of the defined-benefit pension plan was increasingly becoming an albatross around its corporate neck) as "imperious immediacy of interest." By that he was referring to instances in which an organization wants the intended consequence of an action so much that it purposely chooses to ignore unintended effects. That type of willful ignorance, a root cause of unintended consequences, is very different from true ignorance, which would more appropriately characterize the plight of the worker into whose unskilled [investment-wise] hands the proverbial hot potato is summarily dropped. Where the battle-weary sponsors saw risk, the newcomers envisioned the American dream. One man's garbage may be another man's (fool's?) gold ... Please understand that such behavior is not deemed by the writer as malicious, only shirking from responsibility—"passing the buck," if you will. In the name of expediency, responsibility should be delegated as far down the food chain as appropriate but no farther. As to "how far," I suppose the question could be asked: Is the person to whom the duty is conferred able to make rational decisions on his or her own and therefore wholly answerable for his or her behavior? [For a quotation worth repeating, we turn once again to the wisdom of Albert Einstein: "Everything should be made as simple as possible, but not simpler."]

Although an anachronism in the codes of conduct for far too many corporate managers today, perhaps the following will serve as an admonition to the recalcitrant ... Not one to duck the duties that came with the Oval Office, Harry Truman stood stoutly behind the famous sign on his desk "The buck stops here" [as also noted in Chapter Six]. Of course, feisty Harry liked the hot seat! He also purportedly said, "If you can't stand the heat, stay out of the kitchen." Are any members of corporate boards listening?

Mutual Funds: There's Gold in Them Thar Hills!

The vehicle *du jour* to serve as middleman between the newly "empowered" worker and the capital markets where anyone can become a millionaire was the ubiquitous croupier, the mutual fund, offering more flavors than Baskin-Robbins, a smorgasbord of confusing choices cleverly promoted under the intuitively appealing banner of broad diversification. The "manifest destiny" of the individual was in sight. At last the common man would rule the markets—and until the spring of 2000, he felt as if he did. By 1998 approximately three of every four new dollars invested in corporate retirement plans were going into 401(k)'s, indicating a successful passing of the "buck" ("burden" later proving to be a better word). Having come from the "sell" side of the street, it was clear to me that the "packaged product," where commissions and fees in the early years were larcenous, saved the retail-brokerage industry and gave birth to yet another middleman, the financial planner, after stock commissions were deregulated in 1975.

In 1990 and 1991, money that flowed into the funds that invest in stocks averaged barely $25 billion; by 2001 inflows exceeded $260 billion, equal to almost half of the total mutual-fund assets invested in equities in 1990. At the end of the decade, two-thirds of all active workers covered by a retirement plan were responsible for directing their own investments. (Obviously, the vast majority who invested in mutual funds directly had the final say about where their savings were invested.) With interest rates low and stock prices levitating, particularly as the 1990s passed the midpoint, they jumped ever more enthusiastically aboard the stock bandwagon. By the end of the millennium, 401(k) investors had stashed 75% of their assets in equities. (*The Great 401(k) Hoax* by William Wolman and Anne Colamosca does a yeoman's job of painting the backdrop.) Blind inertia was at full throttle as fund investors embraced, as never before, the greatest stock market boom of the 20th century, even as the tech-driven Nasdaq peaked at 5,050 and began its harrowing free fall in March 2000, with 80% of its illusory value popping like a wispy soap bubble, all within two years. Apparently unaware that prices are ultimately tethered to something (is it not so in all other value-for-value transactions in which the reader engages?), however long the rope and therefore oblivious to what lay ahead, retail investors poured $260 billion into U.S. equity funds throughout 2000, fully half of which went into "Aggressive Growth" equity funds, according to the ICI. Saving the most for last, their final splurge in 2000 exceeded the $150 billion that ratcheted its way up the risk chain into equity funds in 1998, followed by $176 billion in 1999. The unfortunate and unintended consequence—widespread financial disaster for millions of retail investors—was born of true ignorance.

From 1980 to 2000, the percentage of U.S. households that owned mutual funds increased almost *10*-fold, from 5.7% to 49.6%, the ICI noted, with a discernible sense of pride. By year-end 2003 the penetration rate had dropped a mere 1.8 percentage points. Stated differently for the writer's emphasis: Household mutual-fund assets were largely committed to fixed-income securities in the earlier years when interest rates were relatively high. Individual investors gradually migrated toward equities in the 1990s as stock prices rose while interest rates were going the other direction. To put things in a broader perspective, in 2003 mutual funds owned 28% ($3.9 trillion) of the $14 trillion in market value of all publicly traded U.S. equities. That's an *18*-fold increase from $216 billion in 1999. About $2 trillion in mutual funds were owned directly by individuals, with the remaining $1.7 trillion held by institutions, approximately half of which on behalf of individuals through such company-sponsored retirement plans as 401(k)'s. As noted above, 75% of 401(k) plan assets were committed to common stocks at the peak. A complementary statistic, the percentage of long-term mutual-fund assets committed to common stocks, rose from 38% in 1990 to 70% in 2003.

The vast majority of the $7.4 trillion invested in mutual funds of all types, including $2 trillion in money-market funds and $1.5 trillion in bond funds, is controlled by individuals. Likewise, a large proportion of the cash flows going into different classes of mutual funds are largely at the discretion of the individual decision maker, frequently aided by financial planners whose models are little more than linear extrapolators. Referring to the oft-quoted metaphor from Benjamin Graham, the mutual-fund investor may indeed be "Mr. Market." For those of you not familiar with this gregarious but naïve fellow, a short paraphrase from the classic *Intelligent Investor* may help.

Imagine that Mr. Market is your partner in a business where you have invested $1,000. Every day he tells you what he thinks your interest is worth and offers to buy your share or sell you more at that price. Some days his offer seems reasonable based on the future prospects of the business, while other days his enthusiasm or fear may cause his offer to seem a bit silly. If you are a sensible businessperson, will you let Mr. Market's daily communication determine your view of the value of a $1,000 interest in the business? You may be interested in his valuation when he offers to buy at a ridiculously high price or sell at a low price, but otherwise you would be better off to value your interest based on the operational and financial reports of the business. With this metaphor in mind, what does Mr. Market look like today? According to demographic information provided by ICI, his or her median age is 48 years; household income, $68,700; household financial assets, $125,000, excluding primary residence but including assets in employer-sponsored retirement plans; household mutual-fund assets, $48,000; number of mutual funds owned, four. Half the decisions are made jointly, the remainder evenly divided between men and women. The average 401(k) account balance, excluding plan loans, was $39,885 at year-end 2002, with approximately 23% of the average household's financial assets, including mutual funds, owned outright. Workers in their 60s with at least 30 years of job tenure at their current employer had an average 401(k) account balance of $146,211.

What about the $37,000 of average household assets that were invested directly—and not through a mutual fund? Exhibiting the "credulity that impedes effective functioning" in the increasingly ethically challenged world of finance, the easily deceived were sitting-duck prey for the disingenuous. Longtime skeptic David Tice, in testimony before Congress in the spring of 2001, illustrated the point by noting that individual investors ended up owning a shocking 75% of all Internet stocks. In order to add some balance to this otherwise discouraging scenario, it seems appropriate to indulge in a little moral reflection and muse for a moment about ultimate consequences.

No Crime Goes Unpunished

Willful ignorance was defined earlier as the desire for an intended consequence of an action that is so strong and overarching that one purposely chooses to ignore any unintended effects ... to put it charitably, to reap what one has not sown. Of this ethical if not legal transgression, many were conflicted, but few were convicted. [Or, as they say in chillier climes, "Many are cold, but few are frozen."] Men and women of power and responsibility—including CEOs and their boards (the order here implying the convoluted power hierarchy), investment bankers and their research affiliates, and mutual-fund companies and their managers—willingly sold their integrity (souls?) for a disproportionate share of the spoils. (The following remarks are not directed at 401(k) plan sponsors who, for the most part, were going with the times. Several independent-minded sponsors with whom I've spoken simply felt they had no other choice.) As for those who, with willful maliciousness, have pillaged with self-enriching stock-option programs and other sleight-of-hand techniques under the guise of the doctrine of (un)just incentives and rewards, "stealth compensation" hardly characterizes the practice with the name plate of injustice that it so richly deserves. We don't quibble with "stealth," as this term befits the conduct, but "compensation" (the return for services rendered) leaves us incredulous at its audacity. In any other venue of misconduct, it would be called larceny—and on the grandest and most socially grotesque scale.

We should not envy the moochers and parasites, nor should we conclude, regardless of the outward appearance of apparent indifference, that they are without conscience. Despite this massive redistribution of wealth, the love of money serves up its own justice for those who come by it dishonorably. Ayn Rand, in *Atlas Shrugged*, points out the true "cost" of ill-gotten gain:

> Money is your means of survival. The verdict you pronounce upon the source of your livelihood is the verdict you pronounce upon your life. If the source is corrupt, you have damned your own existence. Did you get your money by fraud? By pandering to men's vices or men's stupidity? By catering to fools, in the hope of getting more than your ability deserves? By lowering your standards? By doing work you despise for purchasers you scorn? If so, then your money will not give you a moment's or a penny's worth of joy. Then all the things you buy will become, not a tribute to you, but a reproach; not an achievement, but a reminder of shame. Then you'll scream that money is evil. Evil, because it would not pinch-hit for your self-respect? Evil, because it would not let you enjoy your depravity?

What goes around comes around …

Inertia for the Long Term?

Despite warnings to the contrary, bloodied but not broken (yet) mutual-fund investors have not lost faith in common stocks. Due to the combination of 401(k) plan cash flow momentum and seemingly unattractive alternatives, savings continue to flow toward equity funds. Mirroring the market, they fell to a still positive $54 billion in 2001, then turned modestly negative to the tune of $25 billion in 2002, just before the spirited rally that began in the spring of 2003. Based on the latest information provided by ICI, October 2004 year-to-date net new cash flows into stock mutual funds totaled $146 billion, up from $123 billion from the same period in 2003. Tellingly, $1 billion was withdrawn from taxable bond funds by October 2004, compared with a net inflow of $41 billion in a more cautious 2003. No doubt partly motivated by lower tax rates, the pace of net liquidations from tax-free mutual funds quadrupled to $12 billion. Economist Herb Stein's Law, "If something can't go on forever, it will end," originally appeared in the press in the 1980s as a warning about the ever-growing balance-of-payments deficits. He was careful not to say when! As for the mutual-fund mania, I will hide behind Herb to avoid the time trap!

In terms of fund balances, the latest information available is for year-end 2003. One subset, mutual-fund assets invested in 401(k) plans, grew to $1.9 trillion, with an estimated 42 million workers in the United States participating. Equity securities represented 67% of 401(k) plan assets at year-end 2003, up from 62% in 2002, generally reflecting the strong performance of the equity markets relative to fixed-income securities. Equity securities included equity funds, the equity portion of balanced funds, and 16% in company stock. (Steve Leuthold, in the December 2001 issue of *Investment Insights*, reported that the average 401(k) plan had 39% of its investments in company stock, another frequently overlooked item on the hidden agenda.) Equity-fund managers, indicating either their optimism about the markets or their willingness to put investors' money fully at risk to avoid their own professional peril (career risk), maintained a low 4.4% of assets in cash.[75]

Portentous or Poppycock?

Based on the study of mutual-fund data going back to 1980, a couple of conclusions seem to be driven by the facts. First, apart from the growth in popularity of mutual funds as part of a household's portfolio assets, which as warned in last year's report is subject to the law of regression to the mean, fund flows tend to follow the hottest game in town. One can logically draw certain inferences about the finality of a secular financial cycle when mutual-

75 The cash-to-total-assets ratio has proved over the years to be a powerful counterintuitive contrary indicator. During the bear market of 1973–74 the cash ratio rose above 10%, hit 12% just as the great bull market began, then peaked at 13% in the recession of 1990. These were times when prices were so low that one would logically think that mutual funds would commit every spare dollar to the market. On the flip side of the coin, after the sharp rally in 1976, the cash ratio sunk to 4.5%. Likewise it trended downward during the overdrive bull market of the '90s, reaching a low of 4% in March 2000, precisely at the long bull market's peak. In the aftermath it rose to a telltale 6%, only to decline once again to the 4%-plus area at year-end 2004. Some argue that the conversion of cash to stock helped to propel the bull market upward. While it's inappropriate to calculate a historical mean, the reader should not be surprised if the ratio hits 10% again sometime in the future. As for what that should mean for stock prices, I'll leave it to the reader to deduce.

fund investors embrace it *en masse*. To put it bluntly, the behavior of the retail investor today is the mirror image of what we would logically expect of a seasoned, rational investor at the bottom of a secular bear market. Nobody knows how or when (the "if" is not so chancy) we will migrate from a fully priced, widely embraced, retail-driven investment environment that the wise approach with vigilance and restraint to one where the margin of safety is so great that, ironically, nobody cares. Well, almost nobody. The risk-averse investor who, by virtue of the boundless bargains, would be justified in throwing his customary caution to the winds. Buffett's comment elsewhere that *"the hangover may prove to be proportional to the binge"* is all we can bank on—and never with absolute certainty, only with high probability.

Second, the automatic cash-flow programs like 401(k) plans, as noted above, do not represent a commanding portion of mutual-fund cash flows into equities. Like the Baby Boomer cash cow myth [a favorite half-truth flaunted by financial advisors in the late, great "Run for the Roses," the fallaciousness of which was laid bare in Chapter Three], potent were it not for the fact that demand often begets its own supply, the oft-used argument that the cash flows into equities from 401(k) plans will shore up equity prices seems to be a late-in-the-game, seventh-inning credulity stretch. It also is unlikely that hoards of discretionary cash from retail investors will drive the markets upward during the next decade as they did in the 1990s. To the contrary, unless rising prices magically reappear to stimulate their instinct to play "follow the momentum," disaffection may result. Instead of providing incremental demand, they could become the proverbial wet blanket. Who will step up to the plate? Perhaps, as I suspect Buffett fears, foreign investors, loaded with dollars, will eventually assuage their currency losses by buying yet more of American business on the cheap? Congress will surely meddle, smiting those who will be characterized as "infidels" with a new iteration of Smoot-Hawley. After that, "Katie, bar the door ..." But now I'm off on a rant!

Apparently it didn't occur to most market strategists to compare the losses of 2000 with the mauling of 1970—in what turned out to be the first cyclical bear market of several during the aforementioned 1966–82 period when, start to finish, the Dow made as much forward progress as a jogger on a treadmill. Following the crash in 1970, the "Nifty Fifty" of the '70s still stood tall. Those blue chips would not be decimated for another three years. Quoting San Antonio sportswriter Dan Cook (1976), former NBA basketball coach Dick Motta (1978), and countless others since, "The opera ain't over 'til the fat lady sings."

To conclude with a sober observation about the uninitiated, the behavioral propensity of financial cycles can be summed up succinctly: the accumulation by the wise when prices are low, followed by the distribution to the inexperienced when prices are high. The usually hapless *average* mutual-fund investor adds another layer of evidence to reinforce the idea of financial cycles.

What's a Hitter to Do When the Pitcher Is Throwing Junk?

When 'Nothing' Is More Than Something

As an "active manager" with ostensibly unlimited strategic and tactical options before us, we must discuss an "institutional imperative" that narrows, rightly or (mostly) wrongly, the range of practicable options for many in our industry. When a firm is hired to "manage money," in our harried world it is most often judged against the standard of "activity, agency, getting things done." The fearsome S&P 500 benchmark or some other index stalks them like a relentless nightmare. When stocks are moved from prime shelf space to the bargain basement, there are frequently steals galore among the discarded—though not seen as such except in retrospect—for those few who have both the wherewithal and the mindset of a seasoned shopper on the first business day after Christmas. But what course of action do most "wealth managers" take when businesses are richly valued and opportunities scarce? They continue to swing, like the pinch-hitter in the bottom of the ninth a run down, because that's what they are hired to do. There must be a reason why most of them rarely let equities slip to less than 50% of their holdings, even if they fear the worst for their portfolios. At some point the shrinking percentage of equities (perceived as forgone opportunities) prompts the question that managers fear more than losing money for their clients: "Why do I need to pay you a fee when I can buy Treasury bills on my own?" Managers, whose fees are based on their ability to gather and retain assets (the standard construct, though not necessarily an indication of their capacity to preserve and enhance their clients' wealth) will do almost anything to avoid having to field that one-hop line drive.

Seth Klarman, president of The Baupost Group Inc. and author of *Margin of Safety* [published in 1991; some concepts are timeless], is anything but defensive on the subject of holding cash, regardless of the institutional imperative: "You are paying us to decide when to hold cash and when to invest it, to determine when the expected return from a prospective investment justifies the risk involved and when it does not."

We might present essentially the same idea with a different slant. Our long-standing contention is that cash, along with its short-term equivalents, is the default asset class. To the extent that we uncover enough ideas that conservatively promise five-year returns in excess of our 15% threshold rate, cash balances will shrink as cash flows out of safe-harbor, short-term investments toward the higher-return assets, just as water naturally seeks its own level. Conversely, when such ideas are in short supply, as they are today, cash will flow in the opposite direction, toward the default asset class. Portfolio allocation percentages are not set arbitrarily or by formula but rather by the availability of mouthwatering opportunities.

Klarman also addresses the psychological stress on the patient manager who holds cash:

> Emotionally, doing nothing seems exactly like doing nothing: It feels uncomfortable, unproductive, unimaginative, uninspired, and (probably for a while at least), underperforming. One's internal strains can be compounded by external pressures from clients, brokers, and peers. If you want to know what it's like to truly stand alone, try holding a lot of cash. No one does it. No one knows anyone who does it. No one can readily comprehend why anyone would do it. Also, believing that better opportunities will arise in the future [the optimistic bias] than exist today does not ensure that they will. Waiting for bargains to emerge may seem like a better strategy than overpaying for securities today. However, tomorrow's valuations may be higher still.

Klarman's "between a rock and a hard place" (like our president, who's still between "Iraq and a hard place") dilemma is credible, though it comes close to diluting if not contradicting his first straightforward assertion. One can vaguely see the ghost of the imperative shadowing the nervous manager as he makes his every move. Cash is like a burr under our saddle, a constant reminder to redouble our research efforts in search of new ideas that make their way through our filters. We're never working harder than when we appear to be doing nothing. When asked how he discovered the Law of Gravity, Newton said, "I thought about it a lot." There is a great, and often overlooked, gulf between the genesis of an idea and its fruition. The grandeur of the results often makes the enormous effort expended in between seem insignificant in comparison. Thomas Edison said that "genius is 2% inspiration and 98% perspiration." We're human, so we're also most comfortable being fully invested. But in that urge there is too often the tendency to anchor one's thinking in the limited opportunity set of today, forcing "opportunities" that don't really exist, like the parched man who mistakes a mirage for the water that will actually quench his thirst. To put it differently, the best golfers know that birdies come "as they will" as a result of good swings and good strokes; they aren't forced by obsessing about score.

The St. Petersburg Paradox and the Margin of Safety

MCM is a boutique manager catering almost exclusively to a relatively homogeneous group of well-to-do clients. We earnestly believe we have an atypical duty of care to the individuals who make up our client roster, as this aside bears witness. We are not simply one of several hired guns but rather see our relationship or role as more intimate, perhaps equivalent to that of a personal investment steward. Our generally 40-something and mostly much older (the oldest being 94 and going strong) clientele has certain investment proclivities in common, one of which is *not* Russian roulette, as shall become clear below.

Before it was renamed Leningrad, the port in northern Russia was called St. Petersburg. A parlor game ostensibly devised in that fair city en*tails* coin flipping and probability theory. Please bear with as we try to get you from Russia to the point! The "expected value" of the St. Petersburg game is the sum of the expected payoffs of all the consequences (which are potentially infinite in number)—an infinite number of dollars. A rational gambler would theoretically pay any price to enter the game since such price would always be less than the infinite expected value. And yet a respected theorist argues that "few of us would pay even $25 to enter such a game." If so, there must be something wrong with the standard decision-theory calculations of the expected value upon which the game depends. Daniel Bernoulli, an 18th-century Swiss mathematician, discovered the St. Petersburg paradox.

Beyond the obvious practical obstacles to flipping a coin billions of times, there are other explanations that are more reasonable in attempting to resolve the paradox. Bernoulli introduced the now well-known concept of *decreasing marginal utility*. Stated in terms relevant to our use, if one possesses $1 million, one may risk some portion of it in order to double one's sum. On the other hand, if one already has a net worth of $10 million, another million, representing a much smaller (10%) increase, is not likely to have the same marginal usefulness to its owner as in the first example, and the second player would presumably (and rationally) be less inclined to bet as much as the first.

A companion explanation is *risk aversion*. Perhaps we can explain it by examining its opposite. The lottery player and those who gamble at pure games of chance in casinos are not risk-averse but may in fact enjoy risk taking. We would consider such behavior irrational because in these games the entry fee is greater than the expected utility.

Departing from pure games of chance, we believe there is another metric that reconciles decreasing marginal utility and risk aversion for the rational, well-heeled value investor that has a huge influence on the extent to which he or she is in the game. It's the concept of *margin of safety.* Assuming the market is inefficient on occasion—not a heroic assumption for us—the greater the margin of safety implicit in a deeply depressed market or stock, the less the risk and the greater the expected return. At prices low enough, the concept of decreasing marginal utility takes a backseat as part of the decision-making process.

The environment in which we find ourselves is one, in the aggregate, that appears to offer little margin of safety. It is much more appealing for the risk-prone than the risk-averse investor. As the margin of safety increases, perhaps as the result of falling prices, the dynamic changes dramatically in favor of the risk-averse investor. We believe that most of our clients share this mindset.

'Swing, You Bum!'

To be sure, our fee structure intentionally prods us to aggressively search for ideas when we have cash, with the high-water mark acting as a governor on our enthusiasm, to check our swing unless the pitch seems headed for that part of the strike zone where, for us, a hit is most likely. If we are to retain rationality as one of our chief virtues, we must sublimate our natural inclination to keep swinging to the much more demanding calling of remaining patient, of evaluating each pitch with the idea that it's far better to walk to first base than to strike out swinging for the fences. It is no coincidence that Babe Ruth and Ted Williams were third and fourth, respectively, in career bases-on-balls statistics. While the following is an oversimplification, it helps to make the point: Ted Williams' lifetime record of 541 home runs compares with 2,021 walks (8,084 pitches went by that were "called balls"—all the while Williams was poised, at the ready, but checked his urge to swing before the pitch crossed the plate). While I would prefer using his best-ever lifetime batting average of .344 to make the point, the analysis quickly gets too complex. Rather, I roughly estimate that for each home run he hit, Williams watched patiently as at least 30 pitches he didn't like thumped into the catcher's mitt. With steely-eyed determination at the plate, oblivious to an ever-lurking hostile press and tuning out his well-intentioned fans, in a most businesslike manner he let slide by every less than acceptable "pitch" that might keep him from achieving his objectives. He approached every at-bat with the end in mind. It was diligence, determination, and discipline—not destiny—that put Ted Williams in the Hall of Fame.

Many mainstream portfolio managers, judged as they are on short-term performance, feel they must be swinging all the time. They must focus on the present, on survival. If they don't meet the relentless present demands, they'll have no corner office from which to build a great long-term record. Individual investors—or the handful of advisors, such as MCM, who are granted substantial autonomy by their clients whose focus is on building wealth—who aspire to long-term success cannot afford the luxury of impatience (though they usually think the opposite is true). Rather, they must hold their ground in the batter's box until the fat pitch comes over the plate. As Buffett says, "The stock market is a no-called-strike game. You don't have to swing at everything; you can wait for your pitch. The problem when you're a money manager is that your fans keep yelling, 'Swing, you bum!'" Even Ted Williams (or Warren Buffett, for that matter) was not exempt from those cries. He simply ignored them, though not without considerable personal cost: Throughout much of his illustrious career, Williams was pilloried by the press [and booed by a hard-core contingent of leather-lunged Boston "fans"].

The institutional imperative to "do something" does not apply to Buffett, since Berkshire Hathaway's shareholders, like those of a closed-end investment company, can neither cajole nor coerce him, they can only vote with their feet by selling their shares in the open market. In a sense, observing Buffett is an uncompromised "pure play" in rational thinking and acting. Make no mistake about it, Buffett is under a far more stringent, self-imposed imperative than the typical investment managers: to protect and enhance the value of Berkshire Hathaway on behalf of its shareholders, of which he is by far the largest at 32.7%. He is paid as a shareholder on performance, not promises. He knows as surely as night follows day that golden opportunities will appear with time, and he is content to stand, the bat on his shoulder indefinitely, until they appear. At Berkshire's annual meeting in 1998, he remarked, "We're not going to buy anything just to buy it. We will only buy something if we think we're getting something attractive. ... You don't get paid for activity. You get paid for being right." As noted above, we at MCM feel largely free of the institutional imperative, in part because we also are paid for being right and penalized for being wrong—both through our personal portfolios that look very similar to those of our clients (yes, we eat our own cooking!) and our performance-based fee arrangement—but also because our clients are savvy and understand the virtue of patience (of seeming to do nothing) and its positive, and seemingly counterintuitive, effect on long-term compounding.

As for hunkering down in Treasury bills ... that may look to the casual observer in the stands like the equivalent of watching and waiting for the perfect pitch—while sitting on your *gluteus maximus* in the dugout! In reality, about the only thing you can do while standing at the plate, bat poised (if you expect to react quickly in order to take a cut at the ball that crosses the plate in your sweet spot), is be vigilant. Moreover, since the sweet-spot pitches are never telegraphed in advance (unlike batting practice), you must always be at the ready.

Returning to Ted Williams, Buffett metaphorically refers to the Splendid Splinter's swinging methodology to emphasize the importance of patience: In his book *The Science of Hitting*, Ted explains that he carved the strike zone into 77 cells, each the size of a baseball. Swinging only at balls in his "best" cell, he knew, would allow him to bat .400; reaching for balls in his "worst" spot, the low outside corner of the strike zone, would reduce him to .230. In other words, waiting for the fat pitch would mean a trip to the Hall of Fame; swinging indiscriminately would mean a ticket to the minors.

The Mathematics of Patience

Having no interest in the minors, beyond throwing out the first pitch at the Omaha Royals home game during Berkshire's annual "Woodstock of capitalism" weekend, the most successful investor in the world suggests parking your money in cash equivalents and short-term bonds. He'd rather have historically low short-term returns than buy stocks or companies likely to return less than his threshold rate of return "because I'm going to be holding on to those forever ... [E]nough acquisitions like that and you end up with a very average business. So, in this low-interest environment, we have a lot of money in bonds right now."

In responding to a question at Berkshire's 2003 annual meeting about investment hurdle rates,[76] Buffett said, "Ten percent is the figure we quit on. We don't want to buy equities when the *real* expected return is less than 10%, whether interest rates are 6% or 1%. It's arbitrary. Ten percent is not that great after tax." Charlie Munger further qualified his partner's response by adding: "We're guessing at our future opportunity cost. Warren is guessing that he'll have the opportunity to put capital out at high rates of return, so he's not willing to put it out at less than 10% now. But if we knew interest

76 [Original 2004 footnote] The quoted comments were not extracted from a transcript, as no recordings are permitted at the Berkshire shareholders' meeting. Relying on my own memory and the excellent notes taken by Whitney Tilson of Tilson Funds (he played court stenographer at the meeting), the quotations constitute our best approximation of what was actually said.

rates would stay at 1%, we'd change. Our hurdles reflect our estimate of *future* opportunity costs." Warren finished the exchange with a specific example: "We could take the $16 billion we have in cash earning 1.5% and invest it in 20-year bonds earning 5% and increase our current earnings a lot, but we're betting that we can find a good place to invest this cash and don't want to take the risk of principal loss on long-term bonds." The MCM hurdle rate, as noted previously, is 15%, a full 5 percentage points greater than Buffett's minimum. We think it's appropriate for two reasons—one a strength, the other a shortcoming: First, because the assets we manage are minuscule compared with Berkshire's, our universe of investment candidates is so much larger that we stand a better chance of finding pricing inefficiencies and other anomalies. Second, Buffett's finely honed investment prowess gives him a significant edge in qualifying future uncertainty in an investment. Recognizing our relative weakness in that regard, we must insist on a higher margin of safety implicit in a higher hurdle rate.

The mathematics of waiting for fat pitches is quite compelling. Since if you've come this far you no doubt get the gist of the concept, it doesn't seem necessary to inundate you with the numbers we have crunched. Suffice it to say, you can earn a modestly positive return for quite some time while waiting for fat pitches—before your average compounded returns become lackluster. There is a counter argument for those who, apparently unfamiliar with financial cycles, challenge with shrill voices in their impatience, "What happens if those pitches never come your way?" Buffett doubtless feels no obligation to take the challenge, for to reply might dignify a question unworthy of a response (but could have the unintended consequence of sounding a lot like a forecast as well). A market—or an individual company's stock price—is, in most cases, not likely to go from prince to pauper without plenty of price pain. Buffett believes in the tendency of price and value to converge. Buffett's above scenario, namely, the modest return from Treasury bills, is not his worst-case scenario. The math of patience becomes overwhelming if you factor in the possibility of swinging indiscriminately and striking out before the fat pitches come, a risk Buffett has made clear he is unwilling to take. Like the flowers mentioned earlier, sometimes they come in bunches; other times they come one by one.

"We have $16 billion in cash, not because of any predictions [about a market decline]," he says, "but because we can't find anything that makes us want to part with that cash. We're not positioning ourselves. We just try to do smart things every day, and if there's nothing smart, then we sit on cash."

As you may recall from the section on "Financial Cycles," Berkshire's cash hoard as of September 30 totaled almost $40 billion, and Buffett had placed a $20 billion bet against the dollar. Based on what we can infer about the thinking at Berkshire since the annual meeting in May, it would appear that he is laying up stores, girding himself for eventual, but not necessarily imminent, action. Given Buffett's record of snatching victory from the jaws of someone else's defeat (e.g., 1974), his cash cache, supposedly head-in-the-sand benign, looks like enormous potential energy to me. Klarman articulates the logic behind Buffett's actions: "Never limit yourself to the opportunity set of today. Indeed, for almost any time horizon, the opportunity set of tomorrow is a legitimate competitor for today's investment dollars. It is hard, perhaps impossible, to accurately predict the volume and attractiveness of future opportunities, but it would be foolish to ignore them as if they will not exist." The following quotation is from the notes taken by a student who was among a group of University of Pennsylvania and the Wharton School of Business students who spent the morning with Buffett on November 12, 2004. When asked a question about the rich valuation of the market he responded: "We are near the high end of the valuation band, but not really at an extreme. ... I suspect that stocks are too high now. Nothing is cheap, and I am not finding a lot now, but there will be a day when you will be shooting fish in a barrel. The important thing is to be prepared to play heavily when the time comes, and that means that you cannot play with everybody." (The above may not be a verbatim quote from Buffett, but it seems essentially consistent with the way he sees things as interpreted by the writer throughout this report.)

Flashing back to earlier statements, these words fit "hand in glove": "Should tomorrow's opportunity [set] prove superior to today's, when presumably fear will have swept the field, and that perfect pitch finally crosses home plate, swing for the fences." Munger continues: "The wise ones [investors] bet heavily when the world offers them that opportunity. They bet big when they have the odds. And the rest of the time, they don't. It's just that simple."

Likewise, Buffett explains one reason pitches move from the outside edge of the strike zone to what Ted Williams called the "happy zone": "Occasional outbreaks of those two super-contagious diseases, fear and greed, will *forever* [italics added] occur in the investment community." While unsure of the timing or extent of these "outbreaks," Buffett advises investors to "simply attempt to be fearful when others are greedy and to be greedy only when others are fearful. ... Fear is the foe of the faddist but the friend of the fundamentalist."

Marathon Endurance

The message throughout this report, summarized here, is that we are nearer the beginning than the end of the long secular transition from greed to fear, from exhilaratingly high prices to despairingly low ones, from irrational exuberance to levelheaded rationality and perhaps (I say irrespective of how remote the possibility) from a financial economy to real economy. Accordingly, we have, out of necessity, a heightened sense of vigilance, a pervasive but hopefully constructive skepticism. As always, we will focus on individual companies, constantly comparing price and value. Because of the higher-risk environment in which I think we must operate, we will be extra conservative in our calculations of intrinsic value. If, in spite of a possible ebbing tide, our convictions about the value of a company we own are high and a stock gets cheaper, we will buy more. When we're buying something of value, we want the price to keep going down. If the price gets low enough, our average cost will be well below the intrinsic worth of the business. Low prices motivate the value investor to metaphorically grab her purse and make a beeline to the mall the day after Christmas.

Having spent my entire business life in the world of marketable investments, I'm convinced that there are always pricing anomalies in the market. As mentioned in earlier reports, the spring of 2000 was a bonanza for us: We picked up the discards when the players drew from the stacked deck of Nasdaq favorites, which brings to mind the aphorism, "One man's trash is another man's treasure." The Graham-and-Doddsville investors mentioned earlier have made their mark by successfully exploiting gaps between price and value. As Buffett said in 1984, "When the price of a stock can be influenced by a 'herd' on Wall Street with prices set at the margin by the most emotional person, or the greediest person, or the most depressed person, it is hard to argue that the market always prices rationally. In fact, market prices are frequently nonsensical."

I would like to repeat from earlier reports one important factor about risk and reward as it relates to the kind of investing in which we engage. In most games of chance with which we're all familiar, risk and reward are positively correlated—that is, if you want higher returns, you must assume greater risks. The proliferation of casinos and lotteries has done wonders to embed this positive correlation in the minds of millions upon millions of Americans. So ubiquitous is this perception that to suggest otherwise often provokes an incredulous stare, if not glare.

And yet there's a rather simple explanation why Buffett's net worth is $35 billion while the fellow at the lottery window continues to fork over the last few bucks from his paycheck to voluntarily pay the most pernicious and regressive tax of all—shamefully, a tax on ignorance imposed by elected "representatives." (The irony of the lottery system is that the typical state's rake is often "pledged" to support education, of all things. The same vicious circle of catch-22 reasoning is knowingly employed by Congress, permitting

Philip Morris to continue selling cigarettes to a new and nescient generation of smokers to pay the billions in claims from earlier ones.) Buffett's billions seem to suggest that the exact opposite is true with value investing. "If you buy a dollar bill for 60 cents," he says, "it's riskier than if you buy a dollar bill for 40 cents, but the expectation of reward is greater in the latter case. The greater the potential for reward in the value portfolio, the less risk there is."

By contrast, the lotteries and the casinos control the odds and therefore decide who "bears" the brunt of the risk. Is it any surprise that the odds are naturally stacked in favor of the house? It doesn't take a mathematician to understand why casinos and lotteries don't go broke, but gamblers do (as do, some may be surprised to learn, most lottery winners, but for different reasons). On the other hand, the value investor, by his understanding of the relationship between risk and return and his willingness to act independently on that insight, he *becomes* the house. He also controls the odds and (by inference) the risks; if he is skillful and patient, he stacks them in his favor. The markets are open every business day, and the prices are always fluctuating (the only certainty in the marketplace of which I'm aware). The smart investor turns a deaf ear to the crowd and listens to value instead, cherry-picking the best, purchasing them at *his* price. If he is capable of calmly awaiting his moment, unshackled from the ultimatum of the clock and unprovoked by the need to do something, time becomes his ally.

From our bottoms-up perspective, the long-term challenge for us as a small shop doing battle with the New York Yankees of the investment world is to use our minds (we don't have the financial muscle) to do what Billy Beane does so extraordinarily: to find value where no one else can find value. In this picked-over supermarket where every melon has been thumped countless times (you should see the Charmin!), it seems that if, to paraphrase Beane, a company doesn't have something wrong with it, it gets valued properly by the market, and we can't afford it anymore.

Seeing the Tides Through the Heavy Surf

Where some people see a dark cloud, others see a silver lining. Having cast my lot with the value camp almost 40 years ago—at the top of the last great secular cycle in 1966—I'm still amazed by how many opportunities came and went, like the waves, undulating between exuberance and despair, as the tide continued to ebb, oh so gradually and imperceptibly, until it quietly began to reverse its flow beginning in 1982. To capitalize on the post-1966 environment, you could not simply buy and hold, you had to buy cheap so that you could in the not-too-distant future sell dear. The tide was the enemy of those who became enamored with the waves. In most instances, though certainly not all, you "dated" a stock during those days, but you didn't marry it.

The opposite was true after 1982. The ever-present waves continued during the great bull market that ensued, but because of the steadily rising tide, opportunities were more plentiful, of greater magnitude and lasting longer, but also the rising water level buoyed many a less-than-enlightened idea ("a rising tide lifts all ships"). However, the concomitant comeuppance comes in the expression "Genius is before the fall" or, less poetically, "When the tide goes out, you find out who has been swimming naked." (Sadly, for many investors the relentless waves and crashing surf obscured the view of the tide until it had reached the equivalent of a river's flood stage in the late 1990s.) You may want to review the section titled "Run for the Roses" for less-graphic details.

Beyond MCM's non-negotiable allegiance to the basic principles of rational investing as an independent and flexible firm that promotes diversity of thought, we have no other conflicting philosophical loyalties. Period. The man who often sends me a thoughtful note after he reads this report, Peter Bernstein, gave his definition of a new paradigm in a public interview in early 2003. Bernstein's clients, it should be noted, are predominantly institutional managers and pension funds. He said bluntly: "[T]he traditional institutional approach, 'I will structure my portfolio in this way and make variations on the theme,' won't work. So what I'm suggesting is, throw it away. You have to be much more unstructured, opportunistic and ad hoc than you have been in the past." Later in the interview: "... [I]n this looser, more opportunistic environment I foresee the abandonment of the dreadful, depressing, defaulting process of putting managers into cubbyholes—large-cap growth, small-cap value and such foolishness—along with the stifling, stupid obsession with tracking error instead of absolute returns and risks incurred." This kind of diversity of thought is complementary to our philosophical moorings.

From the major bottom (1974) through the end of the secular regression in 1982, the S&P 500 advanced at an annual rate of 8.19% and at 13.7% with dividends[77] reinvested, while the book value of Berkshire Hathaway grew at the stunning compounded rate of 29.12%. Of course, back then Berkshire was the equivalent of a runabout, not a battleship. "Jack be nimble, Jack be quick ..." and don't forget about the candlestick, or you might get burned. In 1977, quoting from the oldest annual report available on Berkshire's Website, Buffett wrote about his investment principles and the opportunities that appeared then in marketable securities:

> We select our marketable equity securities in much the same

77 [Original 2004 footnote] Dividend yields are rarely low at the bottom of bear markets. A word to the wise: The converse also is usually true.

> way we would evaluate a business for acquisition in its entirety. We want the business to be (1) one that we can understand, (2) with favorable long-term prospects, (3) operated by honest and competent people, and (4) available at a very attractive price. We ordinarily make no attempt to buy equities for anticipated favorable stock price behavior in the short term. In fact, if their business experience continues to satisfy us, we welcome lower market prices of stocks we own as an opportunity to acquire even more of a good thing at a better price.

Buffett also is known for having said more recently:

> Our experience has been that *pro-rata* portions of truly outstanding businesses sometimes sell in the securities markets at very large discounts from the prices they would command in negotiated transactions involving entire companies. Consequently, bargains in business ownership, which simply are not available directly through corporate acquisition, can be obtained indirectly through stock ownership. When prices are appropriate, we are willing to take very large positions in selected companies, not with any intention of taking control and not foreseeing sell-out or merger, but with the expectation that excellent business results by corporations will translate over the long term into correspondingly excellent market value and dividend results for owners, minority as well as majority.

Some principles never change ...

Please understand, we can neither forecast the future (Galbraith sums it up by saying, "We have two classes of forecasters: Those who don't know—and those who don't know they don't know") nor expect to be as adroit as Buffett in capitalizing on the "sweet spot" pitches that will sporadically come hurtling our way. Meanwhile, in the future, as in the past, we have a decided preference for learning vicariously rather than firsthand from the school of hard knocks. As U.S. Gen. George Patton used to say, "It's an honor to die for your country, but make sure the other guy gets the honor." Nonetheless, to quote the quixotic Don Quixote from the musical "Man of La Mancha," from which comes the expression "tilting at windmills": "The fortunes of war [investment?] more than any other are liable to frequent fluctuations." More to our immediate need, the dreamer also is recognized for having said, "To be forewarned is to be forearmed." And because of the nature of the business of investing and our relatively diminutive size, we may be able to achieve successful results even if we find ourselves facing a headwind.

Peppered as you've been with baseballs, why not alter course briefly with a h(t?)ide-bound sailing metaphor? ☺ Instead of easing the sheets, engaging the autopilot, and relaxing for a gin and tonic as we would with the wind at our back, working our way "to weather" is not for the fainthearted. It's mentally and physically exhausting, requiring strength, conviction, concentration, and discipline. We must regularly tack to make headway toward our predetermined destination, "coming about" as needed to keep making progress if the winds shift even five or 10 degrees. A sailboat never realizes its maximum speed sailing to windward, but as the old adage goes, we have no control over the wind, but we can and do trim the sails for optimal results under the prevailing conditions. While our compass needle and ship's head (except during tacking) are pointed toward "true north," which we define in this metaphor as first protecting and then enhancing your capital, the winds are *forever clocking.* When they come around to amidships or farther abaft the beam, we'll have all of our canvas flying, and the bow wave will curl high on the prow. Then, and only then, we might grant ourselves the luxury of lacing fingers behind head and leaning back, for a few moments at least, to enjoy the ride.

CHAPTER EIGHT—WHAT HISTORY TEACHES

An Antidote for Speculative Epidemics

Was It All for Naught?

In the Preface, gentle encouragement to stay the course was provided for those who picked up the book, assuring the reader that there are certain truisms that, if applied wisely, will allow one to "eat well *and* sleep well," regardless of the tempests of exuberance or despair that will occasionally rage outside our windows. What follows below are several synthesized proverbs that you may have gleaned as you took the seven-year trek with us through time. I will attempt to list, in no particular order beyond the first one or two (which are foundational), a number of basic truths or practical precepts, in my experience-based judgment, to which you might refer should you become uncertain about which way to turn sometime in the future. The succeeding catalog of aphorisms is by no means all-inclusive nor are they meant to be taken at face value. Readers are encouraged to challenge every statement, extracting for themselves that which they feel will be most meaningful and reject that which they feel is superfluous or simply untrue. Perhaps before readers attempt to navigate their way through the following maxims they should reread the Introduction to Chapter Seven and arm themselves with the words of Ernest Dimnet, author of *The Art of Thinking*, a snippet from which is next: "Nothing is more striking than the absence of intellectual independence in most human beings: they conform in opinion, as they do in manners, and are perfectly content with repeating formulas. While they do so, the thinker calmly looks around, giving full play to his mental freedom. He may agree with the *consensus* known as public opinion, but it will not be because it is a universal opinion. Even the sacrosanct thing called plain common-sense is not enough to intimidate him into conformity."

- Free Markets: Popular Delusions and the Madness of Crowds
- Aspiring to Rationality by Overcoming Heuristic Biases
- Today Is Not Tomorrow: Cycles and Differing 'Opportunity Sets'
- Inverting the Traditional High-Risk/High-Return Paradigm
- The Inevitability of Regression to the Mean
- There Are No Called Strikes in the Investment Ballgame
- Focus on the Important
- The Malevolent Mathematical Mystery of Modern Money Management (a.k.a. MPT)
- The Absurdity of the Collective Wisdom of Individual Irrationality
- Diversification and the Myth of Safety in Numbers
- The New-Era Error

Free Markets: Popular Delusions and the Madness of Crowds

Whether it suits us or not, the free markets will occasionally and forever respond disproportionately to external stimuli so long as they remain unfettered. The antidotes below, deduced from careful examination of this most recent speculative Bubble and the many that preceded it, begin with a lengthy discussion of a supposition that I believe, from years of personal observation, to be a bedrock truism—namely, that crowds can corrupt the capacity for individual reasoning. Much of what follows thereafter is built on that foundation. It is the reservoir of strength that comes from understanding those conditions and circumstances where the individual is mightier than the crowd from which one is able to summon the courage to keep one's head when surrounded by those who are losing theirs.

Though the market mechanism is inherently a methodical system for reconciling supply and demand, behind every order ticket to buy or sell a stock or other security is a human being, most of whom suffer from one sort of affective disorder or another. It is this temperamental link in the chain that causes the system to get downright wacky at times. Worse still, through the process of contagion—disorders like the excessive desire for more than one needs or has earned (more commonly known as greed) or fear of loss—can escalate into epidemics that sometimes spread with shocking speed according to the mathematical laws of geometric progressions, figuratively becoming a "crowd." (Although you may have read this before, the following simple question illustrates the power of geometric progressions. If you give someone a penny on the first day of a 31-day month, 2 cents on the second, 4 cents on the third, continuing to double your gift each day until the end of the month, how much will you have given?)

You may recall reading the section in the last chapter titled "*A Short History of Financial Euphoria*" from the short book by that name written by John Kenneth Galbraith. Both *The Great Crash, 1929* and the above booklet were written years after the fact and were no doubt more thorough and concise because the author had the full benefit of hindsight, including the capacity to research what everyone else had to say on the subject. Because Galbraith was writing from a distance—in another time, if you will—he was able to view the powerful biases that led so many astray with the clinical detachment of a pathologist performing an autopsy. Furthermore, he presumably could have maintained a leisurely pace, motivated to put the pieces of the puzzle together whenever inspiration moved him to take pen in hand. What he didn't venture to do, however, was risk opining on either the present or the future. What his scholarly efforts gained through the focused lens of reflection, they lost in failing to capture the triggering events that gave impetus to the formation of epidemics. Too, he didn't really touch on the insidious way the perception of "reality" migrated with the mood of the crowd as it grew in size and concurrently shrunk in its collective capacity for objective reasoning. Permit me to make an analogy: Subtle is the difference, but the discerning eye can spot the significant dissimilarities between a Broadway play and a movie, though they both take place in a venue somewhat related in appearance.

This effort, then, intends to leave readers with a sense that if they feel they're becoming infected by the next speculative epidemic they will have a place to turn for an antidote that was tested—not on rats in laboratories by men in white coats but by real people in the real marketplace where rampant uncertainty and high emotion are the only realities for many of the participants. What follows are certain generalized truths that may keep an investor away from the edge of the precipice over which he could easily fall into a spiral of irrationality, often leading to great financial and emotional travail—and possibly even a trip to the metaphorical pathologist mentioned above (or to the "smiling mortician" made famous by Lawrence Ferlinghetti's 1955 poem). I hope this book has conveyed how tenuous was the strand of knowledge of history and human behavior that kept us from capitulating to the cry of the crowd as it, like the cartoon of the sheep in Chapter Four, stampeded heedlessly and *head*lessly over the cliff of mindless imitation to their demise. We confess to being investment acrophobics: We fear high places. In investment parlance, we are far less anxious looking up at intrinsic value than looking down at it. Stated another way, our comfort (not to mention our confidence) is inversely proportional to the degree to which common stocks are more or less popular than the norm.

Free markets of all stripes are prone to occasional episodes of extreme detachment from reality, as evidenced by fluctuations in prices that would certainly appear to be wildly disproportionate to the underlying causes. There is little we can do to curb the innate human psyche when, collectively, it is agitated through the process of contagion to the point of irresponsible and often self-destructive behavior. But perhaps by acting independently as individuals we stand some hope of being victors and not victims through the power of knowledge, applied with wisdom. The biographies of Winston Churchill and Teddy Roosevelt would suggest that such a contention is not entirely fallacious. What can we apply that we have observed over the last seven dramatic years to ameliorate the consequences of such flights of fancy in the future? Certainly man is not so inobservant that he is doomed to repeat all mistakes of the past. Wisdom is not cumulative from generation to generation, but information is. Hence, what can be extracted from the information, particularly for those who seek to convert information into knowledge? What is indigenous to all such episodes? In other words, if history is repetitious, despite each event having its own nuances that differentiate it from others, what thread of similarities connects most historical events?

Aspiring to Rationality by Overcoming Heuristic Biases

The word "rational" and its derivatives appear 133 times throughout the text of this book. The call for rationality is found in every chapter. And yet were it not for occasional outbreaks of geometrically progressive epidemics of *irrationality*, the great incidences of speculative euphoria would likely never gain sufficient momentum to become such a force that might threaten to blow your financial house down. There is a world of difference, in terms of consequences, between a tropical depression and a Category 5 hurricane.

Warren Buffett is well-known for imploring investors to be, above all, rational if they are to avoid falling prey to periodic flights of fancy and folly. Buffett himself is the model of self-control and imperturbability, a bastion of reason in the midst of a storm.

Above all other traits necessary for investment success, Buffett emphasizes *rationality,* a form of self-discipline that is part nature, part nurture. Moreover, there are a number of cognitive impediments to rational decision making that must be overcome. Several of the elementary truths are rooted in how the human mind processes information and data. While the following discussion is a little technical, it is essential to understanding why (even when we feel otherwise) we as human beings often make irrational decisions.

It all began in the '70s with a growing field of scientific inquiry regarding how the human mind works. Our brains, it was postulated, use a strict set of compression schemes for abstracting critical features out of vast amounts of incoming sensory data. When new information is abstracted from the surrounding environment, converted into symbolic format, and archived in long-term memory, it becomes subject to certain biasing effects. Decision theorists refer to the hard-wired tendency of humans to perform abstract reasoning in cognitively economical ways as heuristics.

To be sure, heuristics save time and effort, but they often fail utterly when presented with data outside of their "domain of expertise." These failures are difficult to notice, because (1) the thinking processes responsible for judging the overall quality of one's thinking are plagued by these biases as well, (2) they are so widespread and natural that few people notice them, and (3) decisions made based on heuristics feel good; they're intuitively satisfying, regardless of their correctness.

Two of the more easily understood and related heuristics are the "above average" bias, the widespread tendency to categorize oneself as *above average,* and the "optimistic bias," the inclination to view the world through rose-colored glasses. The optimistic bias is often harmless (sometimes it is even helpful), but it's a sure road to ruin in a profession where the gullible are fodder for the occasional vultures who prove time and again that a fool and his money are soon going in opposite directions. Nowhere is the facetious application of the above-average and optimistic biases more obvious than in the outro of American humorist and storyteller Garrison Keillor's widely beloved *Prairie Home Companion* radio show: "That's the news from Lake Wobegon, where all the women are strong, all the men are good-looking, and all the children are above average."

Somewhat more subtle—and clearly more insidious for investors—are the following biases:

- "Anchoring effects" are robust psychological phenomena showing that people adjust insufficiently for the implications of incoming information. We form beliefs around an anchor, and additional incoming data must fight against the inertia of the anchor, even when it is objectively irrelevant to the judgment at hand.
- The availability heuristic results in vivid recent memories overriding normative reasoning. With investing, the urge to either buy or sell is often a function of how good or bad one feels about his most recent experience. The Pavlovian association—two stimuli are associated

when the experience of one leads to the effects of another, due to repeated pairing—reinforces the availability bias.

- "Base-rate neglect" effectively reduces the importance of background frequencies in favor of salient anecdotal evidence.

These biases, either singly or in combination, have the effect of inhibiting impartial judgment. As this relates to the market environment, biased investors can come to believe virtually any environment to be normative—e.g., the seemingly unquestioned acceptance of the reasoning that continued to justify the Bubble months before it burst and logic that would have been rejected as absurd five years before the 2000 implosion. Bias-infected reasoning was proved to be ludicrous in the wake of the collapse. As the market proceeds in its unpredictable and asymmetrical cycles, the vast majority of investors, because of these biases, tend to accept each stage as normative. If this were not so, markets would move forthwith in the direction of what is perceived as normative. The fact that they stand pat tends to be the "pudding proof" of this phenomenon.

Today Is Not Tomorrow: Cycles and Differing 'Opportunity Sets'

Seth Klarman's contention in Chapter Six that tomorrow's "opportunity set" may be different, perhaps radically so, from today's doesn't gain much traction with most investors. And yet, to unquestioningly accept mercurial Mr. Market's judgment as the final arbiter of the fairness of the price-to-value relationship is to mistake a stooge for a sage.

History might suggest that investors anchored in today's opportunity set are a little light on the lessons of history. On the other hand, today's naysayers, including the writer, may simply have their anchors too deeply buried in a past that is never to return. Imagine how agonizing the half-century wait has been for those who still believe that dividend yields will once again eclipse those from bonds. I would counter that argument, claiming the latter phenomenon to be a once-in-a-generation change that took place at a snail's pace, whereas the manic-depressive cyclicality of markets (while unpredictable as to its timing) is still eminently foreseeable as to the inevitability of its place as a permanent feature on the investment landscape.

Those of us who presume to be investment professionals, as well as those who expect to be proficient nonprofessional investors, obviously must acknowledge the existence of biases lurking in our subconscious. One way to minimize the effect of these counterproductive biases is to "back test" our decisions in order to regularly recalibrate our thinking. The process is agonizing and humbling, for most of us tend to handle the truth badly when it conflicts with long-held beliefs. While the expression "no pain, no gain" may sound painfully trite, it is also plainly true. The golfer who disdains systematically going to the practice tee until the hands are blistered—or to the putting green with a pro—is doomed to repeat his mistakes, and thereby habituate them. If he remains steadfastly in denial, once correctable mistakes may become intractable.

Inverting the Traditional High-Risk/ High-Return Paradigm

Moving from the science of the mind to the observable should be less arduous for the reader. Let's begin by attempting to demystify a seemingly inviolable concept. It is generally accepted that risk and return are positively correlated: i.e., in order to earn higher returns one must take on greater risk. That principle is reinforced whenever one participates in commonplace games of chance, such as the lottery. To the extent that a stock market participant transfers that same risk/return paradigm to investment in common stocks—accepting high valuations and extreme volatility as his sole definition of risk—then the assumption of above-average risks can most logically be correlated with the expectation of above-average expected returns. This investor should be anything but venturesome in the markets for intangible assets.

But what happens if he extends his time horizons from the here and now to months or years? What if he buys stocks using the same logic he would apply to purchasing a house? Admittedly, most prospective home purchasers have a notable informational advantage over the investor in intangible assets. They are able to compare the price of a home being offered with others from the same or similar location, size, design, construction quality, and so on. Moreover, they tend to have a good idea of what they're looking for, as well as to shop in a predetermined price range that is congruent with their capacity to service the mortgage loan. The smart shoppers who, based on their own experience, think the house they're looking at is worth, say, $100,000, will become more interested if they conclude that the seller is highly motivated to part with his or her property promptly and offer the home for $90,000. If the buyers can negotiate the price down to $80,000, they may become downright ecstatic! Subconsciously, their brains must reach a logical conclusion: It's less risky to buy the house at $80,000 than it would be, on the flip side of the coin, to impulsively pay $120,000 to a clever seller. They intuitively reason that if they ever have to sell the property, the lower-cost purchase will clearly work to their financial advantage by either minimizing their loss or maximizing their profit. What should be obvious by now is that the buyer has inverted the traditional risk/return paradigm. By purchasing the house at a price deemed to be below its intrinsic worth they have reduced the amount of their risk in the event of a forced sale. On the other hand, if house prices appreciate and they choose to sell, they will have earned a greater profit. Voilà, the wonder of the low-risk/high-return paradigm. It works so well in many of our purchase decisions (the word "sale" is very effective at drawing shoppers' eyes to an advertisement) because the buyers have spent that portion of their lives as consumers accumulating information on the value of real or tangible assets.

The reason this paradigm is less effective in the stock market is because the casual investor has limited skills or experience in pricing assets that one can neither see nor touch. Evidence of ownership is but the name of a company on his brokerage statement, the value of which is wholly dependent on the uncertain proposition that it will return sufficient cash to the investor over the years ahead to justify its purchase price.

If an investor has sufficient skill and experience to first identify companies for which the determination of the range for intrinsic value is even possible and then to make that informed judgment, he has one of the pillars essential to inverting the traditional risk/return paradigm. Good fortune is likely to await this investor.

The Inevitability of Regression to the Mean

Regression to the mean, referred to frequently throughout the book, is a term that has its roots in statistics and probability theory. The example most frequently presented in this book is from physics, the central-tendency movement of a pendulum in, say, a grandfather clock, which, perhaps from personal observation, most readers find to be quite understandable.

So as to avoid unnecessary repetition, a short summary of the simple pendulum phenomenon will lay the groundwork for a number of applications of regression to the mean in the investment world. First, the pendulum will remain motionless, at its position of rest, where opposing forces are equalized, otherwise known as equilibrium. Likewise, the markets or individual stocks would never change in price were it not for the inequality of the actions of buyers and sellers. Unlike the unattended pendulum, the free markets never lacked for those doing the buying and those inclined toward the opposite, the intensity of whose motives and emotions are innumerable in their variations, as well as their capacity to occasionally aggregate. Another striking difference between the rhythmic pattern of the swinging pendulum and the irregular and unpredictable motion of the markets is that the primary force acting on the pendulum is one of the most stable physical powers, gravity.

As noted above, however, not only are markets moved at the margin by many people whose rationality is compromised by a variety of affective disorders, but the movement itself, through a feedback loop, sometimes effects and therefore exacerbates those disorders and behavioral responses to them. In this instance, "at the margin" refers only to that small minority of individuals who are actively buying or selling. Those investors who at present are neither buying nor selling will have no direct effect on the market price of anything. Up to some point, a movement can become a self-reinforcing mechanism. That point, somewhere along the extreme of the pendulum's ark, never known in advance, is where the process of regression to the mean (in mathematics it means the average, while here we're referring to the bottom of the arc, which is the same) begins. Introducing probability theory briefly ... the farther the pendulum moves away from equilibrium or its position at rest, the greater the likelihood that it will reverse its course. Unlike the perfect symmetry of a pendulum, the mean is an ever-changing number because of the irregular movements of the market. The difference does not destroy the analogy but simply makes it a bit more complex. In simple physical terms, gravity eventually overcomes momentum. Finally, once the pendulum reaches the outer limit of its leftward or rightward arc, its course is reversed and its speed accelerates, reaching maximum velocity in the vicinity of the very position where it would be at rest without the motive force of momentum. That is why markets that have swung to extremes rarely come to rest at the mean but, rather, continue well beyond the center, once their course has been reversed by the force of a systemic change in investor sentiment equivalent to that of gravity in the physical realm.

From these observations a host of truisms follows. "This too shall pass" is an aphorism that investors would do well to keep in mind in both good times and bad. It's a reasonable assumption that today's opportunity set, if some distance from the mean, will be quite different from the figurative "tomorrows," particularly to the open-minded investor who is not "anchored" in the present. It should probably hold true as well that markets will cycle in some irregular fashion because the collective psychology of investors that drives markets tends to swing with equal unpredictability from highs to lows and back again.

There Are No Called Strikes in the Investment Ballgame

The business of investing in marketable securities has characteristics that in several ways makes it unique. First, unlike a home, a tract of land, or a private company where ownership changes hands infrequently (and, generally, in its entirety), bite-sized fractional-ownership interests in publicly traded companies are for sale every business day of the year. If a private company or a home you've desired for a long time makes a rare appearance on the market, usually at the seller's behest and price, you either swing at the pitch or head for the showers. In the public market just the opposite is true. There is no need to swing your financial bat until you see the proverbial fat pitch coming your way. Although this characteristic is one of the secondary (not primary, as in IPOs) public market's main attractions, few investors seem to take advantage of the opportunities it presents. Many who never worked through their hyperactivity in their youth might consider a heavy dose of Ritalin. Others are simply compulsive, unjustifiably feeling like a pinch-hitter once they kick the dirt off their cleats at the plate. Think of it. There are no called strikes for the rare breed known as the patient batter. Imagine what Ted Williams' statistics would've been under those rules!

Focus on the Important

Focus, as noted in the Preface, is a term that intentionally limits one's field of vision. Let's say we as a firm have deduced from the study of investment history that businesses possessing competitive advantages sustainable over extended periods of time tend (presuming they are well-purchased) to produce the highest long-term returns. If so, we must consider everything else extraneous and irrelevant to our defined purpose. In order to avoid allowing our gaze to be distracted from that which is important, we focus exclusively on that relatively small subset of the larger investment universe. Even if a particularly compelling investment idea appears outside our subset, we will generally reject it unless we're woefully short of good ideas that fall within the confines of our field of focused vision.

Similarly, in the broader sense of our portfolio management, our focus is on earning above-average investment returns over the years. Many actions that we might otherwise take in the short run suddenly appear superfluous or counterproductive, so long as we look straight ahead and keep our eyes riveted on the well-defined endgame.

The Malevolent Mathematical Mystery of Modern Money Management (a.k.a. MPT)

If you cannot understand a system, particularly one that is esoteric in its complexity, what basis do you have for placing your trust, other than blindly, in it delivering what it proposes? Academia has found a gold mine in transmuting the art of investment (that, at heart, is based on common sense) into the *science* of finance, manifested in textbooks filled with pages and pages of undecipherable equations. The idea that the intricacy of the symbolic logic necessary to solve problems is proportional to the results achieved is woefully misapplied in the world of Main Street investment. What good is the Superman wardrobe if you're not Clark Kent? Countless Nobel prizes in financial mathematics have been awarded by judges who have almost no comprehension of what they're judging. If Nobel prizes were awarded to those who have taken plain, everyday logic to incredible new heights, Warren Buffett's Nobel prizes would soon rival his billions. Buffett would no doubt take his own bounty. Is there a Nobel laureate in finance more highly regarded than the Oracle of Omaha? He makes a mockery out of modern portfolio theory (MPT) by simply proving its relative uselessness with his own results year after year. No less intellectual authority than Albert Einstein wisely noted that "Any intelligent fool can make things bigger and more complex ... It takes a touch of genius—and a lot of courage—to move in the opposite direction."

Harry Markowitz introduced the concept of MPT with his paper "Portfolio Selection," which appeared in the 1952 *Journal of Finance*. In 1990 he shared a Nobel Prize with Merton Miller and William Sharpe for what has become a broad theory for portfolio selection. Concerned with the "random" risks associated with concentrated portfolios, he detailed the mathematics of diversification, proposing that investors focus on selecting portfolios based on their overall risk/reward characteristics, instead of merely compiling portfolios from securities that individually have attractive risk/reward characteristics. In a nutshell, Markowitz theorized that investors should select portfolios, not individual securities.

For many good reasons that do not include the open-ended mandate to maximize "risk-adjusted" performance, MPT has profoundly shaped how institutional portfolios are managed—and spurred the use of passive investment management techniques. The mathematics of portfolio theory is used extensively in financial-risk management and was a theoretical precursor of today's "value-at-risk" measures.

The Absurdity of the Collective Wisdom of Individual Irrationality

Several of the guiding precepts of MPT have been met with some resistance by those *long-term* investors who find them illogical, including the author. First, the Efficient Market Hypothesis states that it is impossible to "beat the market" because existing share prices already incorporate and reflect all relevant information (implying that the prices set are the most reasonable approximation of intrinsic worth because all known information is rationally incorporated in the price). We say it's not the market mechanism itself that casts aspersions on the hypothesis but rather the practical asymmetry of information and the frequently biased buyers and sellers who set the prices. Fighting fire with fire, it isn't unreasonable to assume that asymmetrical information and behavioral dynamics may raise legitimate questions about the market's capacity to set rational prices. The flow of conversation among a group of drunks at the bar near closing time may be quite "fluid," but how much credence would you give to their collective reasoning power? Picture them trying to decide who is the least drunk and who, therefore, should be the "designated driver"!

To be sure, the market mechanism is frequently capable of adjudicating a price that is a fair approximation of intrinsic worth. On other occasions, like the drunks above, emotions and biases overwhelm reason, and wide gaps can and do open between price and value. Never forget "Mr. Market" and his peculiarities.

Diversification and the Myth of Safety in Numbers

Returning to Markowitz's dubious contention that random risk demands broad diversification, simple mathematical modeling seems to have adequately proved through back testing that a concentrated portfolio with as few as 12 truly diversified companies is sufficient in breadth to reduce random risk to a more than tolerable level. One could argue that as you add companies to a portfolio that are of lesser quality and greater future uncertainty than the ones already owned, risks actually rise. So long as you choose to be invested in stocks, there is one risk for which diversification affords no protection. As you increase diversification, you concurrently and inevitably increase your exposure to market risk—namely, the tendency of your portfolio, like an index fund, to mirror the performance of the market. If you owned an index fund that mimicked the Nasdaq 500 as it fell from 5,050 to just over 1,000, you might begin to doubt the concept of the security of principal (or the principle of security!) that is presumed to be found in the safety of large numbers. Let there be no doubt: If you go the route of broad diversification, rest assured that you will never stand out in a crowd. For many investors, particularly of the institutional variety, the desire to be inconspicuous in the comforting gray area of anonymity is greater than the risk of falling below the line in an effort to rise above it.

The degree to which a portfolio can be prudently concentrated among a relatively small number of companies largely rests with the skill, discernment, temperament and experience of the investor. For most, broad diversification is the only commonsensical long-term alternative. If the layperson invests systematically—through thick and thin, no mean emotional feat despite its apparent simplicity—the negative portfolio effect of outlandishly high prices will to some extent be offset by compellingly low prices, such that their long-term results will be acceptably average, particularly when adjusted for the effort expended.

The appeal of a concentrated portfolio is that it is the only chance an investor has to beat the averages by a noteworthy margin. If risk is determined to be a variable, and the amount of assumed risk is a function of the relationship between the market price and the independently determined intrinsic value of the business, then please refer back to the earlier section "Inverting the Traditional High-Risk/High-Return Paradigm" to close the reasoning loop.

The New-Era Error

New eras usually ride into town on the back of a horse mistaken for a golden stallion, transformed momentarily by the brilliance of the afternoon sun. Incredulous onlookers (investors) are thinking riches, when all that's left when the illusion fades is manure. John Kay, the British economist and author of *The Business of Economics,* summed it up succinctly: "If new technologies are *generally applicable* [italics added], then competition means that the benefits will go to consumers. Not just most of them, all of them. New technology has always been better news for customers than shareholders."

Jim Grant has observed that there is nothing ever really new in the world of investment and finance, just old principles dressed up in the latest fashion, often with the sole intent of making a buck from a bumpkin without creating any real value. New investment principles are a contradiction in terms. Notes Warren Buffett: "If principles can become dated, they're not principles." The entire Appendix on Benjamin Graham should leave no doubt whatsoever about this point.

APPENDIX

Figure 1.1

The Illusion of Dilution

Company	1996 Earnings	Adjustment for Option Costs	Earnings Adjusted for Option Costs
Bristol-Myers Squibb	$ 2,850	$ (5,432)	$ (2,582)
Cisco Systems	$ 913	$ (1,569)	$ (656)
Dell Computer	$ 498	$ (1,360)	$ (862)
Eli Lilly	$ 1,524	$ (3,172)	$ (1,648)
Hewlett-Packard	$ 586	$ (616)	$ (30)
Intel	$ 5,157	$ (5,438)	$ (281)
Microsoft	$ 2,525	$ (12,700)	$ (10,175)
Monsanto	$ 385	$ (982)	$ (597)
Texas Instruments	$ 63	$ (131)	$ (68)
Time Warner	$ 191	$ (503)	$ (312)
Unocal	$ 36	$ (88)	$ (52)
Chase/Manhattan	$ 2,461	$ (1,830)	$ 631
Coca-Cola	$ 3,492	$ (1,806)	$ 1,686
Computer Associates	$ 261	$ (214)	$ 47
Gillette	$ 949	$ (822)	$ 127
MBNA	$ 474	$ (263)	$ 211
Merrill Lynch	$ 1,619	$ (1,266)	$ 353
Oracle	$ 603	$ (446)	$ 157
Schlumberger	$ 851	$ (602)	$ 249
Sun Microsystems	$ 620	$ (415)	$ 205
Textron	$ 253	$ (179)	$ 74
Walt Disney	$ 1,534	$ (845)	$ 689
Warner-Lambert	$ 787	$ (559)	$ 228
Waste Management	$ 192	$ (132)	$ 60

Reproduced from *Forbes* Source: Smithers & Co.

Figure 1.2

Dilution Is the Only Option		
Company	Options Allocation as a Percentage of Shares Outstanding	Options Granted in '96-'97 as a Percentage of Shares Outstanding
Delta Air Lines	55.47%	1.24%
Merrill Lynch	53.95%	6.44%
Morgan Stanley	51.22%	3.87%
Microsoft	44.83%	4.45%
Bankers Trust	43.09%	8.79%
Lehman Brothers	42.58%	10.08%
Dell Computer	38.68%	5.73%
Travelers Group	37.06%	5.88%
ITT Industries	36.96%	1.76%
JP Morgan	31.89%	3.91%
Warner-Lambert	29.14%	1.50%
Transamerica	27.93%	2.45%
Time Warner	26.01%	2.19%
Bank America	25.57%	2.70%

Reproduced from *Forbes*

Source: Pearl Meyer & Partners Inc.

Figure 2.1

20 Largest Nasdaq Companies
12/31/99

	Company Name	Market Value $ Mil.	Net Income Last 4 Qtrs	P/E Trailing EPS
MSFT	MICROSOFT CORP	$ 601,029	8,293	72
CSCO	CISCO SYSTEMS INC	$ 355,119	2,016	182
INTC	INTEL CORP	$ 275,006	7,270	43
ORCL	ORACLE CORP	$ 159,540	1,442	115
WCOM	MCI WORLDCOM INC	$ 149,295	3,104	40
DELL	DELL COMPUTER CORP	$ 130,101	1,655	70
ERICY	ERICSSON (L M) TEL -ADR	$ 128,179	1,259	93
SUNW	SUN MICROSYSTEMS INC	$ 120,966	1,189	108
YHOO	YAHOO INC	$ 113,901	35	3,057
QCOM	QUALCOMM INC	$ 113,841	201	520
AMGN	AMGEN INC	$ 61,355	1,053	67
JDSU	JDS UNIPHASE CORP	$ 56,017	(293)	-
SNRA	SONERA GROUP PLC -ADR	$ 49,999	360	110
AMAT	APPLIED MATERIALS INC	$ 47,940	726	66
ICGE	INTERNET CAP GROUP INC	$ 43,012	(4)	-
LVMHY	LVMH MOET HENNESSY -ADR	$ 42,435	-	56
ORNGY	ORANGE PLC -ADR	$ 39,663	(108)	-
NIPNY	NEC CORP -ADR	$ 39,658	(1,653)	-
GBLX	GLOBAL CROSSING LTD	$ 38,395	215	123
CMCSK	COMCAST CORP -CL A SPL	$ 38,007	1,381	28
	TOTALS	**$ 2,603,459**	**$ 28,140**	**93***

* Yahoo P/E reduced to 200x
Source: FactSet Data Systems

Figure 2.2

20 Largest Nasdaq Companies

As of 12/31/1999

(Information Updated 05/30/03)

	Company Name	Market Value $ Mil.	Chg. in $ Value Since 12/31/99	% Chg. in Market value Since 12/31/99	Net Income Last 4 Qtrs	P/E Trailing EPS
MSFT	MICROSOFT CORP	$ 263,868	(337,161)	-56.10%	9,597	28
INTC	INTEL CORP	$ 136,038	(138,968)	-50.53%	3,096	45
CSCO	CISCO SYSTEMS INC	$ 115,165	(239,954)	-67.57%	3,368	36
AMGN	AMGEN INC	$ 83,398	22,043	35.93%	(1,240)	-
DELL	DELL COMPUTER CORP	$ 80,684	(49,417)	-37.98%	2,263	36
ORCL	ORACLE CORP	$ 68,211	(91,329)	-57.25%	-	-
CMCSA	COMCAST CORP -CL A SPL	$ 40,681	2,674	7.03%	(483)	-
QCOM	QUALCOMM INC	$ 26,514	(87,327)	-76.71%	521	53
AMAT	APPLIED MATERIALS INC	$ 25,766	(22,174)	-46.25%	135	202
YHOO	YAHOO INC	$ 18,000	(95,901)	-84.20%	143	127
ERICY	ERICSSON (L M) TEL -ADR	$ 15,931	(112,249)	-87.57%	(2,564)	-
SUNW	SUN MICROSYSTEMS INC	$ 14,049	(106,918)	-88.39%	(2,329)	-
NIPNY	NEC CORP -ADR	$ 7,096	(32,563)	-82.11%	(205)	-
JDSU	JDS UNIPHASE CORP	$ 5,110	(50,907)	-90.88%	(1,915)	-
ICGE	INTERNET CAP GROUP INC	$ 207	(42,806)	-99.52%	(55)	-
WCOEQ	MCI WORLDCOM INC	$ 202	(149,093)	-99.86%	-	-
GBLXQ	GLOBAL CROSSING LTD	$ 15	(38,380)	-99.96%	-	-
SNRA	SONERA GROUP PLC -ADR*					
LVMHY	LVMH MOET HENNESSY -ADR*					
ORNGY	ORANGE PLC -ADR*					
	TOTALS	**$ 900,934**	**$ (1,570,429)**		**$ 10,332**	

Source: FactSet Data Systems

*Acquired at significant discount to 12/31/99 value

Figure 2.3

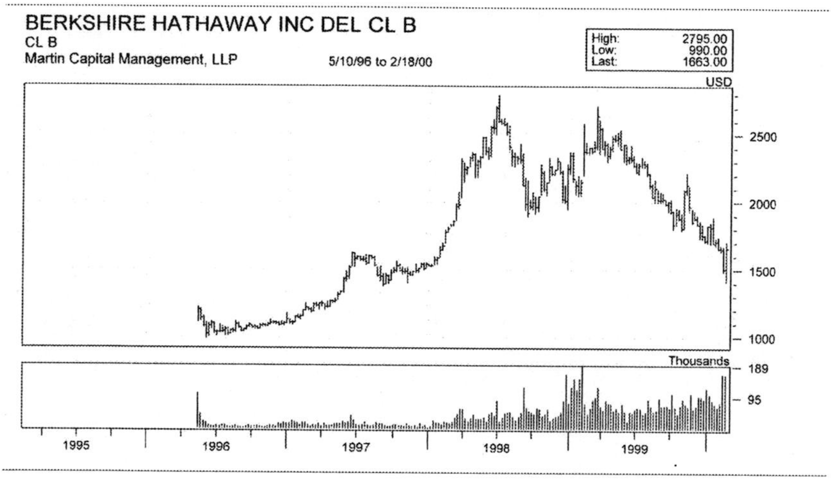
BERKSHIRE HATHAWAY INC DEL CL B
CL B
Martin Capital Management, LLP
5/10/96 to 2/18/00
High: 2795.00
Low: 990.00
Last: 1663.00
USD
2500
2000
1500
1000
Thousands
189
95
1995
1996
1997
1998
1999

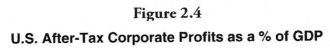

Figure 2.4

U.S. After-Tax Corporate Profits as a % of GDP

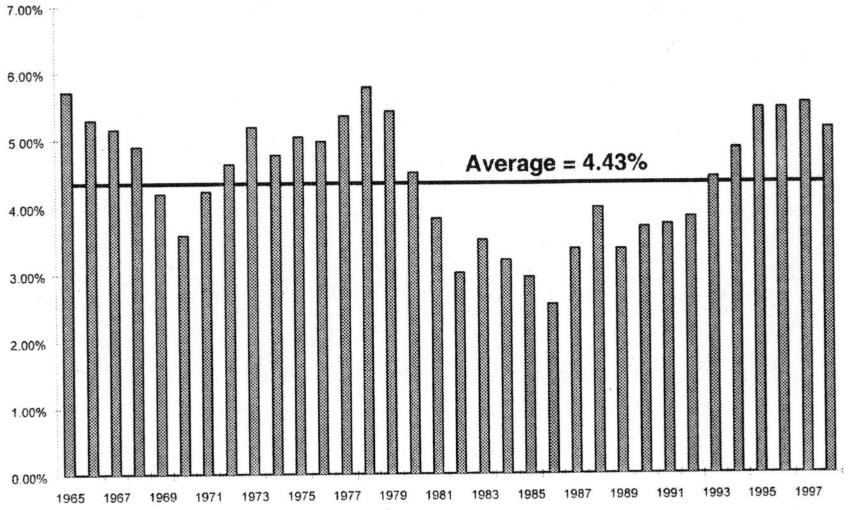

Excerpt 3.1 Business Principles

- Our practice of ethics is quite uncomplicated. We simply conduct ourselves in our relationship with you as if the roles could be reversed at any time. If you would like something more formal, we can send you the Code of Ethics of the Association for Investment Management and Research of which the members of your management team, as Chartered Financial Analysts, are full participants. It is well-thought-out and inclusive.

- We strive to be candid and forthright in our reporting to you. You have placed your trust in us, and we know of no other way to be worthy of that trust. Despite this policy of openness, we will publicly discuss our transactions in marketable securities only when we believe such disclosure will be to your advantage. Good ideas are scarce, and the output of our research efforts is your exclusive property.

- Our portfolio management style is "participatory." We consider it very important for you to be actively involved in the review of our recommended portfolio policy, in mapping out intermediate-term strategies, and in major asset-allocation decisions. Your involvement should not take a great deal of your time, however. The better we get to know you, the more likely we are to appreciate your unique (and sometimes changing) goals, objectives, preferences, biases, and fears, both spoken and unspoken. With your indulgence, we will continue our practice of encouraging frequent face-to-face get-togethers. We also will persevere in communicating our thoughts to you in writing to make it easier for you to get to know us.

- To the extent that security laws and regulations permit, my own portfolio and that of our firm are invested in the same securities as yours, varying only to the extent that our goals and objectives differ. In other words, "We eat our own cooking." It probably goes without saying that such a policy demonstrates the sincerity of our position—not necessarily the soundness of it.

- We are a small organization and intend to remain so. A compact organization makes it possible for us to spend our time managing our business rather than each other. Because everyone has much to do, much gets done. Our design appeals to those for whom form is secondary to substance.

Investment Principles

- Our implicit quantitative performance goal is to maximize long-term portfolio returns.

- The universe of marketable securities from which we select most investments is generally limited to: (1) long-term common-stock holdings, (2) medium-term fixed-income securities, (3) long-term fixed-income securities, and (4) short-term cash equivalents. Beyond respecting the investment-policy guidelines established for you, we are not partial to any one of the above categories. We simply search among them for securities that offer the highest after-tax, risk-adjusted returns as determined by "mathematical expectation."

- We strenuously avoid assuming risks that might result in "permanent" capital loss. We will forgo an outstanding investment opportunity if the flip side of that coin is the risk of an irreversible capital loss. We do expect frequent shorter-term quotational losses as we rarely, if ever, are able to buy a common stock or any other security at its absolute lowest price. So long as we feel our business analysis is sound, further weakness in the market price of a company simply gives us an additional opportunity to purchase shares at an even greater discount relative to its intrinsic value.

- Consistent with our attitude toward catastrophic risk, we have little interest in the use of leverage. We do not margin portfolios and usually avoid making investments in businesses that themselves labor under a heavy burden of debt.

- When we purchase common stocks, we approach the transaction as if we are buying into a private business. We insist on a purchase price that represents a "compelling discount" from intrinsic value. Once a purchase is made, we focus the bulk of our attention on tracking the business itself and ignoring short-term price fluctuations. We are quite content to hold onto our investment in a good business so long as (1) the prospective return on equity capital is expected to be satisfactory, (2) the management continues to conduct itself with competence and honesty, and (3) the market does not become excessively enthusiastic about the future outlook for the business.

- We believe that intrinsic value is in essence the central tendency in the price of an asset. It is the investment concept at the core of our analytical methodology. While intrinsic value is an elusive notion, "earnings power" has become the driving force in fixing a range for intrinsic value. Earnings power allows for the existence of an intangible asset known as "economic goodwill" that can be aggregated with tangible assets to arrive at intrinsic business value. Without such a fundamental benchmark, however vague, one is at risk of becoming awash in the occasional tides of euphoria and pessimism that flood the security markets.

- We generally limit the number of companies we own in any individual portfolio to fewer than 20. Contrary to popular opinion, exceptional investment ideas are uncommon indeed. We do not want to dilute the performance of outstanding investments with potentially mediocre ones purchased solely for the sake of additional, and often redundant, diversification. Despite the intuitive appeal of the broad spreading of your risks, extensive computer-backed testing has demonstrated that 90–95% of all the benefits to be gained from diversification can be achieved with a well-selected portfolio of fewer than 20 businesses.

Figure 3.2

Razed Capital

Performance of Companies That Went Public Between 2/1/00 and 12/15/00

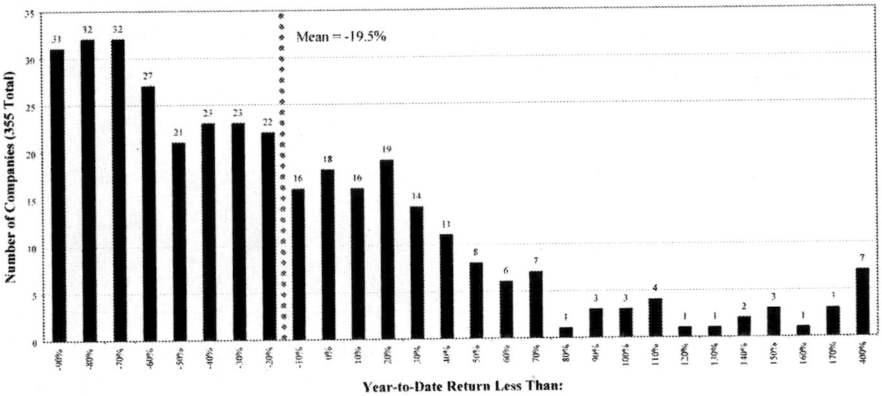

Excerpt 3.3 The More Times Change, the More They Remain the Same

1927–33 Through the Eyes of Benjamin Graham

Despite the periodic celebration of new eras in investment and finance, the verdict of history is not so complimentary to man's capacity to elevate his thinking and behavior in such endeavors beyond the primal states that inevitably lead to follies and flops. To the open-minded and clear-headed student of history, it is a truism that defining moments in finance have a cyclical tendency and, in their essence at least, are rarely without conceptual precedent. If the reader doubts the proposition, he or she need only make note of concrete examples of real progress over the millennia in those human endeavors where emotion did *not* play second fiddle to logic. If the list is as short as I expect it will be, for further confirmation, one might look to *Extraordinary Popular Delusions and the Madness of Crowds*, and read page after page of foolish notions at their repetitious and "sheepish" best. Fear and greed, most notable among counterproductive emotions where money is the object of human desire, can and often do compromise the capacity for rational and orderly thought. To understand why the same person can be calculatingly dispassionate in one instance and blindly irrational in another may well be worth a king's ransom.

Some grasp of history's abundant lessons becomes especially relevant in the examination of the goings-on in the capital markets where emotions, particularly at extremes, run high—and reason often is overwhelmed. Careful study of the past would suggest that it's quite appropriate to argue that there are no "new eras" in finance, only "new errors." An old French maxim may be apropos: "The more things change, the more they remain the same." [I modified the aphorism slightly for the title of this section of the Appendix.] A systematic attempt to study past events to isolate cause-and-effect relationships—so as to apply them to gain a better understanding of the present—is more than simply worthwhile, it's obligatory. No two episodes are alike, but there is often a common thread or two woven through them.

We now turn to the astute observations of Benjamin Graham who had a front-row seat from which he observed the cyclical nature of happenings in finance:

> That enormous profits should have turned into still more colossal losses, that new theories should have been developed and later discredited, that unlimited optimism should have been succeeded by the deepest despair are all in strict accord

with age-old tradition. (Benjamin Graham and David T. Dodd, Security Analysis [New York and London: Whittlesey House, McGraw-Hill Book Company Inc., 1934], 3)

Much of what follows, then, originates in the real-time analysis of the distinctive character of the financial and economic events during the 1927–33 period. Most of what Graham had to say appears in the form of direct quotations from the 1934 edition of *Security Analysis* by Benjamin Graham and David Dodd. While one might argue with such heavy dependence on verbatim observations, our goal is to identify pronounced and often primal patterns of investor behavior unique to exaggerated boom-and-bust cycles, of which that era provided ample supply. Forearmed with such knowledge, we may be able to muster the courage to keep our heads when all those around us are losing theirs, as well as (importantly) the audacity to answer the bell when the majority has thrown in the towel. We also may be able to better understand and avoid the lingering fallout of despair that characterizes the aftermath of booms gone bust if, in fact, that is what is in store: "The swing of a speculative pendulum during this period was of such unprecedented amplitude as to warrant the belief that it will not recur in similar intensity for a long time to come" (ibid., 6). Graham's conclusion was wise in the extreme, and yet investors remained leery of stocks until the 1960s, some 30 years later. To the extent that 70 years is sufficient time for memories of bygone days to have long since faded—and in the belief that there are obvious, more than randomly coincidental, similarities with today—the lessons thus learned can and should be respectfully applied by a manager of wealth to present-day realities.

We also would do well to note that simply because so many years have passed since the last episode of extreme speculative excess, it does not necessarily follow that the risk of recurrence is therefore quite low. On the contrary, to the extent that financial events are cyclical, like a pendulum (in part because the lessons of the past lose poignancy over the years), the mere passage of time actually increases the likelihood that the seeds of a speculative mania will again take root. Witness the outbreak of World War II barely two decades after the conclusion of World War I, "the war to end all wars."

The possibilities for error in endeavors such as these are many. They include the matter of ineffective timing. (The curse of premature caution is one with which this writer is acutely familiar.) Still, when all is said and done, leaving the party early may be better than leaving late. In fact, that is our contention, though it was made almost laughable by a riotous celebration that until 2000 seemed without end. But in 1999, when neither the mountaintop nor the valley had been seen, all that was known was that lots of easy money was being left on the table for those who sat on the sidelines and watched and wondered. In addition, there is a clear risk that judgments will be biased in any number of ways. The search for historical precedent can all too readily compromise objectivity. Our passion in seeking cause and effect may well jeopardize our conclusions. Our minds are calibrated to look for similarities, and our tunnel vision may cause us to overlook critical dissimilarities. If we attempt to limit the primary thrust of our investigation to the attitudes and behaviors that are unique to such highly agitated episodes, we may reduce somewhat the intrusion of unwanted biases. Fortunately, the reader is in all probability not beset with biases that are as threatening as those with which we who present the argument must deal. Thus he or she may be able to absorb what follows with constructive detachment. Therein lies its value to the second party.[78]

Ben Graham Only Human

At the quarter-century mark of 1925, the great bull market was under way, and Benjamin Graham, then 31, developed what he later described as a "bad case of hubris," as he admitted in his memoirs. In early 1929 Graham had a conversation with business associate Bernard Baruch, of whom he disapprovingly observed, "He had the vanity that attenuates the greatness of some men ..." (Benjamin Graham, *Benjamin Graham: The Memoirs of the Dean of Wall Street*, edited by Seymour Chapman [New York: McGraw-Hill Book Company Inc., 1996], 251).

> [Nonetheless they] both agreed that the market had advanced to inordinate heights, that the speculators had gone crazy, that respected investment bankers were indulging in inexcusable high jinks, and that the whole thing would have to end one day in a major crash. (ibid., 251)

Several years later, Graham lamented: "What seems really strange now is that I could make a prediction of that kind in all seriousness, yet not have the sense to realize the dangers to which I continued to subject the Account's capital" (ibid., 252). In mid-1929 the equity in the "Account" was a proud $2,500,000; it had shrunk to a mere $375,000 by the end of 1932 (ibid., x). Of the dismay and apprehension that Graham experienced during those three long years, he summarized by saying:

---

78 If one ever doubts that speculative manias have threads in common, that history rhymes in some fashion, a careful reading of this Appendix should disabuse the reader of such notions. Virtually every section that follows warrants an explanatory footnote to point out the parallels between the late '20s and the late '90s. Rather, it may be much more instructive and revealing for the reader to savor every insight and to imagine the power of such wisdom to protect the knowledgeable from the influences of the great speculative contagions.

> The chief burden on my mind was not so much the actual shrinkage of my fortune as the lengthy attrition, the repeated disappointments after the tide had seemed to turn, the ultimate uncertainty about whether the Depression and the losses would ever come to an end. (ibid., 259)

Graham's memoirs also shed light on his propensity toward delusion, if not a modicum of vanity itself. As noted just below, after the crash in late 1929, a knee-jerk 50% recovery in prices extended until March 1930. While in St. Petersburg, Florida, in January 1930 visiting his wife, Graham was introduced to her elderly friend, 93-year-old industrialist John Dix. Graham recalled the conversation:

> I visited this Mr. Dix at his home in St. Petersburg and found him surprisingly alert for one so close to the century mark. He asked me all about my business, how many clients I had, how much money I owed to banks and brokers, and innumerable other questions. I answered them politely but with smug self-confidence. Suddenly John Dix said, with the greatest earnestness: "Mr. Graham, I want you to do something of the greatest importance to yourself. Get on the train to New York tomorrow; go to your office, sell out your securities; pay off your debts, and return their capital to your partners. I wouldn't be able to sleep one moment at night if I were in your position in these times, and you shouldn't be able to sleep either. I'm much older than you, with lots more experience, and you'd better take my advice." I thanked the old man, a bit condescendingly no doubt, and said I would think over his suggestion. Then I hastened to put it out of my mind. Dix was not far from his dotage, he couldn't possibly understand my system of operations, his ideas were preposterous. As it happened he was 100 percent right and I 100 percent wrong. I have often wondered what my life would have been like if I had followed his advice. That it would have spared me much worry and regret I am sure; but whether my character and later career would have formed as they did after my ordeal by fire is another question. (ibid., 262)

The Years 1927 to 1933: an Aberration

That the six-year span, 1927–33, was a historical aberration is beyond question. From early 1927 until October 1929, the Dow Jones industrial average rose from approximately 150 to exactly 381.17, a gain of 120% over

34 months. During the October-November crash, it fell almost 50% to 198.69. Few people are aware that it regained half of the loss by March of 1930, rising to 294.07. But with the Depression settling in, the market once again dropped, this time sinking relentlessly, hitting its nadir of 41.22 in the summer of 1932, little more than one-tenth of the 1929 peak. At midyear 1932, the Dow was no higher than where it had been in January 1897, some 35 years earlier. It's important to differentiate the violent crash of 1929 (and 50% rebound by March 1930) from what followed. With the benefit of hindsight, the crash was the natural consequence of the speculative frenzy that preceded it, whereas the seemingly endless attrition in stock prices that ensued might be attributed primarily to the emerging business depression.

Falling Fixed-Income Security Yields Abetted the Equity Rationale

> It was the natural disaffection with their experience as bond owners which predisposed investors to embrace the new doctrine of common stocks as the superior form of investment, a doctrine which had a real validity within a limited range of application, but which was inevitably misapplied, with consequences too harrowing to dilate upon. (Graham, *Security Analysis,* 5)

The Dow Jones bond average fell from wartime high of 96.25 in 1917 to a low of 71.96 in 1920, only to rise again to 99.48 in 1928. By the summer of 1932, the bond index had lost a third of its value, plummeting to 65.78, reflecting in large measure the impaired creditworthiness of many issues. As to Graham's reference to the "natural disaffection" investors had with bonds, I must conclude that, at least in the intermediate term, he was referring to the steady decline in bond yields, as the bond average rose in lockstep with the Dow Jones average throughout the 1920s. The concurrent rise in bond and stock prices during the great bull market is not unlike the experience of the last 15 years.

Lowered Standards of Investment Banking Houses

Traditionally, the investment bankers had been able to successfully combine the sometimes conflicting functions of protecting their clients' interests and making money for themselves. They properly thought of themselves as having a quasi-fiduciary relationship with their clients. "The public was safeguarded as much for business as for ethical reasons, since a firm's reputation and continued existence depended on the soundness of the merchandise which it sold" (ibid., 9). Graham traced the relaxation of standards to two causes: (1) the ease with which all issues could be sold and (2) the scarcity of sound investments available for sale. In previous years, investment bankers had the choice between selling good securities and bad, and they generally opted for the good, sometimes at reduced underwriting profit.

> But now they had to choose between selling poor investments or none at all—between making large profits or shutting up shop—and it was too much to expect from human nature that under such circumstances they would adequately protect their clients' interests. (ibid., 10)

The Element of Crowd Psychology

> One of the striking features of the past five years has been the domination of the financial scene by purely psychological elements. In previous bull markets the rise in stock prices remained in fairly close relationship with the improvement in business during the greater part of the cycle; it was only in its invariably short-lived culminating phase that quotations were forced to disproportionate heights by the unbridled optimism of the speculative contingent. But in the 1921–1933 cycle this "culminating phase" lasted for years instead of months, and it drew its support not from a group of speculators but from the entire financial community. The "new-era" doctrine—that "good" stocks (or "blue chips") were sound investments regardless of how high the price paid for them was at bottom only a means of rationalizing under the title of "investment" the well-nigh universal capitulation to the gambling fever. We suggest that this psychological phenomenon is closely related to the dominant importance assumed in recent years by intangible factors of value, viz., good-will, management, expected earning power, etc. Such value factors, while undoubtedly real, are not susceptible to mathematical calculation; hence the standards by which they are measured are to a great extent arbitrary and can suffer the widest variations in accordance with the prevalent psychology. The investing class was the more easily led to ascribe reality to purely speculative valuations of these intangibles because it was dealing in good part with surplus wealth, to which it was not impelled by force of necessity to apply the old-established acid test that the principal value be justified by the income. (ibid., 11–12)

The Rise and Fall of Security Analysis

> But the "new era" commencing in 1927 involved at bottom the abandonment of the analytical approach; and while emphasis was still seemingly placed on facts and figures, these were manipulated by a sort of pseudo-analysis to support the delusions of the period. The market collapse in October 1929 was no surprise to such analysts as had kept their heads, but the extent of the business collapse which later developed, with its devastating effects on established earning power, again threw their calculations out of gear. Hence the ultimate result was that serious analysis suffered a double discrediting: the first—prior to the crash—due to the persistence of imaginary values, and the second—after the crash—due to the disappearance of real values. (ibid., 14–15)

The Concept of Intrinsic Value

One of the many fascinating features of the flashback to 1934 is the absence of any reference whatsoever to modern portfolio theory and, in particular, efficient markets. Those mathematical concepts came into being many years later. In fact, that frequently there was a difference between price and value was central to Graham's thinking. How foreign such thinking must be to the minds of the efficient-markets theorists.

> ... [I]ntrinsic value is an elusive concept. In general terms it is understood to be that value which is justified by the facts, e.g., the assets, earnings, dividends, definite prospects, as distinct, let us say, from market quotations established by artificial manipulation or distorted by psychological excesses. But it is a great mistake to imagine that intrinsic value is as definite and as determinable as is the market price. Some time ago intrinsic value (in the case of a common stock) was thought to be about the same thing as "book value," i.e., it was equal to the net assets of the business, fairly priced. This view of intrinsic value was quite definite, but it proved almost worthless as a practical matter because neither the average earnings nor the average market price evinced any tendency to be governed by the book value.
>
> Hence this idea was superseded by a newer view, viz., that the intrinsic value of a business was determined by its earning power. Since the trend in earnings is far less certain than book value, the concept of intrinsic value thus derived lacks precision and is prone to considerable error. (ibid., 17–18)

No Automatic Relationship Between Value and Price

Investment theory should recognize that the merits of an issue reflect themselves in the market price not by any automatic response or mathematical relationship but through the minds and decisions of buyers and sellers. Furthermore, the investors' mental attitude not only affects the market price but is strongly affected by it, so that the success of a commitment—properly considered—must depend in some part on the subsequent maintenance of a satisfactory market price. (ibid., 12)

And George Soros thought he had an original idea.

The Importance of Price

In the field of common stocks, the necessity of taking price into account is more compelling, because the danger of paying the wrong price is almost as great as that of buying the wrong issue. We shall point out later that the new-era theory of investment left price out of the reckoning, and that this omission was productive of most disastrous consequence. (ibid., 29)

Graham makes a distinction between the untrained and the trained securities buyer by way of analogy:

[The principles that governed their behavior are] applicable to all kinds of merchandise, viz., that the untrained buyer fares best by purchasing goods of the highest reputation, even though he may pay a comparatively high price. But, needless to say, this is not a rule to guide the expert merchandise buyer, for he is expected to judge quality by examination and not solely by reputation, and at times he may even sacrifice certain definite degrees of quality if that which he obtains is adequate for his purpose and attractive in price. This distinction applies as well to the purchase of securities as to buying paints or watches. It results in two principles of quite opposite character, the one suitable for the untrained investor, the other useful only to the analyst.

1. Principle for the untrained security buyer: Do not put money in a low-grade enterprise on any terms.

2. Principle for the securities analyst: Nearly every issue might conceivably be cheap in one price range and dear in another. (ibid., 31–32)

Forces That Militate Against the Indefinite Continuance of a Trend

Abnormally good or abnormally bad conditions do not last forever. This is true not only of general business but of particular industries as well. Corrective forces are usually set in motion which tend to restore profits where they have disappeared, or to reduce them where they are excessive in relation to capital. Industries especially favored by a developing demand [e.g., personal computers] may become demoralized through a still more rapid growth of supply. (ibid., 35)

Distinctions Between Investment and Speculation

.... [T]he cynic's definition [is] that an investment is a successful speculation and a speculation is an unsuccessful investment. ... [T]he failure to properly distinguish between investment and speculation was in large measure responsible for the market excesses of 1928–1929 and the calamities that ensued. (ibid., 50)

Income vs. Profit; Safety vs. Risk

Certainly, through many years prior to 1928, the typical investor had been interested above all in safety of principal and continuance of an adequate income. However, the doctrine that common stocks were the best long-term investments resulted in a transfer of emphasis from current income to future income and hence inevitably to future enhancement of principal value. In its complete subordination of the income element to the desire for profit, and also in the prime reliance it placed upon favorable developments expected in the future, the new-era style of investment—as exemplified in the general policy of the investment trusts—was practically indistinguishable from speculation. In fact this so-called investment could be accurately defined as speculation in the common stocks of strongly situated companies. (ibid., 52)

To be sure, what constitutes safety is highly subjective.

The race-track gambler, betting on a "sure thing," is convinced that his commitment is safe. The 1929 "investor" in high-priced common stocks also considered himself safe in his reliance upon future growth to justify the figure he paid and more.

The concept of safety can be really useful only if it is based on something more tangible than the psychology of the purchaser. [The investor of 1912 relied on established standards and purchased bank stocks] at price levels which he considered conservative in the light of experience; he was satisfied, from his knowledge of the institution's resources and earning power, that he was getting his money's worth in full. If a strong speculative market resulted in advancing the price to a level out of line with these standards of value, he sold his shares and waited for a reasonable price to return before reacquiring them.

Had this same attitude been taken by the purchaser of common stocks in 1928–1929, the term investment would not have been the tragic misnomer that it was. But in proudly applying the designation "blue chips" to the high-priced issues chiefly favored, the public unconsciously revealed the gambling motive at the heart of its supposed investment selections. These differed from the old-time bank-stock purchases in the one vital respect that the buyer did not determine that they were worth the price paid by the application of firmly established standards of value. The market made up new standards as it went along, by accepting the current price—however high—as the sole measure of value ...

It is unsound to think always of investment character as inhering in an issue per se. The price is frequently an essential element, so that a stock (and even a bond) may have investment merit at one price level but not at another. (ibid., 53–55)

History of Common-Stock Analysis

Finally, an impressive theory was constructed asserting the preeminence of common stocks as long-term investments.

> But at the time that the interest in common stocks reached its height, in the period between 1927 and 1929, the basis of valuation employed by the stock-buying public departed more and more from the factual approach and technique of security analysis, and concerned itself increasingly with the elements of potentiality and prophecy. (ibid., 300)

> Analysis was vitiated by two types of instability: instability of tangibles and dominant importance of intangibles. (ibid., 301)

Speculation Characterized by Emphasis on Future Prospects

> In the pre-war period it was the well-considered view that when prime emphasis was laid upon what was expected of the future, instead of what had been accomplished in the past, a speculative attitude was thereby taken. Speculation, in its etymology, meant looking forward; investment was allied to "vested interests"—to property rights and values taking root in the past. The future was uncertain, therefore speculative; the past was known, therefore the source of safety. (ibid., 305)

Buying Common Stocks Viewed as Taking a Share in a Business

If investors would think about buying common stocks in the same manner they think about buying a private business, much trouble would be avoided.

> This meant that he gave at least as much attention to the asset values behind the shares as he did to their earnings records. It is essential to bear in the mind that a private business has always been valued primarily on the basis of the "net worth" as shown by its statement ... An interest in a private business may of course be sold for more or less than its proportionate asset value; but the book value is still invariably the starting point of the calculation, and the deal is finally made and viewed in terms of the premium or discount from book value involved. (ibid., 306)

"It is a significant confirmation of this point that 'watered stock,' once so burning an issue, is now a forgotten phrase" (ibid., 308). Notice how contemporary analysis has moved away from virtually any consideration of book value, even with private companies.

The New-Era Theory

During the postwar period, and particularly during the latter stage of the bull market culminating in 1929, the public acquired a completely different attitude towards the investment merits of common stocks. Two of the three elements above stated [(1) a suitable and established dividend return; (2) a satisfactory backing of tangible assets; and (3) a stable and adequate earnings record] lost nearly all of their significance and the third, the earnings record, took on an entirely novel complexion. The new theory or principle may be summed up in the sentence: "The value of a common stock depends entirely upon what it will earn in the future."

From this dictum the following corollaries were drawn:

That the dividend rate should have slight bearing upon the value.

That since no relationship apparently existed between assets and earning power, the asset value was entirely devoid of importance.

That past earnings were significant only to the extent that they indicated what changes in the earnings were likely to take place in the future.

This complete revolution in the philosophy of common-stock investment took place virtually without realization by the stock-buying public and with only the most superficial recognition by financial observers. (ibid., 307)

The new-era concepts had their root first of all in the obsolescence of the old-established standards. During the last generation the tempo of economic change has been speeded up to such a degree that the fact of being *long established* has ceased to be, as once it was, a warranty of *stability*. Corporations enjoying decade-long prosperity have been precipitated into insolvency within a few years. Other enterprises, which had been small or unsuccessful or in doubtful repute, have just as quickly acquired dominant size, impressive earnings, and the highest rating. (ibid., 307–308)

... [T]here emerged a companion theory that common stocks represented the most profitable and therefore the most desirable media for long-term investment. This gospel was based upon a certain amount of research, showing that diversified lists of common stocks had regularly increased in value over stated intervals of time for many years past. The figures indicated that such diversified common-stock holdings yielded both a higher income return and a greater principal profit than purchases of standard bonds. (ibid., 309)

Stocks Regarded as Attractive Irrespective of Their Prices

The notion that the desirability of a common stock was entirely independent of its price seems incredibly absurd. Yet the new-era theory led directly to this thesis. If a public-utility stock was selling at 35 times its maximum recorded earnings, instead of 10 times its average earnings, which was the preboom standard, the conclusion to be drawn was not that the stock was now too high but merely that the standard of value had been raised. Instead of judging the market price by established standards of value, the new era based its standards of value upon the market price. Hence all upper limits disappeared, not only upon the price at which a stock could sell, but even upon the price at which it would deserve to sell ...

An alluring corollary of this principle was that making money in the stock market was now the easiest thing in the world. It was only necessary to buy "good" stocks, regardless of price, and then to let nature take her upward course. The results of such a doctrine could not fail to be tragic. Countless people asked themselves, "Why work for a living when a fortune can be made in Wall Street without working?" The ensuing migration from business into the financial district resembled the famous gold rush to the Klondike, with the not unimportant difference that there really was gold in the Klondike. (ibid., 310)

Investment Trusts [Mutual Funds] Adopted This New Doctrine

Another irony of the late '20s involved investment trusts.

[They] were formed for the purpose of giving the untrained public the benefit of expert administration of its funds. It was understood that managers of investment funds were to buy in times of depression and low prices, and to sell out in times of prosperity and high prices.

> [They were to diversify and to] discover and acquire undervalued individual securities as the result of comprehensive and expert statistical investigations. The rapidity and completeness with which these traditional principles disappeared from investment-trust technique is one of the many marvels of the period. The idea of buying in times of depression was obviously inapplicable. It suffered from the fatal weakness that investment trusts could be organized only in good times, so that they were virtually compelled to make their initial commitments in bull markets ...
>
> But most paradoxical was the early abandonment of research and analysis in guiding investment-trust policies. However, since these financial institutions owed their existence to the new-era philosophy, it was natural and perhaps only just that they should adhere closely to it. Under its canons investment had now become so beautifully simple that research was unnecessary and statistical data a mere encumbrance. The investment process consisted merely of finding prominent companies with a rising trend of earnings, and then buying their shares regardless of price. Hence the sound policy was to buy only what everyone else was buying—a select list of highly popular and exceedingly expensive issues, appropriately known as the "blue chips." The original idea of searching for the undervalued and neglected issues dropped completely out of sight. Investment trusts actually boasted that their portfolios consisted exclusively of the active and standard (i.e., the most popular and highest priced) common stocks ...
>
> [The final irony was that the] man in the street, having been urged to entrust his funds to the superior skill of investment experts—for substantial compensation—was soon reassuringly told that the trusts would be careful to buy nothing except what the man in the street was buying himself. (ibid., 311–312)

A Sound Premise Used to Support an Unsound Conclusion

While the exponential ascension in stock prices during the late '20s was in large measure a self-fulfilling prophecy, it was not without scholarly explanation, however tenuous. *Common Stocks as Long-term Investments,* by Edgar Lawrence Smith, published in 1924, was often cited as justification for the ownership of common stocks. Unfortunately, the sound premise was rendered unsound by virtue of prices escalating to speculative levels in the late '20s. In practical terms, Smith's supposition was as sensible at 10 times earnings as it was ill-advised at 30 times.

Coincidentally, Professor Jeremy Siegel's book with the nearly identical title, *Stocks for the Long Term,* is the contemporary iteration of the same phenomenon. I listened to Siegel present his case at a conference in December 2000 for the CEOs of investment advisory firms, and he has softened his position somewhat. While he now thinks technology stocks are overpriced, he believes that the S&P 500, exclusive of technology issues, is reasonably priced.

Parenthetically, I remain perplexed that most investors seem predisposed to extrapolating the past in forecasting the future of common-stock price movements. When referring to Roger Ibbotson's *Stocks, Bonds, Bills, and Inflation Yearbook,* a comprehensive statistical analysis of common-stock returns dating back to 1926, why do pundits invariably cite recent or long-term average returns from common stocks as the basis for predicting future returns? Would not a projection based on the post-1928–29 experience be more relevant? *It is a fact, whether we like it or not, that as of the spring of 2000 (and, for that matter, even today) for many stocks the relationship between price and value is more like the late '20s than at any other time in modern history* [italics added].

Average vs. Trend of Earnings

> There are several reasons why we cannot be sure that a trend of profits shown in the past will continue in the future. In the broad economic sense, there is the law of diminishing returns and of increasing competition which must finally flatten out any sharply upward curve of growth. There is also the flow and ebb of the business cycle, from which the particular danger arises that the earnings curve will look most impressive on the very eve of a serious setback. Considering the 1927–1929 period we observe that since the trend-of-earnings theory was at bottom only a pretext to excuse rank speculation under the guise of "investment," the profit-mad public was quite willing to accept the flimsiest evidence of the existence of a favorable trend ...
>
> The prevalent heedlessness on this score was most evident in connection with the numerous common-stock flotations during this period. The craze for a showing of rising profits resulted in the promotion of many industrial enterprises which had been favored by temporary good fortune and were just approaching, or had already reached, the peak of their prosperity. (ibid., 314–315)

> ... [O]ne of the paradoxes of financial history, viz., that at the very period when the increasing instability of individual companies had made the purchase of common stocks far more precarious than before, the gospel of common stocks as safe and satisfactory investments was preached to and avidly accepted by the American public. (ibid., 314–316)

Price an Integral Part of Every Investment Decision

> The price must have a rational basis.
>
> This criterion of reasonableness is vital to all investment methods, and particular to any theory of investing in common stocks. The absence of this controlling test constituted the fatal weakness of the new-era doctrine. (ibid., 318)
>
> An issue is attractive only if the indicated value amply justifies the price paid; hence the price is an integral part of any investment decision. This is true not only at the time of purchase but throughout the period of subsequent ownership. While the expectation may be to hold the issue indefinitely for income and enhancement in value, it will often prove desirable from the investment standpoint to dispose of it should it cease to be attractive—either because its quality has deteriorated or because the price has risen to a level not justified by the demonstrable value. (ibid., 321)

Disturbing Influence of Market Fluctuations

> The wider the fluctuations of the market, and the longer they persist in one direction, the more difficult it is to preserve the investment viewpoint in dealing with common stocks. The attention is bound to be diverted from the investment question, which is whether the price is attractive or unattractive in relation to value, to the speculative question whether the market is near its low or its high point.
>
> This difficulty was so overshadowing in the years between 1927 and 1933 that common-stock investment virtually ceased to have any sound practical significance during that period. If an investor had sold out his common stocks early in 1927, because prices had outstripped values, he was almost certain to regret his actions during the ensuing two years of further spectacular advances. Similarly those who hailed the crash of

1929 as an opportunity to buy common stocks at reasonable prices were to be confronted by appalling market losses as a result of the subsequent protracted decline. (ibid., 321–322)

The Danger of Speculative Contagion in Common-Stock Investment

We doubt, however, whether many individuals are qualified by nature to follow consistently such an investment policy without deviating into the primrose path of market speculation. The chief reason for this hazard is that the distinctions between common-stock investment and common-stock speculation are too intangible to hold human nature in check ... But when the investor employs the same medium as the speculator, the line of demarcation between one approach and the other is one of mental attitude only, and hence is relatively insecure. It is not likely to keep him immune from speculative contagion, especially when this is rampant in the very issues in which he has made his investment. Prior to 1926, a fairly definite separation could be made between investment common stocks and speculative common stocks. The former fluctuated over a much narrower range percentage-wise, since their prices were determined largely by their established dividend rate ...

Hence the issues which the common-stock investor dealt in served to set him apart from the speculative public and make it easier for him to maintain his conservative viewpoint. The new era was marked by a concentration of speculative interest on those issues which had formerly deserved an investment rating. This made for an extraordinary confusion in the mental processes of the entire financial community, and the straightening out of this confusion may be a matter of many years. (ibid., 322–323)

'Stock Watering' Reversed

The new policy of writing off fixed assets bears an interesting relationship to the recent conceptions of stock values. It is a direct outgrowth of the ignoring of asset values and the monopolizing of attention by the reported per-share earnings. A generation ago, when investors consulted balance sheets to ascertain the net worth behind their shares, this net worth was artificially inflated by writing up the book value of the fixed assets far above their actual cost. This in turn permitted a corresponding overstatement of capitalization at par. "Stock watering," as this practice was called, constituted at that time one of the most severely criticized abuses of Wall Street.

It is a striking commentary on the change in our financial viewpoint that the term "stock watering" has practically disappeared from the investor's vocabulary. By a strange paradox the same misleading results which were obtained before the war by overstating property values are now sought by the opposite stratagem of understating these assets. Erase the plant account; thereby eliminate the depreciation charge; thereby increase the reported earnings; thereby enhance the value of the stock. The idea that such sleight-of-hand could actually add to the value of a security is nothing short of preposterous. Yet Wall Street solemnly accepts this topsy-turvy reasoning; and corporate managements are naturally not disinclined to improve their showing by so simple a maneuver. (ibid., 418–419)

Current Earnings Should Not Be the Primary Basis of Appraisal

The market level of common stocks is governed more by their current earnings than by their long-term average. This fact accounts in good part for the wide fluctuations in common-stock prices, which largely (though by no means invariably) parallel the changes in their earnings between good years and bad. Obviously the stock market is quite irrational in thus varying its valuation of a company proportionately with the temporary changes in its reported profits. A private business might easily earn twice as much in a boom year as in poor times, but its owner would never think of correspondingly marking up or down the value of his capital investment.

This is one of the most important lines of cleavage between Wall Street practice and the canons of ordinary business. (ibid., 432)

Other Relevant Topics

For those readers who would like to delve further into this most extraordinary of accounts, I would suggest purchase of *Security Analysis* (1934 edition). A reasonably priced photographic reprint of this collector's edition is available in most bookstores. Among the many *Security Analysis* topics not covered above are:

The hazard of tardy adjustment of price to value (22)
Balance-sheet analysis (485)
Practical significance of book value (491)
Prevalence of stocks selling below liquidating value (498)
Stock-repurchase programs (518)
Officers and directors—summary and conclusion (521)
Discrepancies between price and value (585)
Bargains in a bull market (589)
Mergers and segregations (590)

Conclusion

Of the many factors that contribute to setting the price for a given stock (including management; competition; trends in unit volume, price, and costs; earnings; dividends; assets; capital structure; and terms of the issue), the often emotional attitude of the public in response to those fundamental factors, expressed through their bids and offers in the marketplace, sometimes results in prices that are at significant variance from intrinsic value. By contrast, revolutionary advances have been achieved in communications, the medical sciences, computers, and the whole range of other technologies precisely because they call upon sectors of the brain where emotion does not encroach. To understand the difference is crucial if one is to avoid falling victim to the euphonic contagion common to great speculative booms—and the prolonged despair that invariably follows in their wake.

INDEX

A

B

C

D

E

F

G

H

I

J

K

L

M

N

O

P

Q

R

S

T

U

V

W

Y

Printed in the United States
39632LVS00003B/97-510